Studium Biblicum Franciscanum
Collectio Minor

46

© 2022 Fondazione Terra Santa – Milano
TS Edizioni – Milano

*Per informazioni sulle opere pubblicate
e in programma rivolgersi a:*

TS Edizioni
Via Giovanni Gherardini, 5 - 20145 Milano
Tel. +39 02 34592679 Fax + 39 02 31801980
www.tsedizioni.it
e-mail: info@tsedizioni.it

Leah Di Segni

AN INTRODUCTION TO LATE ANTIQUE EPIGRAPHY IN THE HOLY LAND

Nessuna parte di questo libro
può essere riprodotta o trasmessa in qualsiasi forma
o con qualsiasi mezzo elettronico, meccanico o altro
senza l'autorizzazione scritta dei proprietari dei diritti.

Cover
Fragment of asylia inscription from Galilee
(Photo G. Laron ©Inst. of Archaeology, The Hebrew University of Jerusalem)

Finito di stampare nell'agosto 2022
da Corpo 16 s.r.l., Modugno (BA)
per conto di Fondazione Terra Santa
ISBN 979-12-5471-117-0

PREFACE

The study of Greek and Latin epigraphy requires special training, and everyone who has ever read a paper on the subject, not to speak of approaching an inscription unaided, will freely admit that knowledge of the classical languages, though necessary, is not sufficient. Again, Greek epigraphy requires a different training from Latin epigraphy, for the cultural, historical, geographical, political or other background is completely different. Further, within each wide field, the Latin and the Greek, the archaic, classic and late periods all call for a different kind of expertise. But why is a special introduction to late antique epigraphy in the Holy Land needed?

Putting on for a moment the archaeologist's hat – for which, I admit, I have only a limited right – I'll say that epigraphy resembles pottery in provinciality. Every small area has its own special types, alongside the imports or imitations of types widespread over all its vicinity and the surrounding countries, so that an expert of Galilaean ceramic would find himself/herself at a loss if tasked with classifying the potsherds from a dig in northern Syria or in Asia Minor. The epigraphist meets with the same difficulty. This should be self-evident, for different people, with different traditions, produce both pottery and inscriptions. But let me point out some aspects in which the epigraphic production of the Holy Land is distinguished from that of other regions of the East.

Duration and floruit

Unlike other countries, the peak of epigraphic production here, both in quantity and in quality, occurs in Late Antiquity, and more specifically from the mid-fifth to the early seventh century, with no fall into barbarism (despite some linguistic developments, on which see below); on the contrary, with a marked continuity of earlier traditions, on the one hand, and an innovative push on the other, both exemplified by the dating systems (see Chapter II).

Cultural pluralism

The ethnic pluralism of this region is unparalleled elsewhere. Whatever period of history, or even of prehistory, one chooses to consider, the land, due to its geographical position, was always home to diverse ethne and cultures and a capturer of influences from nearby and faraway countries. In Late Antiquity it also became a focus of pilgrimage and immigration from all parts of the Christian world that further enriched the social texture of the class most active in epigraphic production. The new status of the Holy Land as heart of the Christian world also boosted its economic welfare, augmented the resources available for building and promoted the building of churches, fashionably adorned with inscriptions.

Co-existence of languages

The ethnic pluralism of the Holy Land accounts for an unparalleled co-existence of languages and scripts. Greek and Latin, Hebrew, Jewish, Christian and Samaritan Aramaic, each with its own script, pre-Islamic Arabic in Nabataean and Old Arabic scripts, the occasional Syriac, Palmyrene, Armenian and Georgian inscriptions, Safaitic and Thamudic graffiti in the eastern and southern fringes: all are attested in late antique Holy Land, sometimes influencing one another in vocabulary and formulas (see Chapters III-IV). Still, Greek is the prevailing vehicle of written communication from its first appearance in the region in the fourth century BCE to the end of Late Antiquity in the late eighth or early ninth century, and it will draw most of our attention in the following chapters.

Linguistic developments

Like in other Greek-speaking countries, also in the Holy Land the evolving of Greek brought about changes, most notably confusion of long and short vowels (ε for η, ο for ω and vice-versa), a loss of the sense of grammatical case, and pronunciation and spelling changes due to iotacism. In regard to the cases, in local inscriptions a series of names may show a shift from one case to another, especially with indirect cases (genitive and dative), or the sudden appearance of a nominative after a row of indirect cases.[1] The phenomenon, or rathe the process, of iotacism – the vowel shift by which certain vowels and diphthongs converged towards the pronunciation of iota – can be

---

[1] For instance, a fragmentary epitaph from Jerusalem (*CIIP* I, 2, no. 887) reads: [Θήκη δι]αφέρο[υσα τῷ . . .] ψάλτῃ κ[αὶ ἀναγνω]στου; a dedicatory inscription in the North Church at Lower Herodium (*CIIP* IV, 2, no. 3326) begins with the formula 'Lord Jesus Christ and holy Michael, accept the offering of', followed by a long series of donors' names in genitive, and ends καὶ Ζάνα θυγάτηρ Νόνας.

observed in modern Greek, in which the letters and digraphs ι, η, υ, ει, οι, υι are all pronounced /i/. The spelling of late antique inscriptions attests this process was under way already in the fifth-sixth centuries and even earlier. Lists of vowel exchanges (and of the rarer consonant exchanges), available in several corpora of inscriptions from the Holy Land,[2] show the extent of the phenomenon here, in some details typical of this particular region, most likely due to the influence of Semitic languages spoken by the natives: Arabic and the various Aramaic dialects. Especially noticeable are the shift between /a/ and /o/ and the reduction of diphthongs, which are spelled with a single letter in a great variety of forms beyond normal iotacism. In regard to consonants, double letters may be reduced to single (for instance, ἐκκλησία is consistently spelled ἐκλησία in local inscriptions), and single letters may be doubled (e.g. the name Marinus may be spelled Μαρρῖνος). All these changes should not be viewed as mistakes either of the person who dictated an inscription or of the stone cutter or mosaicist who carried out the job, but as phonetic spellings reflecting the actual pronunciation of the word in that time and place. In the following chapters we shall often remark on the phonetic spelling of different inscriptions. In transcribing them, it is a good practice to correct only those spellings that may confuse the reader, and leave the others unchanged, giving the proper accent if necessary (for instance, τῶν, when spelled with omicron, ought to be rendered as τὸν). Corrections of all types shall be marked with the proper diacritical signs.

Here is a list of the diacritical signs used in the present work:
- ( )   completion of abbreviated words
- [ ]   lost letters, restored by the editor
- { }   superfluous letters, marked as such by the editor
- ⟦ ⟧   letters or words deliberately erased in antiquity
- ⟨ ⟩   correction of one or more letters
- ...   a known number of lost or illegible letters, equal to the number of dots
- - - - an uncertain number of lost or illegible letters
- .   a dot under a letter indicates uncertain reading

---

[2] E.g. *IGLS* XIII, 1 (pp. 35-37), *IGLJ* II (p. 245), Meimaris and Kritikakou-Nikolaropoulou 2005: 55-65, Meimaris and Kritikakou-Nikolaropoulou 2008: 45-47.

ACKNOWLEDGEMENTS

It remains to acknowledge my debt to the many scholars from whose work I have learned; all mistakes are of course mine. I wish to thank the institutions by whose courtesy I was able to enrich this little book with illustrations: the Institute of Archaeology of the Hebrew University of Jerusalem, the Israel Antiquities Authority, the Israel Exploration Society, the Israel Museum, the Studium Biblicum Franciscanum, and their respective archives. My heartfelt thanks are due to their representatives ὧν ὁ Κύριος γιγνώσκει τὰ ὀνόματα, by whose efforts many photographs and drawings were located for me. Several colleagues personally provided me with illustrations and permission to use them: Professors Denis Feissel, Shimon Gibson, Joseph Patrich and Zeev Weiss; Dr. Benny Arubas, Dr. J. Ashkenazi, Dr. Danny Syon, Hanaa Abu-Uqsa Abud, Yigal Ben-Ephraim, Nancy Benovitz, Rachel Chachy-Laureys and the staff of the Herodium. Special thanks to Benny Arubas, whose middle name should be ὁ βοηθῶν, and to two other true friends, Ravit Nenner-Soriano and Shlomit Weksler-Bdolah. Without their help this work would never have been completed.

In this occasion, my grateful thought goes to three scholars who are no longer with us, who touched my personal and professional life: my beloved teacher and mentor, Yoram Tsafrir; my friend Yizhar Hirschfeld, to whose optimistic trust I owe my first epigraphic job when I did not know I was an epigraphist *in fieri*; and Michele Piccirillo, ofm, who opened for me the splendours of archaeology and epigraphy beyond the Jordan. Blessed be their memory.

Leah Di Segni Campagnano
Jerusalem, 9 February 2022

ABBREVIATIONS AND SIGLA

AASOR	*Annual of the American Schools of Oriental Research*
ADAJ	*Annual of the Department of Antiquities of Jordan*
AE	*L'Année Épigraphique*
ANRW	H. Temporini and W. Haase eds. *Aufstieg und Niedergang der römischen Welt*. Berlin-New York 1972-1997
BASOR	*Bulletin of the American Schools of Oriental Research*
BCH	*Bulletin de Correspondance Hellénique*
BE	Bulletin épigraphique in *Revue des études grecques*
CCSL	Corpus Christianorum, Series Latina. Turnhout.
CFHB	Corpus Fontium Historiae Byzantinae. Berlin-New York
CIAP I-III	M. Sharon, *Corpus Inscriptionum Arabicarum Palaestinae, I-III*. Leiden 1997-2004; *Addendum*. Leiden 2007
CIIP I, 1-2	H.M. Cotton, L. Di Segni, W. Eck, B. Isaac, A. Kushnir-Stein, H. Misgav, J. Price, A. Yardeni, *Corpus Inscriptionum Iudaeae/Palaestinae I: Jerusalem*. Part 1: 1-704; Part 2: 705-1120; Appendix 1*-54*. Berlin 2010-2012
CIIP II	W. Ameling, H.M. Cotton, W. Eck, B. Isaac, A. Kushnir-Stein, H. Misgav, J. Price, A. Yardeni, *Corpus Inscriptionum Iudaeae/Palaestinae II: Caesarea and the Middle Coast: 1121-2160*. Berlin 2011
CIIP III	W. Ameling, H.M. Cotton, W. Eck, B. Isaac, A. Kushnir-Stein, H. Misgav, J. Price, A. Yardeni, *Corpus Inscriptionum Iudaeae/Palaestinae III: South Coast: 2161- 2648*. Berlin 2014
CIIP IV, 1-2	W. Ameling, H.M. Cotton, W. Eck, A. Ecker, B. Isaac, A. Kushnir-Stein (†), H. Misgav, J. Price, P. Weiß, A. Yardeni, *Corpus Inscriptionum Iudaeae/Palaestinae IV, Iudaea/Idumaea*. Part 1: 2649-3324; Part 2: 3325-3978. Berlin 2018
CIJ I	J.B. Frey, *Corpus Inscriptionum Judaicarum I: Europe*. Città del Vaticano 1936 (reprinted with a prolegomenon by B. Lifshitz. New York 1975)
CIJ II	J.B. Frey, *Corpus Inscriptionum Judaicarum II: Asie-Afrique*. Città del Vaticano 1952
CIS II, 1	*Corpus Inscriptionum Semiticarum*. Pars secunda, inscriptiones Aramaicas continens, Tomus 1. Paris 1889

CPA	Christian Palestinian Aramaic
CSHB	Corpus Scriptorum Historiae Byzantinae. Bonn
EDCS	Epigraphik-Datenbank Clauss / Slaby (on line)
EDH	Epigraphic Database Heidelberg (on line)
ESI	*Excavations and Surveys in Israel*
GCS	Die griechischen christlichen Schriftsteller der ersten Jahrhunderte (Kirchenväter Kommission der königlichen Preussischen Akademie der Wissenschaften). Leipzig
HA-ESI	*Hadashot arkheologiyot – Excavations and Surveys in Israel* (Hebrew and English)
IEJ	*Israel Exploration Journal*
IGLJ II	P.-L. Gatier, *Inscriptions grecques et latines de la Syrie XXI: Inscriptions de la Jordanie* II: *Région central*. Paris 1986
IGLJ IV	M. Sartre, *Inscriptions grecques et latines de la Syrie XXI: Inscriptions de la Jordanie* IV: *Pétra et la Nabatène méridionale du wadi al-Hasa au golfe de Aqaba*. Paris 1993
IGLJ V	N. Bader, *Inscriptions grecques et latines de la Syrie XXI: Inscriptions de la Jordanie* V: *La Jordanie du Nord-East*, fasc. 1. Beirut 2009
IGLS II	L. Jalabert and R. Mouterde, *Inscriptions grecques et latines de la Syrie* II: *Chalcidique et Antiochène*. Paris 1939
IGLS V	L. Jalabert, R. Mouterde and C. Mondésert, *Inscriptions grecques et latines de la Syrie* V: *Émésène*. Paris 1959
IGLS XI	J. Aliquot, *Inscriptions grecqus et latines de la Syrie* XI. *Mount Hermon (Liban et Syrie)*. Beirut 2008
IGLS XIII, 1	M. Sartre, *Inscriptions grecqus et latines de la Syrie* XIII, 1. *Bostra*. Paris 198
IGLS XIII, 2	M. Sartre, with the collaboration of A. Sartre-Fauriat, *Inscriptions grecqus et latines de la Syrie* XIII, 2. *Bostra (supplément) et la plaine de la Nuqrah*. Beirut 2011
IGLS XIV, 1-2	A. Sartre-Fauriat and M. Sartre, *Inscriptions grecqus et latines de la Syrie* XIV, 1-2. *La Batanée et le Jawlān Oriental*. Beirut 2016
IGLS XV, 1-2	A. Sartre-Fauriat and M. Sartre, *Inscriptions grecqus et latines de la Syrie* XV, 1-2. *Le plateau du Trachon et ses bordures*. Beirut 2014
IGLS XVI, 1	A. Sartre-Fauriat and M. Sartre, *Inscriptions grecqus et latines de la Syrie* XVI, 1. *L'Auranitide. Qanawāt et a bordure nord-ouest du Jebel al-'Arab*. Beirut 2020

IGLS XVI, 2	A. Sartre-Fauriat and M. Sartre, *Inscriptions grecqus et latines de la Syrie* XVI, 2. *L'Auranitide. Suweidā' et la bordure ouest du Jebel al-'Arab*. Beirut 2020
IJO I	D. Noy, A. Panayotov and H. Bloedhorn, *Inscriptiones Judaicae Orientis* I. *Eastern Europe*. Tübingen 2004
IJO II	W. Ameling, *Inscriptiones Judaicae Orientis* II. *Kleinasien*. Tübingen 2004
IJO III	D. Noy and H. Bloedhorn, *Inscriptiones Judaicae Orientis* III. *Syria und Cyprus*. Tübingen 2004
JIGRE	W. Horbury and D. Noy, *Jewish Inscriptions of Graeco-Roman Egypt, with an index of the Jewish Inscriptions of Egypt and Cyrenaica*. Cambridge 1992
JIWE 1-2	D. Noy, *Jewish inscriptions of Western Europe* 1. *Italy (excluding the City of Rome), Spain and Gaul*; 2. *The City of Rome*. Cambridge 1993
JRA	*Journal of Roman Archaeology*
LA	*Liber Annuus*
LCL	Loeb Classical Library
LGPN	*The Lexicon of Greek Personal Names* (on line)
MT	Masoretic (text of the Hebrew Bible)
NEAEHL	E. Stern ed., *The New Encyclopedia of Archaeological Excavations in the Holy Land* I-IV. Jerusalem 1993; V, Supplementary Volume, 2008.
PAES IIIA	E. Littmann, D. Magie and D.R. Stuart, *Publications of the Princeton University Archaeological Expeditions to Syria in 1904-5 and 1909*, Division III, Section A: Greek and Latin Inscriptions: Southern Syria. Leiden 1907-1921
PEF	*Palestine Exploration Fund Quarterly Statement* (1869-1937)
PEQ	*Palestine Exploration Quarterly*
PHI	Searchable Greek Inscription of the Packard Humanities Institute (on line)
QDAP	*Quarterly of the Department of Antiquities in Palestine* 1-14 (1932-1950)
RB	*Revue Biblique*
REG	*Revue des études Grecques*
SBF	Studium Biblicum Franciscanum
SEG	*Supplementum Epigraphicum Graecum*
TAM V, 1	P. Herrmann, *Tituli Asiae Minoris V. Tituli Lydiae, linguis Graeca et Latina conscripti*. Vol. 1, nos. 1-825, *Regio septentrionalis, ad orientem vergens*. Vienna 1981

TB	Talmud Bavli (Babylonian Talmud)
TJ	Talmud Jerushalmi (Jerusalem Talmud)
TMNam	*Trismegistos Names* (on line)
Tos.	Tosefta
TUGAL	Texte und Untersuchungen zur Geschichte der altchristlichen Literatur. Leipzig
Waddington	W.H. Waddington and P. Le Bas, *Voyage archéologique en Grèce et en Asie Mineure: Inscriptions et explications* II. Paris 1870
ZDPV	*Zeitschrift des Deutschen Palästina Vereins*
ZPE	*Zeitschrift für Papyrologie und Epigraphik*

CHAPTER I: INTRODUCTION

Inscriptions do not come down from heaven directly into museums, as many epigraphists and users of epigraphic material seem to believe. Once a toy for antiquarians, later promoted – or demoted – to the status of *ancilla historiae*, epigraphy has finally claimed a place for itself in scholarship, in strict alliance with archaeology, without cutting its ties with history. No inscription can be truly and fully interpreted without its archaeological background, just as no dig where inscriptions are unearthed can be properly understood without a correct reading of the epigraphic finds. Nevertheless, epigraphy has its own independent system of rules and notions.

The study of the epigraphic yield of the Holy Land is a good example. It is a habit of historians and archaeologists to categorize the past into periods in order to facilitate its study: in this region, this periodization usually follows the line of political change. Thus, from the point of view of the student of history or archaeology, the time range that we shall shortly discuss is divided into Hellenistic, Hasmonean, Herodian, Roman, Byzantine and Islamic periods, according to whether the predominant ruler was Alexander and his successors, the Hasmonean kings, Herod, Rome, Byzantium (Constantinople) or the Muslim conquerors (further divided into Umayyads and Abbasids). But to the epigraphist this periodization is unhelpful: there is no 'epigraphic culture of the Roman period' or of any other classified period, but a continuum, in which the proportional impact of different epigraphically attested languages, the predominant types of epigraphic expression and other parameters slowly change. Therefore, we shall use the terms of this periodization as mere flexible frames for epigraphic material sharing some characteristics common to each group but not exclusive of this particular frame.

The geographical framework

The Holy Land is the Promised Land of Israel, but its boundaries are elusive: 'from the Torrent of Egypt to the great river Euphrates', as God promised to Abraham (Gen. 15:18), or 'from Dan to Beersheba including Gilead', the land settled by the twelve tribes (Judg. 20:1)? Jerome further minimized the Dan-to-Beersheba concept by ignoring the region beyond the Jordan ('Gilead') and excluding not only the five city-states of the Philistines but also all the areas occupied by Idumeans, Arabs and Saracens south and around Jerusalem. But Christian pilgrims visited the holy places of the Bible from Sarepta of Sidon, where Elijah raised the son of the widow from the dead (I Kings 17:8-24; Luke 4:25-26), to the land of Goshen, where the Hebrews dwelt for 430 years before leaving Egypt (Gen. 45:10; 47:1-6; Ex. 12:40) and to the place where they had crossed the Red Sea and the Egyptians had been swallowed by the waves (Ex. 14); from the land of Job in Ausitis (southern Syria; Job 1:1) to Mount Nebo where Moses died (Deut. 34:1-7) and Mount Sinai where he received the Tables of the Law (Ex. 34:1-2).[1] For practical purposes (chiefly the accessibility of the epigraphic material for an Israel-based student) we shall focus on the region once forming the Roman provinces of Palaestina and Arabia, with the addition of two fringes: on the north, the southern part of the province of Syria, since ca. 194 Syria-Phoenice, and on the south, the north-eastern margin of Aegyptus. In Late Antiquity, after a partition of Syria-Phoenice, the northern fringe belonged to Phoenice Paralia (Maritima), and the southern fringe, after a partition of Aegyptus, to the province of Augustamnica (Fig. 1). In modern terms this region included the whole of the State of Israel, of the Palestinian Authority and of the Hashemite Kingdom of Jordan, plus southern Syria, the Gaza Strip and the Egyptian districts in the Sinai peninsula.

The chronological framework

'Classical' epigraphy – the epigraphy dominated by the two classical languages, Greek and Latin – begins and ends at different times in different regions. In the Holy Land, the red thread that defines epigraphy in this sense is Greek, which runs throughout a time range of about twelve centuries, from the fourth century BCE to the beginning of the ninth century CE.

During these twelve centuries, three main written languages predominated: Greek, which made its first appearance in the Hellenistic period, Latin, the vehicle of Roman civil and military administration from the first to the fourth century CE, and Aramaic, which was already present before Alexander's conquest but reached a peak in usage and refined into differ-

---

[1] Among the Christian pilgrims who visited these places were the Pilgrim of Bordeaux, 333 CE (*Itinerarium Burdigalense* 583, 12-13), Egeria, 381-384 CE (*Itinerarium Egeriae* 1-5; 7; 13, 1; 16, 5-7), Theodosius, between 518 and 530 (*De situ Terrae Sanctae*) and the Anonymous Pilgrim of Piacenza, ca. 570 (*Antonini Placentini Itinerarium* 2, 10, 37-38, 41). Their reports can be found in *Itineraria et alia geographica*, CCSL 175, Turnhout 1965, pp. 1-26, 37-103, 115-125, 129-153.

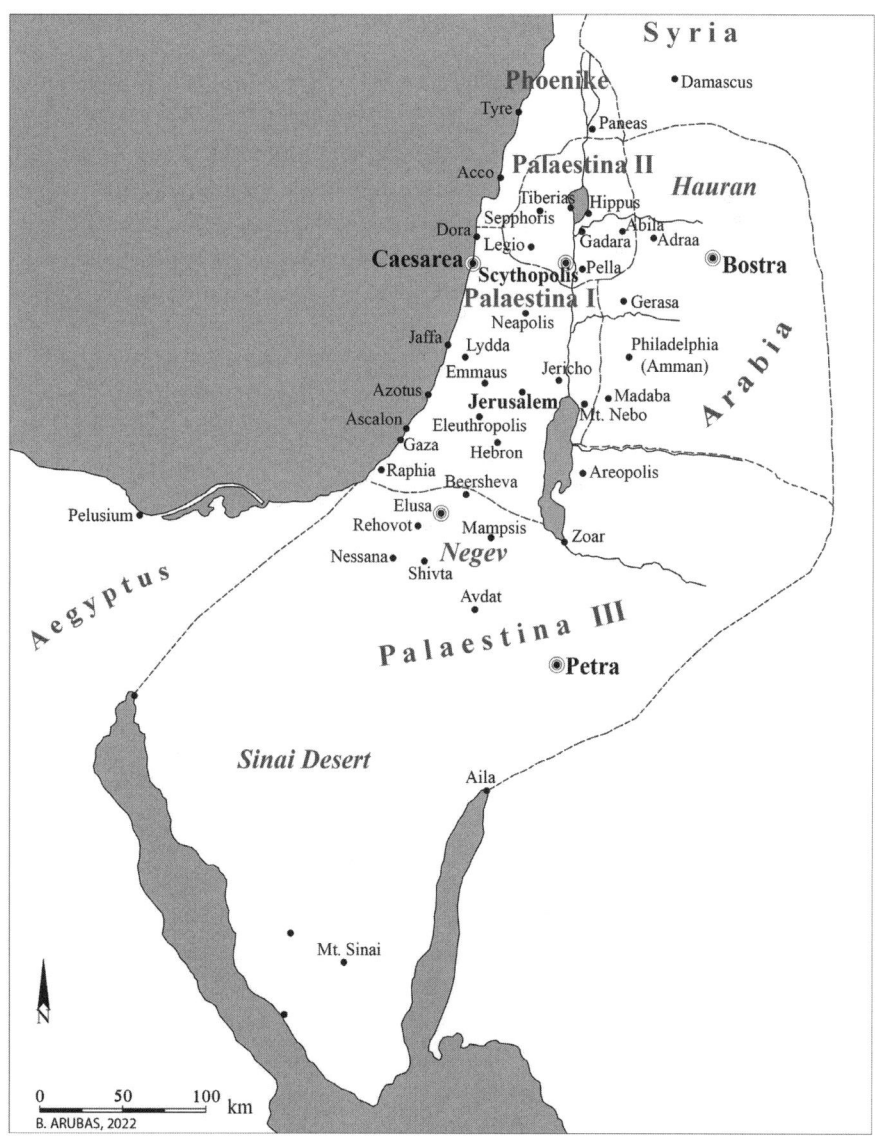

Fig. 1 – The Holy Land in the sixth century (Drawing B. Arubas)

ent dialects and scripts in the course of this period, until it was superseded by Arabic. All three languages ran through most of the historical/archaeological periods listed above: Aramaic was still written long after the Islamic conquest; Greek was still used as a vehicular language by native Christian communities up to the late eighth or the early ninth century, and even later by the Greek Church and its hierarchy; Latin still sporadically occurred in the sixth and seventh centuries and made its comeback in the Crusader period and even in modern times.[2] We shall endeavour to follow their rise and decline, especially for Greek and Latin, less for Aramaic, since its various dialects used in the region require a type of specialization rarely found among classics-oriented students. But the focus will be on Late Antiquity, a chronological term stretching through four of the historical/archaeological periods, from the Late Roman to the first part of the Abbasid period. This time frame must be singled out for two reasons: first, because in Late Antiquity Greek became the main vehicle of public and private expression of the majority of inhabitants in this region, and second, because in the Holy Land Greek epigraphy of this period developed local traits that distinguish it from the Greek epigraphy of other regions, and therefore it needs to be individually studied and described.

A general survey of the epigraphic yield in the Holy Land

During the twelve centuries under consideration, many changes occurred in the frequency and types of the inscriptions found in the Holy Land. Quantitatively, the largest part of inscriptions from the Hellenistic and Early Roman periods are short epitaphs in Greek or Aramaic, and Greek impressions on imported ware (Rhodian and other stamped handles).[3] In the Late Roman period building inscriptions and honorary and dedicatory inscriptions prevail, while the proportion of epitaphs decreases. This points to a change in the epigraphic habit, which also expresses itself in a relative scarcity of finds, especially west of the Jordan.[4] Greek still holds primacy but there is

---

[2] For Crusader inscriptions, see De Sandoli 1974. For an example of modern Latin inscription, see the epitaph of Christopher Costigan from Dublin, explorer of the Dead Sea, who died in the Casa Nova Hostel in Jerusalem in 1835. The tombstone is now in the courtyard of the Flagellation Convent in Jerusalem: Eriksen 1989: 30-32.

[3] For examples of the former, see *CIIP* I, 1 (inscriptions on ossuaries) and of the latter, Ariel et al. 1990 (imported stamped jar handles).

[4] The situation is different east of the Jordan, especially in the cities of the Decapolis, which yielded a wealth of Greek building inscriptions, honorary and dedicatory inscriptions, as well as in the Hauran, where epitaphs and private building inscriptions, including those referring to

no lack of Aramaic inscriptions, mainly dedications in synagogues in villages and minor cities. Latin is mostly represented by military inscriptions (epitaphs of soldiers, soldiers honouring their commanding officers, inscriptions attesting to the presence or the work of army units, dedications of altars by the military), inscriptions honouring the emperor(s) or the provincial governor, and inscriptions produced by the imperial administration and its representatives, as well as by Roman colonies, like Acco-Ptolemais, Caesarea and Aelia Capitolina.[5] But Latin was not habitually spoken by the populace, as is shown by the fact that on milestones, many of which bore long Latin inscriptions naming the emperor who ordered the paving or restoration of the road and the governor or military unit that carried out the work, the lines indicating the distance from the *caput viae* were usually in Greek or at least bilingual.[6] Interestingly, milestones are almost the only example of bilingual Latin and Greek inscriptions in the region,[7] for, as we shall see, the two languages kept functionally and chronologically separate. In Late Antiquity Latin disappears almost completely; Greek flourishes in a great variety of epigraphic types, including large numbers of epitaphs; Aramaic is also well represented in dedicatory and funerary inscriptions. While bilingual inscriptions in Aramaic (or Hebrew) and Greek are not numerous, Aramaic/Hebrew and Greek keep abreast separately in almost all fields in which they are epigraphically attested. Epitaphs in Greek and in Aramaic can be found in the same cemeteries, sometimes on the same ossuary or sarcophagus; dedications in Greek and Aramaic are displayed in the same cult places,

---

funerary monuments, abound in the third – fourth centuries and in the early fifth. For quantitative differences and variations between the West, the East and the Hauran in the Roman and Byzantine periods, see Di Segni 2017a.

[5] Samples illustrating these various types can be found in Kennedy 2004 and in Di Segni and Tsafrir 2017: 780-826 with the bibliography cited there.

[6] For milestones, see Thomsen 1917, Isaac and Roll 1982; Fischer, Isaac and Roll 1996; Isaac 1998; Ben-David 2011. Names of places inscribed in Latin can be found along roads leading to and from forts or garrisoned towns, where more traffic of soldiers and functionaries than of natives was to be expected; see Roll and Avner 2008. The list of milestones, including their inscriptions, is now available on line, care of the Kinneret Roman Roads and Milestones Project (http://milestones.kinneret.ac.il).

[7] Exceptions are rare: the epitaph of a Roman ship-owner working out of Ascalon (*SEG* LI, no. 2016, *AE* 2001, no. 1969; *CIIP* III, no. 2342), a dedication in honour of Trajan set up by a centurion in Gadara (*SEG* LII, no. 1623; *AE* 2004, no. 1584), a graffito of a soldier of the Legio III Cyrenaica in Wadi et-Tuwebe in Jordan (*SEG* VIII, no. 345; *AE* 1936, no. 131); Latin figures indicating value on game counters from Jerusalem (Early Roman period ? *CIIP* I, 2, no. 1115) and on a Byzantine weight from Caesarea (*CIIP* II, no. 1744), whose main inscriptions are in Greek.

be they pagan, Jewish or Christian; even the same type of *instrumenta* may be marked either in Greek or in Aramaic. We shall therefore mention the Aramaic inscriptions alongside the Greek as we encounter them. But for some preliminary explanations about the use of Aramaic in the Holy Land, see below, chapter III.

CHAPTER II: CHRONOLOGICAL SYSTEMS IN USE IN THE HOLY LAND [1]

Of the chronological systems we shall encounter in our survey of the inscriptions of the Holy Land, some came into existence as early as the Hellenistic or the Early Roman periods, others were innovations of Late Antiquity, but since the former continued in use side by side with the latter, we shall treat them all here, before one or the other system will be mentioned in our epigraphic survey.

The topic 'chronological systems' includes two distinct subjects: the calendar, that is, the division of the solar or lunar year into months with a varying number of days, and the era, that is, the counting of years from an agreed starting point. Each era year starts on the first day of the month that is first in the preferred calendar of that particular era (its 'epoch' or New Year Day) but it is important to point out that in inscriptions any era may be found accompanied by a calendar that was not its preferred one but reflected the individual preference of whoever dictated the inscription. For instance, an epitaph from the Negev (Beersheba? *SEG* VIII, no. 293) says that Valentinus son of Petrus died on the 20th of Xanthikos 'according to the Arabs' in the year 605 by the era of Gaza (10 April 545 CE). Gaza used a Macedonian calendar with New Year Day on the 1st of Dios, corresponding to 28 October, in which the 20th of Xanthikos fell on 15 April, while the calendar 'according to the Arabs' (κατὰ Ἄραβας) was an Arabo-Macedonian one, starting on the 1st of Xanthikos, corresponding to 22 March. Another epitaph from the same area (*SEG* XXXIV, no. 1469) bears a date by the era of Eleutheropolis, year 389, with a double calendar date, 23 of the Julian month April and 3 Artemisios κατὰ Ἄραβας, also corresponding to 23 April according to the Arabo-Macedonian calendar, the commonest in use with the era of Eleutheropolis. From these examples we also learn another peculiar aspect of the chronological systems in Late Antiquity: local eras, formerly restricted within the boundaries of their respective cities, can now be found outside the mother territory, so that

---

[1] For a general survey of this topic, see Meimaris 1992; Di Segni 1997a: 3-74; Di Segni 2006-2007.

different eras – the local one and one or more 'intruders' – may be found in use in the same territorial unit.[2]

Calendars

The Macedonian calendar(s)[3]

The most common calendar in epigraphic use in the Holy Land is the Macedonian, originally a lunisolar calendar of twelve lunar months (Dios, Apellaios, Audynaios, Peritios, Dystros, Xanthikos, Artemisios, Daisios, Panemos, Loos, Gorpiaios and Hyperberetaios), adding up to 354 days and therefore needing the addition of extra months roughly every three years to stay in step with the solar year. However, when this calendar reached Syria in the Hellenistic period, it had abandoned the lunar months of 29 or 30 days and found different solutions to end up with a year of 365 days. In addition, though the first month in the Syrian calendars was usually Dios (the moon of October and the first month in the ancient Macedonian calendar), different city calendars started Dios on different dates: at Tyre on 18 November, at Ascalon on 27 November, at Gaza on 28 October, in the Arabo-Macedonian calendar (in which it was not the first month: see below), on 18 October. At the present state of research we have no data for other cities, which prevents our fixing a precise date to an inscription coming from one of these cities even when it gives day and month.

Three types of Macedonian calendar were in use in the Holy Land. In the commonest, the months had an unequal number of days, 30 or 31, bringing the total to 365 days per year. In the south, especially in the coastal region, strongly influenced by Egyptian culture, the twelve month had 30 days each, and to make up the difference, five days – the *epagomenai* or additional (days) – were added between Panemos and Loos at Ascalon, between Loos and Gorpiaios at Gaza. The *epagomenai* corresponded to 24-28 August, leading up to the beginning of the ancient Egyptian year, which was marked

---

[2] For instance, the era of Ascalon appears in inscriptions set up by Ascalonites at Hebron in the territory of Eleutheropolis (*SEG* XLI, no. 1549; *CIIP* IV, 2, no. 3829; 29 July 527) and at Gaza, in the church at Jabaliyye (*SEG* L, no. 1489; *CIIP* III, no. 2452; 548/9 CE), where three mosaicists from Ascalon sign their work and date it by the era of their native city; other inscriptions in the same church (*SEG* L, nos. 1480-1482, 1485, 1487, 1492, 1493; *CIIP* III, nos. 2443-2445, 2448, 2450, 2455, 2456) are dated by the era of Gaza.

[3] On this calendar and its variants, see also Meimaris 1992: 38-41.

by the rising of the star Sirius on 29 August, the beginning of the flooding of the Nile and of the month of Thoth.

The third type of Macedonoan calendar was the Arabo-Macedonian, mostly used with the eras of Arabia and of Eleutheropolis, in the southern and eastern parts of the region. It also had months of 30 days and five *epagomenai*, but unlike the other two Macedonian calendars, it did not start in autumn but at the beginning of spring, on 22 March, and its first month was not Dios but Xanthikos. The *epagomenai* of this calendar fell between 17 and 21 March, before the New Year Day.

In the following table, Tyre is given as example of the commonest type of Macedonian calendar. The New Year Day is marked in bold.

Table I: Summary of calendars in epigraphic use in the Holy Land

Month	Tyre Starting day	days	Gaza Starting day	days	Ascalon Starting day	days	Arabo-Mac. Starting day	days
Dios	**18 November**	30	**28 October**	30	**27 November**	30	18 October	30
Apellaios	19 December	30	27 November	30	27 December	30	17 November	30
Audynaios	17 January	30	27 December	30	26 January	30	17 December	30
Peritios	16 February	30	26 January	30	25 February	30	16 January	30
Dystros	18 March	31	25 February	30	27 March	30	15 February	30
epagomenai							17-21 March	
Xanthikos	18 April	31	27 March	30	26 April	30	**22 March**	30
Artemisios	19 May	31	26 April	30	26 May	30	21 April	30
Daisios	19 June	31	26 May	30	25 June	30	21 May	30
Panemos	20 July	31	25 June	30	25 July	30	20 June	30
epagomenai					24-28 Aug.			
Loos	20 August	30	25 July	30	29 August	30	20 July	30
epagomenai			24-28 Aug.		28 Septemb.	30		
Gorpiaios	19 September	30	29 August	30	28 October	30	19 August	30
Hyperberetaios	19 October	30	28 September	30			18 September	30

Julian calendar

The Julian calendar was well known but never dominant in the land. Only in the territories of Jerusalem and Jericho and on their fringes does this calendar dominate, although the inscriptions mentioning months are too few to prove the point. In most parts of the region Julian months appear sporadically, side by side with Macedonian months, except in Provincia Arabia, where the influence of the Julian calendar is stronger. Indeed, most examples of Julian months are found in inscriptions dated by the era of Arabia, despite the fact that this era, with its New Year Day at the spring equinox, was unsuited to the Julian calendar. The occasional Julian month associated with eras that would normally have employed a Macedonian calendar does not prove that a Julian calendar with New Year on January 1 was in parallel use where the inscription was dictated. However, the adoption of such a calendar is attested in some cities of the Near East, especially those that were Roman colonies, like Sidon and Beirut, and this was probably the case also of Jerusalem, Colonia Aelia Capitolina.[4]

It is worth noting that the acceptance of this Roman chronological system was limited to the adoption of the months – their names, season and duration – but stopped at their subdivision: in inscriptions the days of the month are numbered from 1 to 30 or 31 just as in the Macedonian calendar (or to 28 in the case of February), not according to the Roman system. In the Roman system each month had three reference days: the Kalends (*Kalendae*, the first day of the month), the Nones (*Nonae*, the fifth day of the month, but the seventh on March, May, July and October) and the Ides (*Idus*, the thirteenth day of the month, but the fifteenth on March, May, July and October). These three dates were expressed in ablative, accompanied by the name of the month: e.g. Kalendis Martiis = 1 March; Nonis Maiis = 7 May; Idibus Novembris = 13 November. The days before and after the Kalends, Nones and Ides were known as *pridie* and *postridie Kalendas*, *Nonas*, *Idus*, followed by the name of the month. All the other days were referred to as so many days before the next reference day, by the inclusive system, that is, counting both the day itself and the reference day ahead. For instance, 12 March was referred to as *ante diem quartum Idus Martias* (abbreviated *a.d. IV Id. Mar.*), and 23 April as *ante diem nonum Kalendas Maias* (*a.d. IX Kal. Mai.*). This system is attested in documents of the Roman administration preserved on papyrus but is very rare in inscriptions and only attested in the Hauran.

Babylonian-Aramaic calendar[5]

Jews, Nabataeans and other Semites writing in Aramaic used an Aramaic calendar of Babylonian origin, consisting of twelve lunar months of 29 or 30 days. The lunar year had only 354 or 355 days, and to keep in line with the solar

---

[4] For the Julian calendar in Sidon, see *SEG* LXI, no. 1688. On this calendar and its diffusion in the region, see also Meimaris 1992: 41-45.

[5] On the Jewish calendar, see Meimaris 1992: 45-46; Wiesenberg 2007; Stern 2014.

year an extra month, a second Adar, was added every two or three years. However, the 19-year cycle with seven leap years (the Metonic cycle, discovered in Athens in the fifth century BCE) was only codified by the Jewish leadership in the Middle Ages in the form still adopted by Jews today. In antiquity the Hebrew calendar was mobile, and a new month was announced by the sighting of the crescent. Witnesses posted in high observation points would report the sighting to a rabbinical court, on whose authority Jewish leaders would proclaim the New Moon of the first month, Tishri, to distant Jewish communities by means of bonfires on mountain tops, or by messengers oversea.[6] Intercalation was also fixed empirically year by year, so as to keep the lunar months in step with the agricultural year and the cycle of the seasons (see Table II below for the correspondence of lunar months and the Julian calendar). With Nabataeans, whose calendar is no longer attested after the Late Roman period, it is not quite clear if the leap-year system was applied, and the Nabataean year may have been a purely lunar one, in which months, announced by the sighting of the moon, made the round of the solar year and occurred in turn in all the four seasons, a style persisting to this day in the Islamic calendar.

The year of the Hebrew calendar originally began in spring, with the month of Nisan, but already under the Herodian dynasty the autumnal start in the month of Tishri was adopted. This calendar was applied to different eras in use by the Jews, such as the Seleucid era and the era of the destruction of the Temple (see below): in the latter, the epoch would have been not the 9th of Av 70 CE, but the 1st of Tishri of the previous year, 69 CE. Jews employed the Aramaic-Babylonian calendar when writing Aramaic and Hebrew inscriptions and papyri (e.g. those written by Jewish fighters during the Bar Kochba revolt); but in Greek inscriptions they dated by Macedonian or Julian months, and in Greek papyri by Macedonian months and if official, also by the Latin calendar and consular dates, just like their gentile neighbours. Sometimes a confusion between the Hebrew and the Macedonian calendar is apparent, when an Aramaic name is applied to a Macedonian month,[7] or

---

[6] Tradition ascribes the introduction of the intercalary cycle to Patriarch Hillel II, in 358-359, but during Justinian's reign messengers still travelled from Tiberias to Jewish communities in the Diaspora to announce the beginning of the new year and the expected date of the coming Passover. The Jewish calendar did not reach its final form, in use today, until the tenth century. See Wiesenberg 2007: 357-358.

[7] For instance *P. Yadin* 14, a summons written in Maoza of Ẓo'ar in 125 CE, is dated *ante IV Idus Octobris* and *24 Hyperberetaios called Tishri*, corresponding to October 12 by the Latin calendar, October 11 by the Arabo-Macedonian month. The month is truly Hyperberetaios, for in year 125 11-12 October fell at the end of Tishri, very near the new moon of the next month, Heshvan. This may be the case also of Nabataean months appearing in Greek inscriptions in

the opposite, when a month of the Hebrew calendar is called by the name of the corresponding Macedonian month, as Josephus sometimes does, for instance, in dating the various stages of the siege of Jerusalem and the destruction of the Temple.[8]

Table II: Correspondence of Aramaic, Macedonian and Julian months

Tishri	Hyperberetaios	September-October
Heshvan (Marheshvan)	Dios	October-November
Kislev	Apellaios	November-December
Tevet	Audynaios	December-January
Shevat	Peritios	January-February
Adar	Dystros	February-March
Nisan	Xanthikos	March-April
Iyyar	Artemisios	April-May
Sivan	Daisios	May-June
Tammuz	Panemos	June-July
Av	Loos	July-August
Elul	Gorpiaios	August-September

The days of the Jewish week were simply numbered from the first, Sunday, to the sixth, Friday, while the seventh day was called *sabaton* (σάββατον, Shabbath). Christians continued this tradition, except for changing the name of Sunday to Κυριακή (*kyriaké, dominica*, 'day of the Lord'). They also continued the Jewish system of beginning the day after sunset, so that in

---

the Negev and in southern Transjordan in the third-sixth centuries, long after the creation of Provincia Arabia in 106 CE had displaced the Nabataean kingdom and the Nabataean script had disappeared: examples from 'Avdat (*SEG* XXVIII, no. 1390; Av 241, era of Arabia), Petra (*IGLJ* IV, no. 18; Sivan 256, era of Arabia), Beersheba (*SEG* XLVI, no. 1813; Shevat 537 or Peritios 538). The *communis opinio* is that the Aramaic name was superimposed on a Macedonian month; however, a case can be made for the persistence of the mobile Nabataean calendar: see Meimaris 1992: 170, 172, nos. 30 and 40; Sartre, *IGLJ* IV, no. 18. For a discussion of this question, see Di Segni 1993d: 503-506.

[8] The Passover eve, when John of Gischala entered Jerusalem and seize control of the Temple (*Bell.* V, 98-101), is dated 14 Xanthikos (14 Nisan); the suspension of the sacrifice on the 17th of Tammuz (Mishnah Ta'anith 4:6) is dated 17 Panemos (*Bell.* VI, 94), and the destruction of the Temple, in Jewish tradition commemorated on the 9th of Av, is dated 10 Loos (*Bell.* VI, 249-250).

inscriptions as well as in literary texts written in the Holy Land any event happening after dusk or in the night always bears the date of what in western eyes would be the next day. Day and night were each divided into twelve hours, the first beginning about 6 AM and 6 PM respectively.[9]

The sabbatical year (shevi'it)

In the seventh year of the seven-year agricultural cycle mandated by the Torah (Ex. 23:10-11; Lev. 25:2-7), Jews were commanded to let the land rest and lie fallow (*shmitah*). In Late Antiquity, this rule applied within the boundaries occupied by the people of Israel returning from the Babylonian exile. In the year of *shmitah* only fruits and herbs growing of their own accord and being no one's property, and crops grown in areas entirely inhabited by gentiles were permitted. The seven-year cycle and the seventh year are sometimes mentioned as a chronological device in Hebrew and Aramaic inscriptions written by Jews.[10]

Eras in use in the Hellenistic-Roman period and in Late Antiquity

Inscriptions and documents provide evidence that most eras employed in the Holy Land in the Roman period were still the main means of dating in Late Antiquity, at least until the early seventh century and in some cases long after the Islamic conquest. In Late Antiquity local eras were not restricted within the boundaries of their mother cities but could be found outside them. Therefore, the use of a particular era, while it can be an indication that the find spot was included in the territory of the city whence the era originated, cannot be taken as proof of it. A survey of these eras, in order of antiquity, follows below.

The earliest era adopted in the region was the Seleucid, starting in 312 BCE, which made its appearance after Antiochus III took Palestine from the Ptolemies at the end of the third century BCE. Before that, a chronological system based on the regnal years of the Ptolemaic kings is attested in a few inscriptions from Marisa.[11] The Seleucid era appears on weights and coins

---

[9] On the week, the day and the hours, see Meimaris 1992: 47-50.

[10] For a list of sabbatical years (not always consistent) mentioned in Jewish epitaphs from Zo'ar, see Cotton and Price 2001: 283.

[11] *SEG* XLII, nos. 1439-1440, *CIIP* IV, 2, nos. 3451-3452; Oren and Rappaport 1984: 148-149 = *SEG* XXXIV, nos. 1483, 1492; but see *CIIP* IV, 2, no. 3660 and the commentary there (a foundation era of Marisa by Aulus Gabinius in 57/6 BCE?). Ptolemaic dates were found

in the Hellenistic period but is very rare in the Roman period, when it was supplanted by local eras in the cities of Palaestina, Arabia and Phoenice. However, it remained the dominant chronological system in Syria until the Middle Ages and even became the ecclesiastical era of Jacobites and Nestorians, in use to this day. The Jews too adopted it as 'era of the contracts' (*minyan ha-shtarot*) until the Middle Ages, and even centuries later in some parts of the Diaspora. Its epoch was 1 Dios 312, though peoples of the Near East who preferred a spring calendar started the count on the 1st of Nisan 311. This epoch was adopted by the Jews in the Land of Israel at least until Herod's time, but was later abandoned in favour of the 1st of Tishri. [12]

Tyre had more than a single era, but the main one, and the only one attested in our region, is the era starting in 126 BCE, with an autumn epoch (1 Hyperberetaios, 19 October, or 1 Dios, 18 November). It was used in northwestern and Upper Galilee, which belonged to the territory of Tyre. Its latest appearance (as yet) is in a Greek inscription dated 610/1 discovered on a mosaic pavement at Shelomi, east of Nahariyya.[13] The era of Ascalon, starting on 27 November (1 Dios) 104 BCE, is last attested in an inscription engraved on the chancel screen of a synagogue, dated 605/6 CE, and in a fragment of epitaph from Sawafir el-Gharbiye, dated January 620.[14]

A group of eras starting between 64 and 60 BCE are called 'Pompeian eras', because the cities known to have adopted them appear in the list of Greek cities that Pompey freed from Jewish domination following his campaign in 63 BCE (Josephus, *Bell*. I, 156; *Ant*. XIV, 75-76). All used an autumnal calendar but the exact epoch is unknown, except for Gaza, where the year began on 1 Dios, 28 October.[15] Of the so-called Pompeian eras, those of Gadara, Abila, Dion, Hippos and Scythopolis (Beth Shean) started in 64 BCE;[16] Pella, Philadelphia (Amman) and Gerasa in 63; Gaza in 61; Raphia

---

also on Aramaic ostraca from Marisa: see *CIIP* IV, 2: 941. Regnal years were also used by the Nabataeans in inscriptions and coins until Rome put an end to the independent kingdom with the creation of the province of Arabia in 106 CE.

[12] Grumel 1958: 209-210; Meimaris 1992: 53-54.

[13] Dauphin 1977.

[14] *CIIP* III, nos. 2321, 2578.

[15] On the Pompeian eras and the inscriptions dated by these city eras, see Stein 1990: 26-111; Meimaris 1992: 74-135.

[16] Canatha in the Hauran, a city later belonging to Provincia Arabia, is not mentioned by Josephus among the cities freed by Pompey in 63 (*Bell*. I, 156; *Ant*. XIV, 75-76)) or those restored by Pompey's man, the proconsul of Syria Aulus Gabinius, in 57 BCE (*Bell*. I, 166; *Ant*. XIV, 87-88), but it was certainly included, for on coins its inhabitants are called Gabinii and the city name is Canatha/Canotha Gabinia. However, its era is not 57 BCE as one would ex-

in 60 and so probably Gaba.[17] The era of Dora started between 63 and 61 BCE.[18] An era of 59 BCE, ascribed to Gabinius' restoration of the city, was suggested for Azotos, but has no existence and the inscriptions purportedly dated by this era are really dated by the era of Ascalon.[19]

Most Pompeian eras are still documented in the seventh and even in the eighth century. The era of Hippos appears in an inscription dated July 604 found at Khisfin,[20] the era of Gerasa in the church of Bishop Genesius in the city, 1 September 611,[21] and in the building inscription of a church at Khirbet el-Biddīyah, dated 640/1.[22] The era of Gadara dates the renovation of the bathhouse at Hammath Gader, 5 December 662.[23] The era of Pella

---

pect, but 64 or 63 BCE. Stein (1900: 39), on numismatic evidence, leaves the question open, but Sartre prefers 64 BCE, based on epigraphic evidence (*IGLS* XVI, 1: 159-160). Unlike the other cities with Pomeian eras, Canatha appears to be using an Arabo-Macedonian calendar with New Year Day on 22 March 64; cf. *IGLS* XVI, 1: 180, no. 256.

[17] Gaba, called 'Gaba of Philippus' to distinguish it from several other places of the same name, apparently owed its restoration to Lucius Marcius Philippus, proconsul of Syria in 61-60 BCE, under whose care were the liberated cities; 60 BCE seems therefore more likely than 59, when a new governor, Gneus Cornelius Lentullus, came to Syria. See Stein 1990: 53-56; Meimaris 1992: 134-135; Gitler and Kushnir-Stein 2004: 92-93. Apart from coins, only one example of this era was known (on a weight: *SEG* XXXVII, no. 1480); the discovery of another, still unpublished, has been recently reported in the media.

[18] Stein 1990: 49-52; Meimaris 1992: 117-118. The era of Dora is known through numismatic evidence but is little attested epigraphically: a single example comes from Late Antiquity, a dedicatory inscription from a synagogue discovered at Binyamina, dated 'Year 471', i.e., between 408 and 410 by the era of Dora (Di Segni 1993a; 1994b; 2006-2007:123, n. 53; Barag 1994; *CIIP* II, no. 2080).

[19] For the suggestion see Meimaris 1992: 72-73, and for its refutation Stein 1990: 95-97, 106-109; Di Segni 2008: 33*; 2019: 42. Marisa has an era of 59 or possibly 58 BCE, whose connection with Gabinius' activities is far from demonstrated, though the city is called Gabinia on the few known coins (Gitler and Kushnir-Stein 2004); *contra* Gera 2017, who sets the era to 57/6, under the governorship of Gabinius. It is one of the ephemeral 'Pompeian' eras starting between 61 and 58 (?) that are known only from some early issues of city coins but poorly or not at all epigraphically documented and therefore are not discussed here.

[20] Building inscription in the mosaic pavement of a church: Tzaferis and Bar Lev 1976: 114-115 (= *SEG* XXVI, no. 1676) dated the inscription to June 618 by the era of Antioch, an error corrected by Meimaris 1992: 77, no. 3. Gregg and Urman 1996: 83-84 no. 83 reported this dating but at p. 88, n. 12 suggested a possible dating by a Pompeian era: see *SEG* XLVI, no. 1951 (misleading wording: the era is 64, not 63 BCE).

[21] Mosaic pavement: Welles 1938: 486-487, no. 335.

[22] *SEG* LXIII, no. 1619. There is however some uncertainty whether the village belonged to the territory of Gerasa or to that of Pella, as it is located midway between the two cities.

[23] Inscription engraved on stone, commemorating the restoration of the bathhouse ordered by Caliph Mu'awiya: *SEG* XXX, no. 1687; Di Segni 1997b 237-240, no. 54.

dates two building phases in the church and monastery of Mar Liyas in Jebel Ajlun respectively to 623/4 and 776.[24] The era of Philadelphia appears in the church of St. Varus at Khilda in 687 and in the 'Lower Church' at Quweisme in 718/19,[25] and the era of Gaza in all the building stages of a church at Jabaliyah, the last of which is dated in 732 CE.[26]

Another era came into existence through Roman interference in the land before the establishment of the Roman rule: the era of Acco-Ptolemais, a city of Syria-Phonice (later Phoenice Paralia). This era was long believed to have started in autumn 48, as a result of some benefice the city received from Julius Caesar when he passed through, on his way from Egypt to Antioch, in spring 47 BCE. Now, however, numismatic evidence has proved that the era started in autumn 49, like the era of Antioch, probably as a result of the commitment of both cities in support of Caesar against Pompey immediately before or after the battle of Pharsalus (9 August 48 BCE); on his visit Caesar would have only sealed earlier promises of upgrading the privileges of the cities.[27] This era is little documented on coins, for Ptolemais became a Roman colony (Colonia Claudia Ptolemais Germanica Stabilis Felix) under Claudius in 51 CE and ceased to issue coins dated by its civic era. Its epigraphic documentation is also meagre, not surprisingly, since it is only represented in the territory of Acco, and even here there is evidence that it could be superseded by the era of the metropolis, Tyre. Within the boundaries of the *chora* of Ptolemais, only the inscriptions in the church of 'Evron are dated by the city era (different building stages with dates from 414/5 to 489/90), while an inscription in the church at Shavei Zion is dated 611 by the era of Tyre, corresponding to 485/6 CE.[28]

---

[24] Di Segni 2006a: 579-580; *SEG* LVI, no. 1904; Piccirillo 2011: 107-109; *SEG* LXIV, no. 1799. Two late inscriptions from a church at Khirbet eṭ-Ṭantur in the territory of Pella raise the doubt, whether after all the era might be 64 rather than 63 BCE: see *SEG* LV, no. 1748 (2) and *SEG* LXI, no. 1476, corrected in *SEG* LXIII, no. 1627. The earliest is dated July 688, indiction 13, corresponding to July 625; the later 705, indiction 15, corresponding to 641/2. This, however, may be a case – rare but not unknown – of use of the era of the metropolis (Scythopolis) rather than of the city itself.

[25] *SEG* XLIV, no. 1416; Michel 2001: 283-286, no. 106; *IGLJ* II, no. 53; Michel 2001: 290-293, no. 111.

[26] Saliou 2000; *SEG* L, nos. 1480-1495.

[27] For the old date, 48 BCE, see Schürer 1979: 124-125 and the bibliography there. For the new date, 49 BCE, and the numismatic and historical arguments on which it rests, see Stein 1990: 112-118. Other Syrian cities inaugurated Caesarean eras, apparently following the grant of similar privileges. After 49, Antioch added to its title (metropolis) the attributes *hiera, asylos, autonomous*.

[28] *SEG* XXXVII, nos. 1514, 1516, 1517 ('Evron); *SEG* XXXVII, no. 1509B (Shavei Zion). On this era, see also Meimaris 1992: 136-139. However, Meimaris ascribes to the era of Ptol-

In the north of Israel, one of the sons of Herod, Herod Philippus, was recognized by Augustus as tetrarch of the territories Augustus had granted to his father in the Golan, in southern Syria and in south-eastern Lebanon. Philip established his capital at Paneion, at the sources of the Jordan, and founded there Caesarea Philippi. There is some uncertainty about the era of the city, 3 or 2 BCE. According to Aliquot, in his corpus of the inscriptions in the Mount Hermon region, *IGLS* XI, the era of Paneas-Caesarea Philippi started at some unknown point in the first semester of 2 BCE. Meimaris also opted for 2 BCE, but fixed the epoch in autumn of that year. This, however, is excluded by the numismatic evidence, revised by A. Stein: based on coins, two foundations eras are possible, either autumn 3 or spring 2 BCE.[29] A choice is possible only when this era is attested in late antique inscriptions from the territory of Paneas-Caesarea Philippi, together with the indication (on which, see below). The city territory extended to a large area in northern Golan, as far south as Mount Peres (Kh. 'Asheh) and even farther, to Ramthaniyye and Rafid.[30] On the evidence of an inscription from Quneitra dated 19 Audynaios 463, indiction 15, Stein opted for the era of spring 2 BCE.[31] This epoch is suitable to the Ramthaniyye inscription, dated Panemos 616 CE (both from spring 2 BCE and from autumn 3 BCE, but excluding Meimaris' suggestion, autumn 2 BCE). However, in another inscription dated by the era of Paneas, from Mumsiyye, the era year and indiction fit only by an era starting in autumn 3 BCE. This inscription is dated to a Latin month whose name, partly lost, ends in *-rios* (hence any month between September and February), year 534, indiction 10. By an autumn era of 3 BCE most of these months fell within the 10th indiction (1 September 531 to 31 August 532) in late 531 or early 532, but had the new year begun in spring, all the candidate months would

---

emais also the dated inscriptions from Ḥ. Ḥesheq and Kh. Bata (Karmiel), which are probably dated by the era of the metropolis of Second Palestine, Scythopolis. The territory of Ptolemais was limited to the Plain of Acco, and its eastern frontier was at the village of Chabulon, which belonged to Galilee (Kabul: Jos., *Bell*. II, 503; III, 38; *Vita* 213). Both Ḥ. Ḥesheq and Kh. Bata are deep in the mountains of the Galilee and cannot have been included in the boundaries of Ptolemais. For Ḥ. Ḥesheq, see *SEG* XL, no. 1446, and for Kh. Bata, see *SEG* XLII, no. 1452; corrected date in Di Segni 1997a: 331-333, no. 81.

[29] Stein 1990: 128-130; Meimaris 1992: 142-145; Aliquot 2008: 22.

[30] The latest appearance of this era is in an inscription dated 611 CE: *SEG* LXIII, no. 1582, but most likely in the Ramthaniyye inscription, whose date must probably be read XIH, 618 of the era of Paneas, corresponding to summer 616 CE: see below, n. 82. For incorrect datings of this inscription, see *SEG* XLVI, no. 1987; LV, no. 1719. Boundary stones mentioning the *censitor* Aelius Statutus belong to the territory of Paneas: *SEG* LIII, no. 1818; LVI, no. 1848; Hartal 2006: 281-283.

[31] For the Quneitra inscription, see *SEG* VII, no. 249; Meimaris 1992: 145, no. 4.

have fallen in indiction 11. So also by an era of autumn 2 BCE.[32] In view of these contradictory data, the option of autumn 3 BCE must certainly remain open. A consideration in its favour is that a spring epoch, reflecting a spring calendar, would be an odd choice for the capital of Philip, since it appears that all Herod's successors adopted an autumn calendar in their coinage.[33]

Two other cities had foundation eras starting under the Herodians: Sebaste, founded by Herod in the core of the ancient city of Samaria, probably in 28 BCE, and Tiberias, founded by Herod Antipas between 18 and 20 CE, but neither era is represented in inscription, unless future discoveries hold some surprises.[34] But surprises do happen, as is proved by the era of a rather insignificant city, Capitolias (Beit Ras, 5 km north of Irbid in northwest Jordan). The settlement was probably founded in the late first century CE, and attained the status of *polis* in 97/98; it is first mentioned by Ptolemy (V, 14, 18) as one of the cities of the Decapolis. But its foundation era, known from a few coins, was not epigraphically attested, not even in the Roman period, until 2014, when a fragmentary mosaic inscription came to light at Tell Zar'a, a site in Wadi el-'Arab, some 4.5 km southwest of Gadara. Surprisingly, the date of this inscription, June 612, in the 7th indiction, is not given by the era of Gadara or of Pella, whose territory extended to the south of Wadi el-'Arab, but by the era of Capitolias: June 612, by an epoch of autumn 97, corresponds to June 709, in the 7th indiction.[35] Since it seems unlikely that the era of a modest though prosperous city might have penetrated the territories of its more dominant neighbours, it appears that, when Capitolias was founded, it received as its own territory at least the Wady el-'Arab, a wedge between

---

[32] For the Mumsiyye inscription and its date, see *SEG* XLVI, no. 1969; LVIII, no. 1703.

[33] Kokkinos 1998: 234–235 (Antipas), 237 (Philip), 285 (Agrippa I), 307 (Herod of Chalcis), 398 (Agrippa II]).

[34] Meimaris 1992: 140-141 opts for the epoch of autumn 28 BCE rather than 25 BCE preferred by some numismatics; cf. Schürer 1979: 162-163, n. 410. He ascribes three inscriptions to this era: a stamped amphora dated '(Year) 29', a weight dated '(Year) 88' and a fragmentary base dated 'Year 161' (*SEG* VIII, nos. 99, 99, 104), but there is no certainty that the amphora and the weight belonged to the city, even if they were found there, and the engraving technique and palaeography of the letters on the base point to the second century BCE rather than the second CE. If so, the date on the base is given by the Seleucid era. For the era of Sebaste, based on a study of its coins, see Stein 1990: 120-128, and for the era of Tiberias, based on coins and on Josephus' report of the chronology of Antipas, ibidem: 130-132.

[35] For the era of Capitolias, 97 or 98, based on coins, see Stein 1990: 139-140; for a summary of the history and urban development of the city, see Lenzen 2000: 19-22. For the Tell Zar'a inscription, see Zerbini 2017: 268-270, who mistakenly calculated the epoch as autumn 96, through the common error of forgetting the non-existence of year 0 (zero).

Gadara and Pella, at the head of whose basin the city (itself devoid of water sources) was located on a rocky outcrop.

Two eras were inaugurated by direct Roman intervention. The era of Arabia marked the annexation of the Nabataean kingdom and the creation of the new province of Arabia. The new era, starting on March 22, 106, was not imposed by the Roman rulers but adopted by the local population in exchange for the former dating system by regnal years, which had perforce to be abandoned. The calendar used with this era is the Arabo-Macedonian, with the New Year on the spring equinox, but Julian months are also often associated with it. A notable characteristic of this era is that the digits in the number indicating the year always appear in descending order, first the hundreds, then the tens and finally the units, unlike the earlier eras, in which dates are normally presented in ascending order. The era of Arabia was in use in all the parts of Transjordan and southern Syria that were within the boundaries of Arabia and not included in the territories of the cities of the former Decapolis, which had eras of their own; besides, it also appears in the Negev and in the Sinai peninsula, which belonged to Provincia Arabia from 106 until the late third century, when these regions were transferred to Palaestina.[36] The 'era of the province (of Arabia)' is sometimes called 'era of the city' or 'era of Elusa' when used in the territory of Elusa in the Negev, or 'era of Bostra' when it is used in the territory of Bostra, the capital of the province. This era remained in use long after the Muslim conquest, into the eighth century.[37]

The second era inaugurated in this period is the foundation era of Eleutheropolis, the former village of Beth Govrin which Septimius Severus raised to the status of *polis* under a new name, attested in coins, Lucia Septimia Severiana Eleutheropolis. The epoch of this era is uncertain. The coins allow for a starting point in autumn 199 or in spring 200, and since the calendar adopted with it was the Arabo-Macedonian, it was at first accepted that the epoch was 22 March 200. However, contradictory evidence is offered by a number of inscriptions bearing dates by this era: an unlikely epoch of January 1st was suggested, or more likely, the autumn era of 199. Yet inscriptions dated by this era only appear in the sixth century, and in a vast area that no longer belonged to the territory of Eleutheropolis, or even

---

[36] Tsafrir 1986; Di Segni 2018a: 247-256. On the era of Arabia and its rich epigraphic documentation, see Meimaris 1992: 146-304.

[37] The latest inscriptions dated by the era of Arabia in the Negev is an epitaph from Shivta dated 10 January 679 (Negev 1981: 59-60, no. 65; Meimaris 1992: 302, no. 523), and east of the Jordan an inscription in the church of St. Stephen at Umm er-Rasas, dated 756 (*SEG* XXXVII, no. 1552A; Meimaris 1992: 304, no. 530; Michel 2001:391-394, no. 144c).

to the same province, First Palestine, but had become part of the newly creates Palaestina Salutaris (later Third Palestine) in 357/8.[38] One wonders, therefore, if a change may not have occurred under the influence of the popular eras of the coast (Ascalon, Gaza) or of the indictional year (stating on September 1), causing some users of the era of Eleutheropolis to prefer an autumn epoch. The era of Eleutheropolis continued in use well into the eighth century.[39]

Table III: Summary of the eras of the Hellenistic and Roman periods

Era	Epoch	Calendar New Year	Hell. period	Roman period	4th c.	5th c.	6th c.	7th c.	8th c.
Ptolemaic	Regnal years	Egyptian 1 Thoth (29 August)	√						
Nabataean	Regnal years	Lunisolar or lunar Spring	√	√	(√) (calend. only)		(√) (calend. only)		
Seleucid (era of Damascus)	312 BCE 1 Dios	Macedonian Autumn	√	√	Used by	Jews as	Era of	con	tracts
Tyre	126 BCE	Macedonian Autumn	√	√		√	√	√	
Ascalon	104 BCE 27 Nov.	Macedonian Autumn			√	√	√	√	
Gadara, Dion, Hippos	64 BCE	Macedonian Autumn + Jul. months	√	√	√	√	√		
Scythopolis Palestinian Galilee	64 BCE	Macedonian Autumn + Jul. months	√			√	√		
Pella Philadelphia	63 BCE	Macedonian Autumn	√		√	√	√	√	
Gerasa	63 BCE	Macedonian Autumn	√	√	√	√	√		
Dora	63-61 BCE	Macedonian Autumn	√		√(?)				
Gaza	61 BCE 28 Oct.	Macedonian Autumn	√		√	√	√	√	
Raphia	60 BCE	Egyptian months			√				

---

[38] Di Segni 2018: 254-259.

[39] On the era of Eleutheropolis, see Meimaris 1992: 305-313. The latest inscription dated by this era marks repairs in the mosaic pavement of a church at Yatir and bears the date March 725 (Di Segni 2003: 254; *SEG* L, no. 1498).

Acco-Ptolemais	49 BCE	Macedonian Autumn + Jul. months				√		
Caesarea Philippi	3 or 2 BCE	Macedonian Autumn-Spring + Jul. months	√	√	√	√	√	
Capitolias	97 CE	Macedonian Autumn + Jul. months	√					√
Provincia Arabia	106 CE 22 March	Arabo-Maced. Spring + Jul. months	√	√	√	√	√	√
Eleutheropolis	199 or 200 CE	Arabo-Maced. Autumn or Spring + Jul. months				√	√	√
Destruction of Temple	69 CE 1 Tishri	Jewish Autumn		√	√	√		
Jewish era of creation	1 Tishri	Jewish Autumn					√	

As Table III shows, not all the eras of the Roman period survived into Late Antiquity; yet, those still attested in the fourth and fifth centuries did in most cases survive long after the Islamic conquest, and for those of which no evidence later than the fifth or early sixth centuries is known at the moment, we can confidently expect that such evidence will come to light in the future. The exception, of course, are two chronological systems carried over from the Roman period like the city eras but connected with the political system of the Roman Empire, which inevitably disappeared when the whole Near East – Syria, Palestine, Arabia and Egypt – was cut off from the Empire, first by the Persian invasion in 614 and later by the Islamic conquest in the 630s. These are the dates by consulates and by regnal years of the Roman emperors.

The consuls who came to office on the 1st of January were the eponyms of the year. In the practice of the imperial period, in the following months they were replaced by other consuls appointed as suffects, but dating by suffects' names, occasionally known in other parts of the Roman Empire, is not attested in our region. While consular dates were the same throughout the Empire, regnal years of emperors were counted in different ways in different regions. In the Near East, from Trajan on, they were counted from their first reception of the *tribunician potests* (δημαρχικὴ ἐξουσία), with which the emperor and the emperor designate were invested in order to protect their person from assault or injury.[40] The office was annual and started on December 10, and even a *tribunician potestas* granted a few days before this date was counted as the man's first *tribunician potestas* and his first regnal year.

After an eclipse beginning between the late third and the fourth century, consular dates and regnal years came back into use in the sixth. Due to the short time between their comeback and their forced disappearance, the epigraphic documentation of these systems in late antique Palestine is meagre. Only three Greek inscriptions with consular dates in the sixth century are known at present; a fourth is in Latin.[41] The earliest inscription, from Mount Nebo, has a double date, 425 of Provincia Arabia and the consulate of Lampadius and Orestes, corresponding to 530 CE;[42] next is the Latin inscription from Kh. Batya, dated to the consulate of Justinian (for the fourth time) and Flavius Paulinus, 534 CE;[43] then another inscription from Mount Nebo, dated to the consulate of Flavius Belisarius without a colleague, in 535.[44] Only after a gap of fifty years, in 585, do we find another case, the latest known at present: an inscription from Kursi dated to the second post-consular year of Emperor Mauricius.[45] Dating by post-consulate (first or second year after the last consul) makes its first appearance in the early fourth century, but it

---

[40] *Tribuni plebis* were sacrosanct in republican time and any attack on their persons was punishable with death. Octavianus Augustus was the first emperor who received the tribunician power for life, in 23 BCE. He also started the practice of marking a man as his designate successor by taking him as his colleague in the tribunate. On *tribunician potestas*, see Meimaris 1992: 335-338; on regnal years, see ibidem: 357-380.

[41] For consular dates up to the fourth century, see Meimaris 1992: 340-347, nos. 11-27 (imperial consulates, 114-365 CE); 348-354, nos. 29-43 (civilian consulates, 150-350 CE). Meimaris (355, nos. 44-45) lists as consular dates also two inscriptions commemorating the building of fortifications in Bostra (*IGLS* XIII, 1, no. 9118) and Gerasa (Welles 1938: 467, no. 273), ordered by the *magister militum Orientis* Flavius Anatolius, who was also consul that year, 440 CE; but the date of the inscriptions is given by the era of Arabia and the mere mention of the title does not make them into consular dates. It is worth noting, however, that in Egypt, where evidence for dating systems is enriched by a great number of documents on papyrus, consular dates are common from the fourth to the seventh century without interruption: Bagnall and Worp 2004: 88-98.

[42] *IGLJ* II, no. 74; Meimaris 1992: 355-356, no. 46.

[43] Di Segni and Feissel 2020: 605-606.

[44] *IGLJ* II, no. 100c; Meimaris 1992: 356, no. 47.

[45] Mistakenly described as the first post-consular year in the Greek text and 'first consulate' in Meimaris' comment (but see his discussion at p. 343): *SEG* XXXIII, no. 1270; Meimaris 1992: 348, no. 28; Di Segni 1997a: 275-277, no. 59.

became the prevailing system after the Roman consular office was abolished in 541. After this date, only emperors or members of the imperial family occasionally assumed the consulship; there was no tenure but just an announcement at any time during a calendar year, which made it a consular year. The years between the last consular year and the next were counted as post consulates in two different ways: the first year after a consular year was the first post consulate of the man who had last held the honour, or the consular year itself was considered his first post-consulate. More post-consulates followed until another man was appointed to the consulship. At the time of Mauricius' inscription both systems coexisted.[46]

Little more evidence exists for the revival of dating by regnal years in Late Antiquity. After a gap of about 240 years, the epigraphic use of this style was probably triggered by the publication of Justinian's Novella 47 in 537.[47] Of 60 Greek inscriptions of the Roman and Byzantine periods bearing regnal dates listed by Meimaris, 54 are dated between 45 and 282 CE, and only five between 538 and 592.[48] To this list we can now add a dedicatory inscription discovered in a monastery at Deir Qal'a in northern Judaea, dated to the 18th year of Justinian and the 8th indiction, that is, between 1 September 544 and 31 March 545.[49] One additional case is represented by an Aramaic inscription in the synagogue of Beth Alpha, which dates the mosaic pavement to the reign of Justin, most likely Justin II (565-578).[50]

---

[46] Stein 1934: 887-890. Grumel 1958: 346-347; Meimaris 1992: 343.

[47] In this Novella, issued on 31 August 537, Justinian ordered that all contracts and legal documents from then on should be dated by the regnal year of the ruling emperor, the consul or consuls of that year, the indiction, the month and day, in this order. On this edict, see Bagnall and Worp 2004:45, and on the use of regnal years in Egypt, see ibiden: 43-54

[48] Meimaris 1992: 363-3780, nos. 48-101 are dated between 45 and 282 CE; ibidem: 378-380, nos. 103-107 between 538 and 592. One of the cases listed by Meimaris, no. 102, purportedly dated to the 25th year of Anastasius, must be rejected as its interpretation is incorrect (*SEG* VIII, no. 239; see discussion in Di Segni 1997a: 646-648, no, 223*).

[49] Di Segni 2012a; *SEG* LXII, no. 1682. For the indictional cycle and the use of indiction to determine the right date, see below.

[50] Naveh 1978:72-74, no. 43; on the synagogue, see Sukenik 1932; Avigad 1993). The figure of the year is lost, and the identification of the emperor is problematic. Following Sukenik, both Naveh and Avigad opted for Justin I (518-527), as Justin II (565-578) 'was notorious for his severe anti-Jewish policy' (Avigad 1993:192). In fact, the building of synagogues was forbidden since 439, with Theodosius II's Novella 3, which Justinian incorporated in his Codex (*CJ* 1, 9, 18), published in 533. However, the mosaic pavement with the inscription belonged to a renovation stage of the synagogue, which was permitted by the law. Moreover, the comeback of dating by regnal years began years after Justin I's death, and its anticipation by a Jewish community and in Aramaic seems unlikely.

The innovations of Late Antiquity

Vis-à-vis the continuity described above, also important innovations took place in late antique epigraphy of the Holy Land with regard to chronological systems. At least five new eras appeared here between the late third and the mid-seventh century.[51] Two, the era of Maximianopolis and the Constantinian era, followed the pattern of foundation eras by marking the upgrade of a non-urban settlement to urban status, now highlighted by its elevation to episcopal see. Like other little attested Late Roman foundation eras, these two originated in a long-established tradition and thus, though new, can be considered as still within the continuity frame. The era of Maximianopolis started when the village of Sakkaia (modern Shaqqa in southern Syria) was raised to city status with a new name, honouring M. Aurelius Valerius Maximianus, appointed Augustus as colleague of Diocletian in 286 CE. Two inscriptions from Shaqqa, *IGLS* XVI, 3, nos. 516-517, bearing both the city era and the indiction, allow fixing the epoch in spring 287 or 302, but the later date is excluded, for the toponym Maximianopolis is mentioned in a tetrarchic boundary stone of the land survey order by Diocletian and carried out in 297/8.[52] It is worth noting that another city in the Holy Land was named Maximianopolis after the Tetrarch: Legio in the Valley of Jezreel, an episcopal see as early as 325 or earlier.[53] However, there is no evidence that a foundation era was adopted here.

The Constantinian era was established either under Constantine (324-337) or under his son and successor Constantius II (337-361). Despite its name (adopted in modern scholarship for the sake of convenience), it is not a

---

[51] We leave aside two late foundation eras, that of Philippopolis (Shahba) and that of Neapolis (Sheikh Miskin), both short-lived and only of local importance. The birthplace of Emperor Marcus Julius Philippus (Philip the Arab) was raised to city status in 244, but its foundation era is attested only by a single inscription ('First year of the city': Meimaris 1992 325, no. 1; *IGLS* XV, 2, no. 419). The foundation of Neapolis may have been connected with the activity of the *dux Arabiae* Ulpianus in the area ca. 362: for a discussion of the circumstances, see Sartre, *IGLS* XIV, 2: 372. Like the former, this city era is attested only by a single inscription of year 4 (Meimaris 1992 325, no. 1; *IGLS* XIV, 2, no. 407).

[52] *SEG* VII, no. 1055; *AE* 1936, no. 145; Millar 1994: 539-544, no. 35; *IGLS* XVI, 3, no. 667. On the era of Maximianopolis, see Meimaris 1992: 321-323, 326-327, nos. 3-7; Sartre, *IGLS* XVI, 1: 18-19; *IGLS* XVI, 3: 4-5 (I wish to give my most heartfelt thanks to professor Maurice Sartre for allowing me to read and cite the draft of this volume, which has not yet be published as I write). This era is used also at Hit (ancient Eeitha) in the territory of Maximianopolis: *IGLS* XVI, 3, no. 600 (inscription mistakenly dated according to the era of Arabia by Meimaris 1992 no. 116, with an erroneous reading, corrected by Sartre.

[53] Paul, bishop of Maximianopolis, attended the Council of Nicaea in 325: Fedalto 1988: 1036.

regnal era but marked the creation of an urban entity: this is believed to have been the military and civil settlement of Menois, the administrative centre of an extensive imperial estate (*saltus*) in the western Negev, named *saltus Constantinianus*, whose name implies a (re)organization of this land under Constantine or Constantius. Indeed, three of the four inscriptions dated by this era were discovered at Ḥ. Ma'on (map ref. 093/082); the provenance of the fourth is unknown. All bear both the 'year of the city' and the indiction, allowing to fix the epoch to autumn 331 or 346; all the dates fall in the sixth century.[54] However, bishops of Menois are not attested until 449;[55] it cannot be excluded, therefore, that the new 'era of the city' marked a different event, the constitution of Maiuma, the port of Gaza, as a separate city and episcopal see, ordered by Constantine in the late years of his reign, at least if Eusebius' narrative in his Life of Constantine follows a chronological order. The new city was called Constantia after the emperor's sister.[56] Emperor Julian subjected it again to Gaza, but Maiuma-Constantia was again an independent bishopric immediately after his death.[57] Admittedly, no inscription dated by the Constantinian era was discovered *in situ* at el-Mine, the site of ancient Maiuma, but if the era came into being with its foundation as Constantia, the era must have started in 331 and its adoption in the *saltus Constantinianus* may have come later, with the grant of urban status to Menois. The same reservation should be kept in mind also with regard to the era of Constantiana (or Constantia, Constantina), on the northern margin of the Trachon (Leja Plateau). It may be identified with Buraq (ancient Berroqia), or with nearby Mismiye (ancient Phaene; map ref. 280/282). The best attested name appears to be Constantiana, suggesting that it was more likely a refoundation of Constantius II than of Constantine.[58] Two inscriptions from Buraq (perhaps a village in the urban territory of Constantiana rather than the city itself) bear dates in the years 5 and 8 of the city, but it is impossible to establish an epoch, though Sartre favours the reign of Constantius. Certainly, despite the shared name, there is no connection between the era of the *saltus Constantinianus* and that of Constantiana in southern Syria.

---

[54] Meimaris 1992: 324-325, 328-329, nos. 10-13.
[55] Fedalto 1988: 1027.
[56] Eusebius, *Life of Constantine* IV, 37-38, transl. Cameron and Hall 1999: 167.
[57] Fedalto 1988: 1027; Bagatti 2002a: 171-173. The first known bishop of Maiuma, Zeno, had a long episcopate, from the 370s to the 390s, and lived to be a hundred: Sozomen, *Historia Ecclesiastica* VII, 28, ed. Bidez and Hausen 1960: 345.
[58] Aliquot 2017: 67-70; Sartre, *IGLS* XV, 2: 601-602. For the era and the dated inscriptions, see Meimaris 1992: 323-324, 327-328, nos. 8-9; *IGLS* XV, 2, nos. 527-528.

Unlike the chronological systems rooted in tradition described above, three other systems that came into existence in Late Antiquity – the era of Diocletian, the era of the creation of the world and the Hegira – were rooted in the revolution brought about by the appearance respectively of Christianity and Islam. Despite its name, attested in literary sources, papyri and inscriptions, the era of Diocletian was not based on regnal years, but resulted from a reform of the 19-year lunar paschal cycle, carried out in Alexandria under Diocletian, probably at the initiative of the city bishop Peter (300-311), in order to fix the date of Easter. The first year of the corrected cycle was made to coincide with the first year of Diocletian's rule, and the epoch was fixed on the first of Thoth, the first month of the Egyptian calendar: 29 August 284. This era came into use some time after Diocletian's abdication in 305. In Egypt it was popular in the Byzantine period and long after the Islamic conquest, especially among Christians, who later changed its name into 'era of the Martyrs', in memory of the great persecution against Christians, launched by Diocletian in 303.[59] In our region, except for three or four instances in the south, under Egyptian influence, it was mostly popular among modern scholars who had recourse to it when they could not find an acceptable explanation for some dated inscription.[60]

But the most important innovation with regard to chronological systems was the era, or rather eras, of creation of the world. This is a Christian invention and has nothing to do with the biblical era of creation used by the Jews then and to this day. The Christian era of creation is based on two basic doctrines: the first, an eschatological vision of the world, according to which the world will last 6,000 years, corresponding to the six days of God's creation, after which the Second Advent of Christ will occur and Christ will reign for a thousand years, after which the world will come to an end. The second doctrine taught that the Messiah was born in the middle of the sixth day of

---

[59] On the era of Diocletian, see Grumel 1958: 36-37, 221; Meimaris 1992: 314-318; Bagnall and Worp 2004: 63-87, with an updated list of inscriptions and documents dated by this era between 306/7 and 1166/7, with an isolated example from 1338/9. All listed examples come from Egypt and Nubia, but dates by this era exist also outside Egypt: ibidem: 68, n. 28.

[60] For instance, it was suggested that a lintel from Shivta was dated by the era of Diocletian, while it is probably dated by the era of Arabia or by that of Eleutheropolis (Kirk 1937: 209-211, no. 1; 1938: 163, no. 4; Meimaris 1992: 317, no. 2; refutation in Di Segni 1997a: 821-823, no. 324). The same was suggested for the Beit Safafa inscription (Avi-Yonah 1957; Meimaris 1992: 317, no. 1), really dated by an era of creation (see below). Kirk (1938) listed all the inscriptions from Palestine that, in his opinion, were dated by the era of Diocletian, and rejected several candidates suggested by previous scholars; yet, even his reduced list, like Meimaris' list, includes some intruders.

the world, i.e., around year 5,500 of the creation, and died on the cross at the age of 33,[61] on a Passover Eve (14 Nissan, the date of crucifixion according to the Gospel of John) that fell on a Friday. Given the mobile nature of the Jewish calendar, fixing the date of Jesus' death, and hence of his birth, was a complicated business. Christian chronographers started dealing with it in the third century or even earlier, and by the fifth century several different dates of Jesus' birth had emerged, giving rise to different eras, which were used by Christian chroniclers. The principal ones, and those found in the Holy Land, are the Alexandrian era, which dated Christ's incarnation on 25 March 5493, and the Byzantine era, which dated it in 5509 and placed the beginning of the year on the equinox, March 21. To calculate the corresponding year according to the Common Era, from a date given by the Alexandrian era of creation, one has to subtract 5492 for the period 25/3-31/12, and 5491 for the period 1/1-24/3; when the date is given by the Byzantine era, one has to subtract 5508 for the period 21/3-31/12, and 5507 for the period 1/1-20/3.[62]

Until the late twentieth century it was commonly accepted that creation eras did not appear in inscriptions before the end of the seventh century, and in most places not before the late eighth century; therefore they were believed to be unknown in the Greek epigraphy of Palestine, which was thought to have come to an end by the mid-seventh century.[63] Now, however, a number of inscriptions dated by creation eras have come to light both west and east of the Jordan River, enough to prove not only that these eras were in epigraphic use in the region, and much earlier than the seventh century – in fact, their use developed here long before it reached other parts of the Empire – but also that the Alexandrian era was adopted in Jerusalem and probably in the core

---

[61] This was accepted by the Church Fathers as Jesus' age at the time of his death since a very early period, though there is no basis for this figure in the gospels; on the contrary, the available data for the chronology of the historical Jesus' life indicate that he was older than 33 at the probable date of his execution. For a summary of the question, see Di Segni 2005a: 32-34; 2013.

[62] Why subtract 5492 and 5508 if the incarnation was fixed in 5493 and 5509 respectively? This is because there is no year 0 but the count begins with 1. This mathematical peculiarity has caused not a little confusion in the reckoning of the creation eras, especially leading to identify the incarnation date respectively in 5492 and 5508. On the Alexandrian and Byzantine eras of creation, see Grumel 1958:85-128. In the early Middle Ages, in Constantinople, the beginning of the year of the creation was pushed back to the 1st of September to put the creation year in step with the indiction. This innovation, however, seems to have been already known to Cyril of Scythopolis, a hagiographer writing in the mid-sixth century; this too, therefore, is likely to have been a Palestinian innovation rather than a Byzantine one.

[63] For this opinion, see Foss 1978. Evidence of the use of creation eras west and east of the Jordan was first published in the 1990s: Di Segni 1990a; 1992; 1993b; 1994a.

of the Holy Land west of the Jordan, and the Byzantine across the Jordan; further, that other, less know creation eras were used, seemingly by single religious or ethnic communities.[64] Another peculiarity of the eras of creation in inscriptions is that the dates could be abridged: for instance, an epitaph from Jerusalem dated 'December of the 1st indiction, year 104' can be converted into December 612 CE according to the Alexandrian reckoning by the simple addition of the Greek mark for 6,000,[65] and a dedicatory inscription from en-Nu'eima in Jordan dated 'in the year 8, indiction 8', if interpreted as an abridged reference to year 6008, corresponds to the period between 21 March and 31 August 500 CE, the part of year 6008 of the Byzantine era that was included in the 8th indiction.[66]

It is worth noting that, though chroniclers and historians in Late Antiquity knew an era of Incarnation – different from the Christian era used today – this never came into common use and was never employed in inscriptions. In the sixth century, in Italy, the monk Dionysius Exiguus elaborated the Incarnation era adopted to this day (Dionysian or Common Era), but this was adopted in Europe only in the seventh century and did not reach the East before the Crusader period.

The latest of the new eras that appeared in inscriptions in the region is the era of Hegira, starting in 622 CE, the traditional date of Muhammad's migration from Mecca to Medina.[67] Obviously this era is common in Arabic inscriptions set up by Muslims – the earliest example in the Holy Land an inscription dated 32 AH, 652 CE, found in Jerusalem[68] – but it is unexpected in Greek. Christian inscriptions in Greek dated by a year of the Hegira are rare but not unknown: as a rule, however, the dating formula itself is in Arabic or in Syriac; in other words, they are bilingual inscriptions.[69] At present, only

---

[64] For examples of the various creation eras employed in inscriptions in the region, see Di Segni 2006-2007 and the bibliography there. The earliest examples are from the sixth century (or rather from the end of the fifth, year 500 CE), the latest from the eighth or even from the ninth century.

[65] Di Segni 1993b: 165-167.

[66] Di Segni 2006-2007:117-119; *SEG* LVII, no. 1874.

[67] Grume 1958: 180, 280-296; Meimaris 1992: 330-332; Bagnall and Worp 2004: 300-312. The epoch is 16 July 622, and since this era uses a lunar calendar, hegira years do not keep in step with the years of the Common Era. Concordance tables can be found in both Grumel and Bagnall - Worp.

[68] Sharon 2018.

[69] A lamp with Greek inscription is dated by means of an additional inscription in Arabic to year 211 AH, i.e. 826 CE. A few lamps of this type, often impressed with Greek formulas, bear Kufic inscriptions (an early form of the Arabic alphabet) with dates in the second and third century of the Hegira (eighth and ninth centuries): the earliest date AH corresponds to 723 CE: Loffreda 1989: 187-188.

two cases are known in purely Greek inscriptions. One is an inscription commemorating the restoration of the baths at Hammath Gader by order of Caliph Mu'awiyah in 662; here the date is given by the Hegira as well as by the era of Gadara (Fig. 2).[70] The use of the Hegira seems natural enough when we observe that, despite the opening cross, this was in fact an official text, modelled on the pattern of building inscriptions in Arabic set up by the Muslim

Fig. 2 – The Mu'awiyah inscription, 662 CE (Photo M. Piccirillo, SBF Photographic Archive)
✝ἐπὶ Ἀβδάλλα Μααυϊα ἀμήρα
ἀλμουμενὴν ἀπελύθη κ(αὶ) ἀνε-
νεώθη ὁ κλίβανος τῶν ἐνταῦ-
4 θα διὰ Ἀβδάλλα υἱοῦ Ἀβουασέμου
συμβούλου ἐν μηνὴ Δεκεμβρίῳ
πέμπτῃ, ἡμέρᾳ δευτέρᾳ, ἰνδ(ικτιῶνος) ςʹ,
ἔτους τῆς κολων(ίας) σκψʹ, κατ᾽ Ἄραβα(ς)
8 ἔτους μβʹ, εἰς ἴασην τῶν νοσούν-
των σπουδῇ Ἰωάννου μ(ειζοτέρου) Γαδαρηνοῦ

In the days of Abdallah Mu'awiyah, the commander of the faithful, the clibanus (hot water system) of the (baths) here was cleared and renewed by Abdallah son of Abu Hashim, the governor, in the month of December, on the fifth day, Monday, in the 6th (year) of the indiction, in the year 726 of the colony, according to the Arabs the 42nd year, for the healing of the sick, under the care of John, the Gadarene alderman.

[70] *SEG* XXX, no. 1687; Di Segni 1997a: 237-240, no. 54.

administration.[71] The second and more surprising case is found in an inscription commemorating the laying of a new pavement in a church at Tamra in Lower Galilee, dated in the month of June (?), in the 8th indiction, year 107. The only way to harmonize the year and the indiction is by counting the years from the Hegira. Year 107 AH started on May 19, 725; the 8th indiction fell in 724/5. Year and indiction agree from May 19 to August 31, 725. This date fits the archaeological finds connected with the new pavement.[72]

Table IV: Summary of the eras introduced in Late Antiquity

Era	Epoch	Calendar New Year	3rd c.	4th c.	5th c.	6th c.	7th c.	8th c.
Era of Martyrs (Diocletian)	284	Egyptian 29 August					√	√
Maximianus	287	Julian Spring		√	√	√		
Constantine or Constantius	331 (or 346)	Macedonian Autumn		√		√		
Alexandrian era of creation	Incarnation 25 March 5493	Julian months					√	√
Byz. era of creation	Equinox 21 March 5509	Julian months				√		√
Hegira (in Greek inscriptions)	622	Julian months					√	√

To complete this survey, it is necessary to mention three chronological systems exclusively used by the Jews, not only in their land but also in the diaspora, though we shall cite only local examples. The large majority of Jewish inscriptions are undated. In dated inscriptions, Jews writing in Greek normally adopted any era current in the area where they lived and operated,[73]

---

[71] Not only are some terms of the Muʻawiyah inscription simply transliterated from Arabic, but besides the local person charged with carrying on the task, two authorities are mentioned, the caliph and the emir (district governor), a frequent pattern in official building inscriptions of the early Arab period in this region: see for instance *CIAP* I: 103-106 (Afiq no. 1, 692 CE), 144-146 (Ascalon no. 1, 771/2 CE); *CIAP* II: 216 (Beth Shean no. 2, 753 CE), 275 (Caesarea no. 8, between 878 and 883 CE).

[72] Di Segni and Tepper 2004; Tepper 2018.

[73] For instance, a chancel screen from a synagogue, found near Ascalon, is dated 709 by the era of Ascalon (605/6 CE: *SEG* VIII, no. 267; Roth-Gerson 1987: 25, no. 3; Meimaris 1992: 70, no. 6); a bilingual epitaph from Ẓoʻar bears the date 253 (of Arabia) in Greek and Kislev 290 (of the destruction of the Temple) in Aramaic, corresponding to December 358 CE (Cotton and Price 2001). However, the use of common eras is also present in some cases in Hebrew or Aramaic. The Seleucid era or 'era of the contracts' (*minyan ha-shtarot*) is adopted

while in Hebrew or Aramaic they used the Jewish era of creation or an era of the destruction of the Temple (*minyan hurban ha-bayt* or simply *minyan ha-hurban*). These eras are usually accompanied by the indication of the year in the sabbatical cycle (*minyan ha-shmitah*).[74] The era of creation and the year of the sabbatical cycle appear in a Hebrew inscription in the synagogue of Susiya in southern Judaea.[75] The synagogue of Nabratein in Upper Galilee (ancient Kefar Neburaya) was expanded under Justinian and its lintel bears a Hebrew inscription with the date '494 according to the era of the destruction of the Temple', that is, 562/3 CE.[76] Some doubt existed about the epoch of this era: was it counted from 9 Av 70, the day of the destruction of the Temple,[77] or on the 1st of Tishri 69, the first month of the Jewish calendar? The synchronization of era years and years of the sabbatical cycle may help to answer this question.[78] This era appears in numerous Jewish epitaphs in Aramaic in the cemetery of Ghor eṣ-Ṣafi (Zo'ar), together with *minyan ha-shmitah*. The dates are not always synchronized with the year of the sabbatical cycle, but a bilingual epitaph bearing a double date, of Arabia and of *minyan ha-hurban*, and several synchronized epitaphs, attest that the epoch of the era of the destruction was Tishri 69.[79] It is possible that in the popular memory a full year of *minyan ha-hurban* ran from 9 Av to 8 Av of

in documents, as well as in the synagogue of Dura Europos, together with a regnal year of Emperor Philip (244-249: Naveh 1978: 127-132, nos. 88-89). A regnal date appears in the synagogue of Beth Alpha; see above, text and n. 50.

[74] See above, text and n. 10.

[75] Unfortunately, only the words 'four thousands… since the world was created' survived: Naveh 1978: 116-117, no. 76. On the synagogue, see Gutman et al. 1981; Yeivin 1993:1417-1421.

[76] Avigad 1960; Naveh 1978:31-33, no. 13; on the synagogue, see Meyers 1993. Naveh and Meyers follow Avigad in calculating the date as 564, probably counting 9 Av 70 as the epoch of this era (which would give 563/4, from summer to summer, since Jewish months are mobile), or perhaps just forgetting the non-existence of year 0. But the epoch is most likely Tishri 69, and to reckon the date by the Common Era one has to add 68/69 to 494.

[77] The actual firing of the Temple occurred on the 10th of Av (Josephus, *Bell*. VI, 250), but the firing of the gates that gave access to the Roman attack was ordered by Titus on the 8th, and the fire burned all the following night (*Bell*. VI, 220-235), which was counted as the 9th of Av by the Jewish custom of beginning the new day at sunset. See Schürer 1973: 506, n. 115.

[78] The sabbatical cycle in the first centuries CE can be restored based on information from rabbinical sources and papyri. The second year of Nero, 55/56 CE, was a sabbatical year, and the year of the siege and fall of Jerusalem was a post-sabbatical year: cf. Cotton and Price 2001: 281-282.

[79] Cotton and Price 2001; Misgav 2006. For the bilingual epitaph, see above, n. 73. Though irrelevant to the situation in Late Antiquity, it is still interesting that for Maimonides, writing in the twelfth century, the year of *ḥurban*, the year of the creation and the sabbatical year were completely synchronized.

the following year, and this would explain why in some epitaphs the date and the year of the sabbatical cycle seem to synchronize if the epoch is fixed in Av 70; however, it is clear that in all eras in antiquity the epoch was fixed at the starting point of the calendar year during which the event that triggered the era had occurred. By this rule, and by the above-mentioned evidence, the epoch of *minyan ha-hurban* must be fixed at 1 Tishri 69 CE.

At least in one case there seems to be evidence of the use of this era in a Greek inscription. A synagogue excavated at Deir 'Aziz in the Golan was dated by the excavators to the sixth century, based on coins found under the pavement. But the synagogue had an earlier building stage. Under the niche housing the *aron haqodesh* the fragments of a dismantled arch were unearthed, preserving part of a Greek inscription mentioning the donors, Judah and his brother. One of the fragments shows the letters *qoppa* and *sigma*, in all likelihood the remnant of a dating formula: perhaps the whole figure of the year, 290, or any number up to 299, if the digit of the units is lost.[80] Since the synagogue cannot be earlier than the fourth century, the only possible explanation of this figure is that the date was given according to the era of the destruction of the Temple. Year 290 corresponds to 358/9 (from Tishri 69) or to any date up to 367/8, if one adds a lost digit from 1 to 9 – a dating well in agreement with the palaeography of the inscription and the style of the frieze that adorns the arch.[81]

The indictional cycle and the use of indiction in dates

As we have seen, there were many different chronological systems in use in the Holy Land, and it is not always easy to determine which one is employed in a particular inscription, so that we may be able to calculate the corresponding date by the Common Era. The difficulty is especially felt

---

[80] The two letters can only represent a number, for *qoppa*, a letter of the Greek archaic alphabet, was no longer used as a phonetic symbol in classical Greek but only kept its numerical value: 90. *Sigma* is equivalent to 200. A viable result could also be given by reckoning 290 by the era of Arabia, but this must be excluded as the digits are in ascending order, contrary to the use of the era of Arabia, whose years are consistently given in descending order. Moreover, Deir 'Aziz is very far from the border of Provincia Arabia.

[81] On the building, see Maoz and Ben-David 2003; 2006; Ben-David 2007; on the inscription Di Segni 2006-2007:122-124. In light of this discovery we should perhaps reconsider the date of the Binyamina inscription, also originating from a synagogue and apparently dated by the era of Dora (Di Segni 1993a; 1994b; 2006-2007: 123, n. 53; Barag 1994; *CIIP* II, no. 2080). Barag's suggestion that it was dated by the *hurban* era seemed unlikely at the time, since this era was not attested in Greek, but now this argument is no longer valid.

in Late Antiquity, when not only is the range of possibilities greater than in the Hellenistic and Roman periods, but also eras linked to a particular geographical milieu – urban eras, and even the era of Provincia Arabia – no longer stay always in their proper territory but are sometimes found outside it. Furthermore, urban and even provincial boundaries in the region in Late Antiquity are far from being identified with certainty. Therefore, while proximity to a particular city or supposed location within the boundaries of a particular administrative entity can provide the principal pointer to identify the era used in a specific inscription, nevertheless the answer needs confirmation from additional data. Chiefly, the resulting date must be consistent with the archaeological context and the palaeographical appearance of the dated inscription, as well as with its historical background.[82] Still, the most important tool that helps us to identify the right era is an element of the dating formula that began to appear in inscriptions in the fifth century: the indiction.

The indictional cycle is a cycle of 15 years established for tax purposes in 312/3. It first appeared in Egypt, where a system of tax assessments in 5-year cycles had already been adopted since Diocletian's fiscal reform in 297.[83] The reform required a census of the land to establish the extension of the tilled lands in each administrative entity, the quality of the cultivations and the number of available working hands, so that the tax assessment for each fiscal unit would be fairly proportional to its productivity. The assessments were valid for 15 years, after which they were revised in consideration of changes that might have occurred (e.g. abandonment of agricultural lands, improvement or deterioration of productivity, increase or decrease of hands, and the like). While in Egypt the indiction appears already in 313 in papyri referring to taxes, in our region, where this type of documents is rarely preserved, years of the indictional cycle begin to appear in the fifth century as a dating device in inscriptions and in historical writings. Naturally, saying 'sixth indiction', that is, 'sixth year of an indiction cycle', does not provide

---

[82] For instance, the dedicatory inscription of a martyrium of St. John the Baptist, discovered at Ramthaniyye in the Golan, bore a date read by the editor as Panemos of the 4th indiction, year 688 (ΧΠΗ). The date was reckoned by the Seleucid era, thus equivalent to 376/7, or more precisely summer 377, which fell in the 5th indiction. But, besides the error in the indiction, such an early date is doubtful in view of the progress of Christianization in the Golan, and not consistent with the title of *clarissimus* held by the centurion who paid for the building: such a title for an officer of this rank cannot be expected before the sixth century: see comment in *SEG* XLVI, no. 1987. But a revision of the inscription indicates that the figure should be read ΧΙΗ, 618, and Ramthaniyye is located in the territory of Paneas: thus the date, reckoned according to the era of Paneas, is summer 616, which fell in the 4th indiction.
[83] Bagnall and Worp 2004: 7-35.

an absolute date, but only locates the year at the sixth place within an undetermined cycle, one of a series beginning in 312/3. However, when there is uncertainty about the right era employed in a specific inscription, we can ascertain which era is used by verifying whether the resulting Common Era date fits the indiction year or not. If it does, the era chosen for the calculation is right; if it does not, it will be necessary to try reckoning the date by a different era. Synoptic tables of CE years and indiction years are available in several publications dealing with chronological systems.[84]

The indiction year began on 23 September (Augustus' birthday, which marked the New Year in many city calendars of the East)[85] from Constantine's time to 462 CE; then the beginning of the indiction was anticipated to the 1st of September.[86] Therefore, an indiction year mentioned in inscriptions, documents or literary sources of Late Antiquity never corresponds exactly to a calendar year, be it the Julian, with New Year Day on January 1, to which we refer in converting ancient dates to modern terms, or any of the various Macedonian years in use in the region but is always divided between two successive years.[87]

---

[84] E.g., *Paulys Realencyclopädia*, s.v. Aera (Kubitschek 1893: 666); Meimaris 1992: 393; Grumel 1958: 240-264; Bagnall and Worp 2004:1 29-157. The last two works include also other details, like date of Easter, regnal years and the like.

[85] This calendar, known as Asian calendar, was introduced in Asia Minor by the proconsul of Asia Paullus Fabius Maximus in 9 BCE and was adopted by the cities of the Asian *koinon*.

[86] Grumel 1958: 193-202.

[87] This is obvious wherever a spring calendar was in use (Provincia Arabia, territory of Eleutheropolis), and in any city that adopted a Julian calendar. As to the various local eras associated with a Macedonian calendar, the beginning of the first month, usually Dios, differed from place to place and nowhere coincided with the start of the indiction. For the epoch of the various calendars, see Table III.

CHAPTER III: ARAMAIC DIALECTS AND SCRIPTS

Aramaic was the lingua franca of the Near and Middle East for millennia before and after it was used in the region and period that are the subject of this study.[1] Aramaic is not one language written in one script, but a group of languages belonging to the Northwest Semitic subfamily. Each language, or dialect, developed an alphabet of its own. The Nabataeans adopted Aramaic as their written language and many inscriptions in Nabataean (some of them bilingual in Greek) are found in our region (Fig. 3),[2] but they are out of the

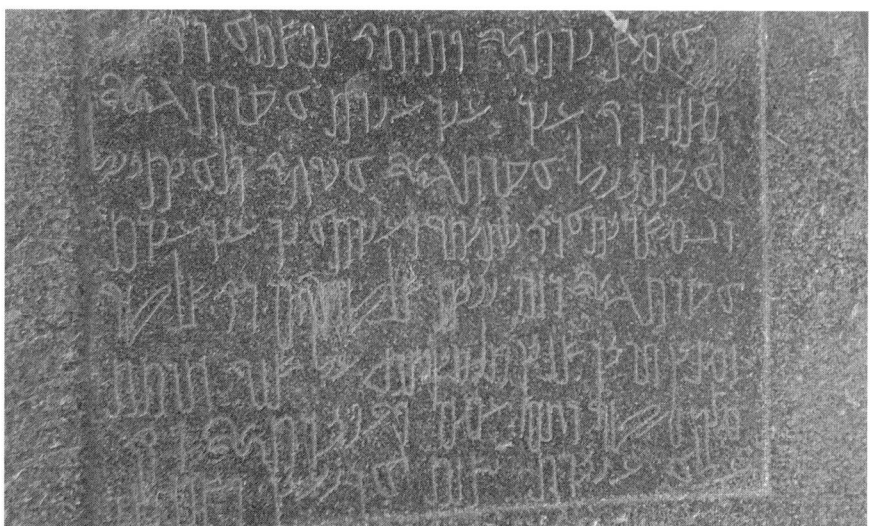

Fig. 3 – Nabataean epitaph from Madaba, 37 CE (*CIS* II, 1, no. 196. By Max.kit – Own work, CC BY-SA 4.0, https://commons.wikimedia.org/w/index.php?curid=58351800 – accessed 21 February 2022)

---

[1] Aramaic originated in Syria about the end of the Late Bronze, in the mid-second millennium BCE, and in some of its various forms is still spoken in some regions of the Middle East: Brock 1989; Aufrecht 2001.

[2] For bilingual inscriptions in Greek and Nabataean, see for instance *IGLJ* II, no. 154 from Zizeh in Jordan; *SEG* XXIX, nos. 1603-1604 from Siʻa and Umm el-Jimal in Hauran. A corpus of Nabataean inscriptions is available on line, as a component of the DASI project (Digital Archive for the Study of Pre-Islamic Arabian Inscriptions). For a corpus of bilingual inscriptions in Nabataean Aramaic and Greek, see Petrantoni 2021.

scope of this chapter, as none is later than the Late Roman period.³ Another variant of western Aramaic is Palmyrene, used side by side with Greek in Palmyra (Tadmor). A number of Jewish epitaphs in Palmyrene were discovered in Jerusalem and Beth She'arim; however we shall not discuss them in this chapter, as they do not belong to the 'native' yield but were dictated by Palmyrene Jews.⁴ Jewish Aramaic was spoken in the Land of Israel in the Second Temple period and written in the Square Aramaic script out of which, in the first century BCE, the Jewish Aramaic script still used in Late Antiquity (as well as in modern Hebrew) developed. Hebrew was still in use but was written in the Jewish Aramaic alphabet, except for sacred texts and divine names, which, as Epiphanius attests, were still inscribed in Paleo-Hebrew in his time, the late fourth century CE.⁵ The Jewish Aramaic script is very well documented in Hebrew and Aramaic inscriptions of all types from the Early Roman period to Late Antiquity and modern times (Fig. 4), but as yet no examples were discovered of sacred names written in Palaeo-Hebrew in that time, surely because such names could not be inscribed on floors or in tombs, considered impure by Jews.

Samaritans spoke their own dialect and continued using a form of Paleo-Hebrew script, as they do to this day (Fig. 5); however, inscriptions in their synagogues are mostly worded in Greek.⁶ Christian Palestinian Aramaic (CPA), or as some prefer calling it, Syropalestinian Aramaic, the dialect used by Christians in the Holy Land in Late Antiquity, developed at a time when Hebrew was still spoken – thus not later than the early third century.⁷ Contrary to the opinion of several scholars,⁸ the beginning of the CPA script must be

---

³ Nabataean inscriptions in our region range from the second century BCE to the third century CE. Some rare examples from the fourth century either are in Arabic, though still using the Nabataean Aramaic script, or come from outside the Holy Land in a proper sense: Naveh 2003.

⁴ For a list, see Ustinova and Naveh 1993: 95, n. 2. A bilingual Greek and Palmyrene acclamation 'To the Most High God' (Θεῷ Ὑψίστῳ) was carved on a block of stone found in the vicinity of Elusa, probably the work of a Roman soldier of Palmyrene origin who served there (Ustinova and Naveh 1993 = SEG XLIII, no. 1053).

⁵ Epiphanius, De gemmis, PG 43, cols. 357-358. The fact is also mentioned in Talmudic literature: Tos. Sanhedrin 4:7; TJ Megillah 1:8; TB Sanhedrin 21b-22a. Cf. Naveh 1973, 1998, with full bibliography.

⁶ Naveh 1998; 2002; Barag 2009. Inscriptions in Samaritan language and script are mostly limited to quotations from the Samaritan Pentateuch: an example at Selbit (Sha'albim) in Judaea, CIIP IV, 1, no. 2756. A building inscription in the same synagogue is in Greek (no. 2755).

⁷ Bar-Asher 1988: 28, 30.

⁸ E.g., Contini 1987; Bar-Asher 1988; Desreumaux 1987a; 1999: 521; Morgenstern 2011: 629-630.

Chapter III: Aramaic dialects and scripts

Fig. 4 – Aramaic inscription from the Sepphoris synagogue, early fifth century (Weiss 2005: 204, fig. 4. Photo G. Laron. Courtesy of Z. Weiss, The Sepphoris Excavations, The Hebrew University of Jerusalem)
Remembered be for good Yudan son of Isaac the priest and Parigri (Paregoria) his daughter. Amen, amen.

Fig. 5 – Samaritan inscription in the synagogue of Selbit in the Shephelah (Barag 1993. Courtesy of the Israel Exploration Society)
The Lord shall reign for ever and ever.

fixed not in the sixth or in the late fifth century, but in the early fifth at the latest, since the earliest dated inscription known so far, in the church of 'Evron (Western Galilee), is firmly dated to year 415 by an adjoining Greek inscription.[9] The inscriptions in CPA come from western Galilee, southern Samaria, Judaea and Transjordan. Most of the inscriptions are epitaphs; some are graffiti on shards, some are inscriptions in churches, mostly in association with Greek inscriptions (Fig. 6).[10] However, the body of CPA inscriptions is meagre, though recently increased by the publication of about 85 epitaphs from Khirbet es-Samra.[11] CPA, in its classical form, was spoken and written until the eighth century at least; later it had a revival, but this is out of the range of this work. By the late eighth-early ninth century it had been superseded by Arabic, which made its appearance in Palestine and Arabia with its own alphabet very soon after the Islamic conquest, in the mid-seventh century.[12]

Syriac inscriptions too are found in the region, but all can be attributed either to pilgrims who left graffiti in holy places,[13] or to Nestorian or Monophysite monks who came as pilgrims and established their own monasteries in the Holy Land (a church at Deir Makr, a hermitage near Jericho, the monastery of Tel Masos in the Negev).[14] The same is true of Armenian and Georgian inscriptions left by pilgrims in holy places and in ethnically-based monastic foundations, especially in Jerusalem and its vicinity (see chapter IV). All are alien to the local culture and will not be treated in this study.

---

[9] Desreumaux 1987b, who dated the inscription to the late fifth century. His dating must be corrected to the early fifth century (Di Segni 1997a: 232-234), for the CPA inscription is located in a room at the northwest end of the church, sharing the same mosaic floor with a Greek inscription dated 415 CE: Tzaferis 1987: 36*, fig. 1 (ground plan); 44*, no. 7.

[10] For a list of CPA inscriptions, see Desreumaux 1987a: 99-101, updated in Di Segni 2009a: 354-355; Hoyland 2010: 37-39, with a map of the distribution of CPA and illustrations.

[11] Desreumaux 1999.

[12] Griffith 1997. Old Arabic, i.e., pre-Islamic Arabic, is attested in the Holy Land as a language at least a century earlier, but it is still written in CPA or in Nabataean script: Hoyland 2010: 34-37.

[13] Examples in Capernaum, Nazareth, Jerusalem: see Brock 1978: 264-266. It is worth noting that some inscriptions, once described as Syriac, are now recognized as CPA.

[14] Naveh 1976 (Deir Makr); Baramki and Stephan 1935 (Jericho); Maiberger 1983 (Tel Masos). On Syrian monks and Syriac manuscripts in monasteries of Palestine and Arabia, see Contini 1987: 56-59; Griffith 1997: 19-20.

Chapter III: Aramaic dialects and scripts 39

Fig. 6 – CPA inscription in the church at 'Uyun Musa, Mount Nebo (Piccirillo 1989: 215. Photo M. Piccirillo, SBF Photographic Archive)
The reader will keep the memory of the benefits of our master, G'N (Gaianos) the priest, and of his heirs who have provided the furnishing (of this church).

CHAPTER IV: LATIN INSCRIPTIONS IN THE HOLY LAND IN LATE ANTIQUITY

The transfer of the political and administrative centre of the Empire from the West to Byzantium, re-founded as Constantinople in 330 CE, brought about a change in the epigraphic use of Latin. Latin was still learned as part of the rhetorical education required from those entering the law schools, and Latin literary texts were discovered in the papyri archive of Nessana; Latin speakers – western pilgrims and temporary residents as well as residents bilingual in Greek and Latin – were common in fourth- and early fifth-century Jerusalem, and we even hear of monks in the late fifth and in the sixth century in the monasteries of Jerusalem, of the Judaean Desert and on Mount Sinai, who spoke and sometimes wrote Latin.[1] But those Latin-speakers were foreigners, not native Palestinians, and probably since the early fourth century the language was no longer spoken or understood except by foreigners and by a small élite of functionaries and jurists or jurists to be. The most famous law school in the Near East was at Beirut, and

---

[1] See in general Eck 2003; 2009; Millar 2006: 223-242; Geiger 1996; 2014: 135-150. For the Nessana literary papyri, see Casson and Hettich 1950; for Latin speakers in Jerusalem and in the Judaean Desert, see Di Segni and Tsafrir 2012: 412-418. Gabriel, a Cappadocian monk in St. Euthymius' laura from ca. 427, was abbot of St. Stephen's monastery in Jerusalem from 456 to his death in 480; Cyril of Scythopolis attests that he could speak and write in Greek, Latin, and in 'the language of the Syrians' – probably Syriac rather than the Aramaic spoken in Palestine, since he had been educated in Syria but had lived in seclusion in St. Euthymius' monastery. Most likely, it was also in Syria that he acquired his proficiency in Latin (Cyril of Scythopolis, *Vita Euthymii* 16, 30, 37, ed. Schwartz 1939: 25, 49, 56; transl. Price 1991: 21, 46, 52-53/Di Segni 2005b: 90, 110, 116-117). The anonymous Piacenza Pilgrim attests that at the time of his visit (ca. 570 CE) Latin was spoken in the monastery of the Holy Bush in Sinai beside Greek, Syriac, Bessian (Georgian) and Egyptian: *Antonini Placentini Itinerarium* 37, ed. Geyer 1965: 148, 171. The anonymous of Piacenza (pseudo-Antoninus) was one of several Latin pilgrims who left written accounts of their visit: the Pilgrim of Bordeaux, Egeria from Spain, Jerome and Paula from Italy in the fourth century; Eucherius bishop of Lyon in the fifth (though his *Epistola de situ Hierosolymae* may be a spurious composition of a later writer); Theodosius and pseudo-Antoninus in the sixth, Bishop Arculfus from Gaul in the seventh, the monks Willibaldus from Wessex in the eighth and Bernardus from Gaul in the ninth century. For the accounts of the Latin pilgrims, see Baldi 1955; Wilkinson 1977, 1981; Limor 1998.

the second most famous at Caesarea, both Roman colonies where Latin was the official language of administration and well represented in inscriptions of the Late Roman period; nevertheless, even in Beirut Latin inscriptions, both public and private, ceased before the middle of the fourth century. Evidently by that time the propaganda value of a public inscription worded in Latin had become nil for there was no longer a public that could read and understand it.

The change was already well under way in the Tetrarchic period. The boundary stones marking the borders between villages for taxation purposes, following Diocletian's fiscal reform of 296/7 CE, are uncompromisingly inscribed in Greek.[2] Inscriptions honouring the members of the first Tetrarchy in Latin were erected in Caesarea, but an inscription honouring Constantius I (Constantine's father, nicknamed Chlorus) Augustus and his Caesar Severus, erected at Elusa in the Negev in 305-306, is worded in Greek.[3] Galerius Augustus was honoured in Latin between 309 and 311 in Beth Shean, by then a *colonia*, by the governor of Syria Palaestina Firmilianus, but the Latin text ends with two lines in Greek. These lines mention the names of the *strategoi* (the Greek equivalent of *duumviri*, the executive magistrates of a colony) who actually carried out the work. Obviously it was the *duumviri*'s desire to have their action noticed by the citizens that prompted them to record their names in Greek.[4] Other inscriptions in Latin from the first and second Tetrarchies all relate to the army: so the inscriptions recording building works at the forts of Udruḥ (303-304 CE) and Yotvata (304 CE), the milestones on the 'Aravah road leading up to Yotvata (293-324 CE), the monumental inscription from 'Aqaba (324-326?).[5] The

---

[2] For the Tetrarchic boundary stones, found in the Huleh Valley and in the Golan, as well as in the Syrian Massif and in the Damascus area, see Millar 1994: 535-552; Syon and Hartal 2003; Hartal 2005: 422-427.

[3] For Caesarea, see *CIIP* II, nos. 1213, 1268, 1272, and for Elusa, Di Segni 2018b.

[4] *SEG* XX, no. 455; XLIII, no. 1073. Galerius was Augustus from May 1, 305 to May 5, 311; Firmilianus succeeded Urbanus at the end of 308: both are well known for the cruelty of their persecution of the Palestinian Christians: see Lawlor 1908: 192-194; Jones et al. 1971: 338, 983.

[5] For the fort and the inscription of Udruḥ, see Kennedy and Falahat 2008; Davenport 2010. Udruḥ, ancient Adru, is located in southern Transjordan and belonged to Provincia Arabia until most of Sinai, the Negev and southern Transjordan were transferred to Palaestina at the end of the third century (Tsafrir 1986; Di Segni 2018a: 247-256). For the Yotvata inscription, see Roll 1989; *AE* 1986, no. 699; 1987, no. 961; 1990, no. 1015; 2002, no. 1563. For the milestones and their connection with the transfer of the Tenth Legion to Aila, see Roll and Avner 2008; Isaac 1998: 72; Kennedy 2004: 205-206. The 'Aqaba inscription is very fragmentary but it seemingly referred to a building erected (by the praetorian prefect?) for the headquarters

one exception, both in its late date and in its lack of connection with the military, is an inscription honouring the emperor Julian (361-363) discovered at Ma'ayan Barukh in Upper Galilee, a region belonging to the province of Phoenice.[6] In fact the inscription was dedicated 'to our lord Julianus forever Augustus, liberator of the Roman world, restorer of the temples, reviver of the city councils and of the State, destroyer of the barbarians' by the people of Phoenice (*Foenicum genus*).[7]

Apart from Jerusalem and its vicinity, where Latin inscriptions of probable foreign origin can still be found (see below), in all the area corresponding to modern Israel the epigraphic habit died out, as far as Latin was concerned, some forty years before the Julianus inscription. Further north and east, in Phoenice and especially in Provincia Arabia, it persisted until the reign of Valens (364-378), always expressing itself in military inscriptions.[8] We can mention the building inscriptions of forts at Qaṣr Bashir (from the first Tetrarchy, 293-305 CE),[9] Deir el-Kahf (306 and 367-375 CE),[10] Qaṣr el-Azraq (under Constantine, 326-333 CE),[11] of a fortified reservoir on a road connecting Late Roman forts in the Basalt Desert (dated 334 CE),[12] of a tower and a *burgus* (outpost?) at Umm el-Jimal (369 and 371 CE),[13] and of an unspecified but probably military building at Kh. es-Samra (under Valentinian, Valens and Gratian, 367-375 CE).[14] The one non-military example is bilingual: a Latin epigram accompanied by a Greek one, engraved on the funerary monument of the former praetorian prefect Maiorinus at Buṣr el-Ḥariri

---

of the Tenth Legion. See *IGLJ* IV, no. 150; Kennedy 2004: 207-208; *AE* 1989, no. 750; 2003, no. 1832.

[6] Ma'ayan Barukh, situated west of the Ḥaṣbani River, was in all likelihood in the territory of Tyre. For the boundaries between the provinces of Phoenice, Palaestina and Arabia, and the cities Caesarea Philippi, Sidon and Tyre, based on era-dated inscriptions, see Aliquot 2008: 17-25.

[7] For this inscription, see *AE* 1969/70, no. 631; 1999, no. 45; 2000, no. 1503. *Foenicum genus* is literally translate 'the race', or 'the people', 'of the Phoenicians', but here *genus* seems to have the same meaning of the corresponding Greek word, γένος, in late antique inscriptions, i.e., 'province'. See Feissel 2006a: 174, no. 551.

[8] Both the chronological limit and the army connection are true for Latin inscriptions in the entire Near East. The rare exceptions are a small number of dedications to emperors and praetorian prefects, epigrams and juridical texts; see Feissel 2006b.

[9] Kennedy 2004: 149-150, no. 3.

[10] Kennedy 2004: 74-76, nos. 4, 6.

[11] Kennedy 2004: 60-62, nos. 3-5.

[12] Kennedy 2004: 71-72, no. 2.

[13] Kennedy 2004: 88-90, nos. 6-7.

[14] Gatier 1999: 381, no. 64; Kennedy 2004: 104, no. 6.

(ancient Bosor in the Hauran), dated to the second half of the fourth century. The choice of Latin was certainly linked to Maiorinus' past function.[15]

Things were somewhat different in the Jerusalem area. As was said above, the holy places attracted pilgrims and short- or long-term residents from abroad, among them many from Latin-speaking countries, and they naturally left some traces of their presence. The earliest epigraphic evidence of a Latin pilgrim is a graffito in a rock-cut cave (the so-called Chapel of St. Vartan) under the Church of the Holy Sepulchre.[16] It reads: *Domine ivimus*, 'Lord, we have come', and is ascribed to Constantine's reign, about the time the church was being erected, between 325 and 335. The graffito is accompanied by the drawing of a ship, no doubt a hint to the sea crossed by the pilgrim on his way to the Holy Land (Fig. 7a-b). In another place frequented by pilgrims, a former *miqweh* (Jewish ritual bath) in the property of the Sisters of Mercy of St. Vincenzo da Paola in Bethany that was transformed into a chapel, two of 71 graffiti on the walls – most of them ascribed to the fifth-sixth centuries – are in Latin, one in CPA, one possibly in Syriac and all the rest in Greek.[17]

Latin monks, nuns and lay people are attested by the sources in Jerusalem and its vicinity, as well as Armenians, Georgians, Syrians and Greeks from various countries,[18] but while Armenian, Georgian and Syriac inscriptions, and Greek ethnics mentioned in Greek inscriptions, substantiate the literary evidence,[19] the epigraphic documentation of the Latins is extremely meagre – and usually in Greek! – perhaps because the Latin immigrants were single

---

[15] Waddingtom, nos. 2474-2475; *IGLS* XV, 1, nos. 241-242. Maiorinus held his post under Constantius II (337-361), before 357, and died in the late fourth century. For the identification and dating of Maiorinus, see Robert 1960: 303-305; Feissel 2006b: 125-126.

[16] Gibson and Taylor 1994: 25-48; *CIIP* I, 2, no. 787, and the bibliography there.

[17] Benoit and Boismard 1951; *CIIP* I, 2, nos. 842.1-67 (Greek); 842.10, 51 (Latin); 843 (CPA); Benoit and Boismard 1951: 241, no. 70 (Syriac?). For a possible identification of the venerated place, see Taylor 1990; *CIIP* I, 2: 160-153.

[18] For the presence of foreigners in Jerusalem, see Di Segni and Tsafrir 2012, and the bibliography there. For the Latins, ibidem: 412-418.

[19] For some Armenian examples, see *CIIP* I, 2, nos. 810A (graffito of a pilgrim); 812, 813, 817, 817B, 837-839 (mosaic inscriptions in chapels); 873, 874, 925-929 (epitaphs); no. 909 mentions a 'monastery of the Armenian women', in Greek. For Georgians in Jerusalem and vicinity, see *CIIP* I, 2, no. 973 (Georgian epitaph from the Umm Leisun monastery); nos. 962, 977, 1000 mention Georgians (Bessian and Iberian ethnics) in Greek. Georgian inscriptions were discovered in the monastery of Bir el-Qutt near Bethlehem (*CIIP* IV, 1, nos. 3201-3204), and an Armenian inscription, no. 3227, in the Church of Nativity. Late antique Armenian and Georgian inscriptions were discovered also in Nazareth and elsewhere: see Stone 1990-1991; 1996-1997 (Armenian); Bagatti 1969: 154 (Georgian). For a general survey of the presence of

Chapter IV: Latin inscriptions in the Holy Land in Late Antiquity

Fig. 7a – Graffito of a Latin pilgrim under the Church of the Holy Sepulchre, in situ (Photo S. Gibson)

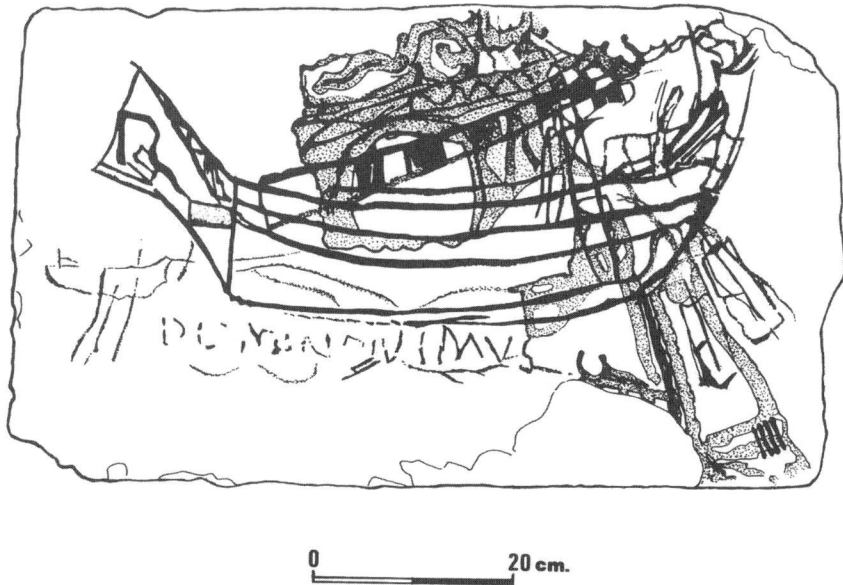

Fig. 7b – Drawing of the graffito, based on early photographs (Drawing S. Gibson)

individuals living in the midst of a Greek or mixed community. So we have the epitaph of one Maria from Rome, possibly a member of the 'monastery of the Apollinarian women', supposedly founded by the daughter of the emperor of the West Anthemius (467-472) with her Roman companions;[20] the epitaph of Thecla daughter of Marulfus from Germany;[21] an inscription marking the tomb of a family probably from Cadiz in Spain[22] – all of them in Greek. This indicates that even if the abbess of the Apollinarian women could have formulated a Latin inscription, she abstained from doing so on the assumption that it would not have been understood.

Only in one case do we have evidence of Latin-speaking residents. A mosaic pavement in a church with attached monastery at Kh. en-Nitle (Jericho) bears two Latin inscriptions, ascribed to the seventh century on archaeological grounds – a date supported by the palaeography and the bastard Latin. One reads *Do(mine) meserere*, 'Lord, have mercy', the other *To(to) feci leto die*, 'I made it all in one happy day'.[23] Even if it could be maintained that the mosaic laid 'in one day' was the work of an occasional pilgrim from a Latin country, he would hardly have inserted two Latin inscriptions without the concurrence of the priest or monks in charge of the church, which points to their being Latin speakers themselves. In Jerusalem there were western monks and nuns even in the ninth century,[24] and the privileged sphere of 'holy places' where foreigners would have wished to settle certainly included also Jericho.

Outside the main area of the holy places, the latest Latin inscriptions before the Crusader period found in Israel belongs to Justinian's reign (527-565). Feissel observed that Latin, the exclusive language of imperial constitutions and administrative acts until Justinian's time, decreases progressively in in-

---

Caucasian pilgrims and monks in the Holy Land, see Tchekhanovets 2018. For Syriac inscriptions, see Chapter III.

[20] *CIIP* I, 2, nos. 900, 901.

[21] *CIIP* I, 2, no. 970.

[22] *CIIP* I, 2, no. 912. Feissel 2012: 676, no. 473 cast doubt on the reading of the last two inscriptions; cf. *SEG* LX, no. 1720.

[23] The church was rebuilt several times with slight modifications. The mosaic pavement belongs to the third-stage church, built in the seventh century, after the second church had been destroyed, perhaps during the Persian invasion in 614. The third church collapsed in the eighth century, probably in the earthquake of 749, and a fourth stage was built over the ruins, reusing the old pavement. In this stage a small monastery was attached to the church. See Kelso and Baramki 1949-1951: 50-56; Foerster 1993; Bagatti 2002b: 103, Pl. 29; *CIIP* IV, 1, no. 2759-2760.

[24] This is attested by the *Commemoratorium de casis Dei vel monasteriis*, a report on the churches and monasteries of the Holy Land ordered by Charles the Great in 808: McCormick 2011: 206-207.

Chapter IV: Latin inscriptions in the Holy Land in Late Antiquity 47

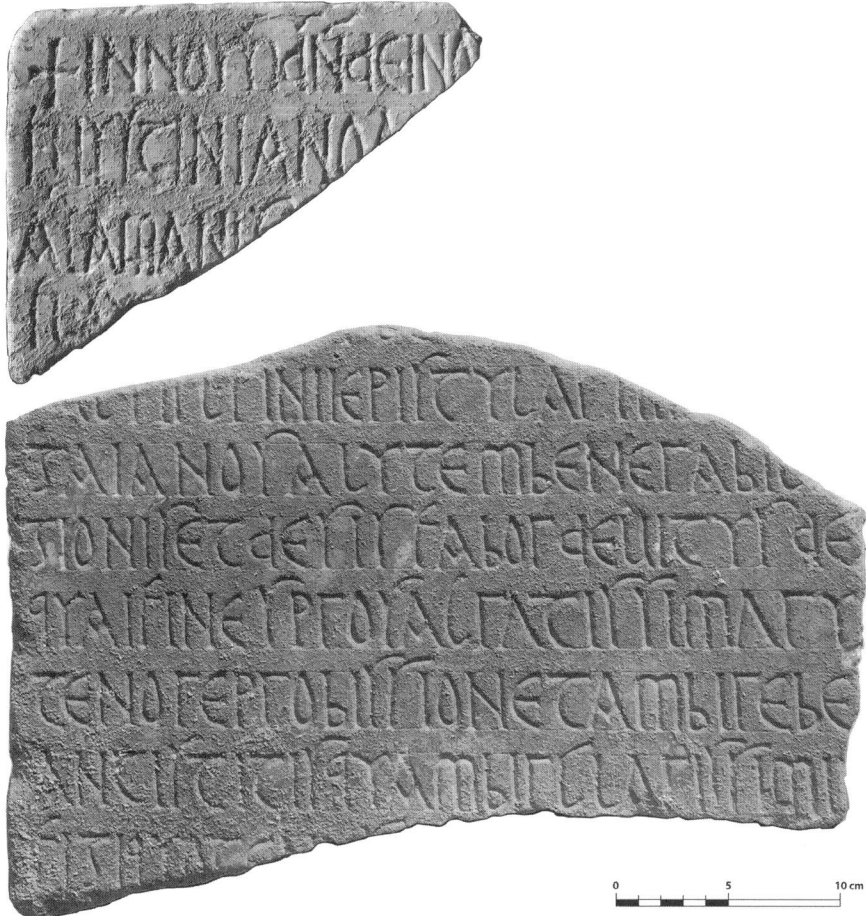

Fig. 8 – The Latin inscription of Kh. Batya (Di Segni and Feissel 2020: 609, fig. 1. Photo D. Syon)

scriptions from the fourth century and only appears in bilingual constitutions on stone in the fifth and early sixth century, the latest example being dated in 527; moreover, in late examples only the emperor's titulature and the date are inserted in Latin, while the text is in Greek.[25] In fact, under Justinian Greek superseded Latin in the use of the imperial chancellery. However, a recent discovery in Upper Galilee demands a slight modification of this view. Two fragments of marble discovered in the ruins of a building at Kh. Batya bear an inscription engraved in the typical Latin semi-uncial script of the

---

[25] Feissel 1995; 2006b: 108-116). See also Amelotti 1985: 102-104, 123-124, nos. 3, 13-14.

sixth century. The text starts with a consular date corresponding to 534 CE; it is addressed to an unknown personage by one of the chiefs of the imperial chancellery and contains an imperial rescript pertaining to the asylum right of churches (Fig. 8), so it was in every sense an official document.[26] No fragment inscribed in Greek was discovered in the excavation; however, the possibility that the Latin text was accompanied by a Greek translation cannot be excluded. If the stone represents part of a bilingual document, it still pushes the upper limit fixed by Feissel several years upward, but if the inscribed document was only in Latin, it would be about a century later than the latest Latin constitutions on stone or other medium. But what is most surprising, this example does not stand alone. A fragment of another Latin inscription dealing with asylum right in almost the same words of other sixth-century *asylia* constitutions, and palaeographically very similar to the Kh. Batya inscription, was found long ago, reportedly in Judaea. It is only known from an old photograph and a partial reading published in the *Revue des études Juives* by Jean Martin (1913), who mistook it for a Late Roman inscription. The exact origin of the fragment, the circumstances of its discover and the identity of the person who committed it to Martin's care are all shrouded in obscurity; nevertheless the fragment is undoubtedly authentic and provides additional evidence that at least imperial constitutions could be still exhibited to the Palestinian public in Latin in the mid-sixth century.[27]

---

[26] Only part of the ancient building was excavated, for most of it is buried under a modern highway. Its function could not be determined, but some finds of ecclesiastical character were recovered from the debris. For the inscription, see Di Segni and Feissel 2020. On the excavation, see Abu 'Uqsa 2006; a final report is forthcoming.

[27] For this fragment, see Feissel in *CIIP* IV, 2, no. 3972 and in Di Segni and Feissel 2020: 621-628. The author of the report, Jean Martin (1888-1914) is little known, for he was killed in the First World War when still at the beginning of his scholarly career. Martin writes that he received the inscription from a Mr Shapira who had bought it from an Arab, who maintained to have discovered it at Yarma in Judaea (no place of this name is known in the entire Holy Land) in a tomb containing a skeleton of gigantic size! The Arab's story not even Martin pretends to believe; as to Mr Shapira, he certainly was not the notorious antiquities dealer and purveyor of fake archaeological artefacts Moses W. Shapira, who died in disgrace by his own hand in 1884. On the identity of Matin's acquaintance see Di Segni and Feissel 2020: 622, n. 8. He was probably Bernard Shapira (1880-1967), an orientalist and a contributor of the *Revue des études Juives* around the same time, and later a lecturer of Hebrew at the École pratique des hautes études in Paris. Given his scholarly interests, he may well have visited Palestine in his youth. In any case, the dubious story of the fragment cannot cast doubt on the authenticity of the inscription: in the Near East at that time there was no known model that could have inspired such a forgery.

CHAPTER V: GREEK INSCRIPTIONS IN THE HOLY LAND IN LATE ANTIQUITY

Greek inscriptions present a very different picture from that presented by Latin inscriptions. While the epigraphic habit in Latin dwindles and disappears in the fourth century, the harvest of Greek finds, already substantial in the Late Roman period, begins to grow in the fourth and fifth centuries and reaches a peak in the sixth and early seventh centuries, as is shown by graphs of dated building inscriptions (Fig. 9) and dated epitaphs (Fig. 10a-b). As far as Greek epigraphy is concerned, Late Antiquity in the Holy Land is a time of great changes on the one hand, and of lively continuity on the other. The changes are rooted mostly – but not exclusively – in the ascent of Christianity, by the mid-fifth century probably the religion of a majority of the inhabitants of the country. The impact of Christianity asserts itself in many ways: from a progressive disappearance of pagan dedications and a multiplication of dedications, invocations and acclamations of Christian character, to a drastic shift of focus in public building and to a profound change in the rhetoric of death as expressed in epitaphs. These phe-

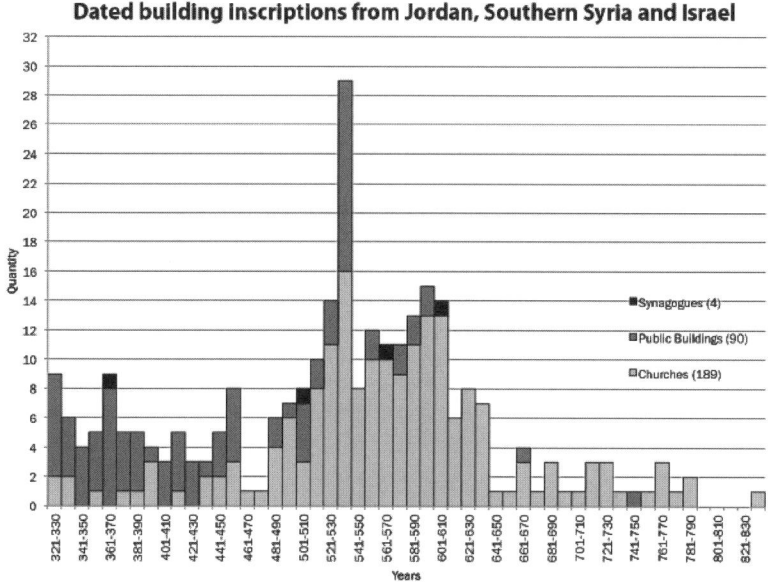

Fig. 9 – Dated building inscriptions in the Holy Land, fourth-eighth centuries (Di Segni 2017a, fig. 7)

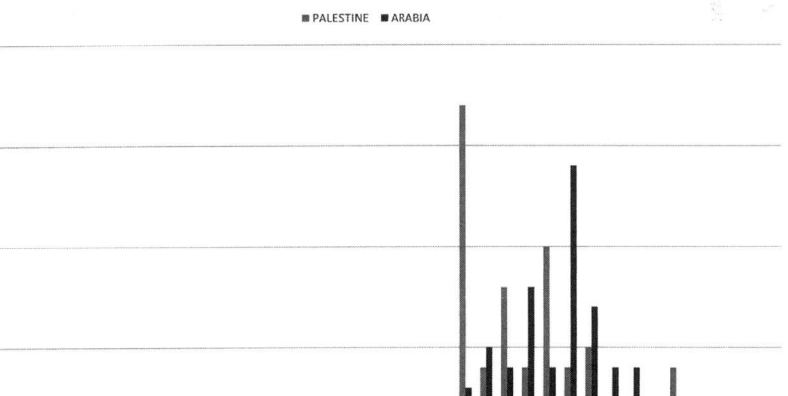

Fig. 10a – Dated epitaphs from the Holy Land, West and East, fourth-seventh centuries, not including the necropolis of Ẓo'ar (Benovitz 2012, fig. 2; cf. Benovitz 2014)

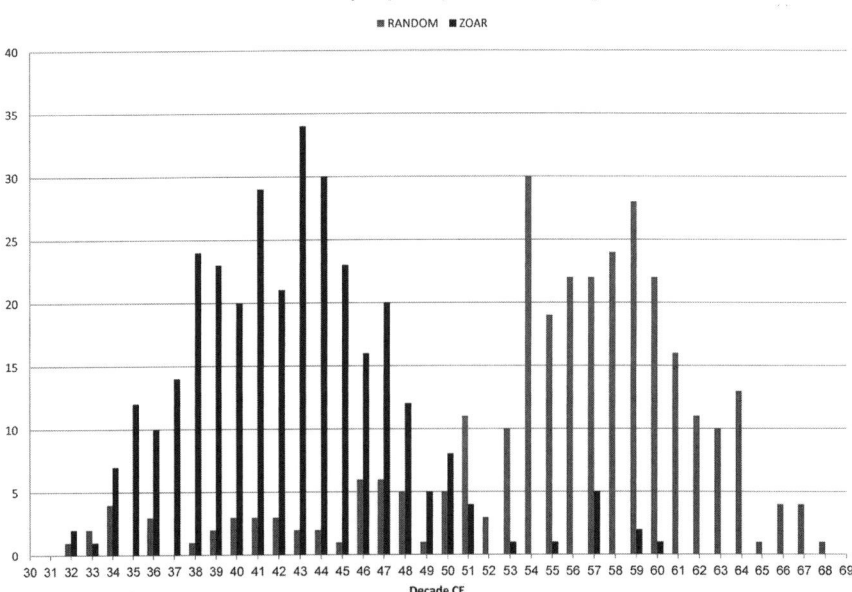

Fig. 10b – Dated epitaphs from the Holy Land, West and East, compared to the epitaphs from the Ẓo'ar necropolis (Benovitz 2012, fig. 1)

nomena will come to our attention in dealing with the various types of inscriptions. As for continuity, its most striking aspect is the persistence of the chronological systems that were in use in the Roman period, some of them originating as early as the Hellenistic period: on this subject, see Chapter II.

Types of finds in the epigraphic yield of the country in Late Antiquity

A typological classification of inscriptions is not an ideal way to gain a full understanding of the complex range of implications a single inscription can convey: who wrote it and why, what it meant to the person who dictated it and to those who read it, and possibly to the worker who executed it; what kind of ethnic, religious, cultural, social and other background can be revealed by it. To gain a real understanding one must read each inscription in its archaeological context and in correlation with other finds associated with it. However, for the present purpose of presenting half a millennium of epigraphic production in the country we shall of necessity introduce the various types out of context and in a somehow rigid framework. As a first step, we shall distinguish two separate categories: public inscriptions – those dictated by authorities or under their aegis, or in homage to figures of authority, and exhibited in the public domain for public consumption – and private inscriptions – those expressing the private feelings and needs of individuals on their own behalf, even when exhibited in the public domain.

V. 1 Public inscriptions

V. 1. 1 Imperial edicts

In our region, royal and imperial communications on stone are known in the Hellenistic and Roman periods mostly in the form of letters sent by the king, the emperor or his representative, to an individual or a community in answer to a request or a query addressed to the supreme authority.[1] In Late Antiquity the range

---

[1] For instance, the Hefziba inscription (an exchange of correspondence between Antiochus III and his general Ptolemy, ca. 199 BCE: *SEG* XXIX, nos. 1613, 1808; XXXIX, no. 1636; XLI, no. 1574; XLVII, no. 2056), the Yavne-Yam inscription (Antiochus V and the Iamnites, 163 BCE: *SEG* XLI, no. 1556; XLVII, no. 2050; *CIIP* III, no. 2267); the *Diatagma Kaisaros* (the so-called Nazareth inscription), an early imperial edict on tomb violation, erroneously believed to be connected with the removal of Jesus' body from the tomb (*SEG* VIII, no. 14; Robert 1946:132-133; for a summary of bibliography see *SEG* LI, no. 2029), and the letter of Julius Saturninus, legate

of ordinances on stone is wider and preserves edicts emanating from the two legislators of the Byzantine Empire: the emperor and the *praefectus praetorio*. Some of the emperor's edicts were constitutions, i.e., laws issued on imperial initiative; many were rescripts, i.e., responses to queries sent him by local officials; as to the *praefectus praetorio*, each of the *praefecti praetorio* (of the East, of Italy, Illyricum and Africa) could issue regulations, under imperial guidance, but their edicts were always issued in the name of all colleagues together.[2]

The earliest attestation of an imperial ordinance on stone is offered by the Tetrarchic boundary stones. These inscriptions marked the borders between agricultural lands belonging to different villages; they were set up following a survey of fields subject to the land tax, ordered by Diocletian in 296/7 in connection with his reform of the taxation system. Many of these stones are found in the Golan and in the Huleh Valley, as well as in the Damascus area and in the Syrian Massif near Antioch; a fragment was also discovered in secondary use at 'Ein Jedide near Jerusalem and another was seen by Clermont-Ganneau at Deir Nidham in southern Samaria.[3] The inscriptions are usually engraved rather carelessly on rough boulders, rarely more carefully on a dressed slab (Figs. 11-12). They appear in two different versions: a full one and an abbreviated one. The full formula reads: 'Diocletian and Maximian the Augusti, Constantius and Maximian the Caesars, have ordered this stone to be set up, marking the boundaries of the villages (or the fields) of X and Y, under the supervision of (name of the official in charge of the census in the province)'. In northern Golan, in the Huleh Valley and in the territory of Damascus, all belonging to the province of Phoenice, the name is that of the *censitor* Aelius Statutus, *vir perfectissimus* (a man of the highest rank of the equestrian class), while in southern Golan, included in Palaestina, and in Trachon, included in Arabia, the stones mention the names of two *censitores* working together.[4] The

---

of Syria under Commodus, to the people of Phene in Trachon, on the *metatum*, the obligation to give lodging to travelling soldiers and state officials (Waddington, no. 2524; *IGLS* XV, 1, no. 13).

[2] Italy, Illyricum and Africa, and later Italy and Africa, were under one *praefectus praetorio* for some time in the fourth century; then each had its own prefect, except when Italy and Africa were not under Byzantine control. See lists in Grumel 1958: 369-372. The collegial publication of edicts was the norm also for emperors during the periods when there were two or more recognized emperors (e.g. Constantine II, Constantius II and Constans between 337 and 340), as is shown by legal sources, but the only evidence of this rule in our region is offered by the Tetrarchic boundary stones.

[3] Millar 1994: 535-552; Syon and Hartal 2003; Hartal 2005: 422-427. On the fragment found near Jerusalem, see *CIIP* I, 2, no. 772, and on the one observed in Samaria, Clermont-Ganneau 1899: 231, note 1.

[4] Syon and Hartal 2003: 236, fig. 4; 238-239.

Chapter V: Greek inscriptions in the Holy Land in Late Antiquity

Fig. 11 – Boundary stone from Kibbuz Shamir in northern Golan (Aharoni 1955: 109, no. 1, pl. IX; courtesy of the Israel Antiquities Authority)
[Dio]cletian and Maximian the Augusti, Constantius and Maximian the Caesars, have ordered this stone to be set up, marking the boundaries of the fields of the villages of Galania and Migerame, under the supervision of Aelius Statutus, vir perfectissimus.

Fig. 12 – Boundary stone from 'Ashshe, SSW of Quneitra (*SEG* LVII, no. 1825. Photo Y. Ben Ephraim)
[Diocletian and Maximian the Augusti, C]onstantius and Maximian the Caesars, have ordered this stone to be set up, marking the boundaries of the village of Agrippina, under the supervision of Aelius Statutus, vir perfectissimus, censor. Stone marking the boundaries of the fields of Radanes.

abbreviated formula reads simply: 'Stone marking the boundaries of the villages (or the fields) of X and Y'.

Two important imperial edicts on stone found in our region were issued respectively by Anastasius (491-518) and most likely by Justinian (527-565). Anastasius' constitution deals with a wide range of issues pertaining to the military administration of the East, and copies were displayed in many places, as is evident from the fact that fragments are found in various locations: Bostra, Qasr el-Hallabat, Imtan, Umm el-Jimal and Salkhad in ProvinciaArabia, and Jerusalem in Palaestina.[5] The tax schedule known as the Beersheba Tax Edict (Fig. 13) was ascribed first to Emperor Anastasius, then to Theodosius II (408-450), but indubitably belongs to the sixth century and is almost certainly to be attributed to Justinian, though this cannot be proved for the inscription – in common with several edicts on stone surely or confidently ascribed to Justinian – lacks both the heading and the date.[6] The heading would have contained the name and titulature of the emperor and the name of the addressee, and would have been followed by the text of the imperial edict; at the end, the date. However, though the Beersheba inscription is fragmentary, it is quite certain that it included nothing but a list of communities and amounts in gold coins (*nomismata*) to be paid by each, preceded by a short introduction, from which we learn that the addressee was a *dux* (the

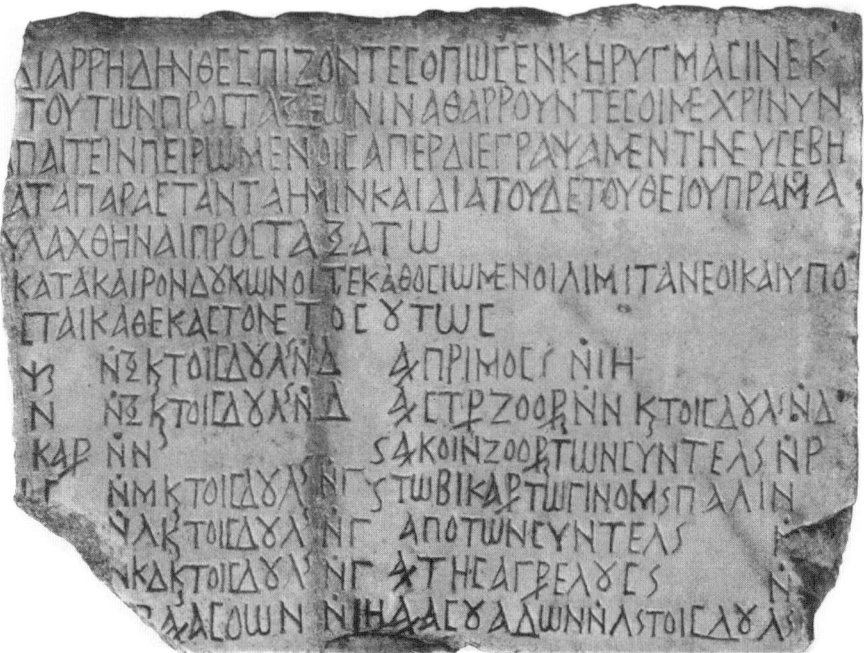

Fig. 13 – Fragment of the Beersheba Tax Edict (Abel 1909: photo in front of p. 89)

---

[5] *IGLS* XIII, 1, nos. 9045-9046; Feissel 2010; *CIIP* I, 2, no. 784.
[6] Cf. Amelotti 1985: 89-127.

military governor of a province of the *limes*), and that the schedule was to be attached to the edict, so that taxpayers would not be unfairly made to pay more than the prescribed amounts (a hint that it may be a rescript, issued in response to complaints addressed by the communities to the emperor). From the names of the towns and villages that are preserved in the seven pieces of marble slab, which join into four fragments, it appears that the *dux* to whom the edict was addressed was the *dux Palaestinae*; hence that the tax pertained specifically to the three Palaestinae (First, Second and Third or *Salutaris*). The old interpretations of the figures as assessments of the *annona* (the land tax levied for the maintenance of the army), or of the 1/12 deduction from the soldiers' pay in favour of the *dux* and his staff, must be abandoned; however, there are indications that this tax had some connection with the army, though the introduction specifies that it was exacted from both soldiers and civil landowners. Firstly, the official in charge of its collection was the *dux*, while all regular taxes were the responsibility of the civil governor or of imperial agents; secondly, most of the settlements mentioned are known to have had military units stationed there; and most significant, some amounts are ordered to be paid to commanding officers of regiments (*vicarii*). An alternative interpretation has been suggested, that the tax was meant to pay for the hospitality and assistance given to travellers and pilgrims in *burgi* or in public *xenodochia* – part fortresses and part caravanserais – by state servants subject to the authority of the *dux*, as well as to finance a task formerly imposed on soldiers, namely, escorting the caravans in insecure areas.[7]

Emperor Justinian is also the source of other rescripts on stone discovered in the Holy Land. Many rescripts are known from Justinian's *Novellae Constitutiones*, and since all are built along similar lines, their structure is well known: they open with the *invocatio* ('In the name of Our Lord Jesus Christ our God'), followed by the name and titles of the emperor, including his triumphal attributes,[8] then the *salutatio*, giving the name of the addressee of the rescript. Throughout the text the emperor speaks in the first person directly to the addressee in a courtesy third perso (e.g., 'Your Holiness', if the correspondent is a bishop; 'Your Magnificence', if he is a governor). After this heading there is an introductory part explaining the reason for issuing this order and its circumstances (*arenga* and *narratio*), after which are the constitution itself and any sanctions imposed on transgressors; finally, a command to the proper

---

[7] *SEG* LIV, no. 1643, and see Di Segni 2004a for a discussion of different interpretations.
[8] Justinian's triumphal titulature made its first appearance in constitutions issued in November-December 533 and became an obligatory part of all legal documents: Amelotti 1985: 102-103; Feissel 1992: 393-394; 1993.

authorities to have the edict published and observed, and the date. In inscribed format, however, rescripts are usually summarized or abridged and lack, or only present very concisely, one or more of these elements. For instance, no less than five inscriptions dealing with asylum rights granted to churches were discovered in the region (six when we count one from the vicinity of Tyre).[9] All are fragmentary, but even in their mutilated form some decurtation shows. None, for instance, has the obligatory date at the end; one, the Latin inscription discovered at Kh. Batya (see Chapter IV), is dated but the date is given as a consular formula attached to the titulature of the emperor; on the other hand, it has the required heading (*invocation*, *intitulatio* and *salutatio*) and the preserved part of the text starts with the *arenga* and *narratio*. Fragments of another *asylia* inscription, this one in Greek, were discovered in secondary use in the Church of the Holy Sepulchre: here the heading can be completely restored, with the *invocatio* and *intitulatio*, but no *salutatio*; then the short *arenga* ('The zeal due to the most holy churches of the orthodox faith was displayed') and the beginning of the *narratio* ('The borders of *asylia* that … to the church of the First Martyr…' – all the rest is lost).[10] Perhaps the best known *asylia* inscription from the Holy Land is the one originating from a church dedicated to the prophet Zechariah in north-western Galilee; the church itself was not located, but two large fragments of the inscription were reported found at el-Bassa (Bezeth, near the Israeli-Lebanese border). This inscription lacks the heading, so the rescript cannot be ascribed to Justinian with certainty but may have been issued by one of his successors: Justin II (565-578), Tiberius (578-582) or Mauricius (582-602). Its left side and some of its bottom are lost, but many lines survive, and thanks to the fact that the structure of these rescripts is known and the wording follows formulas shared by several such inscriptions, most of the text can be restored down to the threat of sanctions to transgressors. The last partly preserved lines dealt with an additional privilege conferred upon this church, permission to hold an annual five-day fair, which would have provided an income to the foundation.[11] A similar privilege seems

---

[9] Four come from Phoenice (el-Bassa, an unknown site in the same area in northwestern Galilee, Kh. Batya, and the vicinity of Tyre), two from Judaea (Jerusalem and the unknown 'Yarma', see Chapter IV). All six are published or republished together in Di Segni and Feissel 2020.

[10] *SEG* LVI, no. 1896; *CIIP* I, 2, no. 785; Di Segni and Feissel 2020: 613-619. The expression 'First Martyr' may refer to the Protomartyr Stephen, to whom were dedicated the church and monastery built by Empress Eudocia outside Damascus Gate; but the title was also given to Jesus himself, and since the fragments were discovered in the Holy Sepulchre, it is more likely that the church whose asylia was ensured was this same church.

[11] Di Segni and Feissel 2020: 557-576.

to have been granted together with the right of asylum also to another church, as attested by a fragmentary *asylia* inscription whose origin is not known with certainty, though is certainly comes from the Holy Land and possibly from north-western Galilee like the el-Bassa inscription. Here the final part of the rescript is partly preserved: the prohibition to security personnel to harass the clergy of the site or to draw away by force any person who had taken refuge in the church; the threat of punishment for transgressors and the conclusion, commanding the proper authority (unfortunately the address identifying the office is lost) to have the edict observed – but no date.[12]

Another imperial edict, communicated through an otherwise unknown *silentiarius* Flavius Aeneas, was discovered near Bethlehem, in the vicinity of the aqueduct to Jerusalem (Fig. 14).[13] The edict forbade sowing and planting within a distance of 15 feet from the aqueduct, under pain of death and confiscation of property. A shallow groove 30.9 cm long, engraved under the text, indicated the length of the foot. The emperor who issued this edict is not named but referred to as ὁ θιότατος καὶ εὐσεβ(έστατος) δεσπότης ὅλης οἰκουμένης ('the most divine and most pious master of the whole world'), a title sometimes given to Justinian but more often to later emperors.[14]

A notable example of praefectorial edict is the schedule of fees for official services (*sportulae*) discovered in the *praetorium* of Caesarea (Fig. 15).[15] It is engraved on a large slab on grey marble, broken in several pieces, not all of them recovered. The heading refers to the *praefecti praetorio* in the plural but mentions only the name of the *praefectus praetorio* of the East Flavius Pusaeus, which dates the inscription to 465-467. Under the heading, several columns of scripts list different types of official services, mainly judicial, with the price of each in *nomismata* or in *keratia* (1/24 of *nomisma*).[16] A sizable part of the text, both entries and amounts, is lost, but much of it can be restored based on written legal sources. The judicial fees were valid for all

---

[12] Di Segni and Feissel 2020: 577-585.
[13] Abel 1926; *SEG* VIII, no. 171; Di Segni 2002a: 58-60; *CIIP* IV, 2, no. 3431. A *silentiarius* was a high functionary of the private household of the emperor.
[14] Cf. Bagnall and Worp 2004: 47, 52. A date under Anastasius (491-518) has been suggested, but the emperor is more likely to be Mauritius (582-602).
[15] Di Segni, Patrich and Holum 2003; *SEG* LIII, no. 1841; Di Segni 2006b; *CIIP* II, no. 1197.
[16] The *solidus*, called in Greek *nomisma*, was the gold coin of the Late Roman Empire. It was introduced by Diocletian in place of the old *aureus*, and became widespread since Constantine ruled that all taxes and official payments should be paid in gold. Its weight, 4.54 g (1/72 of the Roman *litra* of 327 g), remained almost precisely the same in the golden coinage of the Byzantine Empire, and its purity was not debased until the early eleventh century.

Fig. 14 – Imperial edict for the protection of the aqueduct to Jerusalem (Abel 1926: 284, tb. V)

Fig. 15 – Schedule of judicial fees for the governor's court, Caesarea (Di Segni et al. 2003: 296, fig. 2. Photo G. Laron. Courtesy of J. Patrich, The Joint Expedition to Caesarea Maritima)

court proceedings, both civil and criminal, and from the total amounts we learn that appearance in court was rather expensive, so that only the well to do could afford it. On the other hand, only litigations for a value of 50 *solidi* and more appeared in the governor's court: lesser causes were discussed at no expense in front of the city advocate or in the bishop's court.

Another as yet unpublished praefectorial ordinance pertaining to taxes was discovered engraved on a column at Beth Shean.

V.1.2 Building inscriptions in civil and military buildings

We call 'building inscriptions' all epigraphic texts pertaining to the erection, decoration or renovation of an edifice. To better understand this type of inscriptions we should ask a preliminary question: who paid for public buildings in late antique Palestine? Unlike other parts of the Roman Empire, in our region inscriptions attesting to euergetism (the phenomenon of wealthy persons paying for public building or public entertainment to enhance their status and gain political influence in the city) are rare in the Hellenistic and Roman periods,[17] and are practically non-existent in Late Antiquity.[18] With

---

[17] Herod was the most prominent local *euergetes* in this period, but even when he paid for lavish buildings outside the boundaries of his kingdom – in Rhodes, Asia Minor and Syria – he acted as a king, not as a private citizen, and his activity cannot therefore be classified as typical euergetism.

[18] A possible exception may be the fragmentary epigram praising Orion, who provided the money for the renovation of the walls of Petra, perhaps in the late fourth century or in the early fifth (Merkelbach and Stauber 2002: 445, no. 22/71/01; *SEG* LII, no. 1732). The inscription was discovered out of context in Petra and has not yet been properly published and illustrated. It is impossible to ascertain who was this Orion, to whom the epigram also ascribes a victory against barbarian attackers. He may have been a wealthy citizen of Petra, but it is much more

the advent of Christianity, private donations became very visible in the Holy Land, as everywhere else, in the construction and adornment of religious foundations, but in the area of civil and defensive public building, both literary sources and inscriptions attest that financing came from public money rather than from euergetic supplies. The money was provided by three main sources – the city coffer, the provincial coffer and, in special cases, imperial grants – through different procedures.

Many building inscriptions of this period mention the name of the governor in office at the time of building, or even of the emperor, but this does not mean that the money for building came from the provincial coffer, for which the governor was responsible, or from imperial liberality (*philotimia*). The norm, inherited from the Roman period, was that public buildings in a city were erected or restored at the expenses of the city itself, and therefore inscriptions of this type sometimes mention a city officer called λογιστής ('inspector of the accounts'), and by the sixth century πατὴρ τῆς πόλεως ('father of the city'), who was the controller of the city finances.[19] Two building inscriptions from Caesarea mention the πατὴρ τῆς πόλεως immediately after the governor.[20] In the first, dated to the late fifth-early sixth century, the name of the father of the city follows that of a 'most magnificent *comes*' (the governor of First Palestine) in connection with the building of a civil basilica and a flight of steps. In the second, dated to the sixth century (after 536 CE as the governor bears the proconsular rank), the father of the city, who built a monumental entrance to the Byzantine Esplanade east of the Crusader city, bears a double title: πατὴρ καὶ πρωτεύων. The πρῶτοι or πρωτεύοντες (members of an inner circle of prominent citizens who managed the city affairs) are also mentioned in building inscriptions as supervisors of the work: one of them, Silvinus son of Marinus, appears in two building inscriptions at Beth Shean, one commemorating the building of a *sigma* (semicircular piazza) in 506/7 and the other the paving of a street and the laying down of a water conduct in 521/2 (Fig. 16).[21] This is but the continuation of the practice

---

likely that he was a *dux Palaestinae*, in which case the funds he gave came not from his own purse but from the provincial coffer with imperial permission. Since the text is an epigram, its language cannot be as explicit as in similar cases. For the erection of defensive structures by military or civil governors, see Di Segni 1995: 317-322.

[19] For this office, see Appendix A. For the question of the different authorities involved in public building, see Di Segni 1995, and for other examples of *pater poleos* in building inscriptions, see ibidem: 325-326.

[20] *CIIP* II, nos. 1262-1263.

[21] Di Segni 1999a: 636-627, 642, fig. 3; *SEG* XLIX, nos. 2082-2083. For more examples of *protoi* involved in public building, see Di Segni 1995: 323-324, and for this office, see Appendix A.

Fig. 16 – Paving of a street and building of a new water conduit under the governor of Second Palestine Orestes and Silvinus, comes and prôtos of Scythopolis (Beth Shean) (Di Segni 1999a: 642, fig. 3. Drawing B. Arubas. Courtesy of B. Arubas, The Hebrew University Expedition to Bet Shean)

of councilmen supervising the erection of public monuments, usual in the Roman period, when planning and financing building in the city was the sole prerogative of the city council. We still find councilmen – since the fourth century called πολιτευόμενοι (*politeuomenoi*) – in building inscriptions of the fifth century, for instance at Elusa in the Negev and at Bostra in Arabia.[22] Notably, in all building inscriptions the names of all these officials follow the name of the governor in office at the time. The mention of the governor's name may be just a dating device, but it may also reflect a measure of responsibility of the governor who, being in charge of the provincial coffer, probably had to sanction the outlay of city funds to avoid overspending, which might impair the city's ability to pay its taxes. But could governors also initiate the erection of public buildings? From fourth-century legislation it appears that they were eager to do so in order to extoll their successful leadership in the province. The legislator had to curb their enthusiasm and to compel them to direct the now limited resources of the city[23] first of all to maintenance and repairs of existing building, and to complete those left unfinished by their predecessors. As an inducement, they were permitted to inscribe their names

---

[22] Elusa, 454/5 CE: *SEG* XXXI, no. 1401; Bostra, 490/1 CE: *IGLS* XIII, 1, no. 9123.
[23] Since the fourth century imperial edicts forced the cities to give up a large proportion of their revenues to the imperial treasury: see Appendix A.

on buildings they had only brought to completion. By the end of the fourth century, however, the governors were forbidden to initiate new constructions, except by special permission of the emperor, and to put their names on any public work they might have completed: only the emperor's name was to appear on it. This edict, issued in 394, was included in the Theodosian Code and later in the Justinian Code, but epigraphic finds show that at least its second part was not observed: governors' names continue to appear in building inscriptions, either because the building was only restored, or because the governor had found a way to act on his own, or because he had been instrumental in getting imperial permission, or – last but not least – simply as a dating device when the city had been able to act on its own initiative, under the aegis of its 'father' or *prôtoi*.[24] Differently worded inscriptions hint to a variety of situations. For instance, a more direct involvement of the governor seems to be implied when his name appears as the grammatical subject of the sentence, as in the inscription of Silvanus of Scythopolis, probably a governor of all Palaestina except *Salutaris* in the late fourth or at the beginning of the fifth century, who 'built his own mother city in imitation of Hadrian'.[25] Some decision making on the governor's level may be implied also in another inscription from Beth Shean, commemorating the erection of a portico in the palaestra of the western bathhouse by the governor Flavius Nysius Sergius, a native of Scythopolis, 'without touching municipal funds'.[26] The date of the inscription, 534/5 CE, may explain who paid for it if not the city: after the Samaritan revolt of 529-530 was crushed, Justinian gave tax exemptions to the provinces of First and Second Palestine, as well as some leeway to the governor of First Palestine to use money from the provincial coffer and from the confiscation of Samaritan property to restore buildings damaged by the rebels.[27] Most likely the same arrangement was made also with the governor of Second Palestine, and he stretched a point in favour of his home city by using some of these moneys to erect the portico. In other cases, in which no local official's name is mentioned but only the governor's, it is impossible to establish with any certainty whether this points to his direct involvement or the name just served as a dating device, and if the former, whether the governor's involvement always implied specific permission or even instructions from the emperor. In these cases, in which city magistrates do not ap-

---

[24] On the changing role of the governor in public building, see Di Segni 1995: 317-322.
[25] Di Segni and Arubas 2009; *SEG* LIX, no. 1718.
[26] *SEG* XLII, no. 1471.
[27] Cyril of Scythopolis, *Vita Sabae* 73, ed. Schwartz 1939: 176-177; transl. Price 1991: 186/ Di Segni 2005b: 205-206.

pear, a direct involvement of the governor seems indicated, especially as we notice that inscriptions pertaining to civil buildings, like the aqueduct or the *burgus* in Caesarea, mention civil governors, while inscriptions pertaining to fortifications or to structures serving the military mention the *dux*. The inscription discovered near Channel D of the high-level aqueduct to Caesarea reads: 'Under Flavius Florentius, the most magnificent proconsul, the two aqueducts were renovated from the foundations.' It is dated ca. 385 by the name of Florentius, known as governor of Palaestina from an edict dated 25 August 385, included in the Theodosian Code (X, 16, 4).[28] The inscription of the *burgus* (a public inn or caravanserai) was discovered near the city wall of Caesarea; it ascribes the construction to the governor Flavius Procopius Constantius Severus Alexander and probably dates from the early years of the sixth century.[29] On the other hand, the building inscription of a hostelry for travelling officers, erected at Eleutheropolis in the 360s or 370s, bears the name of the *dux Palaestinae* Flavius Quintianus, and a fort renovated at Jiza in Jordan that of the *dux Arabiae* Flavius Paulus.[30]

Not a few building inscriptions refer to donations or grants of the emperor as the source of the expenditure. As we have already observed, this is not necessarily an expression of imperial liberality, in the sense that gold reached the province from the emperor's private purse, his *patrimonium*, administered by a special department called *res privata*;[31] rather, it means that the monarch authorized the local governor to use tax money levied in the province to pay for the building (for an example of this type of imperial *philotimia* in Jerusalem, see Appendix A). Nevertheless, in certain cases the inscriptions seem to attest a real transfer of money from an imperial source.[32]

---

[28] *SEG* XVIII, no. 626; *CIIP* II, no. 1259. For the structure to which the inscription was attached, see Porath 2008: 1663-1664. Contrary to Porath's opinion, the inscription cannot date the construction of Channel D and Channel C, which carried the water from the spring of 'En Ẓur, for it speaks explicitly of a renovation.

[29] *CIIP* II, no. 1261, but contrary to Ameling's interpretation there, a *burgus* is not a tower (πύργος) but a khan, a public inn or caravanserai managed by the State along the public roads or, as in this case, before a city, to provide secure overnight stay to travellers arriving after the gates were closed. *Burgi* are mentioned in inscriptions as well as in the Talmud: Isaac 1990: 176-186. See also comment in Di Segni 1997a: 450-455, no. 126.

[30] For the former, see Di Segni 1995: 321; *SEG* XXXV, no. 1537; *CIIP* IV, 2, no. 3479. For the latter, see *IGLJ* II, no. 155; Di Segni 1995: 321.

[31] Jones 1990: 411-427; Sarris 2018.

[32] A transfer of imperial money does not mean necessarily that gold would be moved from Constantinople to the province. The emperor had immense estates in the region, the revenues of which went to the *res privata*. Those estates were usually leased, and it would have been easy to divert the rents to selected building projects.

This is the case, for instance, of two inscriptions, both in verse, commemorating repairs and restructuring in the Hall of Fountains of the thermal baths at Hammath Gader by Mucius Alexander, whose governorship is dated ca. 506, based on historical considerations. In one epigram the work is ascribed to Emperor Anastasius, by the care of Mucius Alexander, governor of Second Palestine;[33] the other (Fig. 17) says:

> Mucius Alexander, supreme governor, accomplished this wondrous work,
> he whom Caesar's city nourished,
> having received a great gift from Emperor Anastasius.[34]

The 'great gift' might well be the governorship, but for the wording of the other epigram and for the fact that literary sources inform us that in 504/5, in the aftermath of a Saracen invasion, the *praepositus sacri cubiculi* (the emperor's Grand Chamberlain) Urbicius travelled through Syria and Palaestina disbursing large sums of money for the relief of the country.[35] Some of this money could have been given to the governor of Second Palestine for the restoration of the baths of Hammath Gader, the most famous health resort of the region, which was located in his province.

Imperial grants are also mentioned at Beth Shean. Two building inscriptions, one in verse, the other in prose, commemorate the rebuilding of a civil basilica by two lawyers, Silvanus and Sallustius, sons of Arsenius, 'with the riches of Anastasius, the wealthy king', 'with a grant of Emperor Flavius Anastasius Augustus', in 515/6 (or less likely in 500/01).[36] Silvanus son of Arsenius is well known from the sources as a wealthy Samaritan who held office in Scythopolis in the first third of the sixth century. Evidently he had personal or political connections at court in Constantinople that enabled him to fulfil the function of city patron and to obtain special grants for the capital of Second Palestine. His son, Arsenius, was a senator in Constantinople and intimate with Justinian and his wife Theodora.[37] Arsenius too obtained grants to restore the city wall of Scythopolis, as is attested by three building inscrip-

---

[33] *SEG* XXXVI, no. 1344; Di Segni 1997b:233-234, no. 50. This epigram says:
(This place) which Time crushed, revolving in its cycle,
Raised Anastasius, king-hero with a great name,
Under the care of Alexander, the thoughtful governor,
Dweller of Caesarea, who obtained the reins of Nysa.
Nysa is the ancient name of Scythopolis-Beth Shean, the capital of Second Palestine.
[34] *SEG* XXXVI, no. 1345; Di Segni 1997b:234-235, no. 51.
[35] Martindale 1980: 1188-1190, Urbicius 1.
[36] Di Segni 1999a: 638-639; *SEG* XLIX, nos. 2084 A-B.
[37] Procopius of Caesarea, *Arcana* XXVII, 6-9; Cyril of Scythopolis, *Vita Sabae* 61, 70, ed. Schwartz 1939: 163, 172-173; transl. Price 1991: 172, 182/Di Segni 2005b: 196-197, 203.

Chapter V: Greek inscriptions in the Holy Land in Late Antiquity

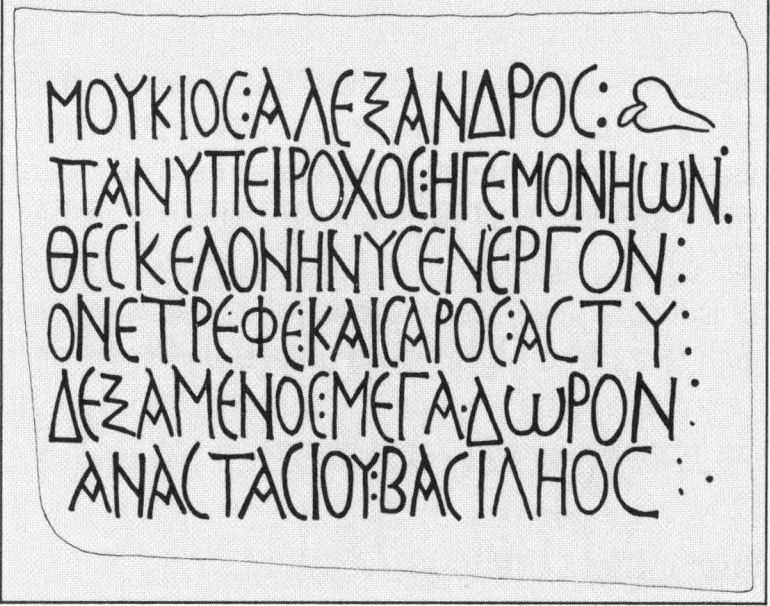

Fig. 17 – Mucius Alexander's inscription in the bathhouse of Hammath Gader (Di Segni 1997b: 235, fig. 47. Photo Z. Radovan; drawing T. Gorenstein. Reproduced with the permission of the Israel Exploration Society)

tions dated 524/5 and 525/6.[38] All three open with the phrase: 'From a grant given by the imperial liberality at the request of the most glorious Flavius Arsenius...' and end with the names of the governors in office respectively in the third and the fourth indiction, preceded by the formula 'in the time of' – namely, as a dating device. All this, in conjunction with Arsenius' known position in Constantinople, points to a real allotment of extraordinary funds, rather than to imperial permission to use tax money from the provincial coffer. A similar formula: 'From the liberality (*philotimia*) of our master, Emperor Justinian... accomplished through John the archbishop...' (in one text: 'by the intercession of John the archbishop') opens no less than ten building inscriptions found in Bostra, the capital of Arabia, pertaining to the erection of a variety of buildings, civil, military and religious. Four of the inscriptions are dated 540 CE.[39] One (no. 9137), commemorating the erection of a church of St. Job, ascribes the liberality to Justinian and Theodora his wife; none mentions the governor. These data tempt to interpret the *philotimia* as a real donation; however, the example of Justinian's *philotimia* in the matter of the construction of the Nea, the foundation of a hospital in Jerusalem and the erection of a fort in the Judaean Desert, at the request of the archbishop of Jerusalem through the saintly monk Sabas,[40] teaches us that buildings of all kind, funded by the intercession of the most influential patrons, were still paid for with tax money from the provincial coffers. It is possible, therefore, that also the great wave of public building that hit Bostra around 540 was financed with provincial funds.

The mention of the bishop as an active party in civil (and military) building in the city reflects not only his function as a patron and intercessor. Inscriptions attest that bishops built on their own steam. They built churches, of course (see below), but also civil buildings. For some of them the bishop's initiative may have been motivated by compassionate concerns, as in the case of the bath for lepers restored by Theodore, archbishop of Scythopolis, in 558/9,[41] or the prison for persons awaiting trial built by Paul, bishop of

---

[38] Avi-Yonah 1942: 166-169; *SEG* VIII, nos. 34-35; *AE* 1948, no. 140, and see comments in Di Segni 1997a: 393-399, nos. 103-104.

[39] *IGLS* XIII, 1, nos. 9128-9137, and see Sartre's comment there, pp. 209-212. The inscriptions are fragmentary and many lack a date, but the similar formula points to their belonging to the same short period, except no. 9135, which mentions the successor of Archbishop John, Thomas.

[40] Cyril of Scythopolis, *Vita Sabae* 73, ed. Schwartz 1939: 176-178; transl. Price 1991: 186-187/Di Segni 2005b: 205-207. See the discussion of the topic in Appendix A.

[41] Avi-Yonah 1963; *SEG* XLIX, no. 2086.

Gerasa, in 539;[42] but the bath built by Bishop Placcus in Gerasa in 454/5 and inscriptions attesting the involvement of Bishop Eutropius in the laying of mosaic pavements in sidewalks at Sepphoris indicate that bishops were active not only for the welfare of their flock but also for the beautification of their city.[43] Their concern is attested also in literary sources: for instance, Cyril of Scythopolis reports that, during a severe drought that hit the region for five years (516-520 CE), John, the patriarch of Jerusalem, organized the digging of pits in various low places in and around the city in the hope of finding water.[44] The rhetor Choricius praises Marcianus, bishop of Gaza in the first half of the sixth century, for having built not only churches but also porticoes, baths and old age homes for the poor, and for having restored the city walls.[45] Some epistles of Theodoretus, bishop of Cyrrhus in Syria Euphratensis, attest that the bishop build two bridges, an aqueduct and other public structures from the revenues of the Church.[46] Moreover, as the Church held real estate in every city, it was obliged to contribute its share in any repairs of roads and public buildings in the city, like any other landowner, as is confirmed by Justinian in Novella 131, ch. 5, issued in 545.

All the examples presented above refer to civil buildings in the cities or in their suburbs. Though many inscriptions attest to the erection of cult buildings in villages, we have hardly any epigraphic documentation of public building with no religious affinities in the villages of western Palestine.[47] However,

---

[42] *SEG* XXXV, no. 1571. Persons awaiting trial, namely, defendants in litigations or in criminal cases, were obliged by law to give security or bail, and if they had no adequate property to give it, they were subject to preventive arrest; cf. Di Segni et al. 2003: 287-288 and n. 45. The bishop showed concern for their relief by lodging them in a special prison, which they would not have to share with criminals expecting death sentences, insolvent debtors and similar wretches.

[43] Welles 1938: 475, no. 296 (bath of Placcus); *SEG* XLIV, no. 1371; XLV, no. 1945 (sidewalks at Sepphoris). A similar case, the paving of a portico, is attested in an inscription at Souq Wadi Barada in southwestern Syria, ancient Abila Lysaniae (Waddington, no. 1878). On the involvement of bishops in public works see Feissel 1989: 820-825; Di Segni 1995: 332; Hamarneh 2013a.

[44] Cyril of Scythopolis, *Vita Sabae* 67, ed. Schwartz 1939: 167-169; transl. Price 1991: 177-178/Di Segni 2005b: 199-201.

[45] Saliou 2005; Hevelone-Harper 2005: 112-113.

[46] Feissel 1989: 823.

[47] An inscription copied by the Colt Expedition in Shivta mentions a work carried out by the officers of a military unity (*priores*) and their commander (*vicarius* – both Latin terms are transliterated in Greek), which may point to a communal building (e.g. a dining hall or a clubhouse) for the use of the *limitanei* in the village. However, nothing is known of the find spot or archaeological background of the inscription, and thus the nature of the building cannot be

there is abundant evidence of the erection of communal structures – meeting halls, stables, bathhouses, spring houses and cisterns, public hostels for travelling officers, workshops for hire, and other buildings whose function is not specified in the inscription – across the Jordan and especially in the Hauran, during the third- early fifth centuries. Officers stationed in the village (usually centurions) or village magistrates, often described as προνοηταί (curators) or πιστοί (trustees), were in charge of these works, and the money apparently came from the village communal coffer (κοινόν).[48] Some evidence from literary sources pertaining to western Palestine confirms the epigraphic evidence from the east, indicating that village magistrates – both headmen of free villages and stewards of privately owned villages – were instrumental in initiating building.[49]

We have already noted the existence of building inscriptions in verse, namely, in the form of epigrams. In some cases, the epigrammatic form – common to many types of inscriptions – encounters a literary genre more often found in rhetoric compositions in prose: the *ekphrasis*. The *ekphrasis* ('description') is a favourite genre in Byzantine literature, describing works of art, monuments and magnificent buildings, real and sometimes imaginary. The fourth volume of the corpus of epigrams engraved on stone and mosaic, collected by Merkelbach and Stauber (2002), contains epigrams from the provinces of Palaestina and Arabia, about half of which are epitaphs, some dedications of altars or statues; the rest are building inscriptions of churches or other edifices. Two of the last can be ascribed to the *ekphrasis* genre: a poem by Eudocia Augusta, describing the baths of Hammath Gader, which the empress, Theodosius II's wife, visited probably during her first journey to

---

ascertained. See *SEG* XXXI, no. 1453; Meimaris 1992: 224-225, no. 238, and for a corrected interpretation and dating (599, not 505 CE), Di Segni 1997a: 814-819, no. 323. Military buildings in the countryside, or buildings erected for the relief of officers and soldiers, cannot be included, for they were the responsibility of the *dux*: so for instance the decorated dome of a bathhouse (?) built in Beersheba, the headquarters of the military command of the province, by Antipater, probably the *dux Palaestinae* ca. 522 (Martindale 1980: 106, Antipater 2). See below, text and n. 51.

[48] For village magistrates involved in building in the Hauran, and their buildings, see MacAdam 1986. For dated examples since the fourth century, see Di Segni, 2017a: 307-309, List II. For examples of buildings erected 'at the expenses of the *koinon*', see *SEG* VII, no. 1154; *IGLS* XV, 2, nos. 458-459.

[49] See for instance Cyril of Scythopolis, *Vita Euthymii* 12, ed. Schwartz 1939: 22; transl. Price 1991: 18/Di Segni 2005b: 88; *Vita Sabae* 35, ed. Schwartz 1939: 120-121; transl. Price 1991: 130/Di Segni 2005b: 169. In both cases, however, the buildings were religious (monasteries).

Jerusalem in 439.[50] The other describes a map of heaven, probably adorning the dome of a building erected by the *dux Palaestinae* Antipater in Beersheba ca. 522. This kind of work of art, depicting the cosmos, is known from literary descriptions of real or imaginary monuments as well as from archaeological finds.[51]

V.1.3 Building inscriptions in cult buildings

In Late Antiquity three religious groups erected cult buildings in the Holy Land: Jews, Samaritans and Christians. The inscriptions found in Jewish and Samaritan synagogues are of a private character, at least in the sense that, even when they are dictated by the community or the village, they involve no authorities of the religious or civil hierarchies. In the case of churches, only public, only private, or both public and private inscriptions together can be found in one and the same church, depending on its status, namely, whether it was a parochial church, a pilgrimage or a roadside church, a monastic, or a private church. Since it is difficult to separate the public and private realms in the epigraphy of religious buildings, this topic will be treated below, within the category of private inscriptions.

V.1.4 Honorary inscriptions

In the Roman period, honorary inscriptions, usually attached to statues, were common: not only cities freely honoured their patrons with statues, but so did also private persons for their friends or benefactors. The pattern of honorary inscriptions was fixed: if public, they opened with the formula ἡ βουλὴ καὶ ὁ δῆμος ('The city council and the people') in nominative, followed by the name of the honorand in accusative; if private, the name of the honorand in accusative came first, followed by the name of the dedicator in nominative; in both types, a short phrase at the end indicated the reason for the dedication. The verb 'honoured' (ἐτίμησαν/ἐτίμησε) was most often implied rather than expressed.

---

[50] *SEG* XXXII, no. 1502; Di Segni 1997b: 228-233; Merkelbach and Stauber 2002: 346-348, no. 21/22/01. For the date of Eudocia's visit, see Laurence 2002: 67-75.
[51] *SEG* VIII, no. 281; Merkelbach and Stauber 2002:323-324, no. 21/07/01; and see comment in Di Segni 1997a: 703-707. The building was probably a bathhouse, for domes are mostly a feature of baths or temples, and the decoration described in the epigram is suitable to an edifice built for pleasure, not for religion. Moreover, temples were no longer built at the probable date of the inscription.

Not so in Late Antiquity. Since the mid-fourth century bronze statues could be erected only by imperial permission, and in 394 a law of Arcadius and Honorius extended the obligation to marble statues. The inclusion of this law in the Justinian Code (*CJ* I, 24, 1) indicates that it was still enforced in the sixth century. Often the imperial permission was even mentioned in the dedicatory inscription of the statue as a γέρας ('gift') received by the honoured person. This is the case, for instance, of an epigram engraved on a marble plaque, from an unknown provenance in the Negev,[52] which reads:

✝Οὐδὲ λιπὼν λιμίτοιο Παλεστ(ίνης) χθόνα δῖαν |
Δωρόθεος γεράων πέλεν ἄμμορος ἐκ βα|σ[ι]λῆος ✝

(cross) Although he has left the divine soil of the *limes* of Palestine, Dorotheus was not without a share of rewards from the emperor (cross)

In this case, the epigrammatic form disrupted the classical pattern of honorary inscriptions described above, but in the following examples the basic format – honorand in accusative, dedicator in nominative, rationale – is preserved. Again *geras* appears in a fragmentary epigram engraved on a column from Caesarea, on whose top holes indicate that it supported a statue; the honorand was apparently a governor of First Palestine named Eusebius, and his statue was dedicated, and paid for, by a certain Alypius, a private citizen.[53] Another governor, Nomos, was honoured in Caesarea with a golden statue, ca. 443-446; also in this case the dedicatory epigram is engraved on a column on whose top are holes to secure a statue.[54] A metric inscription engraved on an octagonal pedestal, discovered at Beth Shean (Fig. 18), tells us that the governor Artemidorus 'has erected a golden (statue of) Eudoxia, queen of the whole earth'.[55] Full-body statues or busts of emperors were probably present in

---

[52] *SEG* VIII, no. 296; XXXIV, no. 1506; XXXVIII, no. 1587; Feissel 1984: 545, 556-557; Merkelbach and Stauber 2002: 454, no. 22/81/01. The epigram means that Dorotheus, who according to literary sources served as *dux Palaestinae* in 452-453 (Martindale 1980: 377-378, Dorotheus 7), was honoured with a statue by imperial permission, after he had left his post as commander of the *limes* of Palestine. Feissel 1984 (*SEG* XXXIV, no. 1748) described the procedure and collected many examples of *geras* in the sense of honorary statues in inscriptions and in literary epigrams.

[53] Lehmann and Holum 2000:57-58, no. 26, Pls. XXVI-XXVII; Merkelbach and Stauber 2002: 317, no. 21/03/03; *CIIP* II, no. 1264.

[54] Lehmann and Holum 2000: 56-57, no. 25, Pls. XXVI; Merkelbach and Stauber 2002: 316-317, no. 21/03/02; *CIIP* II, no. 1260.

[55] Di Segni 1999a: 631; *SEG* XLIX, no. 2076. Eudoxia was empress between 395, when her husband Arcadius ascended the throne of the eastern half of the Empire, and her death in 404,

Chapter V: Greek inscriptions in the Holy Land in Late Antiquity 71

Fig. 18 – Pedestal of Eudoxia's statue, Beth Shean (Photo G. Laron; courtesy of B. Arubas, The Hebrew University Expedition to Bet Shean)
Ἀρτεμίδωρος ἄνασ|σαν
ὅλης χθονὸς | Εὐδοξίαν
χρυσεί|ην ἔστησε
περισκέ||πτῳ ἐν χώρῳ (hedera)
Artemidorus has erected a golden (statue of) Eudoxia, queen of the whole earth, in a far-seen place (Homeric quotation: *Odyssey* 1, 426; 10, 211).

every important city as a matter of course: for instance, the 'divine images' are mentioned in a sixth-century inscription from Sepphoris commemorating the restructuring of the civil basilica and mentioning the governor and the father of the city.[56] If the 'divine images' that stood near the basilica in Sepphoris were accompanied by inscriptions, these inscriptions did not survive; but emperors of the first and second Tetrarchies were honoured with statues whose inscribed pedestals came to light not only in the capital, Caesarea, but even in Elusa, the only *polis* of the Negev, as well as in Gerase in Provincia Arabia.[57]

V.1.5 Acclamations

Acclamations represent a personal expression of political, religious or sporting support, and should therefore be considered as private inscriptions. However, the most common acclamations in this period (all in Greek) are

---

but the inscription may be dated after 400, when she was granted the title of Augusta.
[56] *SEG* XX, no. 417; XXVI, no. 1667; Di Segni 1997a: 343-348, no. 85*.
[57] For Caesarea, see *CIIP* II, nos. 1213, 1268, 1272 (in Latin); for Elusa, Di Segni 2018b (Greek); for Gerasa, Welles 1938: 414, nos. 105-106 (Latin); 431, no. 161 (Greek).

Fig. 19 – Stamp on amphora (Clédat 1916: 20, fig. 11)

expressed in fixed formulas and represent adhesion to a party, and therefore they belong to the public rather than the private domain. For instance, the acclamation Εἷς θεός· νίκα, Ἰουλιανέ (God is one. Conquer, o Julian!), incised on a column discovered in Ascalon,[58] was not simply an expression of respect and admiration for Emperor Julian (361-363), but most likely represented the war-cry of the pagan population who supported his anti-Christian policy. This is apparent from similar acclamations ('God is one, one emperor Julian'; 'God is one, Emperor Julian conquers'; 'Julian, you were born to conquer' and the like) that appear on milestones in the vicinity of Jerash and Amman.[59] Clearly the victory formula was adopted in response to the slogan launched by the Christians: Τοῦτο νικᾷ; Χριστὸς νικᾷ, 'This (the cross) conquers', 'Christ conquers'. These acclamations originate from Constantine's dream at the eve of the battle at the Milvius Bridge, reported by Lactantius (De mortibus persecutorum XLIV, 5) and by Eusebius (Vita Constantini I, 28). Constantine saw a chi-rho sign and heard a voice from heaven telling him: 'With this sign you will conquer'; he put the sign on his banners and defeated his rival, the pagan Maxentius. The Christians adopted the symbol and the phrase in their struggle against paganism, and the cross and the acclamations, in full or in abbreviated form, are present in a great many inscriptions, from lintels to bread stamps. By the time Christianity had prevailed and had become the religion of the majority in the Holy Land, as in the whole empire, the acclamations 'The cross conquers', 'Christ conquers'

---

[58] SEG XLI, no. 1544; CIIP III, no. 2326. The acclamation is accompanied by the date 'Year 465' of the era of Ascalon, corresponding to 361/2 CE. Julian rejected Christianity but as a Neoplatonic philosopher he supported a fundamental monotheism, in which the ancient gods were seen as allegoric aspects of the one divinity.

[59] Welles 1938:489-490, nos. 345-348. For no apparent reason Welles omitted the word 'conquer' from some of the inscriptions, though it was read on the stone, in abbreviated form, by the first editor. Cf. Di Segni 1994c: 107, nos. 40-41 and n. 86. On the pagan background of the acclamation 'God is one', see below.

had exceeded the significance of a declaration of loyalty to the Christian side and had become rather an apotropaic formula. They can be viewed as such in many cases, when they appear over the entrance of churches, monasteries and private houses,[60] in public buildings,[61] in sacred places[62] and tombs[63], and on objects of everyday usage (Fig. 19).[64]

The Blue and the Green factions of the hippodrome also had their war-cry: Νικᾷ ἡ τύχη τῶν Βενέτων or νικᾷ ἡ τύχη τῶν Πρασίνων (May the Fortune of the Blues – or of the Greens – win!). This cry, attested in wall graffiti as well as in literary sources, was not only in support of charioteers of one or the other colour, but also the slogan of political parties, a cry raised in bloody riots not only in the races but in the theatres and in city streets in all parts of the empire.[65] An acclamation for the victory of the Blues is framed in

---

[60] E.g., a lintel from a monastery or church in the Armenian Quarter in Jerusalem, *CIIP* I, 2, no. 862; lintels at Khisfin, Rafid and Ramthaniyye in the Golan, Gregg and Urman 1996: 85, 156-157, 187, nos. 86, 120, 154; in various sites in Hauran, Dunand 1939: 562, no. 257; 1950: 160, no. 359; *SEG* XXXII, no. 1481.

[61] E.g. *IGLJ* II, no. 129, on the wall of a cistern in Madaba; Welles 1938: 490, no. 350, in the hippodrome of Jerash; *IGLJ* V, no. 110, on the tower of the barracks at Umm el-Jimal.

[62] E.g. in monastic caves in Naḥal Mukhmas, *SEG* XXXIV, no. 1503 and at Muallaqah in Jordan, *IGLJ* II, no. 65a; in an underground church at Ḥorvat Qaẓra near Beth Govrin, *SEG* XL, no. 1460; in the atrium (the Fountain Court) of the cathedral in Jerash, Welles 1938: 491, no. 352; in a chapel at Petra, *IGLJ* IV, no. 90.

[63] E.g. at Luzit near Beth Govrin, *SEG* XL, nos. 1490-1491; at Ghor eṣ-Ṣafi, Meimaris and Kritikakou-Nikolaropoulou 2008: 143, no. 66.

[64] E.g. on bread stamps (a stone stamp from Petra, *IGLJ* IV, no. 90, and a wooden one from Jerusalem, *CIIP* I, 2, no. 1077), on a painted bowl from Jerash (*SEG* XXXIX, no. 1660, 6), stamped on an amphora from northern Sinai (Clédat 1916: 20, fig. 11).

[65] Cameron 1976; Dan 1981. The once popular hypothesis that the Green supported Monophysitism and the Blues the Chalcedonian creed, or that the Greens represented the populace and the Blues the upper classes, was challenged by Cameron and is no longer upheld by most historians. However, political strife often burst out within the framework of the two factions. This is illustrated in a Greek text written in 640 CE, *Doctrina Iacobi nuper baptizati* (ed. and French transl. by Déroche 1991), purportedly addressed by a converted Jew to his brother Jews. Jacob, forcibly baptized and secretly still a Jew, enjoyed causing blood shedding among the Christians in the cities he visited as a merchant, and did so by feigning enthusiastic support here for the Blues, there for the Greens, at a time when the two factions took opposed sides in the riots against Phocas in Africa, Palestine and Syria in 608-610. Also disorders started by the Greens in Antioch against the governor were sometimes funnelled into violence against the Jews, who were considered supporters of the Blues: Joannes Malalas, *Chronographia* XV, 15, (under Zeno: ed. Dindorf 1831: 389-390; ed. Thurn 2000: 316-317; fuller version in *Excerpta*, ed. De Boor 1905: 166-167; Thurn 2000: 316); XVI, 6 (under Anastasius: ed. Dindorf 1831: 396; ed. Thurn 2000: 324), and cf. X, 20 (ed. Dindorf 1831: 244-245; ed. Thurn 2000: 185), where the same pattern is anachronistically ascribed to riots under Caligula.

a round medallion in the mosaic pavement along a colonnaded street in Beth Shean (Fig. 20).[66] A graffito on a stone reused in a wall in Jerusalem probably contained the acclamation 'May the Fortune of the Blues win!', followed by another common acclamation formula: Πολλὰ τὰ ἔτη, 'Many be the years', that is, 'Long live' the acclaimed party.[67] This too is a well-known acclamation in honour of emperors, governors, bishops and other illustrious personages who had gained the goodwill of the populace, as well as factions, as we have seen above. In Caesarea the governor Andreas 'lover of building' is so acclaimed (Fig. 21);[68] at Bostra it is an archbishop whose name is lost,[69] at Sepphoris Bishop Eutropius,[70] at Beersheba one Anastasius 'illustrious and *euergetes*' – judging by the title *illustris* perhaps a man of senatorial rank rather than Emperor Anastasius.[71]

A particular type of acclamation is Εἷς θεός, 'God is one', alone or accompanied by μόνος, 'the only one'. It is essentially a private acclamation, often assuming an apotropaic or supplicatory character, when accompanied by ὁ βοηθῶν, 'who helps', or βοήθει, 'help!'.[72] But the acclamation Εἷς θεός often appears in the public domain and thus it must be presented here. Studying its appearance in Syria, Prentice ascribed the earliest occurrences to Jews, on the assumption that Εἷς θεός represented the proclamation of monotheism contained in the Jewish *Shemaʻ* prayer; through Jewish-Christian usage, it would have been adopted by the Christians, to whom Prentice ascribed the later occurrences.[73] On the other hand, Peterson (1926) collected a large number of examples from Syria (including Phoenice, Palestine and Arabia) and Egypt, and concluded that Εἷς θεός was a typical Christian formula. Peterson's conclusion was widely accepted and became a self-fulfilling prophecy, inasmuch as any inscription containing this formula is automatically classified as Christian, even if no other detail points in this direction, and sometimes even despite contrary pointers. However,

---

[66] Syon 2004: 13*; 14, fig. 17; *SEG* LIV, no. 1678.
[67] *SEG* VIII, no. 213; *CIIP* I, 2, no. 1026. The inscription has now disappeared. For other examples of acclamations of the Blues, see *IGLJ* V, nos. 147-148, from Umm el-Jimal in northern Jordan.
[68] Holum 1986: 62, fig. 1, pl. 12A; *SEG* XXXVI, no. 1341; *CIIP* II, no. 1331.
[69] *IGLS* XIII, 1, no. 9442.
[70] In an unpublished inscription, mentioned by Weiss and Netzer 1994: 43; *SEG* XLIV, no. 1371.
[71] *SEG* XXXVI, no. 1326.
[72] For a *corpusculum* of the various types of Εἷς θεός inscriptions found in the region, see Di Segni 1994c. The formula with the additional invocation for help is often followed by a person's name: these types will be treated below.
[73] Prentice 1908: 18-19, 50-51.

Chapter V: Greek inscriptions in the Holy Land in Late Antiquity

Fig. 20 – Acclamation for the Blues, Beth Shean (Syon 2004: 14, fig. 17. Photo D. Syon, The Israel Antiquities Authority)

Fig. 21 – Acclamation for the governor Flavius Andreas (Holum 1986: 62, fig. 1. Drawing K. Wanous. Courtesy of the Israel Exploration Society)

we should not neglect the fact that Εἷς θεός is also an expression of pagan monotheism, as attested by the acclamations to Julian mentioned above, by an acclamation to Kore found at Sebaste and by others from the West and the East of the Roman Empire.[74] Εἷς θεός is certainly not a translation of the first verse of the *Shemaʿ* (at least, not in the Septuagint, the most authoritative Greek translation of the Bible circulating in the relevant period),[75] and it is doubtful if it was a typical Jewish expression. In the region inhabited by Jews and Samaritans – roughly in Judaea, Samaria and Galilee – it appears mostly in a Samaritan context. Many examples, most of them still unpublished, come from the Samaritan holy place on Mount Gerizim, prior to its appropriation by the Christians under Emperor Zeno (474-491), from the Samaritan synagogues at el-Khirbe near Shechem and Raqit on the Carmel.[76] Other examples come from public and private buildings in cities with a strong Samaritan community: notably, these examples lack Christian symbol, unlike contemporary Christian inscriptions.[77] The exceptions that may be assigned to a Jewish or Christian milieu are few and not totally incontrovertible. For instance, one is a tablet originating from a synagogue probably located in Caesarea; only the name of the dedicator, Judah, tips the scales in favour of a Jewish rather than a Samaritan synagogue.[78] In another unclear case, the acclamation is engraved on the

---

[74] Flusser 1975. Flusser (p. 16) cites a parallel to the Sebaste acclamation, a twin inscription from Rome acclaiming Zeus Helios Sarapis Mithras as only god. An inscription from Lydia acclaims the local god, Men Uranius (god of the sky) as only god: *TAM* V, 1, no. 75.

[75] The first verse of the *Shemaʿ* (Deut. 6:4), in the Septuagint translation, reads: Ἄκουε Ισραηλ· κύριος ὁ θεὸς ἡμῶν κύριος εἷς ἐστιν, 'Hear, o Israel: the Lord is our god, the Lod is one'.

[76] Di Segni 1990b; 1993c; 1994c; 2004c; *SEG* XL, nos. 1502-1503; XLII, nos. 1426-1429; LV, no. 1732.

[77] E.g. in the *praetoriun* of Caesarea, where Samaritans served in the governor's office (*CIIP* II, nos. 1184, 1342); two other acclamations incised on columns, nos. 1177, 1183, were not found in situ. W. Ameling, in his comments to two of these inscriptions (*CIIP* II, nos. 1177, 1342) denies the Samaritan character of the formula, apparently being unaware of the many Samaritan examples and of Samaritan life in Caesarea and in other Palestinian cities, but see Di Segni 2000: 786-787; Patrich 2001: 81. A capital (from a synagogue?) in Emmaus is engraved with the acclamation in Greek and a devotional formula in Samaritan (Vincent and Abel 1932: 235-237, fig. 10; *CIIP* IV, 1, no. 3079; see also nos. 3080-3082, more Samaritan inscriptions from Emmaus). Two acclamations come from Apollonia: one in a winepress (Roll and Tal 2009; Tal 2009), the other from a building whose function is unclear: this inscription is bilingual, with the acclamation in Greek and an additional text in Samaritan language and script (Tal 2015).

[78] Di Segni 1993a; 1994b; Barag 1994.

door of a tomb at Belah in Western Samaria, which was ascribed to Christians because of the addition of the letters ΧΜΓ, often interpreted as the abbreviation of Χ(ριστὸς Μιχαὴλ Γαβριήλ, 'Christ Michael Gabriel', or Χ(ριστὸς ἐκ) Μ(αρίας) γ(εννηθείς, 'Christ born of Mary'; but they represent also a number, 643, the isopsephic value of Θεὸς βοηθός, 'God who helps', which may be used by Samaritans or Jews as well as by Christians.[79] In another case the acclamation appears in the mosaic pavement of the church at 'Evron on the northern coast, where, however, an inscription invoking God's help writes the sacred name in Paleo-Hebrew, an indication that the community may have originally been Samaritan or Jewish, recently converted to Christianity.[80]

In short, it would be foolhardy to automatically ascribe *Eis theos* acclamations to Christians, when they come from the mainland of Palestine, as opposed to its periphery; for indeed this formula does appear on Christian lintels in the Golan, in inscriptions from the Hauran, some of them Christian, others pagan or Jewish/Samaritan, and on many Christian tombstones at Ghor es-Safi (Zo'ar), as well as in Christian graffiti and in churches in the Negev and in Sinai.[81]

V.1.6 Other inscriptions in public buildings

Some inscriptions, though not rare, escape the categories described above. They belong to various types that appear in public buildings and even more frequently in religious buildings and in the private sphere. We shall discuss them in more detail below, but some examples will be presented here to illustrate their use in a public environment.

---

[79] Bagatti 2002b: 166; Di Segni 1994c: 100, no. 16; for the figure/abbreviation ΧΜΓ, see Avi-Yonah 1940: 111. Isopsephism is the Greek equivalent of the Hebrew gematria, the practice of adding up the numerical value of the letters in a word or sentence to form a single number, which stands for the word or sentence. The commonest example in late antique Christian inscriptions is 99 (ϙθ) for Ἀμήν (1+40+50+8).

[80] *SEG* XXXVII, no. 1518; Di Segni 1994c: 96-97, no. 3. The church was erected in 414/5 and went through several stages: the inscription with the name of God in Paleo-Hebrew (*SEG* XXXVII, no. 1520) belongs to the first stage, while the mosaic pavement with the acclamation was laid in 443. Paleo-Hebrew is the script used by the Samaritans until today, but was sometimes used by Jews for sacred names until the late fourth century at least: see Chapter III, n. 5.

[81] For the Golan, see for instance Urman 2006: 81, 148, 154-155, 212; for Negev, Sinai and Hauran, Di Segni 1994c: 105-111; for Ghor es-Safi, Meimaris and Kritikakou-Nikolaropoulou 2005 and 2008, passim.

One of the effects of the spreading of Christianity in the Roman Empire was making the Bible more visible through the epigraphic use of scriptural quotations – in the East, and specifically in the Holy Land, drawn from the Greek translation of the Septuagint or, in less proportion, from the New Testament.[82] The purpose behind the choice of a particular verse varied: the text could have a didactic or hortative aim, or an apotropaic or augural function. For instance, in the wing of the praetorium complex in Caesarea known as the Revenue Office, the mosaic pavement of Room V is embellished with a quotation from Paul's Epistle to the Romans 13: 3, framed in a medallion: 'Do you want to be free from fear of the one in authority? Do what is right and you will receive his approval'. A shorter version of the same text ('Do you want to be free from fear of the one in authority? Do what is right') within a medallion occupies the centre of another room in the same office.[83] The text is well chosen to admonish tax payers and tax collectors against cheating in their dealings with the Revenue Office. In Room VII of the same office, a blessing is inscribed in mosaic within a *tabula ansata* just inside the threshold: Εἰρήνη ἡ εἴσοδός σου καὶ ἡ ἔξοδός σου, 'In peace be your coming in and your going out' – a modified quotation from I Kingdoms 16: 5 (MT I Sam. 16:4). The same verse is quoted in two other rooms in the praetorium compound, one giving access to a bath.[84] Its purpose appears to be apotropaic, to wish the visitor a good result of his visit and to ward off evil. Another example is found at the entrance of a multi-room building at Tel Malḥata in the northern Negev, a civil settlement attached to a fort. A *tabula ansata*, the right-hand part of which is lost, occupies the threshold of the entrance hall and contains a two-line inscription: in the first line is the quotation Εἰρήνη ἡ (ε)ἴσοδό[ς σου], 'In peace be your coming in'; there appear to be no space for the second half of the blessing. The second line reads: ΠΛΗΡΩΘΗΣΕΤΑΙΑΙ - - , and one may wonder if this was another quotation: πληρωθήσεται π[ᾶς ἀσκὸς οἴνου], 'Every wineskin shall be filled with wine' (Jeremiah 13: 12). The function of this building is unclear, but a second inscription at the centre of the lavish mosaic pavement of this room may point to some kind of resort, perhaps an inn. The central medallion features a figure holding a flower and flanked by a partly fragmentary

---

[82] See the list of quotations in Felle 2006: 522-526. The number of quotations from the Old Testament is almost double the amount of those drawn from the New Testament.

[83] *SEG* XLV, no. 1937; *CIIP* II, no. 1334 (Room V); *SEG* XLV, no. 1935; *CIIP* II, no. 1335 (Room I). The name 'Revenue Office' is based on an inscription in Room VIII of the same complex, an invocation to Christ by the 'accountants and clerks of this bureau' (*CIIP* II, no. 1339).

[84] *CIIP* II, nos. 1338, 1344, 1345.

text, probably to be read Καλὸς | [κα]ιρός, 'Good time'.⁸⁵ At Umm el-Jimal in northern Jordan, a town and military base in the Roman and Byzantine periods, a profusion of protective inscriptions is engraved on all sides of the tower of the so-called Barracks: they include crosses and christograms combined with the names of the archangels, Gabriel, Michael, Uriel and Emmanuel; the formula 'This (the cross) conquers and helps'; scriptural quotations (Ps 21 [MT 22]: 10-11; 34 [MT 35]: 1) and various liturgical formulas.⁸⁶

Apotropaic and augural inscriptions at the entrance of public buildings were not limited to scriptural quotations. Protective words or wishes of pleasure are especially common at the entrance of baths, a place that promised enjoyment but also threatened real or imagined danger. For instance, in a bath south of the temple platform at Caesarea two inscriptions were found: 'Grace and health to those who are here' and 'Envy, I shall tread you underfoot'; a bathhouse at Tel Tanninim presents the inscription 'Enter with good omen'. The notion of 'entering gladly' and 'casting away jealousy and the evil eye' appears in one of the mosaic panels in the hall of the so-called House of Nestor at Sheikh Zuweid near Raphiah, and another small inscription in its bathhouse wishes the visitor: 'Wash pleasantly'.⁸⁷

A different type of inscriptions is captions, that is, names or words inscribed beside figures in a mosaic pavement to identify them. Two mosaic panels in the hall at Sheikh Zuweid feature mythical scenes, the story of Phaedra and Hippolytus and a triumph of Dionysus: in each, every figure is accompanied by a label (Phaedra, Eros, Hippolytus, Nurse, Hunters; Dionysus, Eros, Telete, Skirtos, Heracles).⁸⁸ The myth of Hippolytus is represented also at Madaba, in the central panel of the mosaic floor called 'The Hippolytus Hall'. The mosaic lies partly under the Church of the Virgin and was dated to the first half of the sixth century on stylistic grounds. The figures in the central panel are tagged Handmaids, Phaedra, Attendants, Nurse, Hippolytus, Slave. The side panel fea-

---

⁸⁵ A large quantity of cooking pots and storage jars were discovered in one of the rooms; Eldar and Baumgarten 1993. Tel Malḥata, ancient Malatha (Tsafrir et al. 1994: 176), was situated on the junction of two important roads: the road from Jerusalem through southern Judaea to Aila (Eilat), and the road from Beersheba to the Dead Sea. Both roads connected many forts and military bases and would have seen intense military traffic, so the erection of a hostel for travelling officers would not be an unlikely provision.

⁸⁶ *PAES* III A, nos. 245-255; on the site, see Kennedy 2004: 86-91.

⁸⁷ *CIIP* II, nos. 1419-1420 (Caesarea); 2090 (Tel Tanninim); *CIIP* III, nos. 2568-2569 (Sheikh Zuweid). In a mosaic inscription in Jerusalem the bathhouse itself addresses its builder exhorting him to wash with good health and to enjoy his foundation: *CIIP* I, 2, no. 796. For baths seen as scary places, see Dunbabin 1989; Eliav 2009.

⁸⁸ *SEG* XXIV, no. 1197; *CIIP* III, no. 2568.

tures a country scene with a peasant, three Erotes, three Graces, Aphrodite and Adonis, each accompanied by its proper label (Fig. 22), and the border on the east side shows three personifications of cities wearing mural crowns and seated on thrones, labelled Roma, Gregoria and Madaba.[89] Both the Hippolytus Hall and the complex at Sheikh Zuweid may be private mansions, or habitations for the use of public officials. Similar figurative mosaics with captions identifying the figures appear in sumptuous houses, often not easily distinguishable from public buildings,[90] as well as in churches and synagogues, on which see below.

Fig. 22 – Aphrodite and Adonis in the Hippolytus Hall at Madaba (Photo M. Piccirillo, SBF Photographic Archive)

[89] Piccirillo 1982: 386-396; 1989: 50-60; *SEG* XXXII, no. 1547; *IGLJ* II, nos. 125-128.
[90] For instance, the bathhouse, or more like the palatial mansion with private bathhouse, at Caesarea, where a personification of Summer is labelled Καλοκερία, 'Good Season' (*CIIP*

V.1.7 Instrumenta

The category of *instrumenta* includes objects of all types, both in everyday use and in cultic or liturgical use, some of which normally or occasionally bore inscriptions. Weights are the main type of *instrumenta* belonging to the public domain, inasmuch as, even when privately manufactured, they were controlled by the city or the state authorities. Late antique weights, made of lead, bronze or glass, were marked in various ways, but always in Greek. Two lead weights of the Late Roman-Early Byzantine period, one found at Caesarea, the other at Mishmar ha-Negev, bear the specification of their weight, one *litra*, and the name of inspectors of the market – the *episkopos* who had supplanted the *agoranomos* in the Late Roman period.[91] A group of bronze weights found at Ascalon are marked with a cross and their value in multiples of *solidus* (*nomisma*, 4.54 g, 1/72 of a Roman pound) or of ounce (*ounkia*, 27.25 g, corresponding to 6 *solidi* or 1/12 of a Roman pound) (Fig. 23).[92] Similar weights, in multiples of *solidus*, ounce and scruple (*gramma*, ¼ of *solidus*), were also found in Caesarea.[93] Three small bronze weights from Caesarea bear the name of the governor in office when the weight was cast, and their value in scruples; they are dated to the mid-sixth century.[94] Finally, a glass weight found at Beth Shean bears the name of one Simeon, *eparchos* (*praefectus urbis*) of Rome.[95] The urban prefect was responsible for the control of the administration of the capital of the Roman Empire, keeping the peace and supervising market activities, including checking the weights. The language of the inscription indicates that it did not refer to Latin-speaking Rome but to the urban prefect of 'New Rome', i.e. Constantinople.

II, no. 1347a), vignettes of cities are identified as Birsama, Mampsis and Epikairos and a galloping horse is labelled Eutychios, 'Lucky' (*CIIP* II, no. 1347b; Di Segni 2020: 324-325). In Jerusalem, a labelled personification of Γῆ ('Earth') adorns the floor of a Late Roman-Early Byzantine mansion on the southwestern slope of Mount Zion: *CIIP* I, 2, no. 731.

[91] Lifshitz 1970: 80, nos. 18-19, pl. VIII a-b; *CIIP* II, no. 1735. They weigh 240 and 250 g, perhaps a local standard or an Italian *litra* of ten ounces, 270 g, slightly underweight. The editor of the Caesarea weights in *CIIP* II, A. Kushnir-Stein, did not understand the significance of the term *episkopia* – the office of the *episkopos* who had supplanted the *agoranomos* – and thus dated this weight to the second century. Literary sources attest this office in the fourth century, while in the second we are still confronted with *agoranomoi*.

[92] *CIIP* III, nos. 2363-2366.

[93] *CIIP* II, nos. 1742-1748; the first bears the portraits of two emperors.

[94] *CIIP* II, nos. 1730a-b, 1731.

[95] *SEG* VIII, no. 51. Identical weights were found also in other parts of the Byzantine Empire: cf. *SEG* XXXVI, no. 666; XLV, no. 708, as well as bronze weights bearing the same title but the name of a different *praefecti urbis Romae* (Constantinople): *SEG* XLIV, no. 558; LI, no. 2009; LXI, no. 554. Glass weights were in use also in the Early Islamic period (Allan 2001).

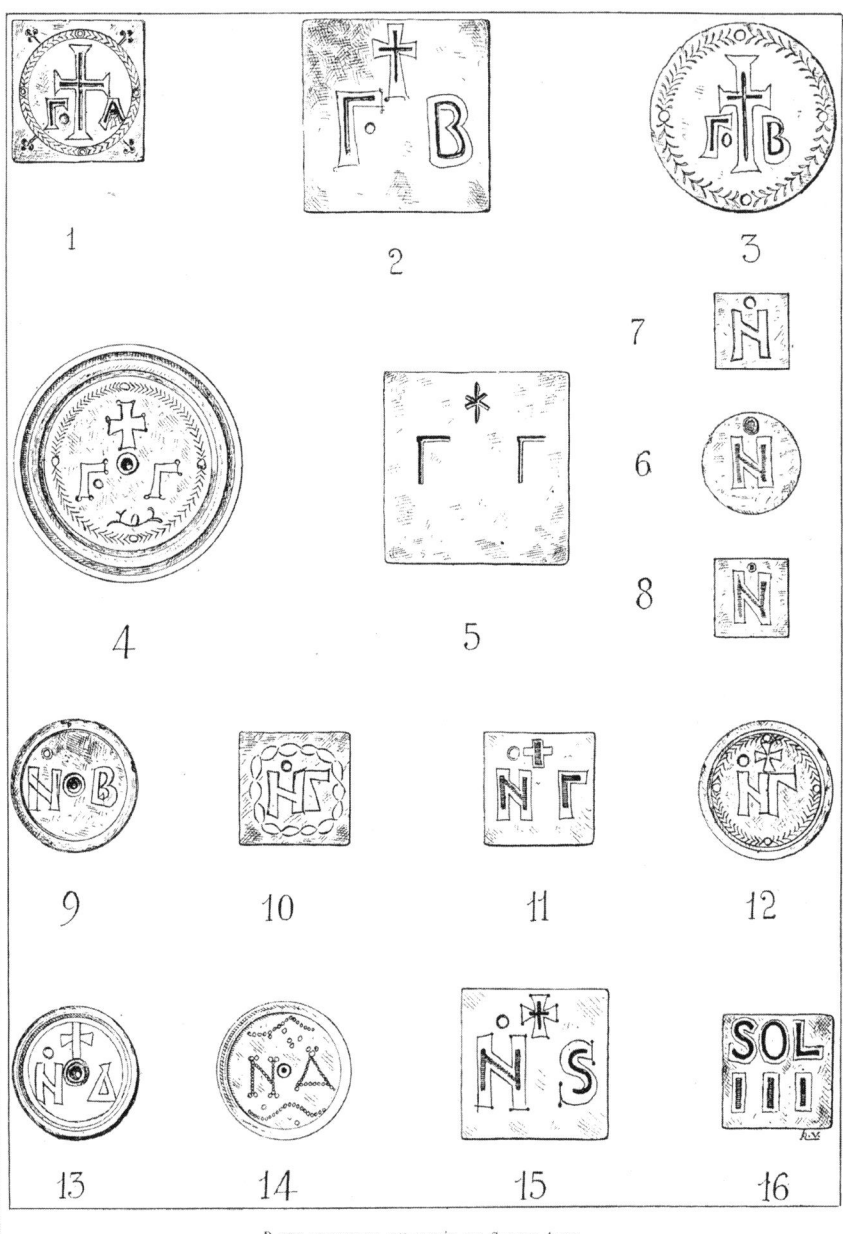

Fig. 23 – Weights from Ascalon (Decloedt 1914: 553-555)

Other types of *instrumenta* will be treated below, in the subchapter dedicated to private inscriptions.

V. 2 Private inscriptions

A large proportion of private inscriptions in the Roman period expressed aspect of the religious experience: invocations and prayers, dedications of altars and statues of gods, as well as inscriptions connected with urban cult, e.g. dedications of priests of the city Tyche, of the imperial cult etc. With the spreading of Christianity, expressions of pagan religiosity were no longer publicly displayed in epigraphic form, though there is abundant evidence to show that paganism was still very much alive in the private sphere. In their place, a great variety of Christian inscriptions make their appearance: building inscriptions and dedications of private donors in churches, prayers and invocations for divine help, apotropaic formulas, and others. For the sake of convenience, and to present a truer to life picture of the variety of epigraphic expressions that may be found in a single complex, we shall treat together different types of inscriptions in some ecclesiastical buildings of the Holy Land.

V. 2. 1 Inscriptions in ecclesiastical buildings

A. Monasteries and charity foundations

There are various types of ecclesiastical buildings, and inscriptions therein vary according to their type. Monasteries and service structures belonging to them sometimes contain building inscriptions referring to the entire structure or parts of it. The main location of inscriptions in monasteries is the church and its annexes (e.g. baptistery or *diakonikon*), or any chapel added to the compound, but inscriptions can also be found in burials (see below) and in service spaces, e.g. a refectory,[96] a reception room,[97] a bakery or a wine press.[98] In many cases, when the remains are not sufficiently

---

[96] Examples in the monastery of Martyrius at Ma'ale Adummim (*SEG* XL, no. 1498) and in the monastery of Kyra Maria in Beth Shean (FitzGerald 1939: 16, no. 7).

[97] In the 'parlour' or reception room of the head of the monastery of Kyra Maria (FitzGerald 1939: 16, no. 6; *SEG* VIII, no. 38); in a reception room for guests near the entrance of the monastery recently excavated on Mount Scopus, north of Jerusalem (*SEG* LIII, no. 1854; *CIIP* I, 2, App. no. 10*).

[98] In a bakery in the coenobium at Kh. Siyar el-Ghanam near Bethlehem (Corbo 1955: 40); in a winepress belonging to a monastery at Tel Ashdod (Di Segni 2008; *SEG* LVI, no. 1890).

preserved or not properly excavated, the mention of an abbot (*hegoumenos* or *archimandrites*)[99] in the inscription identifies the building as a monastery church, or at least as a church with attached monastery.[100] Invocations for the community or for specific members of it are frequent, often in the form of a quotation or paraphrase from the Scriptures (mainly from the Book of Psalms). Scriptural quotations appear in monasteries also for their didactic or apotropaic value (see below).[101] Pleading for divine blessing upon benefactors may also be present, often on objects offered to the monastery church, like chancel screens or altar tables.

The monastery of Theoctistus, Deir Mukallik, was a coenobium located in a deep gorge (Naḥal Og, Wadi Mukallik) in the Judaean Desert east of Jerusalem. The building, supported by massive retaining walls, leaned against the face of the cliff in front of the original cave of the founders, the saintly monks Euthymius and Theoctistus, which was made into a church. The entire fabric collapsed in the Islamic period, leaving only the cave church and the built path that led to the entrance of the monastery. Along this path, a small 'waiting area', with a rock-hewn bench and a water cistern, had been arranged by the monks for the relief of visitors and pilgrims, especially women, who were not permitted to enter the monastery. Their visits are attested here by many Greek graffiti scratched on the cliff face, with invoca-

---

[99] The two terms are equivalent in the largest part of the Holy Land as well as in Syria, but not in the Jerusalem area. Here the title of archimandrite was reserved for the head of the monastery of Theodosius, who was responsible for supervising *coenobia* (communal monasteries), and for the head of the laura of Sabas, who was responsible for supervising *laurae* (monasteries of hermits) and hermitages, as well as for their seconds-in-command, the head of the monastery of Martyrius and the head of the laura of Gerasimus near the Dead Sea. Note that the title of Abbas (from Aramaic *Abba*, 'father'), from which the term 'abbot' later originated, did not indicate the head of a monastery but applied to any monk or priest as a respectful address.

[100] Some churches, especially pilgrimage churches, had an attached monastery for the service of pilgrims and visitors, even if they were not monastic churches. However, in examining the plan of an excavated church it is important to keep in mind that a couple of rooms attached to the body of the church are not enough to declare it a monastic church or a church with an attached monastery. On the problem, see Di Segni 2016.

[101] Quotations from the psalms were common in churches, and especially in monastic churches, where psalms were chanted at all the seven prayer hours of the day and the night, and one of the perquisites for becoming a monk was to learn the Psalter by heart; Cyril of Scythopolis, *Vita Sabae* 28, 75 (ed. Schwartz 1939: 113, 180; transl. Price 1991: 122, 189/ Di Segni 2005: 163, 209). For a collection of scriptural quotations in Greek and Latin, from churches and other locations, see Felle 2006; and for the same in Palestine and Arabia, Di Segni 2017b.

tions to Christ for help or protection, crosses and drawings.[102] More graffiti and dipinti of the same supplicatory character, these probably left by the monks themselves, filled the walls and ceiling of the cave church.[103] A burial crypt opened in the depth of the cave church: a panel over its entrance bears a painted inscription: 'Tomb of the saintly fathers and brothers. Lord, if you had been here, my brother would not have died. Lazarus, come out!' – a quotation from the scene of Lazarus' restoration to life by Jesus (John 11: 21, 32, 43).[104] The eastern wall of the church was plastered and covered with frescoes; on one wall, three layers were identified, the earlier showing a bust of Christ, the uppermost, and probably also the middle one, presenting an Ascension scene with Christ and angels. The two upper layers belong to a later period of occupation of the cave in the early Middle Ages. Christ holds an open book on whose pages are painted quotations from John 11: 25-26 and other Johannine passages, and Matthew 11: 28.[105] At the foot of the Ascension scene is a painted quotation of Ps 23 (MT 24): 7, 9, and below the Ascension is a row of thirteen figures identified by painted labels as apostles and evangelists.[106] Like this painting, other figures and quotations, some fragmentary, on the walls of the cave church belong to the medieval phase (eleventh-early twelfth centuries), but the general effect they offer illustrates what the inner space of a monastic church may have looked like also in Late Antiquity. Such late antique examples are not readily available, for walls are usually robbed of the stones and rarely stand at their original height; and even when some portion still stands, it is usually stripped of the original plaster or marble facing. However, there is sufficient evidence that inscriptions painted on plaster or engraved on marble facings of walls, as well as graffiti, did appear in monastic churches and perhaps also in rooms where the members of the community would meet, like refectories and *diakonika*. Written texts with a didactic function may well have been more common in in monastic than in parochial churches, for a larger part of the faithful could be expected to be literate in the former than in the latter. Fragments of marble panels on which quotations from psalms can be identified were discovered

---

[102] Patrich and Di Segni 1987; *SEG* XXXVII, nos. 1502-1505; *CIIP* IV, 1, nos. 3172-3181.
[103] Goldfus et al. 1995; *SEG* XLV, nos. 1958-1972; *CIIP* IV, 1, nos. 3155-3164, 3169.
[104] *SEG* XXXVII, no. 1508; XLV, no. 1958; Goldfus et al. 1995: 283-284, no. 1; *CIIP* IV, 1, no. 3153.
[105] Felle 2006: 117, no. 177; *CIIP* IV, 1, no. 3166. Fragments of the 'book' were looted by antiquities robbers and resurfaced in the antiquities market at Bethlehem.
[106] *SEG* XLV, nos. 1963-1964; *CIIP* IV, 1, nos. 3167-3168. Five of the labels are legible: Philippus, Marcus, Mattheus, Andreas, Petrus.

in the monastery on Mount Scopus known as 'monastery of Theodorus and Cyriacus'.[107] At Rehovot-in-the-Negev personal names, appeals to God for help and other undeciphered graffiti were incised on stones of the walls and jambs in the Northern Church – a pilgrim church apparently served by a team of monks; in a side room, fifty-three fragments of an inscription in black ink on white plaster were recovered together with the remains of a figure painted in fresco.[108] A quotation from Ps. 90 (MT 91):4-7, was painted on plaster in the monastery church on Jebel Harun near Petra. It reads: 'His truth will encircle you with an armour; you will not fear the terror of the night, nor the arrow that flies by day, nor the (evil) thing (pestilence in the Hebrew text) that walks at night, nor the destruction and the demon of noonday. A thousand shall fall at your side, ten thousand at your right hand, but it will not come near you'. The editors interpreted it as a protective prayer against the plague that raged in the Holy Land in 541-542 and did not spare the monasteries of the desert.[109]

There is some evidence, both literary and epigraphic, that in monasteries a special place was reserved for the tomb of the founder, of the abbots and of priests and elders of the community.[110] Examples can be seen in the few monasteries that have been completely excavated. In Martyrius' monastery at Ma'ale Adummim a stone slab marks the opening of the tomb of the ab-

---

[107] *CIIP* I, 2, no. 817A.

[108] Tsafrir 1988: 176, nos. 37, 39 (the only legible graffiti); 178-182, no. 45, ill. 270 (fragments in ink); *SEG* XXXVIII, nos. 1633, 1635, 1639.

[109] Frösén et al. 2008: 279-280, no. 18; *SEG* LVIII, no. 1775. The medium itself, paint on plaster, indicates that the inscription was not planned with the building, like those engraved on lintels or set in mosaic pavements, but was written impromptu to fit the occasion. The Justinian plague entered southern Palestine from Egypt in 541 and spread all over the Byzantine Empire and beyond its borders for several years. For the scourge reaching the monasteries of the desert, see Cyril of Scythopolis, *Vita Cyriaci* 10 (ed. Schwartz 1939: 228-229; transl. Price 1991: 252/Di Segni 2005: 244).

[110] Some examples from hagiographic sources: a special tomb for the founder Theoctistus and for his successor in the abbacy, Maris, in the monastery of Theoctistus, and for the founder Sabas and his successors in the Great Laura of Sabas: *Vita Euthymii* 36; *Vita Sabae* 77-78 (ed. Schwartz 1939: 55, 184; transl. Price 1991: 52, 193/Di Segni 2005: 116, 211). In the latter, presbyters were buried separately, and a monk who had led a particularly ascetic life was privileged with burial with them: *Vita Sabae* 44 (ed. Schwartz 1939: 135; transl. Price 1991: 145/Di Segni 2005: 179). The mortuary chapel in the monastery of Euthymius was so planned that burials for abbots, priests and specially venerable elders were prepared around the grave of the founder, set in the centre: *Vita Euthymii* 42 (ed. Schwartz 1939: 61; transl. Price 1991: 58/Di Segni 2005: 121); the arrangement can still be seen today. A side room contains the communal burial of the simple monks, who were laid one next to the other on the crypt floor. For the archaeological evidence, see Hirschfeld 1992: 130-143.

bots in the atrium of the church. It bears the inscription: 'Tomb of Paul, priest and archimandrite'.[111] A cave between the main entrance of the complex and the church is identified as the burial vault reserved for the monastery priests by a mosaic inscription opening with a quotation from the Gospel ('Lord, remember in thy kingdom'; Luke 23:42), followed by the names of three priests, Elpidius, Ioannes and Georgius, 'and the other priests who rest here, whose names Thou knowest'.[112] Only few skeletons were found in this crypt, confirming that the mass of simple monks were buried elsewhere, most likely in the ground outside the compound. The three priests were probably responsible for the transformation of the cave into a burial vault covered with a mosaic pavement, as well as for the paving of another chapel in the monastery, where a mosaic inscription says: 'O Lord our God, remember in thy kingdom Elpidius, Ioannes and Georgius the priests and all their community in Christ'.[113]

To complete the dossier on this monastery, we shall mention three other epigraphic finds. A fragmentary inscription in the second-stage mosaic pavement of the church informs that the work was done 'at the time of our saintly father Genesius, priest and archimandrite', a successor of Paul in the second half of the sixth century. The same abbot is mentioned in the refectory, a splendid mosaic pavement made 'for the salvation of himself and of his community in Christ'.[114] A fragment of chancel screen from the church bears the engraved names of two donors, a woman and a man, more likely mother and son than a married couple, since the woman's name precedes the man's.[115]

A cliff coenobium was excavated at Khirbet ed-Deir in the Judaean Desert, east of Hebron. Here too separate burial places were reserved for the head of the monastery and for the priests and elders. A cave between the

---

[111] *SEG* XL, no. 1493. Martyrius founded his coenobium along the Jerusalem-Jericho road in the late 450s and left it permanently when he became patriarch of Jerusalem in 478. Paul, his successor, was the first abbot who died and was buried in the monastery (at the end of the fifth century or in the early sixth), for Martyrius was duly buried in the tomb of the patriarchs on the Mount of Olives. Paul rated the title of archimandrite as head of the monastery of Martyrius: see above, n. 99. On the monastery of Martyrius, see Magen 2015.

[112] *SEG* XL, no. 1497. This is the only cave on the site and must therefore be the original cave chosen by Martyrius for his hermitage before he founded his coenobium: Cyril of Scythopolis, *Vita Euthymii* 32 (ed. Schwartz 1939: 51; transl. Price 1991: 48/Di Segni 2005: 112).

[113] *SEG* XL, no. 1499.

[114] *SEG* XL, nos. 1494, 1498.

[115] *SEG* XL, no. 1496. When a married couple is mentioned, the man's name as a rule comes first.

outer and the inner gate of the monastery was made into a tomb by the construction of burial troughs within and of a small chapel paved in elegant geometric mosaic in front of its entrance. A *tabula ansata* under a conch at the inner end of the mosaic carpet contains the inscription: Ἅγιοι π(ατέ)ρες πρεσβε(ύετε) τὴν | εἰρήνην τῷ τόπῳ τού|τῳ κ(αὶ) τ(αῖς) ψυχαῖς ἡμῶν, 'Holy fathers, intercede for peace for this place and for our souls' (Fig. 24). The prayer is addressed to the priests and probably to other dead elders; the cave, ca. 5 × 5 m, contained about ten troughs, and even if they were used for repeated burials, this space is unlikely to have been planned for burying all the members of the community.[116] A smaller cave near the church, more like an alcove, perhaps the original founder's cave, was made into a tomb for him and probably for his successors by blocking its opening with a built door that could be locked; a cross was engraved on it and a mosaic panel was laid in front of the entrance, adorned with a Greek cross, a *crux ansata* and a nine-line inscription quoting a passage from the First Epistle to the Corinthians

Fig. 24 – Khirbet ed-Deir monastery: inscription in the funerary chapel (Hirschfeld 1999: 102, fig. 5. Photo Z. Radovan. Reproduced with the permission of the Institute of Archaeology, The Hebrew University of Jerusalem)

[116] *SEG* XXXVII, no. 1496; *CIIP* IV, 2, no. 3820. On the burial arrangement at Kh. ed-Deir, see Hirschfeld 1992: 139-141, and on the whole coenobium, Hirschfeld 1999.

Fig. 24 – Khirbet ed-Deir monastery: inscription in front of the burial cave of the founder (Hirschfeld 1999: 51, fig. 74. Photo Z. Radovan. Reproduced with the permission of the Institute of Archaeology, The Hebrew University of Jerusalem)

Δεῖ τὸ φθαρτὸν
τοῦτο ἐνδύσασ-
θαι ἀφθαρσίαν
4 καὶ τὸ θνητὸν
τοῦτο ἐνδύσασ-
θαι ἀθανασίαν·
σαλπίσει γὰρ
8 καὶ οἱ νεκροὶ
ἀναστήσονται.

This perishable nature must put on the imperishable, and this mortal nature must put on immortality. For the trumpet will sound and the dead will be raised (I Cor. 15: 52-53).

(15:52-53) that proclaims the resurrection of the dead (Fig. 25).[117] This text was certainly suitable to a tomb, but it presents an additional point of interest: the Pauline verses are not quoted verbatim but the order of the verses is inverted and the words 'and we shall be changed' are omitted. This seems to hint to a didactic approach or perhaps a political strategy on the part of the monastery leadership: in the climate of violent controversy between Origenists and their opposers that raged in the monasteries of the Judaean Desert between ca. 532 and 555, these words could have been perceived as endorsing the Origenist concept of resurrection of the body as ethereal rather than

---

[117] SEG XXXVII, no. 1495; *CIIP* IV, 2, no. 3819: 'This perishable nature must put on the imperishable, and this mortal nature must put on immortality. For the trumpet will sound, and the dead will be raised'. I Cor 15: 52-53 reads: 'For the trumpet will sound, and the dead will be raised imperishable, and we shall be changed. For this perishable nature must put on the imperishable, and this mortal nature must put on immortality'. This quotation is unique: the only other partial example (I Cor 15: 53) in all the *orbis Christianus* is in a tomb (?) at Sidon: Felle 2006: 141-142, no. 251. For a discussion of the significance of the omitted words, see Di Segni 1999b: 99-101.

corporeal as it was in life. The members of the coenobium, who passed the tomb on their way between the church and the refectory, were reminded by the inscription that St. Paul's words, which they surely heard uncensored in church, were not to lead to unorthodox interpretations.

A large cave in the centre of the complex was made into a church and paved with a splendid mosaic. An inscription at the foot of the chancel reads: 'Remember us, o Lord, with the favour thou hast for thy people, visit us with thy salvation, that we may behold the good of thy elect'. This is the Septuagint version of Ps. 105 (MT 106): 4-5.[118] An altar table recovered in the church bears an engraved dedication on its edge: 'O Lord, remember the donors, Alafeos deacon and Aianos, monks' – probably members of the Khirbet ed-Deir coenobium.[119]

Urban monasteries are not well known, archaeologically speaking: in the densely populated cities of the Holy Land, they were destroyed or superseded by later building activity. Even when a monastery in urban context is identified on the ground, often only part of it can be excavated, by choice the church or chapel. An exception is the monastery of Kyra Maria at Beth Shean, which was entirely excavated in the 1930s. It is a small coenobium attached to the inner side of the northern section of the city wall, though in an uninhabited part of the ancient and the modern city. The monastery seemingly originated from a recluse's cell in one of the wall towers and was built in two main stages, documented by inscriptions (Fig. 26).[120] In the first stage, a chapel was built parallel to the city wall, with some rooms south of it for a few monks serving the holy man. An inscription in the mosaic pavement of the portico that functioned as a narthex reads: 'O Christ the god saviour of the world, have mercy upon the Christ-loving Lady Mary (*Kyra Maria*) and her son Maximus, and grant rest to her forefathers, through the prayers of all the saints, amen' (no. 1 in Fig. 26).[121] Within the church, the recluse made arrangements for two tombs, one in the south-eastern corner, reserved for the future burial of the benefactress and her family, the other in the north-eastern

---

[118] *SEG* XXXVII, no. 1493; *CIIP* IV, 2, no. 3818. This quotation too is rare: Felle (2006: 189, no. 394) cites only one other example, from Syria, a mixture of Ps. 102: 4 and 105: 4-5.

[119] *SEG* XXXVII, no. 1494; *CIIP* IV, 2, no. 3821. This dedication confirms what we know from literary sources: in this period, monks were not obliged to give up all their property on entering a monastery. They could keep money and ever real estate yielding an income.

[120] The terrain south of the city wall drops steeply to the streambed of Naḥal Ḥarod and is unsuitable for domestic building. Part of the upper area was used as a necropolis in the Late Bronze Period and Early Iron Age. For the excavation report, see FitzGerald 1939, and for a reassessment of the different building stages, Di Segni 1997a; 401-414; 2017b: 67-68.

[121] FitzGerald 1939: 14, no. 3, pl. XX.

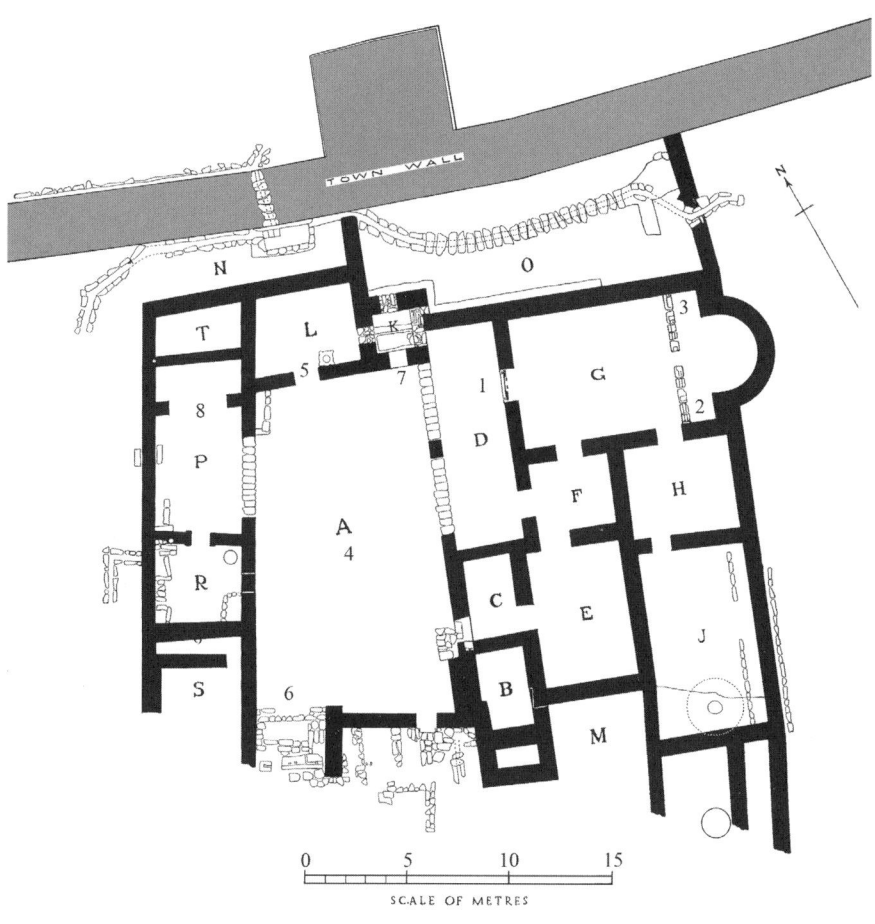

Plan of the Monastery, by Mr. E. F. Beaumont

Fig. 26 – Plan of the monastery of Kyra Maria at Beth Shean (Drawing B. Arubas, modified from FitzGerald 1939, pl. II)

corner, presumably reserved for himself. The former (no. 2 in Fig. 26) was identified by the following inscription, set in the mosaic pavement: 'Where the wreathed cross is, [there] lies the lid of the mouth of the tomb, which has rings. Whoever wishes shall lift the wreathed cross, and he will find the lid and bury. And if the Lady Mary, who founded this church, should desire in future to lay down (a dead) in this tomb, she or anyone of her family at any time, I Elias, by the mercy of God a recluse, in the name of the Father, the Son and the Holy Ghost curse and anathematize whoever after me hinders her or any of hers, or removes this inscription of mine'. At least two dead were laid in this tomb. This text illustrates not only the phenomenon of privileged laypersons being secured burial space in a monastery, even in the church itself, in exchange for their patronage, but also the protection of private tombs against alien occupation through curses and anathemas.[122] The other tomb was also marked with a mosaic inscription, which was damaged when the tomb was reopened for more burials and was restored by a later and less practiced hand (no. 3 in Fig. 26). Probably, but not certainly, the restored text was the same as the broken one. The inscription reads: 'Where the wreathed cross is, there lies the lid of the mouth of the tomb, which has rings. There have I laid my Christ-loving sister Georgia, I, Elias, by the mercy of God a most lowly recluse [break] (she?) died on the fourth day in the month of May of the fifteenth indiction, the day of mid-Pentecost'. The date corresponds to 4 May 567. At least four bodies were laid in this tomb.[123] Some time later, but still in Elias' lifetime, a new wing was added, separated from the east wing by a hall paved with a splendid mosaic representing the zodiac, with the personifications of the Sun and the Moon in the centre and of the months, each labelled with its Roman name, all around (no. 4 in Fig. 26). On the north side of the hall a room lavishly paved in mosaic (Room L) may have served as a reception room where visitors could talk with the recluse through a window opening in his adjoining cell; in front of its entrance an inscription announced that 'The work was completed with God's help in the time of Elias, the most God-loving priest and recluse, in the year 6[. .], indiction 2' – probably 568/9 CE (Fig. 27; no. 5 in Fig. 26).[124] The entrance to the coenobium was on the south side of the hall and an inscription in front of the entrance (no. 6 in Fig. 26) tells us that a different patron had paid for the new wing or at least for its superb mosaic pavements. It reads: 'Offering for the memory and the perfect rest in Christ of the *illustris* Zosimus, and the preservation and succour of John, the most glorious ex prefect, and of Peter and Anastasius, Christ-loving counts, and of all their blessed house, through the prayers of the saints, amen'. The titles show this was a senatorial family of the highest rank. John, the most glorious ex prefect (or honorary prefect),

---

[122] FitzGerald 1939: 14-15, no. 4, pl. XXI; *SEG* VIII, no. 39. For the protection of tombs through funerary curses, see Di Segni 2009b; *CIIP* I, 2, no. 985 and the bibliography there.

[123] FitzGerald 1939: 15-16, no. 5, pl. XXI; *SEG* VIII, no. 40.

[124] FitzGerald 1939: 16, no. 6, pl. XXI; *SEG* VIII, no. 38; Meimaris 1992: 86, no. 19. The figure indicating the year lost the digits for the tens and the units. Fitzgerald restored 6[17], corresponding to 553/4, which fell in the second indiction, in the belief that this inscription was earlier than the one in the church. Meimaris suggested 617 or 632, the latter corresponding to 568/9, also in a second indiction. This is most likely the right date, considering both the architectural history of the building and the fact that Elias is now a priest.

Fig. 27 – Inscription 5 in the monastery of Kyra Maria at Beth Shean (Courtesy of B. Arubas)

and his family again pray for God's help through the prayers of the saints in another inscription on the northern edge of the mosaic carpet of the hall, in front of a small room (Room K: no. 7 in Fig. 26) that at some point was blocked and made into a tomb, probably for the holy man Elias himself.[125] At a later sub-stage a long room in the west wing (Room P), most likely the refectory, was restructured; an inscription in its mosaic pavement reads: 'The whole work of laying the mosaic was completed in the time of the priest and *hegoumenos* George and of the *deuterarius* Comitas' (no. 8 in Fig. 26).[126]

Lay benefactors are mentioned also in other monasteries, though their presence is less dominant than in parochial churches. Again at Beth Shean, an isolated fragment of mosaic pavement on the northern bank of Naḥal Ḥarod, east of the necropolis, bore this inscription: 'The monastery of Abba Iustinus the recluse was built in the time of the 15th indiction, on the 2[?] of Panemos of the year 585, and he was enclosed in the same year, on the [?]

---

[125] FitzGerald 1939: 13-14, nos. 1-2, pl. XX.
[126] FitzGerald 1939: 16, no. 7, pls. XXI-XXII. A *deuterarios* was the second in command of the abbot in a coenobium.

of September [of the 1st indiction]. An offering of Anoisius the advocate. Lord, help!' (June-July and September 522).¹²⁷ An interesting abbreviation is used for the word 'monastery': MONT, μον(ασ)τ(ήριον). In the Greek of this period this term – like the corresponding Latin *monasterium* – often indicated a single monastic cell rather than a monastery: in this case it seems clear that the building was the hermitage of a recluse, built for him by a local patron. In Mar Liyas, the famous monastery dedicated to the prophet Elijah in the Jebel Ajlun in the bishopric of Pella (Jordan), an inscription at the entrance to some rooms south of the church reads: 'With the help of Christ, the mosaic pavement has been laid under Esion (?), the most God-loving priest and abbot, by the care of John, pulse merchant (φακοπώλης), for the succour of himself and (his) wife (σύνβιος) and his children, in the month of June (or July) of the 14th indiction, year 838 [of the city] of Pella' (June-July 776 CE; Fig. 28). Another inscription, in the southern aisle of the church, though fragmentary, can be partly deciphered; it ascribes the work to Sabas, priest (and abbot – this part is lost) and to a benefactor, possibly a craftsman of some kind, who invokes the Lord's mercy upon himself and his wife, and asks Saint Elijah's intercession for his workshop. The greatest part of the last lines is lost except for the invocation ἅ]γιε Ἠλία, the word ἐργαστή[ριον] (workshop) and the date, year 686 of the city era, corresponding to 623/4 CE (Fig. 29). Attached to the northern side of the church is a baptistery: here too a mosaic inscription in the font mentioned an anonymous benefactor: 'Offering of one whose name the Lord knows, for the remission of his sins and for a long life'.¹²⁸

As we have seen, except for some inscribed artefacts, like altar tables and chancel screens, inscriptions are mostly set in mosaic pavements, for walls rarely stand at more than a negligible height and more often the stones are looted down to the foundations. Nevertheless, we have presented evidence of graffiti and inscriptions painted on plaster or engraved on marble facings of walls. In addition, some elements of church architecture are often preserved, which display engraved inscriptions. Lintels adorned with crosses and sometimes bearing also inscriptions, set above the entrances of churches,

---

[127] FitzGerald 1939: 19, no. 7, pl. XXII *SEG* VIII, no. 37; Meimaris 1992: 86, no. 17.
[128] Di Segni 2006a: 579-580; *SEG* LVI, no. 1904; Piccirillo 2011: 107-110; *SEG* LXIV, nos. 1799-1800. This reference to anonymous benefactors 'whose name God knows' is more frequent in churches than in monasteries, and appears also in a synagogue (e.g., at Beth Shean: *SEG* XXXVII, no. 1532). See for instance *CIIP* I, 2, nos. 812 (in Armenian), 854 (with a list of occurrences from other sites on both sides of the Jordan), 869, 1084; *CIIP* II, no. 1152 and comment there.

Chapter V: Greek inscriptions in the Holy Land in Late Antiquity

Fig. 28 – Mar Liyas, 776 CE (*SEG* LVI, no. 1904. M. Piccirillo, SBF Photographic Archive)

Fig. 29 – Mar Liyas, 623 CE (*SEG* LXIV, no. 1799. M. Piccirillo, SBF Photographic Archive)

monasteries or monastic structures, are the commonest find of this type. For instance, a fragmentary lintel discovered in secondary use in the Old City of Jerusalem bears a large cross in the centre, flanked by the engraved inscription: 'Monastery of the Mother of God and of Saint John, established by... and Sophia, children of the blessed Ioannes'.[129] Another lintel bearing a building inscription, found out of context at Hesban in Jordan, reads: 'Under the most God-fearing George, presbyter and *hegoumenos* of this [house] of salvation, the church was renovated on the first of the month of September, indiction - -'.[130] The lintel at the entrance of a baptistery attached to a small monastery at 'Ein Ma'amudiye in southern Judaea is adorned with a central cross, geometric patterns, and the inscription: 'Jesus Christ, help thy servant Demetrius and his community. This is the gate of the Lord. The Lord will protect your coming in and your going out'.[131] These two verses, 'This is the gate of the Lord, the righteous shall enter in it' (Ps. 117 [MT. 118]: 20) and 'The Lord will protect your coming in and your going out' (sometimes: Lord, protect etc., or May the Lord protect etc.) (Ps. 120 [MT. 121]: 8) have an apotropaic function and are very common at the entrance of churches, including monastery churches.

Another typical place where inscriptions were set up are cisterns both of monasteries and of churches. This may seem strange for – in the profound darkness of a cistern – these inscriptions were never seen. The usual text is Ps 28 (MT 29): 3: 'The voice of the Lord is upon the waters', sometimes with the second part of the verse: 'The God of glory thunders'. This quotation was erroneously connected with the liturgy of baptism, but it is always found moulded in the hydraulic plaster of cisterns or engraved on lids covering the mouths of cisterns, and its function was obviously apotropaic, to defend the precious water from malignant spirits lurking in the dark. An example can be seen in the cistern of the monastery of St. Aaron on Jebel Harun near Petra;[132] another at el-'Aleiliyat in Wadi Suweinit in the Judaean Desert north of Jerusalem. Here the quotation is engraved in CPA over the entrance of an ancient miqveh, reused as a cistern by the monks of the Laura

---

[129] *CIIP* I, 2, no. 858.
[130] *SEG* LVI, no. 1918. Instead of Σωτηριώδ[ους δώ]ματος, 'house] of salvation', a generic designation of a monastery, it was suggested to read Σωτηριώδ[ους Μνή]|ματος, 'Salutary Tomb' which would be the name of this monastery.
[131] Stève 1946: 569–571; *CIIP* IV, 2, no. 3816.
[132] *SEG* LII, no. 1733 (11); Frösén et al. 2008: 277–278 no. 12. For a discussion of the function of this quotation and a list of its epigraphic appearance in the Holy Land, see Di Segni 2017b: 71, tb. 4; 80.

of Firminus, who occupied the caves some four centuries after Jewish rebels had hidden there from the Romans and left Aramaic inscriptions.[133] The same apotropaic role was filled by crosses painted or moulded on the thick layer of waterproof plaster that covered the walls of a cistern, for instance in the same cave at el-'Aleiliyat, in the reservoir of the laura of Suca near Teqoa and in the one created in the vaults under the Nea Church and monastery in Jerusalem.[134] In the Nea, the cross is exceptionally accompanied by a building inscription. Cross and inscription are moulded in the plaster high up in the southern wall of the reservoir, about 8 m above floor level, opposite the opening of a stepped gallery that entered the vaults (Fig. 30). Like in other cisterns, the cross was obviously intendent to remain above water level even when the reservoir was full, but cross and inscription would probably have been seen only on the inauguration of the structure, if such an even was celebrated. Why, then, was it important to set up this inscription? Unlike most dedications, which must be read by the public to maximize their impact on the status of the dedicator – what in modern terms we would call their publicity value – the point in this case seems to be having it known that such inscription was there. It reads: Κ(αὶ) τοῦτο τὸ ἔργον ἐφιλοτιμή|σατο ὁ εὐσεβ(έστατος) ἡμῶν βασιλεὺς Φλ(άουιος) Ἰουστινιανὸς προνοί|ᾳ κ(αὶ) σπουδὶ Κωνσταντίνου ∥5 ὁσιωτά(του) πρεσβ(υτέρου) κ(αὶ) | ἡγουμέ(νου) ἰνδ(ικτιῶνος) ιγ' (This work too was donated by our most pious Emperor Flavius Justinian through the provision and care of Constantine, most saintly priest and abbot, in the 13th indiction).[135] With these words the abbot expressed both his thankfulness for the imperial liberality and his gratification for the special honour shown to the monastery by the personal intervention of Justinian. In fact, while the honour was there – for the church

---

[133] The CPA inscription, together with Christian graffiti in Greek and crosses, were inscribed by the monastic community, which was apparently composed of both Aramaic and Greek speakers, as in attested by another CPA inscription on the mosaic pavement of a small building in the core of the laura, which says that the cell was built by a priest named Silas: *CIIP* IV, 1, nos. 2800-2803 (first-century Jewish inscriptions), 2504-2806 (Christian inscriptions). Marcoff and Chitty, who first explored the site, mistakenly interpreted the miqveh as a baptistery (Marcoff and Chitty 1929: 169); Patrich and Rubin (1984) explored the cave again and recognized the true function of the cistern in its different stages.

[134] Hirschfeld 1992: 63-64, 157-158. For a history of the construction of the Nea and of the vaults that supported it, see Procopius of Caesarea, *Aed*. V, 6; Di Segni 2012c.

[135] *SEG* XXVII, no. 1015; *CIIP* I, 2, no. 800. The 13th indiction occurred three times under Justinian, in 534/5, 549/50 and 564/5, and the absolute date of this inscription was left undecided until lately, when a similar inscription by the same abbot, dated to the 14th indiction, confirmed the most likely date for the inauguration of the Nea cistern: 549/50 (Di Segni and Gellman 2017).

Fig. 30 – Building inscription of the reservoir in the vaults under the Nea Church (Photo M. Suchowolski © The Israel Museum, Jerusalem)

and its annexes were built following a request of the venerated monk Sabas to the emperor – the liberality was less real, for though Justinian did send an architect to build the church, he ordered the money for the building to be taken from the provincial coffer.[136]

Capitals and baptismal fonts sometimes bore engraved inscriptions, but since they are often discovered out of context, and it is therefore unclear if they belonged to a monastic or a parochial church, we shall treat them when discussing the latter.

As we have seen, there is evidence that in monasteries separate tombs were marked out for the founder and his successors in the abbacy, and the priests and

---

[136] So we learn from Cyril of Scythopolis, *Vita Sabae* 73 (ed. Schwartz 1939: 177; transl. Price 1991: 186/Di Segni 2005: 206).

elders. Simple monks could be buried in vaults within or without the precinct, or in trough graves in the open fields.[137] In an urban monastery, however, burying within the compound was not possible, for the Roman law that forbade burial within the city limits was still enacted in Late Antiquity. In Jerusalem, epigraphic evidence attests that many monasteries had their own cemetery outside the walls: west of the city was the cemetery of the monastery of the Iberians at David's Tower;[138] in the Kidron Valley was the 'Tomb belonging to the monastery of the Apollinarian women' and probably the cemetery of the Probatica Church;[139] in the Valley of Hinnom (Wadi er-Rababi), south of the city wall, were the burial caves owned by the monastery of Juvenal, a nunnery, the monastery of St. Sergius and the Hagia Sion, as well as by the Patriarchal Hospital and by the hospice and hospital of the Nea Church.[140] The church and monastery of St. Stephan, located north of the city gate (today's Damascus Gate), had its burial grounds within its precinct and adjoining it.[141]

Charity foundations, like hostels and hospitals, alms houses, old age homes, orphanages etc., were often managed by monks. We have already mentioned the two hospitals attested by inscriptions in Jerusalem, both attached to foundations that had their own crews of *spoudaioi*. Another inscription, engraved on a lintel reused in the Turkish wall of Jerusalem near Herod's Gate, reads: 'Home for elderly, poor women, established through the holy (church) of the Mother of God by Ioannes and Verina from Byzantium'.[142] A fragmentary

---

[137] As we have seen above, the inscription of the crypt in the monastery of Theoctistus shows that elders and simple brothers were burials together in it. However, literary sources indicate that the founder and his successors in the abbacy were buried separately. The monastery of St. George in Wadi Qelt has a burial vault just outside its gate, where Greek inscriptions on the walls identify different deceased (Schneider 1931). To this day monks who die there are first buried in the ground in a small cemetery outside the gate; then their bones are translated to the burial vault. The founders of the monastery and specially venerated monks, however, were buried in a separate chapel, today's chapel of St. Stephen; see Antonius Chozibita, *Vita sancti Georgii Chozibitae* 57; *Miracula Beatae Virginis in Choziba* 6, transl. Di Segni 1991: 55, 124, 130-131. Trough graves near monasteries are not identified either epigraphically or archaeologically, but literary sources hint at the existence of such a solution.
[138] *SEG* VIII, no. 205; *CIIP* I, 2, no. 1000, cf. no. 977. On this cemetery, see Tchekhanovets 2017.
[139] For the former, see *CIIP* I, 2, no. 901, and for the latter, *CIIP* I, 2, no. 980 and cf. p. 275, introduction to nos. 894-901.
[140] *CIIP* I, 2, nos. 962 (monastery of Juvenal), 963 (St. Sergius), 965, 968-971 (Holy Zion), 967 (Patriarchal Hospital), 1008 (hospital of the Nea).
[141] *CIIP* I, 2, nos. 883-893.
[142] *CIIP* I, 2, no. 859. The church in question may be the one dedicated to the Virgin near the Probatica Pool, or the church of Mary Theotokos called Nea, both with their attached monasteries.

inscription from Caesarea mentions an orphanage (*orphanatrophion*).[143] The founding inscription of a hospital, worded in CPA, was discovered in Jordan, seemingly at Shuneh.[144]

B. Building and dedicatory inscriptions in churches

As in the case of monasteries, because of the settlement history of the country we have much more material evidence from churches in villages or in isolated spots than from those located within the cities, most of which disappeared under later development.[145] Of necessity, therefore, we shall focus on churches in rural areas. Churches belonging to lay congregations were of two types: parochial and private. Parochial churches were built by the villagers, often with the help of the bishop of the diocese in which the village was located – help that could be expressed in money for the work or in guidance for planning the building, as well as in the appointment of a priest.[146] In many cases the building inscription, usually located in front of the entrance or at the foot of the chancel, mentions the bishop's name, either because of his involvement in the work or as a dating device. In the former case, the bishop would most likely act through his *chorepiscopus* (country bishop) or through a visitor (*periodeutes*), his helpers in charge of the countryside; in which case their names would appear after his in the building inscriptions. If a priest had been appointed to the church, his name usually appears too, but inscriptions lacking it are far from rare, attesting that in some circumstances the bishop and his helpers could build a church for a community that still had no shepherd. If there was no one in a village with the qualifications required for the priesthood, the bishop would ordain deacons among the villagers and put the church in their charge, while leaving to visiting priests the duty to celebrate the Eucharist, the unique part of the cult that only a priest could perform. We shall survey some examples of building and other inscriptions in rural churches.

---

[143] *CIIP* II, no. 1168.
[144] Milik 1953: 530-533; cf. Di Segni 2009a: 355, n. 11.
[145] This description holds true for the western part of the country but not for the eastern part. In what is now southern Syria and Jordan, cities declined in the Islamic period and most of them were abandoned until modern times; so urban churches, though usually looted of stones, can be excavated and several have been, especially in Jerash, Madaba, Amman and Abila (Tell Abil, Umm el-'Amad). Still, the great majority of excavated churches there is located in ancient villages: see Michel 2001: 467-471.
[146] For an example of this process, see Cyril of Scythopolis, *Vita Euthymii* 15 (ed. Schwartz 1939: 24-25; transl. Price 1991: 20/Di Segni 2005a: 90), and for an example of financial help, see Cyril of Scythopolis, *Vita Sabae* 36 (ed. Schwartz 1939: 123; transl. Price 1991: 132-133/ Di Segni 2005a: 171).

A double church was excavated at Ḥorvat Karkara in Upper Galilee.[147] The older building was almost square, with two rows of columns and three entrances in the western wall. No apse or narthex were located by the excavators. In front of the main entrance a two-line inscription was inserted between the mosaic carpet of the nave and the threshold. It is oriented to the west, facing people coming out of the church – a rare but not unknown orientation in Palestinian churches. The first line quotes Ps 117 (MT 118): 19, 'Open to me the gates of righteousness'. The function of this verse, a favourite at the entrance of churches, was to define the sacred space and to separate it from the profane.[148] The second line contains the signature of the mosaicists: Ἔργον Εὐθυμίου δὶς κὲ Ἰωάνου ψηφ(ο)θετ(ῶν), 'Work of Euthymius the third and John, mosaic workers'.[149] A larger basilica was later attached to the northern wall of the earlier building: a wide opening in this wall connected the two wings into a single unit. The northern church had a single entrance at the west end from the narthex, and three projecting apses at the east end. An inscription in the centre of the nave reads: 'In the time of our most holy and God-loving archbishop Longinus and of the most God-fearing country bishop Polychronius and the most pious visitors Gaianus, Dorotheus and Bassus, the mosaic was completed, on the 30 of the month of Dystros of the year 603'. This dates the pavement of the northern church to 16 April 478 by the era and calendar of Tyre, in whose territory the village was located. Interestingly, 16 April of that year was the first Sunday after Easter, a significant date.[150] Two inscriptions in the nave, on the edge of the bema just above the step and in front of the entrance, are too fragmentary for reconstruction, but the latter seems to mention an *oikonomos* (ecclesiastic steward) and a

---

[147] Kohn-Tavor et al. 2020: 1-5 (excavation); Di Segni and Ashkenazi 2020: 303-310 (inscriptions).

[148] The next verse ('This is the gate of the Lord, the righteous shall enter through it', Ps 117: 20), was more common, in the mosaic floor at the entrance or engraved on the lintel of the door of a church; see list of occurrences in Felle 2006: 523. It appears in front of the entrance of the Northern Church at Herodion, facing people coming out of the church. The text is framed in a panel in the narthex imitating a door ajar (*SEG* XL, no. 1472; Felle 2006: 112, no. 165; *CIIP* IV, 2, no. 3325).

[149] Di Segni and Ashkenazi 2020: 304-305, no. 1. Δίς means 'twice', but is used in inscriptions after a personal name to indicate that the man had the same name as his father and grandfather. Ἰωάνης with a single N, instead of the correct Ἰωάννης, is quite common, as is the phonetic spelling κέ for καί.

[150] Avi-Yonah 1966; Di Segni and Ashkenazi 2020: 308-309, no. 5. In Byzantine Palestine, catechumens received baptism on Easter Sunday and wore white clothing for eight days, a custom still maintained by the Eastern Orthodox Church. Therefore, the first Sunday after Easter was the day when they came to communion and ceremonially took off their baptismal garment.

subdeacon.¹⁵¹ In the centre of the bema was a cross with the letters IX AΩ ('Jesus Christ, the beginning and the end', Ap. 1: 8), of which only the alpha-omega survived. Once it was believed that crosses in a mosaic floor could date the floor before 427 CE, when Theodosius II issued a law, preserved in the Justinian Code (*CJ* I, 8, 1), forbidding the representation of crosses on pavements; but there is abundant evidence that crosses continued to appear on floors after the law.¹⁵² Another inscription, skirting the back wall of the northern apse, prayed for a woman, surely a benefactress: 'Lord, remember your servant Sousan' – the Aramaic form of the biblical name Susanna.¹⁵³

Not far from Ḥorvat Karkara to the north-east, two churches were excavated at Ḥorvat ʿErav. The Eastern Church is a basilica with three apses (the lateral ones built in a later stage) and a narthex, whence three entrances led into the church; the northern entrance and part of the pavement of the northern aisle and of the nave are lost due to erosion. A long rectangular panel stretched across the entire width of the nave. Its central part is occupied by a *tabula ansata* with an eight-line inscription, flanked by peacocks, of which only the right-hand one remains with an accompanying text (Fig. 31). The left-hand part of the panel, presumably with another peacock and possibly another inscription, is lost.¹⁵⁴ The central inscription reads:

> Under the most holy bishop Ireneus and under the country bishop (χωροεπίσκοπος) Thomas and (the country bishop) Achillios, and under the most pious visitor (περιοδευτής) of the village Ioannios the mosaic pavement of the holy church was completed in the year 570, in the month of Loos. Deacon Barochi(u)s gave alms of 1/2 (*solidus*), Deacon Symeon 1 *solidus*, Deacon Apson 1 *solidus*, Deacon Dipheos 1 *solidus*, Deacon Gaion 1 *solidus*, Deacon Macedonius 1/2 *solidus*, Megistianus 1 *solidus*, Kaiumos 1 *solidus*.

The inscription on the right lists two more donors, laymen, who gave additional sums of money. The date is given according to the era of Tyre, in whose territory Ḥorvat ʿErav was located, and corresponds to August-

---

¹⁵¹ Di Segni and Ashkenazi 2020: 306-308, nos. 3-4.
¹⁵² All the mosaic floor of the bema of the northern church was decorated with a pattern of crosses in circles: Kohn-Tavor et al. 2020: 3. This combination – cross and the letters adapted from Revelation 1: 8 – is very common on mosaic pavements as well as on lintels, and not only in churches. When it appears in the domestic sphere, its role is merely apotropaic. For crosses on floors in the Holy Land, see Habas 2015.
¹⁵³ Di Segni and Ashkenazi 2020: 305–306, no. 2.
¹⁵⁴ On the church, see Kohn-Tavor et al. 2020: 5-9; on the inscription, Di Segni and Ashkenazi 2020: 310-315.

Fig. 31 – Ḥorvat ʿErav: building inscription in the Eastern Church (Di Segni and Ashkenazi 2020: 311, fig. 8. Photo Y. Drey. Courtesy of J. Ashkenazi)

September 445. Ireneus is known from literary sources: he was metropolitan of Tyre for a few years between ca. 444 and 448, though in the inscription he is described simply as 'bishop' – not unusual in early inscriptions and literary sources.[155] But this is not the only noteworthy detail in this text. One is the great number of deacons, surely many more than the service of this modest church needed. We note the same multitude of deacons and other low clergy, like subdeacons and lectors, in another early church in the Galilee, at ʿEvron: a possible explanation may be that a recently converted community could be made to develop stronger ties to the new faith through an active involvement in the ritual. Two other peculiarities in the ʿErav inscription: first, the church had no priest but no less than two country bishops are mentioned: perhaps one was involved in a former stage, erecting the building, and the other in the final stage, the laying of the mosaic pavement. Secondly, the visitor was apparently specifically assigned to this village (περιοδευτὴς τῆς κώμης). If he was a priest, his task presumably was to visit this church on a regular basis to celebrate the sacraments.

At ʿEvron, also situated in Western Galilee, but in the territory of Acco-Ptolemais, the village church went through various stages. The earliest inscription dates the mosaic pavement of the early baptistery to March-April 415 and mentions the bishop (of Ptolemais), a *chorepiscopus*, a priest named Samakon and a long list of archdeacon, deacons, subdeacons and readers. Clearly the community already had an organized clergy when the church was first built. A later inscription, in the new mosaic pavement of the nave of the same church, dated 10 February 443, again mentions the bishop of Ptolemais but no *chorepiscopus*, the same Samakon, explicitly described as

---

[155] Ireneus was *comes Orientis* in 431-435; a friend of Nestorius, he was stripped of his rank and exiled following Nestorius' condemnation for heresy, until the patriarch of Antioch Domnus ordained him bishop of Tyre, ca. 444. He was deposed in 448 due to the hostility of the Monophysite Dioscorus of Alexandria: Martindale 1980: 624-625.

'priest of the village', and a long list of lesser clergy, while another inscription in the same pavement, in front of the entrance, contains the usual blessing on coming in and going out, and the name of a visitor. A still later inscription, in the new pavement of the narthex, dated 489/90, only mentions priests and two laymen who probably had paid for the work.[156] Seven of the thirteen Greek inscriptions in the church (*SEG* XXXVII, nos. 1511, 1516-1517, 1519-1522) contain the formula: 'Lord, remember..' or 'Lord, help..', followed by names of clerics or laypersons, most likely donors, as is explicitly attested by two inscriptions: no 1511 commemorates a group of deacons and a lector 'who offered the two service rooms (καρποφορισάντων τὰ δύο διακονικά) and no. 1518 contains the invocation of Valentinus 'who offered one *solidus*'. An exception is represented by nos. 1516 and 1520, where the invocation to God is on behalf of the mosaic workers. Another inscription, belonging to the early stage of the church, is in CPA: it mentions the names of two women and a man, clearly benefactors, accompanied by the blessing 'May they live'.[157]

While the *chorepiskopos* is mentioned in many inscriptions of the fifth-seventh centuries throughout the Holy Land, both east and west of the Jordan, the *periodeutes*, common in Syria and Lebanon, appears almost exclusively in the northern part of the region in the fifth-sixth centuries.[158] The old theory upheld by Avi-Yonah and Meimaris, that the role of the *chorepiskopos* as representative of the bishop in rural congregations was taken over by the *periodeutes* in the sixth century, must be abandoned.[159] The former was not

---

[156] Tzaferis 1987; *SEG* XXXVII, nos. 1510-1522. The three inscriptions cited above are nos. 1514-1517, but for the last, see Meimaris 1992: 139, no. 3 and Di Segni 1997a: 257, no. 50 for corrected readings. The excavation was not properly published, and there are a number of inconsistencies between the excavators' journal and sketches and Tzaferis' published plan and interpretation of the building stages of the church. For a reassessment of the building stages based on the excavators' journal, see Di Segni 1997a: 230-258. Interestingly, the earliest mosaic contained crosses and christograms, and the new pavement in the nave, the aisles and two rooms on the northern side of the church covered most of them: this would be an unique case of obedience to Theodosius II's edict of 427 that forbade the picturing of crosses and sacred images on pavements.

[157] Desreumaux 1987b.

[158] Di Segni 2019: 44-45 and n. 7 (*chorepiskopos*); Di Segni and Ashkenazi 2020: 310, table 1, summarizing the appearance of *chorepisckopos* and *periodeutes*, to which add a *periodeutes* at Riḥab in northern Jordan: *SEG* LI, no, 2040. In most cases the *periodeutes* is attested in that part of the Holy Land that was included in the province of Phoenike. The only appearance of a *periodeutes* south of the Galilee is at 'Ein Samiye in southern Samaria, in an inscription dated to 557 (Macalister 1907: 237-238; Abel 1907; Meimaris 1992: 379, no. 104).

[159] Avi-Yonah 1966: 210; 1967: 59; Meimaris 1986: 214-215, 254-255.

superseded by the latter but continued to fulfil his duties in large dioceses, sometimes assisted by the *periodeutes* in the north. Other officials mentioned in building inscriptions in other parts of the country – the *oikonomos* and the *paramonarios*, were most likely locals attached to their own village church.

The title of *oikonomos* (οἰκονόμος) in an ecclesiastical context applies to three different offices: the steward in charge of the revenues and property of a diocese on behalf of the bishop, the administrator of an individual church, and the steward of a monastery.[160] Whenever an *oikonomos* appears in the epigraphical samples from our region, he can usually be identified as the steward of the church where he is mentioned. Whether the bishop's name heads the inscription or not, the *oikonomos*' name does not follow his but is listed with the clergy of that church; he may be a deacon or subdeacon or even a layman, and his name comes second after the priest, or third if an archdeacon is listed as well; in any case, last of the men in charge of the church but before any donors. In some cases the *oikonomos* dedicates an inscription of his own, not one of the main inscriptions in the more visible parts of the building.[161] The case of Suḥmātā is slightly different. Here the persons under whose auspices the church was paved with mosaic are listed in three separate groups, each introduced by the preposition ἐπί, 'under' or 'in the time of': the diocesan authorities, the priest and *oikonomos*, and two laymen. The inscription is rather fragmentary but can be restored as follows:

---

[160] On the office of *oikonomos*, see Meimaris 1986: 256-259, with a collection of epigraphic examples from Palestine and Arabia. The office of steward of a bishopric was made obligatory for every diocese by canon 26 of the Council of Chalcedon, but Justinian's legislation deals also with the *oikonomos* of single churches or religious institutions. For instance, *CJ* 1, 3, 45 establishes the right of testators to have a steward appointed for the church or pious institution they endow: the official was called *oikonomos* or *paramonarios* or by other specific names, according to the type of charitable activity in which the foundation specialized. In the Holy Land, only *laurae* (communities of hermits) had an *oikonomos*, while in the *coenobia* (communal monasteries) the task fell upon the deputy of the abbot (*deuterarios*): Patrich 1995: 174-77 (Palestine), cf. 15-17 (Egypt), 26 (Syria).

[161] Examples from Suḥmātā in Upper Galilee (*SEG* VIII, no. 21), Beit 'Anun north of Hebron (*SEG* LXII, no. 1654), Beersheba (*SEG* LXIV, no. 1670), Jābir in the territory of Adraa (Provincia Arabia: *SEG* LIX, no. 1722), Khirbet el-Maqati and Khirbet el-Wahadneh in the territory of Pella (*SEG* XXXII, nos. 1492, 1513), Mount Nebo (*SEG* XXXVIII, no. 1659; *IGLJ* II, no. 100), el-Quweismeh (Amman, 717/8 CE: *SEG* XXXIV, no. 1517; *IGLJ* II, no. 54), Umm er-Rasas (in the principal church, St. Stephen's, *SEG* XXXVII, nos. 1552 [March 756], 1553 [1 September 718-21 March 719]). At Quweismeh the priest of the church is also its *oikonomos*; at Umm er-Rasas, the *oikonomos* in 718/9, a deacon, is also one of the town leaders (*archontes*).

(This place) was beautified in the month of Loos of the (year) 680, in the [?] indiction. The mosaic was made with God's help in the time of the most saintly archbishop John and of the country bishop Cyriac, and in the time of our lord Stephen, the archpriest and church steward, and in the time of the *clarissimi* Marinus *comes* and Diobius. Lord Jesus, help this village and bless it. Having contributed Theodorus and Theodora [(his) wife], and Elias and Theodorus and John - - and Timotheus and Elias - - - deacons [of the most holy church].[162]

The date is given by the era of Tyre, in whose territory Suḥmātā was located, and corresponds to August-September 555, at the end of the 3rd or at the beginning of the 4th indiction; the archbishop is that of Tyre. The two laymen, who bore the title of *clarissimi*, much depreciated in this period but still carrying local prestige, were presumably the village leaders. The archpriest and *oikonomos* was revered as 'our master', an indication that he was based locally, though in this case the epithet cannot indicate ownership of the village itself, since the village had high-status leaders and the church had a large number of benefactors, more likely free farmers than tenants.[163] Thus we can conclude that also at Suḥmātā the *oikonomos* presided on the village church and his name was separated from those of the local people to set apart the ecclesiastical authority from the lay leadership. But in the church of Ḥorvat Gerarit near Gaza, the *oikonomos* is grouped with the bishop and the *chorepiscopus*, as third in a hierarchic order, presumably that of the diocese. The dedicatory inscription reads: 'Under our most holy bishop Misael and Zacharias, priest and *chorepiscopus*, and Alphios deacon and *oikonomos*, this mosaic was made in the month of Panemos of the year 659, indiction 2' (by the era of Gaza, corresponding to June-July 599 CE). This church was built at some distance from the village, which had its own parochial church, but this was not a monastic church. Possibly it was founded by the bishop of Gaza to provide an alternative cult place to a minority of villagers who did not communicate with Miaphysites, at that time a majority in southwestern Palaestina; if so, presumably Alphios

---

[162] My reading is based on the *editio princeps*, Avi-Yonah 1933a, rather than on the reading in *SEG* VIII, no. 21, which resolves the abbreviation ΑΡΧSΠΡΒ into ἀρχ(ιμανδρίτου) (καὶ) πρ(εσ)β(υτέρου) instead of ἀρχ(ι)πρ(εσ)β(υτέρου). There is no justification for an abbreviation ΑΡΧS for ἀρχ(ιμανδρίτης, while the use of stigma (S) in place of a single letter is well attested.

[163] The village is described as κώμη rather than κτῆμα, 'estate', a term found in Palestinian sources of this period to indicate a privately owned village. For a discussion of *despotes* referring to an abbot in a village possibly belonged to a monastery, see Di Segni 2016: 187*-188*.

was the steward of the church of Gaza, which had provided the funds for the building.[164]

A function similar to that of *oikonomos* of a single church, and mentioned in parallel with it in Justinian's Code, is that of *paramonarios* or warden.[165] This office is well attested in the region, especially in the southern part of Palaestina and in Provincia Arabia. Mainly a *paramonarios* appears in mosaic inscriptions commemorating the building or paving of a church that was carried out under (ἐπί) him or by his efforts (σπουδῇ); the name of the bishop as eponym may head the inscription. The *paramonarios* was often a priest,[166] sometimes a mere deacon,[167] but in several cases he is given no ecclesiastical title and we must conclude that he was a layman.[168]

---

[164] For this church and its inscription, see Di Segni 2004b: 56-58 (= *SEG* LIV, no. 1656); Hirschfeld 2004: 70-72. Hirschfeld views the church as part of a monastery, but there are no structures attached to it, except for two cisterns, nothing unusual in a non-monastic church. Besides, the inscription mentions clergy but no monks, while as a rule building inscriptions in monasteries mention the abbot's name.

[165] For *paramonarios* in the Justinian Code, see above, n. 160.

[166] So in a mid-sixth century phase of the church at Jabaliyye (Gaza: *SEG* L, no. 1490); at Shellal, south of Gaza, 561/2 CE (*SEG* VIII, no. 279; Avi-Yonah 1933: 42, no. 306); in the Church of the Trinity at Beer Shemaʻ (ancient Birsama in the western Negev: *SEG* XLVI, no. 2009 [8]); in Provincia Arabia in St Mary's Church at Riḥab, between 1 September 582 and 21 March 583 (*SEG* XXX, no. 1715; Meimaris 1992: 232, no. 267); at el-Husn near Irbid, 1 April 535 (*SEG* XLVII, no. 2064); on the lintel over the entrance of St. George's Church at Jizeh in the diocese of Adraa, 538/9 CE (*SEG* L, no. 1590); in St. Sophia's Church at Gerasa, 542/3 (*SEG* LIII, no. 1890); in two churches at Mekhayyet on Mount Nebo, SS. Lot and Procopius' and St. George's (*SEG* VIII, no. 336, *IGLJ* II, nos. 97, 100) – all building inscriptions. Abba Zenobius the *paramonarios*, who invoked the Lord's help in an inscription at the foot of the bema in the West Church at Kurnub (Mampsis in the eastern Negev: Negev 1981: 70-71, no. 84; *SEG* XXXI, no. 1414) was also most probably the church priest, though Negev misunderstood the term Abbas and translated 'Abba son of Zenobius'.

[167] So at Gerasa, in a church founded by a benefactor named Procopius in autumn 526 (*SEG* VII, no. 872; Welles 1938: 378-379, no. 304; Meimaris 1992: 108, no. 74); it was most likely a private church with no incumbent priest. At Kissufim, south of Gaza, the *paramonarios* who supervised the laying of the mosaic pavement in the nave was a deacon, monk and abbot of St. Elijah in 576. He was still in charge when the northern aisle was paved in 578, but in this case the title *paramonarios* is omitted (*SEG* XXX, nos. 1688-1689). The church later acquired a priest who was not a monk (*SEG* LX, no. 1716). The scenes depicted in the mosaic floor are more suitable to a private estate of a wealthy family than a monastery, and it is possible that St. Elijah was not the title of the church but of a nearby monastery whose abbot was temporarily put in charge of the building while it was completed: see discussion in Di Segni 2016: 188*.

[168] So at Riḥab in the churches of St. Paul, St. George and St. Constantine (*SEG* XXX, no. 1711; LI, no. 2045; LXIV, no. 1854: in the latter, two *paramonarii* were in charge together); at Gerasa in the church of SS. Cosmas and Damianus (Welles 1938: 482, nos. 315-316), in the

In his discussion of the Shellal inscription, Avi-Yonah translated the term as 'sacristan', but while the office of a *paramonarios* surely included the care of the furnishings and sacred vessels of his church, his involvement in building activities shows that he fulfilled an administrative role, financing and supervising the construction and adornment of the church. When he was a priest, he most likely was the incumbent, who took upon himself the stewardship of his church in addition to his religious duties. It is perhaps significant that this office appears to be widespread especially in those parts of the Holy Land where the *periodeutes* is absent or less represented. This may point to a different organization of rural congregations in the north and in other parts of the country. Here the custom seems to have been that the villagers presented their candidate to the bishop for ordination to the priesthood in their parochial church;[169] so the 'priest and *paramonarios*' would have been a locally elected leader rather than a representative of the bishop, as apparently was the *periodeutes*.

Since the financial support of the villagers was essential for the erection and maintenance of the church, inscriptions mentioning benefactors are frequently found both on mosaic pavements and on chancel screens and other items of church furniture, in the formula 'Lord, accept the offering of…', or with invocations for their succour, remission of sins, remembrance, repose, and the like. When many donors were involved, and more were expected to donate, they were left anonymous and the blessings or prayers are invoked in behalf of 'those who have given offerings', 'those who have given and give/will give – offerings', 'those whose names God knows' (Figs. 32-34), and sometimes simply 'the village', as in the building inscription of the church at Khirbet el-Maqati mentioned above (n. 161).[170]

Among the excavated churches, not a few were erected not by a community and for it, but by private persons, and more often by families and clans. The existence of private churches is quite evident wherever a village boasts of such a number of prayer houses that it is quite impossible to explain them as representing different denominations of Christianity. This plurality of churches is particularly striking in Transjordan, where some large villages count more

---

Church of Bishop Isaias and in a church outside the city wall (*SEG* XXXVII, no. 1543; LIII, no. 1893); possibly also at Mekawer (Machaeron: *SEG* XLV, no. 2021).

[169] Barsanuphius, *Questiones et responsiones* 814-817.

[170] 'All the inhabitants of the village' appear also in a fragmentary inscription in the Samaritan synagogue of Zur Nathan, apparently a building inscription (*SEG* XLII, no. 1474).

Chapter V: Greek inscriptions in the Holy Land in Late Antiquity

Fig. 32a – Madaba, Church of the Apostles: mosaic in the northwestern chapel (*IGLJ* II, no. 143. M. Piccirillo, SBF Photographic Archive)

Fig. 32b – Madaba, Church of the Apostles: the inscription in the northwestern chapel (Piccirillo 1989: 106. Drawing C. Florimont, SBF Photographic Archive)
Lord, accept the offering of those who have offered and offer to the church of the Holy Apostles, in memory of John, priest, by the efforts of Anastasius, deacon.

Fig. 33 – 'Offering of those whose names the Lord knows' – to a church in Caesarea (*CIIP* II, no. 1152. Photo M. Salzberger. Courtesy of the Israel Antiquities Authority)

than a dozen churches,[171] but even in western Palestine there are small settlements with two or three churches; e.g. Lower Herodion and Ḥorvat Malḥata, with three churches each.[172] Inscriptions found in the building can clinch its private nature. A good example is the church of Ḥorvat Ḥesheq in Upper Galilee. This church is part of an isolated structure, some 200 m distant from the remains of the late antique settlement of Ḥorvat Maḥoz. It was erected above a rectangular building, part of which was occupied by a barrel-vaulted burial chamber, the rest by a reservoir. The chamber was apparently a family tomb, and the church was a private church, built and used by an extended family,

---

[171] E.g. Riḥab with at least fifteen and possibly more than twenty; Umm er-Rasas with fifteen, Umm el-Jimal with fourteen, Kh. es-Samra with eight; Hamarneh 2013a: 419-422.

[172] On Lower Herodion, see below; on the churches of Ḥorvat Malḥata, see Ovadiah 1970: 121-122, nos. 119-121. On private churches, see Ashkenazi 2018, 2019.

Fig. 34 – 'Offering of those whose names the Lord knows' – in the 'House of Leontis' synagogue at Beth Shean (*SEG* XXVI, no. 1683. Photo D. Bahat. Courtesy of the Israel Antiquities Authority)

four generations of which are mentioned in the inscriptions.[173] Neither bishop, country bishop, visitor or priest is mentioned anywhere; instead, the building inscription in front of the bema (no. 1444) reads: 'Lord God of the holy and glorious martyr George, remember for good your servant Demetrius the deacon who built this holy house, and George his son and all their household'. In front of a reliquary sunk in the floor of the southern apse, no. 1445 prayed 'For the salvation of Demetrius, deacon, and of George his son, and for the repose of Somas his father and of his grandparents Demetrius and Theodora'.[174] This apse was dedicated to the cult of another martyr, saint Sergius, and the reliquary presumably contained some relics of him, for inscription 1447 at the entrance of the apse reads: 'Lord God of saint Sergius, have mercy upon your

---

[173] On the church, see Aviam 1990; on the inscriptions, Di Segni 1990c; *SEG* XL, nos. 1444-1448. A new excavation recently carried out (Ashkenazi 2020) brought to light an additional inscription and enabled the excavators to make a small but significant correction to inscription no. 1445, on which see below. On Ḥorvat Maḥoz, see Tsafrir et al. 1994: 175.

[174] The last word of this inscription was erroneously read τ[έκν]ων, 'children', and corrected to πάππων, 'grandparents', when the mosaic was cleaned in the course of the recent excavation; see Ashkenazi 2020: 136.

servant Demetrius the deacon and George his son and all their household'. Near the southern of the three entrances from the narthex into the church an unframed inscription (no. 1448) quoted Ps 86 (MT 87): 2: 'The Lord loves the gates of Zion more than the tents of Jacob'. A new inscription, discovered in a recent campaign in the northern aisle, contains a long list of male and female names, members of the extended family of Demetrius.[175] The building is dated by an inscription in the centre of the nave (no. 1446): 'For the salvation of Demetrius, deacon, and of George his son and of all their household this entire work was completed in the month of April of the year 582, indiction 12'. Since the site was certainly included in Second Palestine, in the territory of Sepphoris, which had no era of its own, the date must be reckoned by the era of the metropolis, Scythopolis, 64 BCE, and corresponds to April 519, in the 12th indiction. As we have seen, this church was a private foundation in charge of the paterfamilias who was a deacon, but showing no dependence from the ecclesiastical authorities: we are left to wonder whether the family had some kind of arrangement with a priest from the neighbourhood to come from time to time and administer the sacraments, or if they attended a parochial church in the area for this need.

Another clear example is the northern church at Lower Herodion, dedicated to saint Michael.[176] Its mosaic pavement bears three inscriptions: the main one, at the foot of the chancel, prays Christ and saint Michel to accept the offering of a brother and sister, Anael and Saphrica, with their households, and of other families, all probably members of the same clan. A second inscription, in a side room (Fig. 35), again prays saint Michael to accept the offering of Anael, his wife Saprica and his son Mamas, and a third, in front of the entrance, contains the usual quotation from Ps. 117 (118):20 ('This is the gate of the Lord, the righteous shall enter in it') and an invocation to Christ to remember his servants, Anael and Saprica (the wife or the sister?). Like at Ḥorvat Ḥesheq, there is no mention of a priest, but here there is not even a member of the lower clergy in charge of the church. Nor is the bishop or a representative of the diocese mentioned anywhere in either church, another strong indication of their private character. However, the mere mention of a patron who claims to have been responsible for building and/or paving a church is not sufficient evidence that it was a private foundation: see the examples of a church at Mukhmas whose erection and paving with mosaics

---

[175] Ashkenazi 2020: 137-138.
[176] *SEG* XL, nos. 1470-1472. A final report on the church and its inscriptions is forthcoming: Roi Porat and Rachel Chachy-Laureys, *Herodium* II.

Fig. 35 – Herodium, Northern Church. Inscription 1 (*SEG* XL, no. 1471. Photo Z. Radovan. Archive Ehud Netzer. Courtesy of Chachy et al. eds. *Herodium* II).
Holy Michael, receive the offering of Thy servant Anael and of his family, Saprica and Mamas, amen.

was promoted by one Valentinus and his family,[177] and of St. Andrew's in Jericho, where an inscription in front of the main entrance reads: 'Magnianus the soldier, in thanksgiving to St. Andrew, built (this church) and had it paved, by the care of Heraclius the priest, Constantinus the deacon and Polychronius'.[178] The eastern part of the nave, where possibly another building inscription may have been located, is lost. The wording of the inscription and the several burials under the pavement indicate that the church was not the property of a family, but it cannot be excluded that it belonged to a specific group, perhaps the garrison stationed in Jericho.

Beside private churches, there are other kinds of cult buildings not intended for a congregation, like roadside churches and pilgrimage churches. The former could be in the charge of a monastery in the vicinity, as in the case of

---

[177] Avi-Yonah 1933: 35-36, no. 266. The church is located in the ancient village, and its inscription speaks of Valentinus' zeal (τῷ σπουδάσαντι) for the work, a language more fitting a benefactor than a proprietor. The status of this church is therefore unclear.
[178] *SEG* XXXVII, no. 1492B. On the church and its date (637 CE?) see Augustinovic 1951: 77-83; Di Segni 1997a: 602-607, no. 206; Bagatti 2002b: 98-99.

Ḥorvat Ḥanot, Khirbet el-Khan on the Jerusalem-Beth Govrin road,[179] or it could have a small team of living-in monks to serve travellers, like St. Peter's Church at Qasr 'Ali on the Jerusalem-Jericho road.[180] The function of such cult buildings usually cannot be identified by inscriptions but only through their location and archaeological settings.[181] The same is at least partly true for pilgrimage churches. Many churches have been unwarrantedly described as such simply because they were, or seemed to be, in an isolated spot, or because they had a crypt with entrance and exit through separate staircases that permitted a steady flow of visitors.[182] But more evidence is needed to confirm this description: a tradition of sacrality attested by literary sources and/or graffiti left by pilgrims. These preconditions are present, for instance, in the church recently discovered at Banyas (Paneas-Caesarea Philippi), in the little underground church of Saint Salome in the Judaean Shephela (a Second Temple period tomb that was made into a church by carving a nave and apse out of the soft rock) and in the former mikveh at Bethany, identified by pilgrims as the room where Mary and Martha hosted Jesus.[183]

C. Other inscriptions in churches and monasteries

We have already mentioned in passing two types of inscriptions that are often combined with dedications of buildings or mosaic pavements: invocations or prayers and artists' signatures. In many cases both are tantamount

---

[179] Radashkovsky 2020. There was a winepress attached to the church, but no remains of a monastery were uncovered around it, though the Greek inscription in the church mentions an abbot. The only structure beside the church, a caravanserai (khan), dates from the Ottoman period: Avner 2021.

[180] Hirschfeld 1990: 19-21, no. 8, fig. 24; 1992: 130. Hirschfeld misinterpreted this foundation as a coenobium; see discussion, Di Segni 2016: 185*-186*.

[181] For a general discussion of the contribution of epigraphy – cautiously read and interpreted – to the identification of the different functions of churches, see Di Segni 2016.

[182] An example is the church at Dor (Dauphin 1993), a roadside church whose connection with Byzantine Dora cannot be easily ascertained, since the Byzantine settlement was scattered. It certainly served travellers but there is no reason to view it as a pilgrimage destination. The crypt accessed from north and south is found in several churches, e.g. at Ḥorvat Berachot (Tsafrir and Hirschfeld 1993), Ruḥeibe (Tsafrir 1988; 1993) and in the recently discovered 'Church of the Glorious Martyr' at Ramat Beth Shemesh (Storchan 2021), and certainly answered a need to facilitate the transit of visitors, but these churches may well have been simply centres of local veneration.

[183] For the church founded on the spring of Paneion, see Brown 2020; for St. Salome, Patrich and Di Segni 1990. The mikveh at Bethany, too small to be restructured as a church, was made into an oratory by depicting a large cross and an altar on its east wall; all the walls and the lower soffit are full of graffiti in Greek, Latin and CPA: see Benoit and Boismard 1951; Taylor 1990; *CIIP* I, 2, nos. 842-843.

to building inscriptions, for the person or persons who dictated the prayer or signed the work intended to publicize their contribution to the erection or adornment of the church in this way.[184]

The most common formulas of prayer may be categorized into three main groups:

(1) 'Lord/Lord Jesus Christ/Lord God/God of saint ...' (followed by the name of the patron saint of the church: in Greek Κύριε, Κύριε Ἰησοῦ Χριστέ, Κύριε ὁ Θεός, Θεὸς τοῦ ἁγίου/τῆς ἁγίας - -), 'remember/ help/ have mercy upon/ give rest to', more rarely 'save' or 'protect' (μνήσθητι, βοήθει, ἐλέησον, ἀνάπαυσον, σῶσον, φύλαξον) 'your servant/handmaiden so-and-so'. A subcategory of this group is the simple petition, found in synagogues as well as in churches, 'May so-and-so be remembered' (Μνησθῇ - -), often accompanied by the mention of a sum of money the subject offered to the holy place.

(2) Invocation as in (1), accompanied by the formula 'accept the offering of - -' followed by the name(s) of the donor(s); in Greek πρόσδεξαι (often phonetically spelled πρόσδεξε) τὴν καρποφορίαν/προσφοράν - - .

(3) Petitions without invocation to the deity: 'Offering (προσφορά) for the salvation/help/succor/remittance of sins/remembrance/rest': in Greek, ὑπὲρ σωτηρίας, βοηθείας, ἀντιλήμψεως, ἀφέσεως τῶν ἁμαρτιῶν, μνήμης, ἀναπαύσεως, and similar combinations, followed by the name(s) of the donor(s); the word 'Offering' is often omitted.

Sometimes prayers were not dictated by donors or by members of the church clergy, but were inscribed by those who had contributed their skills as builders, mosaicists or marble workers, and not only in churches but also in synagogues. See for instance the prayer of a father and son, both mosaic workers, in the synagogue of Beth Alpha (Fig. 36),[185] of the mosaicist (ψηφοθέτης) Paulus at 'Evron,[186] of the mosaicist and craftsman (τεχνίτης) Zosys in the Early Northern Church at Shiloh, where the man also added a small inscription in a corner of the nave, saying that he had built the benches, probably as a gift to the church.[187] Two brothers mosaicists pray the Lord for

---

[184] This subject is discussed at greater length in Di Segni 2017b.
[185] Sukenik 1932; *SEG* VIII, no. 93; Roth-Gerson 1987: 29-32, no. 4.
[186] *SEG* XXXVII, no. 1516; other names after the prayer formula may belong to his fellow-workers. The inscription belongs to the early stage of the church, 415 CE. The usual term for this profession is ψηφοθέτης; ψηφιστής is rarer.
[187] Di Segni 2012b: 211-213, nos. 3-4; *SEG* LXII, nos. 1688-1689; on the church see Magen and Aharonovich 2012. The early church is dated to the late fourth-early fifth century. The term *tech-*

Fig. 36 – Beth Alpha synagogue (*SEG* VIII, no. 93. Photo J. Schweig. Courtesy of the Archive of the Institute of Archaeology, The Hebrew University of Jerusalem)
May the craftsmen be remembered who have labored at this work, Marianus and Aninas his son.

remembrance in a church at Bahan in Samaria; three pray for life at 'Anab el-Kabir in Judaea; one asks God's help in the church of St. Sergius at Nitl in the diocese of Madaba (Fig. 37).[188] A group of mosaicists joined the clergy and monks of the Memorial of Moses on Mount Nebo in a prayer inscribed in the pavement of the diakonikon-baptistery.[189] Sometimes the mosaicist simply signs his work with the word Ἔργον and his name, or just by inscribing his name, as at Karkara, Kissufim, Jabaliyye (Gaza), el-Rashidiyye in southern Jordan, Deir 'Ain 'Abata (St. Lot on the Dead Sea): more than thirty names of these artists are epigraphically attested in Israel and Jordan.[190] But not only mosaic artists signed their work. A marble worker (μαρμαράριος) signed a capital from a synagogue in Tiberias and a stone carver (λατόμος) the arch of a synagogue at Deir 'Aziv in the Golan.[191] Several names incised on dressed blocks and capitals in churches on Mount Nebo must belong to the stonecutters who carved them, though they do not mention their profession.[192] In the Northern Church at Nessana, the master-builder (οἰκοδόμος)

---

nites seems to apply to various specializations: Zosys was a mosaicist and so were Marianus and Hanina, the *technitai* who worked in the synagogue of Beth Alpha (above, n. 185), but Stephanus, who added the words Στεφάνου τεχ(νίτου) γραφ‹ή› ('Signature of Stephanus craftsman') to a dedicatory inscription on stone in an unidentified ecclesiastical structure at Ruḥama in the western Shephela, must have been a stonecutter or a mason (*CIIP* IV, 2, no. 3838; 600 CE).

[188] *SEG* LXIV, no. 1804 (Bahan); LXII, no. 1660 ('Anab el-Kabir); LI, no. 2068 (Nitl).
[189] *SEG* XXVII, no. 1020; *IGLJ* II, no. 75.
[190] Di Segni and Ashkenazi 2020: 304, no. 1 (Karkara, early fifth century); *SEG* XXX, no. 1693 (Kissufim, 578 CE); *SEG* L, no. 1489 (Jabaliyye, 548/9 CE); *SEG* LVI, no. 1913 (el-Rashidiyye, 574 CE); *SEG* LVIII, no. 1779 (Deir 'Ain 'Abata). The names of 29 artists were collected by Talgam 2014: 170-171, 576; update in Di Segni and Ashkenazi 2020: 317, n. 8.
[191] *SEG* XLVI, no. 1810(1) (Tiberias); LVII, no. 1826 (Deir 'Aziz). The arch belongs to an early synagogue dated between 358/9 and 367/8.
[192] *IGLJ* II, nos. 88, 90, 94. For a list of professions and crafts related to building activities in Palaestina and Arabia, see *SEG* XL, no. 1433.

Fig. 37 – Nitl, Church of St. Sergius (*SEG* LI, no. 2068. M. Piccirillo, SBF Photographic Archive)
God of saint Sergius, remember Ammonius and his children, the mosaicist, for I have labored in this place.

Flavius Sergius son of Victor gives the date of the completion of the work, 18 September 605, on a stone slab, while invoking salvation for himself, his son Victor and his hired man (μισθωτός), Abramius son of Abuzonainos.[193] Another *oikodomos*, Maximus 'who also wrote this', invokes the Lord's help on the lintel of a church at Ramthaniyye in the Golan.[194] A τέκτων, more likely a carpenter than a builder or architect, prays for salvation and mercy in the church of St. Catherine's monastery on Mount Sinai.[195] Two contractors (ἐργολάβοι) inscribed their names on the city wall of Gaza, which they

---

[193] Kirk and Welles 1962: 165, no. 72. Note the name of the master-builder, a Latin name preceded by the 'Flavius' that indicates his superior social status, while the labourer bears an Arab name and patronymic. A similar phenomenon can be observed in the inscriptions from Mount Nebo: clergy and donors bear Latin or Greek names (possibly Hellenized Semitic names), while the simple workers bear Arabic names: Di Segni 1998a: 458.
[194] Gregg and Urman 1996: 188, no. 155; *SEG* XLVI, no. 1991 (2). Apparently Maximus was also proficient in stonecutting.
[195] *SEG* XXXIX, no. 1634.

renovated in the early seventh century, and another signed the pavement of a church at Yatir (ancient Iethira) in 725 CE.[196]

As in monasteries, the pavements and architectural elements of parochial, private and other churches were often adorned with quotations, mostly biblical, sometimes as an expression of devotion or supplication (e.g. Ps 30 [31]:2; 58 [59]:2), or with a didactic function (e.g. Ps 50:21 [51:19]; Is 65:25), or, when inscribed on thresholds or lintels, with an apotropaic function (e.g. 1 Kgdms [1 Sam] 16:4; Ps 120 [121]:8) or to define the sacred space (e.g. Ps 64 [65]:5; 117 [118]:19-20). We have already given several examples above.[197]

One last kind of inscriptions found in churches is the informative one: inscriptions imparting plain information, of which there are two different types. The first type is sometimes encountered on the lintel above the entrance of a church, where the name of the church is engraved, alone or accompanied by further information about it. For instance, a basalt lintel from Juwezi in the Golan held the following inscription on two sides of a central circle, originally containing a cross: 'The consecration of Saint Mark is in the month of August, the 15th'.[198] Another lintel, found in secondary use at Jizeh in the diocese of Adraa, bears a long inscription with all the details of the building: 'Under the most holy bishop Euphrasius (the church of) Saint George was built and completed, by the efforts of Thomas priest and warden, in the year 433 (538/9 CE), in supplication to saint George, for this village of Ameda (or Amera, Amela?) and for Saedos'.[199] Another lintel, still unpublished, from the South Church at Shivta in the Negev, reads simply: 'Hall (αὐλή) belonging to the most holy church'. The second type appears on mosaic pavements and consists of captions identifying personifications of months, seasons, Earth, Sea and the like

---

[196] *SEG* VIII, no. 268 (Gaza); L, no. 1498 (Yatir).

[197] Supplication: Ps 30:2 (In Thee O Lord I have hoped, let me never be put to shame); Ps 58:2 (Deliver me from my enemies, O my God; protect me from those who rise up against me); didactic: Ps 50:21 (Then bulls will be offered on Thy altar); Is 65: 25 (The lion shall eat straw like the ox); apotropaic: I Kgdms 16:4 (In peace is your coming in); Ps 120:8 (The Lord will guard your coming in and your going out from this time forth and for evermore); definition of the sacred space: Ps 64:5 (Holy is Thy temple, admirable in justice); Ps 117:19-20 (Open me the gates of righteousness, that I may enter through them and give thanks to the Lord. This is the gate of the Lord; the righteous shall enter through it). For more examples from single churches, see Di Segni 2017b: 70-79, tb. 4. For biblical quotations Felle 2006 is an invaluable instrument.

[198] *SEG* VIII, no. 29; Gregg and Urman 1996: 198, no. 161. The specification of month and day served as a reminder of the anniversary of the consecration of the church, which by custom was celebrated with a yearly festival.

[199] *SEG* L, no. 1520). Saedos (Sa'id) may have been the headman of the village, a wealthy villager who contributed to the building, or even the stonecutter who engraved the inscription.

(Fig. 38),²⁰⁰ cities, villages, holy places and geographical features,²⁰¹ biblical figures,²⁰² and personages who probably gained the privilege of being portrayed in a church by giving substantial donations to it.²⁰³ At least in one instance,

Fig. 38 – Zodiac in the monastery of Kyra Maria (Beth Shean). Months are labelled with their names and the number of days, ἡμέ(ραι), in each (SEG VIII, no. 42. Courtesy of B. Arubas)

²⁰⁰ See for instance the zodiac with names of the Julian months in the courtyard of the monastery of Kyra Maria in Beth Shean (FitzGerald 1939: 7, pls. VI-VIII; *SEG* VIII, no. 42); the Macedonian months at Gerasa (Welles 1938: 475, no. 295; *SEG* LXIV, no. 1843), the seasons, Ocean, Earth and Wisdom in the early church in Petra (*SEG* XLIII, no. 1096; LV, no. 1760); Γῆ (Earth) in the Chapel of Priest John on Mount Nebo and Θάλασσα (Sea) in the Church of the Holy Apostles at Madaba (*IGLJ* II, nos. 108, 142).
²⁰¹ Best known are the Madaba map of the Holy Land in St. George's Church in Madaba (Avi-Yonah 1954; *IGLJ* II, no. 153, 1-154; Piccirillo and Alliata eds. 1999) and the vignettes of cities in churches at Maʿin (*IGLJ* II, no. 157) and Umm er-Rasas (*SEG* XXXVII, nos. 1569-1595; Piccirillo 1994b).
²⁰² E.g. Jonah in the mosaic pavement of a church north of Beth Govrin: *CIIP* IV, 2, no. 3471. For biblical figures in synagogues, see below.
²⁰³ So the *paramonarios* Theodorus and his son in the church of SS. Cosmas and Damianus at Gerasa (Welles 1938: 482, nos. 315-316), Elias, Mary and Soreg in a church called after them in the same city (Saller and Bagatti 1949: 268-289, pls. 45-51; *SEG* LXIV, no. 1842).

however, the portraits seem to have a funerary function: this is most likely the case of the two ladies, Theodosia and Georgia, pictured in the mosaic of the Orpheus Chapel in Jerusalem.[204] Sometimes captions appears in frescoes on walls, though this occurrence is rare for walls, and particularly their plastered and painted surfaces, rarely survive. We have already mentioned the row of figures labelled as apostles and evangelists in the church of Deir Mukallik.[205] In Caesarea, among several fragmentary frescoes in the area of the praetorium, one, in a vault perhaps adapted for some religious function, depicted three haloed saints labelled Ares/Sergius, Promos and Elias, three famous martyrs of Diocletian's persecution.[206]

V. 2. 2 Inscriptions in synagogues

Inscriptions from Jewish synagogues in Israel were collected in two volumes, both in Hebrew: Naveh 1978 for Aramaic and Hebrew inscriptions,[207] Roth-Gerson 1987 for Greek ones. New synagogues discovered thereafter have increased the epigraphical yield not only with inscriptions dictated by Jews in Greek, Aramaic and Hebrew, but also with those of Samaritans, who favoured Greek in their sacred places, with very few exceptions.

The synagogue at Sepphoris is among the most prominent new discoveries of epigraphic significance published until now. It was built in the early fifth century over the remains of a structure of the Roman period, which may have dictated its unusual plan and orientation (not towards Jerusalem, as was customary). The synagogue is an elongated building consisting of a nave and a single aisle separated by a row of columns, with an entrance room at the short south-eastern end. The aisle is paved with geometric mosaics framing nine dedicatory inscriptions in Aramaic, all beginning with the formula 'Remembered be for good', followed by the name of the dedicator, sometimes with members of his family. The nave is paved with a figural carpet divided broadwise into seven bands, some of them subdivided into panels containing biblical scenes as well as Greek dedications of single donors or families who paid for each panel. Nine such dedications survived, some of them beginning with the same formula 'Remembered be for good', in Greek, and all ending with

---

[204] *SEG* VIII, no. 96; *CIIP* I, 2, no. 878, with ample bibliography.
[205] See above, n. 106, *CIIP* IV, 1, no. 3168. In a crucifixion scene in the same church St. John the Evangelist is also identified with a vertical caption Ὁ ἅ(γιος) Ἰω(άννης) ὁ Θεόλογος, *CIIP* IV, 1, no. 3171.
[206] *CIIP* II, no. 1165.
[207] For an update, see Naveh 1989a.

the words Εὐλογία αὐτῷ/αὐτοῖς, 'A blessing upon him/them'.[208] The first band, starting from the west, is partly destroyed: it depicted a wreath framing a Greek inscription and flanked by two lions. The second band showed a temple façade, a *menorah* and other Jewish symbols. The third band illustrates the consecration of Aaron (Exodus 29): an altar stands in the middle, a water basin on the right, a bull and a lamb on the left; above the lamb a Hebrew caption reads 'the one lamb' (Ex. 29: 39; Num. 28: 4). Between the altar and the sacrificial animals a human figure stands, of which only part of the garment and the Hebrew label 'Aaron' remain. The fourth band is divided in three panels: in the left, the daily sacrifice in the Temple, with Hebrew labels identifying the various objects; in the middle, the shewbread table, in the right panel a basket with the offering of the first fruits. Two Aramaic dedications were included in the left and middle panels. The fifth and widest band contains a zodiac, with the sun riding a quadriga at its centre, all around the personifications of the months, each labelled in Hebrew, and at the corner the four seasons, labelled in Greek and Hebrew. The sixth and seventh bands pictures scenes of the life of Abraham: the binding of Isaac and the visit of the three angels.[209]

Two other synagogues recently discovered, both in eastern Galilee, also have splendid figural mosaic pavements with biblical scenes and inscriptions: the Late Roman synagogue at Wadi Hamam, with four fragmentary Aramaic inscriptions (dedications and captions),[210] and the fifth-century synagogue at Huqoq, with a few very fragmentary inscriptions, not yet completely understood.[211] Biblical scenes with captions identifying figures are found in other synagogues: for instance Noah's story in the synagogue of Gerasa, which was transformed in a church in 530/1 CE, and David portrayed as Orpheus in the synagogue of Maiuma, the port of Gaza.[212] Other biblical scenes have no cap-

---

[208] This blessing appears also in other synagogues, in Hebrew or in Aramaic: at Bar'am, Hammath Gader and Susya: *CIJ* II, nos. 856-857, 974; Naveh 1978: 19-20, 54-58, 121-122, nos. 1, 32-33, 82-83.
[209] Weiss 2005: 199-203; 2008: 2033-2034; Di Segni 2005c.
[210] Miller and Leibner 2018; Leibner 2018. The synagogue is dated by the excavators to the third century.
[211] A blessing, perhaps upon those who gave charity to the foundation, probably in Hebrew rather than in Aramaic; Hebrew labels of months in a zodiac, perhaps passages from Gen. 49 associated with each of the twelve tribes. See Magness et al. 2014: 2018.
[212] On the Synagogue Church of Gerasa and its captions, see Crowfoot 1938: 234-241; Welles 1938: 473, no. 286; on the synagogue of Gaza, Ovadiah 1969: 195, pl. 15A; Magen 2010: 106-109.

tions. In general, while biblical quotations, so common in churches, are rare in synagogues, the opposite is true in the case of pictorial representation.[213]

Signatures of craftsmen appear in synagogues as in churches. We have already mentioned the marble worker (*marmararios*) who engraved a blessing in Greek on a capital from a synagogue in Tiberias, the stone carver (*latomos*) who did the same on the arch of a synagogue at Deir 'Aziv,[214] and the mosaicists (*technitai*) Marianos and Hanina who signed their work both in the Jewish synagogue of Beth Alpha and in the Tell Istaba Samaritan synagogue at Beth Shean (Fig. 39).[215] A lintel from Dabbura in the Golan bears two engraved inscriptions, one in Aramaic, 'Eleazar son of - - made the columns above the arches and beams. [May he be blessed]', the other in Greek: Ῥούστικος ἔκτισεν, 'Rusticus built (this)'. The verb in Aramaic, עבד (*'avad*, 'made'), indicates that Eleazar paid for the columns – probably of the gallery – while Rusticus was the builder who carried out the actual work.[216]

Like in churches, donors appear in many inscriptions in synagogues, both in Greek and in Aramaic, sometimes with the simple name of the benefactor and the phrase 'who made (this)', sometimes with specification of the part of the building they paid for (a mosaic pavement or part of it, a single column or an architrave),[217] sometimes with expressions of prayer. Among the favourite formulas, in both languages, are 'May so-and-so be remembered' or 'remembered for good' or 'for good and for blessing'; 'May a blessing be upon him/them'; 'May he live'. The phrase 'for the salvation of..' is sometimes used, just as in churches. Donations in money are also mentioned, though not in Greek, at least so far. In the synagogue of Hammath Gader a family gave five *dinarin de-zahav* (golden *nomismata*, a hefty sum), a benefactress gave one *dinar* and two other families gave half *dinar* and a *tremissis* (one third of *nomisma*); a family gave a *tremissis* to the synagogue of

---

[213] Cf. Weiss 2016, especially pp. 124-126; but see Hamarneh 2013b (the binding of Isaac in the mosaic floor of a church at Ya'amun), Cascianelli 2013 (a young David in the chapel of Priest John at Kh. Mukhayyet).

[214] See above, n. 191.

[215] *SEG* VIII, no. 93; XXVIII, no. 1450 (b).

[216] Urman 1972: 17-19; Naveh 1978: 26-27, no. 7. In fact, ἔκτισεν is most often used in the sense of 'had this made, i.e., paid for the part of a building where the dedication is inscribed (see for instance Πρόκλος Κρίσπου ἔκτισεν on the mosaic pavement of a synagogue at Tiberias (Roth-Gerson 1987: 61-64, no. 15; *SEG* XLVIII, no. 1906), but comparison with the Aramaic inscription entails interpreting the Greek term in its literal sense.

[217] Lifshitz 1967; *SEG* XXXIII, no. 1299 (στοά); *CIJ* II, no. 987; Naveh 1978: 52-53, nos. 30-31 (*tabla*, mosaic panel); 23-24, 44-45, 70-72, nos. 4, 22, 42 (architrave); *SEG* LV, nos. 1734-1735, 1738, 1740-1742 (τάβλα); *CIJ* II, no. 983; *CIIP* IV, 2, no. 3468 (column).

Fig. 39 – Beth Shean, Samaritan synagogue (*SEG* XXVIII, no. 1450 (b). Photo N. Tzori. Courtesy of the Israel Antiquities Authority)
Work (χιροϑεσία) of Marianus and of his son Aninas

Eshthemoa in southern Judaea and other donors gave three *dimarin* to the synagogue of Ma'on in the southern coastal plain.[218]

Some inscribed objects represent votive offerings given to synagogues: e.g. a basin from Gaza, a marble plaque from Binyamina near Caesarea, engraved with a *menorah*, *shofar* and *lulav*, and the inscription Εἷς Θεὸς βο⟨ή⟩θι Ἰούδα πρεσ(βυτέρῳ)· ἔτ(ους) αου' (One God, help Judah the elder; year 471;)[219] a bronze plaque found in the sea near 'Atlit, dedicated by a member or members of the Jewish congregation in ancient Sycamina.[220]

---

[218] *CIJ* I, nos. 856, 858, 859; Naveh 1978: 54-56, 60-65, nos. 32, 34-35 (Hammath Gader); 92-93, no. 57 (Ma'on); *CIIP* IV, 2, no. 3868 (Eshthemoa).

[219] *SEG* XLI, no. 1545; *CIIP* II, no. 2080. The date is discussed above in Chapter II, nn. 18 and 81.

[220] *SEG* XLIV, no. 1368. The plaque is adorned with vines and grapes as well as with the usual Jewish symbols, *menorah*, *shofar* and *lulav*, and the inscription Ὑπὲρ σωτηρίας Συκαμίνω[ν]. Sycamina on the Cape Carmel is now within the boundaries of modern Haifa. Another bronze object that may come from a synagogue is a door knocker inscribed 'Offering of Marcellina (daughter) of Felfelas for the salvation of her son Barachos, written in November 636, indiction 6', i.e. November 572 CE by a Pompeian era of 64 BCE; the artefact

Some synagogues uncovered in recent years have been identified as Samaritan and inscriptions have been found in them, mostly in the mosaic pavements: among the best documented are those of el-Khirbe, Zur Nathan and Raqit.[221] Most common here are the acclamation 'May so-and-so prosper' (αὐξίτωι) and the invocation 'One God help so-and-so', all apparently mentioning donors who contributed to the building. The latter is also the favourite formula in the dedications on stone slabs that must once have been set up in the sacred place of the Samaritans on Mount Gerizim and were reused for paving the church built there around 484 CE.[222] Here the donation was in money, and in several cases the dedicators specified the number of gold coins (*nomismata*) they gave to the holy place, 'following a vow' (εὐξάμενος), 'in thanksgiving' (εὐχαριστῶν), on behalf of themselves and of members of their family. From the information available today it appears that in late antique Samaritan sacred places the chosen language for dedicatory inscriptions was Greek. Unlike Jewish synagogues, where Greek and Aramaic are equally popular, not half a dozen inscriptions in Samaritan Aramaic have been discovered in synagogues, and none in the sacred precinct on Mount Gerizim.[223] The sample dwindles even more on closer examination. A bilingual capital from Emmaus and a lintel from 'Ein Beith el-Ma near Shechen are of uncertain date, and the Samaritan text in both is a biblical quotation; moreover, it is far from certain that the lintel belonged to a synagogue.[224] The mosaic pavement of Sha'albim featuring a *menorah* certainly belonged to a Samaritan synagogue, for it bears a fragmentary Greek inscription mentioning the renovation of the prayer hall and quotation from the Sa-

may come from Beth Shean (*SEG* XLIV, no. 1364). It is clearly a votive offering and since it bears no Christian symbols it is more likely to come from a synagogue than from a church, especially considering the names of Marcellina's father and son.

[221] *SEG* XLII, nos. 1423-1429; 1474; LV, no. 1732; on the sites, see Magen 1993a; 1993b; 2002; 2010: 127-165; Dar 2004.

[222] Magen 1990; 2010: 166-179; *SEG* XL, nos. 1501-1506; many are still unpublished.

[223] Besides the Greek dedications, all dating from the early Byzantine period except for one, of the Hellenistic period, a large number of inscriptions in Paleo-Hebrew, early Jewish Aramaic and Samaritan script were discovered in the excavations of the sacred precinct on Mount Gerizim, but those of the first two groups belong to the Hellenistic period, and the Samaritan fragments are very late, possibly medieval: Naveh and Magen 1997: 10*.

[224] The capital (Vincent and Abel 1932: 235-237, fig. 105; *CIIP* IV, 1, no. 3079) bears the Greek acclamation Εἷς θεός and a blessing attached to the Shema' verse from Deut. 6: 4; it was dated by most scholars to the Roman period. The lintel bears a Decalogue and was dated to the Roman period, or to the fifth century, or to the medieval period (Ben-Zevi and Albright 1941; White 1993). On re-examining the evidence Barag (2009: 311-316) opined that both are not earlier than the fourth century, but they may be later, even much later, especially the lintel.

maritan Pentateuch (Ex. 15: 18) in Samaritan script.[225] The only non-biblical inscriptions in Samaritan script are a rathe cryptic one in the mosaic pavement of a synagogue at Tell Qasile (Ramat Aviv), probably commemorating two benefactors,[226] and the invocation to the Lord of two persons, most likely donors, in a side room of the Tell Istaba synagogue at Beth Shean: but this is really a Greek inscription transcribed in Samaritan letters.[227] Two other inscriptions in the same synagogue – a basilica with an apse oriented to the northwest – were in Greek: a building inscription near the central entrance to the main hall and the signatures of the mosaicists in a side room (Fig. 36): Marianos and Hanina, the same father and son who worked in the synagogue of Beth Alpha, probably under Justin II (565–578). This, and the inscription in Samaritan letters, belong to the second stage of the synagogue, while the building inscription belongs to a previous stage, dated to the early fifth century or even earlier, on archaeological grounds.[228] Besides the Samaritan letters, several other clues contribute to the identification of this basilica with a Samaritan synagogue. A panel in front of the apse depicts a Torah shrine, *menorahs*, *shofars* and incense shovels, but no *lulav* or *etrog*, which were typical of the Sukkot ritual in the Temple of Jerusalem. The mosaics in all the building are floral or geometric, with no human or animal figures. The prayer hall is not oriented towards Jerusalem (nor east like a church). Last but not least, the building is located in an isolated spot outside the city, which seemingly answered a peculiarly Samaritan fear of contracting impurity.[229]

A location at the edge of a settlement is shared by other synagogues recognized as Samaritan, like those of Khirbet Samara, el-Khirbe and Sha'albim, also decorated with the same motifs (Torah shrine, *menorah* and other ritual objects) and lacking figures of any type. These are in Samaria and their orientation is toward Mount Gerizim.[230] The mosaic pavement of el-Khirbe contains several Greek inscriptions scattered between the decoration: augural acclamations for various persons, obviously donors, and invocations of

---

[225] Barag 1993; Magen 2010: 164-165; *CIIP* IV, 1, nos. 2755-2756.
[226] Tsafrir 1981; Macuch 1985; *CIIP* III, no. 2168. The pavement includes two other inscriptions in Greek, nos. 2166-2167, one the dedication of a benefactor who paid for the mosaic floor, the other a blessing: 'Blessing and peace upon Israel and upon this place, amen'. The Samaritans referred to themselves as 'Israel'.
[227] Naveh 1981. The Greek text is: Κύριε βοήθει Εφραι(μ) καὶ Αναν.
[228] *SEG* XXVIII, no. 1450, a-b. For the synagogue, see Tzori 1967 and for the date see Ch. II, n. 50. Of the building inscription only the words Ἔτους . . . μη(νὸς) Ἰανουαρ[ίου] survived.
[229] Cf. *Antonini Placentini Itinerarium* 8 (ed. Geyer 1965: 133).
[230] Magen 1993a; 1993b; 2002; 2010: 127-165. For Sha'albim, see above, n. 225.

the type 'Only God, help so-and-so' (Εἷς Θεός, βοήθι - - -). One such invocation is engraved on a lintel.²³¹

The appeal or acclamation to the 'Only God' (Εἷς Θεός, Εἷς Θεός μόνος), so common in the Samaritan holy place on Mount Gerizim, is typical of a Samaritan context in Palestine. It appears also in a small synagogue, a simple rectangular room surrounded by stone benches and paved in mosaic, located at the southern edge of a walled estate at Raqit on Mount Carmel. At the centre of the floor, a medallion encloses an inscription oriented to the south, the approximate direction of Mount Gerizim: Θ(εὸς) β(οήθει). Εἷς Θεός μόνος ('God helps. One (is) the only God'). A lintel once standing over the entrance showed an elaborated carved decoration including a *menorah*, a conch, rosettes and geometric shapes.²³²

Several quotations from the Samaritan Pentateuch engraved in Samaritan script on stone were discovered in Shechem and its vicinity, Emmaus, Yavne, Gaza and other sites, but their date is uncertain and seemingly they came from private houses where they fulfilled an apotropaic function.²³³ As Barag (2009) has shown, the Samaritan script derived from Paleo-Hebrew did not emerge before the fourth century CE, which may explain why it is so little represented in Samaritan synagogues. Legal disabilities were enforced against Samaritans even more severely than against the Jews, and probably they were unable to build new synagogues under Byzantine rule in the sixth century, and possibly even in the second half of the fifth, after the publication of Theodosius' Novella III in 439.

---

[231] *SEG* XLII, nos. 1423-1429.

[232] *SEG* LV, no. 1732. A burial cave at the opposite end of the estate bears a Greek inscription above the entrance (*SEG* LV, no. 1731): Μαρείνου μνημῖον, 'Tomb of Marinos', a name frequently borne by Samaritans, although common also among other Semites. For the synagogue, see Dar 2004: 120-151, and for the lintel, Gersht 2004. For the Samaritan use of the acclamation Εἷς Θεός in Palestine, see Di Segni 1994c. In Syria and Egypt the acclamation is usually associated with Christian inscriptions; so also on the fringes of the Holy Land, e.g. in the Golan Heights and at Zoʻar (Ghor eṣ-Ṣafi) on the Dead Sea.

[233] A marble slab with a complete Samaritan inscription, found in unknown context but seemingly in Yavne in 1913, contains two lines of dedication and 18 lines of the Samaritan version of the Ten Commandments, dated to the Late Byzantine-Early Muslim period (*CIIP* III, no. 2265). Another Samaritan fragment, containing three lines of the Ten Commandments, was discovered in Yavne in 1982 among the ruins of an Arab house, and was dated to the Byzantine period (*CIIP* III, no. 2266). According to Naveh, however, Samaritan inscriptions of this kind, mainly those inscribed on building stones and slabs, were not put up in synagogues but in private houses as a protection against the evil eye, illness and other misfortunes (1989b: 62; 1998: 95-98).

V.2.3 Inscriptions in private buildings

Inscriptions in private (residential or commercial) buildings are not easily identified. Modest private dwellings are rarely excavated, and therefore architectural elements bearing inscriptions are mostly discovered out of context, scattered on the ground or in secondary use in later structures. For instance, lintels or blocks bearing apotropaic inscriptions, or inscriptions proclaiming the name of the builder(s), are frequently found especially in the Golan and the Hauran, but either they are clearly not in their original place, or their setting is not properly investigated and described; therefore it is impossible to show to what kind of structure the inscription belonged, unless this is declared by the inscription itself. Only by exclusion, if the inscription does *not* describe the edifice as a tomb or a public building of any kind and does not mention authorities of any kind, can we suggest that it was a private building. Some such examples come from Rafid in the Golan, where several houses have lintels, probably reused, with acclamations charged with apotropaic power like 'One is God who helps so-and-so' or 'One is God who helps so-and-so the builder', 'In this sign (cross) conquer!', 'The Lord is light and life' (John 8: 12), 'Alpha-Omega' (Rev. 1: 8), or invocations, e.g., 'Jesus Christ, help so-and-so'.[234] The quotations from the Samaritan Pentateuch not found in the remains of a synagogue (above) also belong to this class of private apotropaic inscriptions.

Sumptuous mansions are excavated oftener than modest dwellings and their mosaic pavements sometimes contain inscriptions; but even in this case their identification as private houses is not always clear. This is the case of a small mosaic floor uncovered on Mount Zion, which is decorated with inhabited vine-scrolls and bears the inscription "Good luck, Stephen!', flanked by a pair of sandals, symbol of fortune and success.[235] The room was interpreted as a tomb but in fact belongs to a house, most likely a private one to whose owner the augural inscription was addressed. A similar inscription, 'Good luck to those who live here', decorated a simple mosaic floor in the anteroom of a private house uncovered south of the Temple Mount.[236] We have already mentioned the splendidly decorated pavements of Sheikh Zuweid and of the Hippolytus Hall at Madaba (above, ch. V.1.6): both are mostly regarded as belonging to private mansions, but it can-

---

[234] *SEG* XLVI, no. 1985; LVI, no. 1874.
[235] *CIIP* I, 2, no. 802. On the symbolical meaning of sandals at the entrance of a building, see Habas 2009.
[236] *CIIP* I, 2, no. 792.

not be excluded that they were official residences and if so, they should be viewed as public buildings.[237]

Two other types of private structures are documented by inscriptions: private baths and places of business. Two baths attached to private mansions are adorned with inscriptions. A mosaic pavement in Jerusalem bears a building inscription in which the bath addresses its builder, Count Eugenius, and wishes him to wash in good health and enjoy his foundation together with his family. In Caesarea, the building identified as a (public) bathhouse, whose mosaic pavement is adorned with augural inscriptions and labelled figures, is now recognized as a wing of a sumptuous private mansion.[238] The building inscription of a bath in Ma'in (Jordan) describes it as πριβᾶτον (*privâton*, 'private (bath)'), as opposed to the usual name of public baths in late antique Palestine, δημόσιον (λουτρόν) (*dêmosion [loutron]*, 'public [bath]').[239] This does not mean that it was part of a private home, but that it was privately built as a business venture; still, the inscription belongs to the private sphere. Shops and workshops (*ergasteria*) were usually held on a lease from the local authority;[240] so owners' inscriptions are rare. Tanneries were kept out of the inhabited area because of the smell, and a tanner's workshop in Hebron – apparently a simple shed made of perishable material – was privately erected in an isolated spot. A modest inscription engraved on the rocky surface on which the vats stood reads: 'This is the shed of Master Zonenos, tanner of Ascalon, year 630, the 5th of the month of Panemos' (29 July 527, reckoned by the era of Ascalon).[241]

The scanty sample of inscriptions attached to private business places may reserve some surprises. For instance, a mosaic medallion at the entrance of a shop in Beth Shean encloses the following text, under a cross and an

---

[237] Inversely, the 'House of the Nile' at Sepphoris, identified by the excavators as a public building, has been interpreted as a private mansion by Bowersock (2004) and Feissel (2006a: 248-250, no. 793), through a different reading of the inscription in front of the entrance, unwarranted by the remains of the letters in the opinion of the present writer. Moreover, the building lacks the domestic facilities common in private dwellings and especially in mansions, like a latrine and a kitchen. See Weiss and Talgam 2002; Di Segni 2002b; 2005d; Weiss 2008: 2033.

[238] *CIIP* I, 2, no. 796; *CIIP* II, nos. 1345-1347; Patrich 2011: 138.

[239] *IGLJ* II, no. 162.

[240] Cities and towns built or acquired workshops and even houses with public funds, as a source of income. This is shown by inscriptions attesting the purchase of a shop (e.g. *IGLS* XIII, 1, no. 9439 from Bostra) or its building, sometimes as an act of *philotimia* of a wealthy citizen (e.g. *IGLS* XVI, 4, nos. 878-879 from Busan, ancient Bosana, dated 378/9 and 386/7 CE, and *SEG* VII, no. 1105 = *IGLS* XVI, 1, nos. 122–123 from 'Atil, ancient Atheila, both in the Hauran).

[241] *SEG* XXXIX, no. 1625. Tanners soaked the hides in urine to soften them and produce leather; it was therefore a proverbially smelly occupation.

alpha-omega: 'Lover of building, behold the wares for you'. The first part has an apotropaic function, the second is an advertisement of the wares on sale inside – tools or samples of building materials? Another street in Beth Shean seems to have hosted some entertainment spots: several inscriptions in verses (still unpublished, like the former one) invited the menfolk of the city to come and enjoy themselves with Venus and Dionysus. One mosaic inscription reads: 'This path leads to desire and to amorous pleasure'; another 'This hall Megas has adorned for friends, that in it they may enjoy all night long with tender-hearted girls'. A Flavius Megas was governor of Second Palestine at the end of the fifth century, but he is unlikely to have built brothels as part of his beneficence to the metropolis. The name Megas is common, and he was probably the owner, advertising his business.

V.2.4 Funerary inscriptions

There are different kinds of funerary inscriptions. The most common is the epitaph engraved on a stele, a headstone or a tombstone on the burial place of one or more individuals and announcing the name of the deceased, often with added personal details, e.g. his/her/their age, date of death, profession or position in life. A second type is represented by epigrams lamenting the death of a beloved person. A third type includes inscriptions proclaiming the private ownership of the tomb: the owner may be an institution, or more often a private individual, in which case he or she is buried in it (though not necessarily at the time the inscription was engraved) and the inscription serves as his or her epitaph. A fourth type of funerary inscription is in fact a building inscription commemorating the construction of a burial vault or mausoleum for an individual, or more often for a married couple or an entire family. The founder or founders are mentioned by name but are not necessarily the first buried in the tomb, and may even not be buried there at all.

Funerary inscriptions tend to follow fixed formulas or at least similar patterns, but formulas and/or patterns vary with their chronology and region, as well as with their type. However, establishing a chronology is not easy, since many funerary inscriptions are not dated even in a general way by internal evidence (e.g., pagan or Christian character), and palaeography – the changing form of the script in different periods – is often the only way to propose a chronological frame to a specific inscription. Nevertheless, a development in the wording of epitaphs can be suggested, based on a sufficient number of samples with a shared wording that do have dates, and undated epitaphs with similar wording can most likely be ascribed to the same periods, though regional variations must also be considered. For instance, as we shall see, the epitaphs in the cemetery of Ghor eṣ-Ṣafi (Zoʻar) notably deviate from the pattern commonly adopted in the rest of the country in the same time range.

Fourth- and early fifth-century epitaphs are usually very simple, in the tradition of Late Roman epitaphs. They open with the name of the deceased, often accompanied by his patronymic and age, rarely also the date of death.[242] The name of the deceased may be preceded by "Here lies ' or 'Tomb of'"; or these words may be implied, as is clearly the case when the name appears in genitive. Sometimes the inscription addresses the dead himself, whose name is then given in the vocative, accompanied by one or more augural formulas: θάρσ(ε)ι or εὐψύχει ('Be conforted'), εὐτύχει or εὐμοίρει ('Fare thee well') (Fig. 40).[243] Most fourth-century epitaphs end with the formula Θάρσ(ε)ι, οὐδ(ε)ὶς ἀθάνατος, 'Be comforted: nobody is immortal', which becomes less and less common in the fifth century and rare in the sixth, with the spread of Christianity and its promise of immortal life.[244] The parting phrase χαῖρε, 'farewell', addressed to the dead and often accompanied by attributes referring to his youth or good character (ἄωρε, χρηστέ. ἄλυπε, 'untimely dead', 'good', 'innocent'), typical of epitaphs of the Roman period, disappears almost totally in the fourth-early fifth centuries.

In the course of the fifth, and still more in the sixth century, epitaphs become longer and more varied. The great majority are Christian and open and/ or end with crosses. Besides the formulas formerly in use new ones appear, all metaphors for 'died': ἐτελεύτησεν ('came to an end'), ἀνεπάη ('came to rest'), ἐκοιμήθη ('fell asleep'), κατετήθη ('was laid to rest'), ἐτέλεσεν τὸν δρόμον ('finished the race', Epistle to Timothy 4:7). The name of the deceased is usually accompanied by ὁ μακάριος/ ἡ μακαρία ('the blessed') and sometimes by a title indicating his position in the Church, if he was an ecclesiastic or a monk, more rarely by his profession.[245] Age is often indi-

---

[242] For examples of dated epitaphs of this period, see *SEG* XLVI, no. 1995 (Ṣurman, Golan: years 367, 410 and 415 of the era of Paneas = 364/5, 407/8, 412/3 CE); *SEG* LXV, no. 1772 (Raphia, 411 CE); Meimaris 1992: 178-208, nos. 63, 86 (with a pagan invocation), 89, 92, 101, 122, 147 (south-east of Jerash), 161 (Moab), 162 (306-399 CE: all from the Hauran except 147 and 161); Meimaris and Kritikakou-Nikolaropoulou 2005: 91–184, nos. 1-90 (Ghor eṣ-Ṣafi, 309-405 CE).
[243] See for instance Meimaris and Kritikakou-Nikolaropoulou 2005: 108, 111, nos. 16, 18 (Ghor eṣ-Ṣafi, 356 and 359 CE); *SEG* XXVIII, nos. 1459-1468; XLVII, no. 2094; LIX, nos. 1873-1882 from el-Huweinat, the necropolis of Ostracine in northern Sinai, fourth-fifth centuries. These formulas were current in Egypt already in the Roman period.
[244] With the exception of the necropolis at Ghor eṣ-Ṣafi (Zoʻar) where dated epitaphs show that the formula is common in the fourth and fifth centuries and continues in use in the sixth; see below.
[245] For instance, a vault in a complex of burial caves at Ḥorvat Luzit, north of Beth Govrin, has inscriptions engraved on the wall with only crosses, names and professions of the dead, a

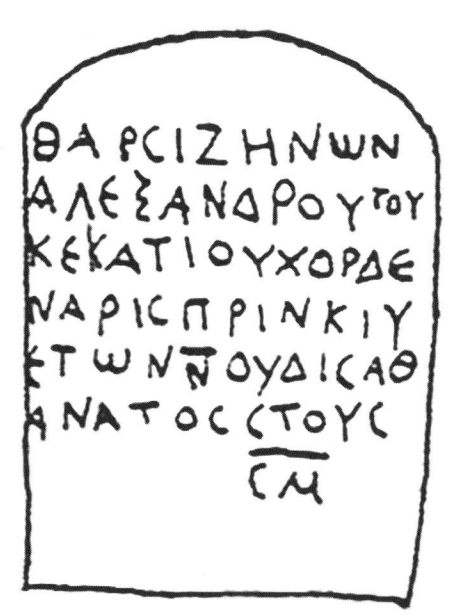

Fig. 40 – Funerary stele from 'Anz in the Hauran, 345/6 CE (Dunand 1939: 565, no. 271)
Be comforted, Zeno son of Alexander also (called) Katios, senior centurion, 50 years old. Nobody is immortal. Year 240 (of the era of Arabia).
Note the abbreviation for ἑκατοντάρχης, 'centurion', represented by X surmounted by a small vertical stroke (lost in the drawing).

cated, and the date of death, when it appears, is usually given with great precision: day and month, sometimes also weekday and even hour, indiction, and if the date is absolute, also year by the local era.[246] The addition of invocations for the repose of the dead's soul is not rare. In addition to crosses and christograms, palm branches sometimes appear, presumably as a symbol of virginity, on tombstones of persons who died unmarried.

Jewish epitaphs were worded in Greek, Aramaic or Hebrew and were usually undated, with the exception of those in the cemetery of Ghor eṣ-Ṣafi

goldsmith (χρυσόχοος) and a chief-physician (ἀρχιατρός): *SEG* XL, nos. 1487, 1489. The tombstone of another physician, probably from Beersheba, bears his epitaph: 'Here lies the blessed Abraamios, physician; he died on the 8 of the month of May, 18 of Artemisios, of the 12th indiction, year 365', by the era of Eleutheropolis, 564 CE (Alt 1921: 19, no. 22; Meimaris 1992: 311, no. 6). Two bakers and a κωμερκιάριος (an official of the fiscal service) are mentioned in burial inscriptions from Jerusalem (*CIIP* I, 2, nos. 880, 978), and a worker in gypsum (plasterer?) in Gaza (*CIIP* III, no. 2492): all these epitaphs date from the sixth-early seventh centuries.

[246] Apart from the necropolis of Ghor eṣ-Ṣafi (Zo'ar), epitaphs including weekday and hour of death are found only in the Negev, with the sole exception (at the actual state of knowledge) of a burial in Jericho dated 637 CE (*CIIP* IV, 1, no. 2810). Two tombstones from 'Avdat bear the weekday and hour not only of the death but also of the burial (*SEG* XXVIII, nos. 1395-1396; no. 1395 has also a double date, the day and month by the calendar of Gaza and by that of Elusa). For other examples from the Negev: *SEG* XXVIII, no. 1398; XXXIV, no. 1469.

(see below). Jewish epitaphs in Greek follow simple formulas, similar to the pagan and Christian epitaphs of the early period: name, patronymic, sometimes a title or profession or a term of kinship.[247] They can be distinguished from non-Jewish ones only because of the presence of a Jewish element (a *menorah*, a Jewish office, the word *shalom* in Hebrew) or Jewish names, as can be seen from the cemeteries of Beth She'arim, Caesarea, Jaffa or Tiberias.[248] Epitaphs in Aramaic or Hebrew, and also some bilingual in Greek and Aramaic, were discovered at Sepphoris and in southern Judaea,[249] as well as in the cemeteries of Beth She'arim, Caesarea, Jaffa and Tiberias.

The cemetery at Ghor eṣ-Ṣafi (Zo'ar) merits special attention, in the first place because of the great number of epitaphs it yielded and still yields, for more and more come to light in museums, private collections and in the antiquities market;[250] moreover, a large proportion of them is dated.[251] Secondly, this cemetery contains both Jewish inscriptions in Aramaic or Greek, and Christian inscriptions in Greek;[252] and finally, the epitaphs are much richer in

[247] Several examples from the necropolis of Jaffa (between the third and the sixth century: *CIIP* III, Introduction to nos. 2174-2254, p. 38): positions in the Jewish community (priest, i.e., *cohen*; rabbi; elder; *phrontistes*, i.e. *parnas*, the chief administrative official of a Jewish congregation), professions (bakers, fishermen, a labourer, a carder, a pedlar, a cumin seller, a merchant of linen), and two members of the lower Roman officialdom (*centenarius*, *magistrianus*). In Caesarea only one of four individuals buried under the same headstone bears a typically Jewish name, Ἰακώ, a hypocoristic form of Ἰακώβ, but another is styled αζάν, *hazan*, 'cantor' (*CIIP* II, no. 1490).

[248] But defining what makes a name a 'Jewish name' is far from simple. Many names can be shown to have been adopted by Jews, but no name, with the probable exception of Judas, can prove by itself that a particular inscription is Jewish. The Jewish epitaphs from Palestine were collected in *CIJ* II (1952). Later discoveries are published in Schwabe and Lifshitz 1974 and Avigad 1976 for Beth She'arim; *CIIP* II, nos. 1445-1667 (Jewish and not Jewish epitaphs are mixed) for Caesarea and *CIIP* III, nos. 2174-2255 for Jaffa; Di Segni 1998b for Tiberias. We leave aside epitaphs on ossuaries and in *kokhim* tombs, all earlier that the period we are treating.

[249] Sepphoris: Naveh 2005; Ustinova 2005; Aviam and Aharoni 2012; southern Judaea: *SEG* XXXV, no. 1542; Avni, Dahari and Kloner 2008; *CIIP* IV, 2, nos. 3847, 3848, 3850.

[250] Archaeological looting, feeding the illicit trade of antiquities, has been, and still is, the main industry of the local population, and since the Ghor eṣ-Ṣafi tombstones are very characteristic both in the type and colour of the stone (purple or pink sandstone) and in their contents and decoration, they are easily recognized when they are noticed.

[251] Counting only the legible tombstones of the main corpus of Greek epitaphs, published by Meimaris and Kritikakou-Nikolaropoulou 2005, 279 out of 358 are dated. Nos. 1, 3-79 and 1-8 of the Appendix bear dates in the fourth century, nos. 2, 80-252 and 9-22 (Appendix) in the fifth, and only fourteen, nos. 254, 256-264 and 24-26, in the sixth. For a summary of the various components of the Ghor eṣ-Ṣafi epitaphs, see *SEG* LV, no. 1764.

[252] Ghor eṣ-Ṣafi is not the only necropolis where Jews and Christians both buried their dead: the same is true of those of Eleutheropolis (Avni et al. 2008) and Caesarea (*CIIP* II, nos.

details than any found everywhere else in the Holy Land. We shall consider first the Christian epitaphs, which are by far more numerous than the Jewish ones. The great majority open and/or end with crosses. All begin with μνῆμα or μνημ(ε)ῖον, 'Tomb of..', and give the name and patronymic of the deceased, his or her age and in most cases the date of death not only by the year but also by the month and day, very often even adding the day of the week. Ecclesiastical titles, from bishop down to the lower clergy, and military and civil offices appear in several cases.[253] While the former is common in Christian funerary inscriptions of the same period, the latter is unusual elsewhere in the Holy Land. Even more unusual is the mention of the cause of death: three tombstones, dated 28 Artemisios 258, corresponding to 18 May 363, reveal that four persons buried under them had perished ἐν τῷ σιζμῷ (σεισμῷ), 'in the earthquake'.[254] With a few exceptions, all the epitaphs end with the sentence Θάρσ(ε)ι, οὐδ(ε)ὶς ἀθάνατος, which even appears in several dated in the sixth century.[255] The acclamation Εἷς θεός, rare elsewhere in a funerary context, especially Christian,[256] first appears here in the second half of the fourth century and becomes dominant in the fifth and sixth in a number of variants: Εἷς θεός, Εἷς θεός μονος, Εἷς θεός ὁ βοηθῶν, Εἷς θεός ὁ πάντων δεσπότης and the like.[257] Also in the late fourth century a new formula, with no parallels anywhere else in the Holy Land, appears in most epitaphs dated to the two following centuries: the deceased died 'with a good name', or 'with a good name and a good faith' (μετὰ καλοῦ ὀνόματος καὶ καλῆς πίστεως), or 'in holiness' (ἐν ὁσιότητι).[258]

Most Jewish epitaphs in the cemetery of Ghor eṣ-Ṣafi are in Aramaic, but some are in Greek or bilingual in Greek and Aramaic. The Greek epi-

---

1443-1678), though the latter cannot be proved because the tombstones were usually found out of context, scattered on the ground or reused in later buildings, mostly as mere fragments.
[253] Meimaris and Kritikakou-Nikolaropoulou 2005: 41-42.
[254] Meimaris and Kritikakou-Nikolaropoulou 2005: 116-121, nos. 22-24. The famous earthquake under Emperor Julian destroyed many cities in Syria, Palaestina and Arabia, and put an end to the Jewish hope to rebuilt the Temple in Jerusalem: Brock 1977; Russell 1980.
[255] Meimaris and Kritikakou-Nikolaropoulou 2005, nos. 253, 257, 258, 260, 262, 264 (502, 506, 516, 571, 576, 591 CE).
[256] Excluding the necropoleis of Ghor eṣ-Ṣafi and Feinan in the 'Aravah (Meimaris and Kritikakou-Nikolaropoulou 2005; 2008), only four examples are found in the region: Di Segni 1994c: 111-113, nos. 5 (Jewish), 16 (Samaritan or Christian), 21 (Samaritan), 26 (Christian).
[257] Meimaris and Kritikakou-Nikolaropoulou 2005: 417, Index 1b.
[258] The earliest examples of Εἷς θεός are Meimaris and Kritikakou-Nikolaropoulou 2005, nos. 23 (363 CE) and 71 (394 CE), and the earlies of μετὰ καλοῦ ὀνόματος are nos. 75 and 78 (395 and 397 CE). From the beginning of the fifth century both formulas become common. Ἐν ὁσιότητι appears in nos. 22 (363 CE), 61 (389), 89 (405), 95 (408).

taph of Saridas the *archisynagogos*, who died on 11 November 345, can be confidently assigned to a Jew, though it differs in nothing from the Christian epitaphs of the same period, except, of course, for the absence of crosses.[259] In fact, many tombstones inscribed in Greek in the Ghor eṣ-Ṣafi necropolis, from both the dated and the undated group, lack Christian symbols and might well have marked the burial places of Jews or even pagans.[260] The Aramaic epitaphs reflect the presence of the Jewish community that lived in Ẓoʻar from the Roman period until the eleventh century at least;[261] they belong to the fourth to early sixth century and many are dated according to the era of the *hurban* (destruction of the Temple in 70 CE) and the sabbatical cycle.[262] They are now collected in Meimaris and Kritikakou-Nikolaropoulou 2016. A bilingual, Greek-Aramaic epitaph dated 358/9 shows an interesting parallel between the two languages as the Semitic term for 'sabbatical cycle', *shabuʻa*, is transcribed in Greek σαεβυη.[263]

A cemetery with a mixture of pagan and Christian epitaphs, part of them in Greek, part in CPA, was explored at Khirbet es-Samra in northern Jordan. The Christian epitaphs were inscribed between ca. 450 and 680, the pagan ones are earlier. Desreumaux (1999) published about 85 CPA epitaphs, and Gatier (1999) 66 in Greek, as well as 61 from the cemetery of Riḥab in northern Jordan. The formulas are of the simplest: in the Greek epitaphs, name alone, name and patronymic, name, patronymic and age; sometimes with the addition of θάρσι, 'Be comforted'. The CPA epitaphs are even simpler: a cross and a name, rarely with the addition 'for eternity'.

Epitaphs in epigrammatic form, which were popular in the Late Roman period, still appear in the fourth century but become less and less common in the fifth and sixth. Since epigrams are rarely dated, it is not easy to distinguish between those of the Roman period and those of Late Antiquity.

---

[259] Meimaris and Kritikakou-Nikolaropoulou 2005, no. 7.

[260] On one, dated 20 December 388, the reading Μνημῖον Αἰνίου Ἰουδέου proposed in *SEG* VIII, no. 334 was rejected by Sartre 1993b: 136 and Ἰουδέου is now read as a patronymic, Γοδέου: Meimaris and Kritikakou-Nikolaropoulou 2005, no. 59. I do not find the new reading totally convincing.

[261] For the early period, see for instance *P. Yadin* 16, in which Babatha declares her property in Ẓoʻar for the census of Arabia of 127 CE. For the later period, see Alon 1945; Goitein 1975.

[262] For these chronological systems, see above, chapter II. The chronological systems adopted in the Jewish inscriptions of Ẓoʻar were first studied by Akavia (1945) and Cassuto (1945; for the epitaphs on which these studies were based, see Sukenik 1945 and Fraenkel 1945). All these papers are in Hebrew; for more recent consideration in English, see Cotton and Price 2001; Misgav 2006.

[263] Cotton and Price 2001, Greek corrected in *SEG* LI, no. 2082.

In the volume of *Steinepigramme* that contains the yield from Palaestina and Arabia the great majority of epitaphs is dated generally to the imperial period, up to the third century, rarely to the late third-possibly early fourth century; only a handful out of about 150 can be dated with certainty to the Byzantine period.[264] The metre is usually hexameters or elegiac couplets (alternate hexameters and pentameters) and the language is characterized by the use of epic forms of the verb and of the declension of nouns (e.g. aorist without augment, genitive in -ῆος instead of -έως). Mentions of Moira, the personification of Fate, and of other pagan or mythological figures are common in spite of the dead being Christian. The epigrammatic form is most often chosen for persons who died young.

Inscriptions proclaiming the private ownership of the tomb follow different patterns, depending on whether they belonged to an institution or to an individual. We have already spoken of inscriptions identifying tombs reserved for a particular class of members of a monastery (e.g. abbots, priests and elders), or for specific benefactors, as well as cemeteries belonging to a particular church, monastery or charity foundation (Ch. V. 2. 1). In the case of privately owned burials, the simplest formula, most common in Jerusalem but found also elsewhere, is represented by the words 'Tomb belonging to' (Θήκη διαφέρουσα, or Μνῆμα/μνημόριον διαφέρον) followed by the owner's name in genitive or dative, indicating that the tomb was reserved for the owner alone, or for the owner and his spouse, or for the owner and his family.[265] In some case the right of burying is explicitly granted or denied, as in an inscription from Caesarea that reads: 'It is permitted to all my descendants to be buried near (me)', while an inscription from Jerusalem explicitly forbids burying anyone else in the private tomb of Euphemia.[266] The owner,

---

[264] Merkelbach and Stauber 2002: 321, 325, 385-386, 393-394, 403-404, 416, 417, 430, 437, 448, 449, nos. 21/05/2 (Gaza, 569 CE), 21/07/2 (Beersheba, sixth c.), 22/15/01-02 (Buṣr el-Ḥariri, ca. 357 CE, bilingual in Latin and Greek), 22/21/01 (Shaqqa-Maximianopolis, 356/7?, erection of a funerary tower), 22/33/02-03 (Mejdel, ca. 360?), 22/40/04 (Orman, 401/2, building of family tomb), 22/41/01 (Salkhad, 419/20, building of family tomb), 22/42/98 (Jemerrin, 410/11), 22/45/01 (Kerak in Hauran, 497/8), 22/71/04 (Petra, 537/8), 22/76/01 (Avdat, fourth-seventh c.). A group of funerary epitaphs from Moab (ibidem: 436-444, nos. 22/61-22/65) are dated to the fifth-sixth c. either by years of the era of Arabia or by their palaeography and Christian symbols.

[265] See for instance *CIIP* I, 2, nos. 877, 879, 883, 885, 887-888, 892, 898-899, 901, 909, 912-913 and others (Jerusalem); *CIIP* II, nos. 1514, 1533, 1548, 1552, 1565, 1614-1616, 2086 (Caesarea); *CIIP* III, nos. 2186, 2217, 2218, 2228, 2236 (Jaffa), 2575 (Gaza); *SEG* LIII, no. (Beit Lid).

[266] *CIIP* II, no. 1613 (Caesarea); *CIIP* I, 2, no. 986; *SEG* LIX, no. 1713 (Jerusalem). Cf. also the inscription from the monastery of Kyra Maria in Beth Shean that gives instructions on the

Euphemia, reinforces her prohibition with a funerary curse: 'From the hour in which I am buried in this tomb, do not open it or bury another body. Whoever tries to do such a thing has to answer for it towards the coming Judgement' (ἕκαστος δὲ ἐπιχειρῶν ποιῆσαι τί ποτε τοῦτο ἔχει πρὸς τὴν κρίσιν τὴν μέλλουσαν). This wording belongs to a particular type of inscriptions aiming to protect the privacy of the burial, already well attested in the Hellenistic and Roman periods. These inscriptions contained a warning against opening the tomb to bury another body, strengthened with imprecations against violators, which in the early period threatened the vengeance of the gods, or more prosaically, a fine to be paid to the public coffers (*fiscus*, city treasury or the communal funds of a funerary association).[267] The funerary curses of Late Antiquity projected the threat to the afterlife (Last Judgement for both Jews and Christians, oaths in the name of the Trinity for the latter).[268] For instance, the epitaph of a father and son who died in 564 and 570, found in Beersheba, ends with the sentence: 'A curse (ἀνάθεμα) be on whoever opens this grave, for it is full and cannot take in any other'. Another epitaph, also from Beersheba, marks the tomb of a child who died on 23 April 588, aged five years and seven months. It ends with the words: 'A curse be from the Father, the Son and the Holy Ghost upon whoever opens this tomb, for it is full' (Ἀνάθεμα δὲ ἔστω ἀπὸ τοῦ Π(ατ)ρ(ὸ)ς κ(αὶ) τοῦ Υἱοῦ κ(αὶ) τοῦ Ἁγίου Πν(εύματο)ς πᾶς ἀνύγων τὸ μνῆμα τοῦτο, ἐπειδὴ γέμει).[269]

---

way to open the tomb for subsequent burials and threatens with curses whoever should dare to challenge the founder's right of burying there (*SEG* VIII, no. 39). Curiously, an inscription of uncertain date (Late Roman? Early Byzantine?) from Mejdel in the Hauran, after stating that four brothers built a family tomb at their own expenses, explicitly debars their daughters from any right on it (Waddington, no. 2403; *IGLS* XVI, 1, no. 45).

[267] Examples of threatened fines seem to cease in the fourth century, since the fine is normally expressed in *denarii*: see for instance *IGLS* XVI, 1, no. 221; *IGLS* XVI, 2, no. 367; *IGLS* XVI, 3, no. 607; *PAES* IIIA, no. 23 (Qasr el-Bai'j, north Jordan). An exception is the building inscription of a tomb in Harran (Hauran) by one Maior, who reserved it for himself alone, imposing a fine of three ounces of gold upon whoever violated his injunction (*IGLS* XV, 1, no. 269). This is probably later that the others, since the fine is given in gold; still, it is not calculated in *nomismata*, the golden coin that superseded the *denarius* under Constantine.

[268] For funerary curses in Jewish and Christian inscriptions, see Di Segni 2009b: 142*-145* and the comment in *SEG* LIX, no. 1713.

[269] Alt 1921: 20, nos. 23, 25; *SEG* XXXIV, no. 1469. Similar examples come also from Jerusalem and the Emmaus area. For the former, see *CIIP* I, 2, nos. 986, 990, 997. In Jerusalem, a Second Temple period example in Aramaic points to the existence of a Jewish tradition of curses for whoever disturbs the grave of the dead: see no. 1088 and the comment there. For Emmaus, see *SEG* VIII, no. 162 = *CIIP* IV, 1, no. 3099.

Despite the religious awe these inscriptions strove to arouse, their aim was not to prevent sacrilege but to protect the private enjoyment of an expensive piece of property, the burial cave, vault or monument, and all its parts. Another type of funerary inscriptions served the same purpose by explicitly declaring that the burial was purchased by the person who inscribed his name on the entrance. The simplest example appears on the stone door of a sixth-century tomb in Beth Shean: - - νος τὸ ἀγόρασμα Ἀμοῦς ('- - the purchased property of Amos').[270] In the Abu Kabir necropolis in Jaffa two slabs, not discovered in situ but most likely originally affixed to the entrance of a burial chamber, bear the following inscriptions: 'Burial place which I, Nonnus, bought' (Τόπος τὸν ἠγόρασα ἐγὼ Νόννος), and 'I, Saul, have purchased (this) tomb in Jaffa from Baruch' (Ἠγόρασα ἐγὼ Σαοὺλ ἐν τῇ Ἰόππῃ παρὰ Βαρουχίου μνῆμα).[271] Most famous is the inscription of the tomb of the Monastery of the Iberians in Jerusalem. It reads: Μνῆμα διαφέρ(ον) Σαμουὴλ ἐπισκόπου Ἰβέρων κ(αὶ) τῆς μονῆς αὐτοῦ, ὃ ἠγόρασαν ἐν τῷ πύργῳ Δαουίδ, 'Tomb belonging to Samuel, bishops of the Iberians (Georgians) and to his monastery, which they purchased in the (area of) David's Tower'. Despite the opinion held by some scholars that the property purchased was the monastery, not the tomb, the neuter pronoun can only refer to μνῆμα, the tomb. And this interpretation seems to be confirmed by another inscription discovered in Jerusalem, in which two deacons of the Holy Sepulchre declare themselves co-heirs of the Iberians in the 'tomb of David's Tower'. Apparently this tomb in the vicinity of the so called 'Tower of David' near Jaffa Gate was the property of the monastery of the Iberians and the two deacons, perhaps Georgian themselves, had, or had purchased, burial rights in it.[272]

---

[270] *SEG* VIII, no. 49.

[271] *SEG* LIII, no. 1848 = *CIIP* III, no. 2181; *CIJ* II, no. 953 = *CIIP* III, no. 2234. In the latter, under the first well-spaced lines, three more crowded lines were added, saying: 'We first buried (here) Saul and Syncletica', probably an addition by Saul's children or heirs who first used the family tomb for the head of the family and his spouse. Also a broken stone, seen in secondary use in the mosque at Misiliyeh, south of Jenin, seemingly contained the phrase [ἠγό]ρασαν [τὸ μνημεῖον], 'purchased this tomb' (*SEG* VIII, no. 94).

[272] *CIIP* I, 2, no. 1000. This interpretation was offered in the *editio princeps* (Iliffe 1934) and supported by Tsafrir 2012: 253-256). For the second inscription, see *CIIP* I, 2, no. 977. No. 1000 was discovered in one of the funerary structures excavated by Iliffe at the YMCA site, located opposite the Citadel ('Tower of David') across the Valley of Hinnom. The tomb of the monastery of the Iberians can probably be identify with the cemeterial enclosure there or part of it; for a revaluation of Iliffe's finds and conclusions, see Tchekhanovets 2017.

Inscriptions proclaiming the private ownership of a tomb are sometimes properly building inscriptions, in which the person who commissioned the tomb set up his name on it just as if it were his dwelling, often adding that he built it while still living, how much it cost him, who was the master-mason, to whom the tomb was reserved. Several examples come from the Hauran. In an inscription dated 389/90 a man and his wife erected a tomb, reserving it for themselves and their children, and adding the names of two builders; in another, dated 390, a veteran of the Third Legion Cyrenaica specifies how much he paid from his own pocket for the tomb he built (τὸ μνη[μεῖον ἐξετέλεσεν] ἐκ τῶν ἰδίων ἀναλώσας δ[ηνάρια - -]) and forbids burying anyone else in it, except his brother.[273] In a third, dated 401/2, three brothers renovated a tomb, presumably the family vault, 'at their own expenses' (ἐκ τῶν ἰδίων ἀνενέωσαν), dividing the burial rights in it between them: 6/12 to one and 3/12 to each of the other two.[274]

Despite the fact that the greatest concentrations of funerary inscriptions that can be dated with certainty to Late Antiquity come from a limited number of areas (Caesarea, Jerusalem, Gaza and the Negev, Moab, Ghor eṣ-Ṣafi),[275] while other parts of the country are represented only by scattered samples or by small groups, we can identify local preferences in the choice of terms, as well as in the habit of dating. For instance, θήκη is by far the commonest term for tomb in Jerusalem, where μνῆμα is much less used and μνημεῖον or μημόριον are quite rare. In Caesarea too θήκη is the commonest term, followed by μημόριον, and other terms, like μνῆμα or τόπος, are rare. Τόπος in a funerary sense is popular in Jaffa; but almost nowhere else in the Holy Land;[276] μνῆμα and μνημεῖον are current in the Hauran, where μημόριον is rare and θήκη almost unknown.[277] Θήκη is rare also in the eastern part of the Holy Land, now included in the Hashemite Kingdom of Jordan: a case from the vicinity of Madaba is unusual in appearance too. It is an epitaph in mosaic, surrounded by a circular frame in the centre of the nave of a church, and

---

[273] Meimaris 1992: 202, nos. 151-152.

[274] Meimaris 1992: 205, no. 163; *IGLS* XVI, 4, no. 895.

[275] We shall leave aside the inscriptions from Beth She'arim (Schwabe and Lifshitz 1974), for though the corpus is conspicuous, many of the items belong to earlier periods, and it is impossible to isolate those of the period considered here.

[276] *CIIP* III, nos. 2181, 2192, 2195, 2231 (Jaffa). Τόπος occurs also at Beth She'arim, but the date of the inscriptions in which it appears may be earlier than the period considered here. Most of the few examples from Caesarea appear in epitaphs of Jews: *CIIP* II, 1483, 1490, 1524, 1661, 2151. For a case from Kibbutz Shomrat, north of Acco, see *SEG* L, no. 1511, and for another from Mount Tabor, Ovadia and Pierri 2019: 387, no. 12.

[277] For the Hauran, see Waddington and *IGLS* XIII, XIV, XV and XVI.

it reads: Θήκη τῶν ἁγίων πατέρων Εὐστρατίου Μαγνου καὶ λοι(πῶν) (Tomb of the holy fathers Eustratius, Magnus and the others).[278] In the great necropolis in Ghor eṣ-Ṣafi the dominant term for tomb is μνημεῖον, constantly used in various spellings;[279] on the contrary, in Moab, scarcely 20 km to the east, almost all epitaphs start with 'Here lies' (Ἐνθάδε κεῖται) and there are very few references to the tomb (στήλη or σῆμα, both meaning 'tomb marker'), with just one occurrence of μνημεῖον.[280] Another term, τύμβος, occasionally appears, but only in funerary epigrams, whose date cannot always be ascertained, though they seem to have been still popular in the fourth century.[281]

In the Gaza region and in the Negev the name of the deceased is accompanied as a rule by the epithet 'the blessed one' (ὁ μακάριος, ἡ μακαρία) and often also by 'servant/handmaid of Christ' (δοῦλος/δούλη Χριστοῦ), but these epithets are rare in the rest of the country, including Transjordan. For dying, the favourite term in the Negev and the Gaza region is 'came to rest' (ἀνεπάη), the second favourite is 'fell asleep' (ἐκοιμήθη), but in Nessana the most used verb is 'came to an end' (ἐτελεύτησεν). In Ghor eṣ-Ṣafi the metaphors 'coming to rest' or 'to an end' are known, but by far the most common verb is the unadorned ἀποθνήσκειν, 'to die'. Like in most of the country, here too the age of death, when given, appears in the genitive: he/she died ἐτῶν x, sometimes down to the number of months and days (μηνῶν, ἡμερῶν), especially if the deceased is a child or youngster. On the contrary in Moab the age of the deceased is consistently given in term of his lifetime, and the usual formula is 'Here lies so-and-so, having lived so many years', in many cases followed by the date of death given without introductory verb, except in a limited area between el-Mota and Mahatij in southern Moab, where the date of death is preceded by 'came to an end' or less often 'fell asleep'.[282] As for the dating habit, this is prominent in the south: Gaza and the Negev, Moab and Ghor eṣ-Ṣafi. In Golan and Hauran dated epitaphs

---

[278] *IGLJ* II, no. 116.
[279] Meimaris and Kritikakou-Nikolaropoulou 2005: 24, 91-92.
[280] Canova 1954, passim. Μνημεῖον at el-Mota: ibidem, no. 306.
[281] Some examples: *SEG* XXXVII, no. 1488, from Karmil in southern Judaea; Welles 1938, no. 211 from Gerasa; *IGLS* XIII, 1, nos. 9393, 9410, from Bostra; *IGLS* XIV, nos. 177, 189, 338, 428, 519 from the Bashan (Batanaea); *IGLS* XV, nos. 115, 241, 369, from the Leja (Trachon).
[282] Reginetta Canova collected a total of 428 inscriptions, most of them (415) epitaphs. Out of the 415 epitaphs, only twelve lack the age of the dead, and those are fragmentary; 145 have dates, and more were probably dated but are fragmentary. The dates range from the second half of the fourth century (only two cases) to the eighth century (two cases), with the largest concentration in the fifth and especially in the sixth century, and only six in the seventh:

of the fourth-seventh centuries are not rare but neither are they as common as dated inscriptions of other types.

Funerary inscriptions are very often found not in situ, but it cannot be doubted that most of them were originally located in cemeteries. Inscribed tombstones are found in situ or near their original location when burial occurred in churches, usually in the atrium, narthex, side rooms or aisles, rarely in the nave or the presbytery. Epitaphs in mosaic, though hardly common, are well attested.[283] It is important to remember, however, that inscriptions containing the formula ὑπὲρ ἀναπαύσεως, or ὑπὲρ μνήμης καὶ ἀναπαύσεως, frequently found in the mosaic pavements of churches, are not epitaphs but invocations and are not, as a rule, set above a tomb.

V.2.5 Instrumenta

Ceramic and similar objects

Objects created for home use (*instrumenta, instrumenta domestica*) were sometimes inscribed by means of various techniques. The largest proportion of *instrumenta* preserved for study are made of clay, the cheapest and most durable of substances, for metal, more expensive as raw material as well as in processing, was often melted and reused.[284] Clay objects could be stamped, or imprinted in a mould; inscriptions could be incised on the soft surface with a pointed tool before firing, or they could be made after firing at any moment during the service of the artefact, by scratching the hard surface with a sharp implement or by drawing with ink or paint. Inscriptions stamped on a ceramic object before firing probably refer to the potter's workshop where the object was manufactured, while those made by any technique after firing are more likely to refer to the owner, the contents or anything else, and must be examined singularly for meaning.

Painted inscriptions (*dipinti, tituli picti*) appear mostly on storage jars and may refer to the producer, owner or recipient of the contents, or to their nature,

---

Canova 1954: xci-xcvii. The inscriptions from el-Mote are nos. 301-321 and those from Mahaij nos. 350-418.

[283] See for instance *SEG* VIII, no. 40 (Beth Shean); *CIIP* I, 2, nos. 875, 1006 (Jerusalem); *CIIP* IV, 1, nos. 2810, 2833 (Jericho), 3313 (Kh. Shuweika); *IGLJ* II, no. 116 (Madaba).

[284] This is not only a reasonable surmise but is actually documented by finds of broken metal objects gathered together. A spectacular treasure of about 1,000 bronze objects, metal scraps and coins were found stored in three large pithoi in a workshop in Tiberias. The collection is dated to the eleventh century by a coin of Emperor Michael VII (1071-1078): Hirschfeld and Gutfeld 2008: 20-24; Ponting 2008. A similar hoard was discovered in Caesarea: Shalev 1998.

quality or quantity. The painted letters are often interrupted by a break or too faint to be read, and even when legible, they cannot always be interpreted.[285] Personal names in genitive can be understood as referring to the owner; in dative, to the person to whom the jar, or rather its content, was intended for.[286] A small group of dipinti on fragments of amphoras, discovered in the excavations of the Nea Church and its vicinity, contain names in genitive referring to persons who gave the jar and its contents as an offering to the church. One reads [Ἀ]πὸ προσ[φορᾶς | Ἀντ]ωνίν[ου], 'From the offering of Antoninos'; another [Προσφορὰ Εὐδο]ξίου, 'Offering of Eudoxios'; a third simply ΠΡΣ, Πρ(οσφορά), unless the name of the almsgiver is lost in the break under the letters. The abbreviation ΡΘ, Ῥ(όγα) Θ(εοτόκου), 'Alms of the Mother of God' is painted on several other sherds.[287]

Both liquid and dry goods were transported in jars, and dipinti on the jar may describe the contents, especially if they were not the commonest products carried in that particular type of container, like oil or wine: examples discovered in excavations at Jaffa, Jerusalem and En Gedi (still unpublished) include special wines, various kinds of *garum* (fish sauce), almonds, preserved foodstuff produced from pigs (lard? pickled trotters?) and mineral pitch.[288] Quantities and prices are sometimes marked in the same way. In Late Antiquity quantity was normally expresses in *sextarii*, a ξέστης or *sextarius* corresponding to 0.54 litres. The term ξέστης is usually abbreviated ξέ(στης) or ξέσ(της) in inscriptions.[289] Prices were expressed in νο(μίσματα), the golden *solidus* weighting 4.54 g or, when cheaper, in the smaller silver coin, the κεράτιον (Latin *siliqua*), which was one twenty-

---

[285] For examples of the difficulty in reading and interpreting dipinti, see *CIIP* II, nos. 1784, 1791 (ΡΚ = 120?), 1792 (ΟΙ - - = οἴ[νος -]?), 1793-1794, 1795 (Ξ Θ = ξ(έσται) θ', 'Nine *sextarii*'?), 1796-1797, 2106, 2107, 2114. Of these eleven cases, from Caesarea and Mount Carmel, not one can be interpreted with certainty. Of twelve examples from Jerusalem (*CIIP* I, 2, nos. 1047-1058), a probable interpretation can be suggested only for three or four.

[286] See for instance *CIIP* I, 2, no.1051: [Θεο]δόρῳ, 'For [Theo]dore'.

[287] *CIIP* I, 2, nos. 1047 -1050, 1054.

[288] *Garum* and special wines also appear in dipinti on jars of the Roman period: see for instance Cotton and Geiger 1989: 166-167, no. 826, pl. 24 (Masada); Ecker 2013: 306-308 (Jericho); Zissu and Ecker 2014: 308-309 (Beth Govrin).

[289] Avi-Yonah 1940: 89; examples of abbreviation reduced to a single *xi*, ξ(έστης) are also known: cf. *CIIP* I, 2, no. 1093, and other cases still unpublished. In papyri and ostraca ξέστης is abbreviated with the single letter ξ crossed with a diagonal stroke or with the four letters ξέστ(ης), alone or followed by a *stigma* indicating truncation: McNamee 1981: 67.

fourth of a *solidus*. Figures representing year of production are also known, as well as augural formulas.²⁹⁰

Another technique for writing on a vessel while it was in use was by scratching the hard surface with a sharp implement. The resulting graffiti are mainly personal names in the genitive, which most likely refer to the owner of the artefact,²⁹¹ but in some cases the name may belong to a foundation rather than to a private person. For instance, a fragment of platter bearing the inscription [- - Παυλο[υ -]], found in Caesarea, may have belonged to a chapel dedicated to St. Paul rather than to a man called Paul, since it was discovered among the debris of what seems to have been a chapel at the upper floor of a warehouse, together with a bread stamp engraved with a blessing (*eulogia*) of St. Paul.²⁹² Another find from Caesarea, the base of a bowl with a graffito incised after firing, Ἁγήου Θεοδό[-], surely belonged to a church or monastery of Saint Theodore rather than to one Agias son of Theodore!²⁹³ As in *tituli picti*, also in graffiti letters may represent a figure indicating a quantity, the serial number of an amphora included in a particular cargo, or a date. For example, the letters ΡΠΑ, '181', incised on the shoulder of an amphora dated between the late first and the early fourth century, found in Caesarea, may refer to year 55/6 CE by the era of Tyre, 77/8 CE by the era of Ascalon or 120/1 by the era of Gaza, all cities linked by maritime commerce to Caesarea.²⁹⁴ As the graffito is often found on a sherd, it is not always possible to establish the type of vessel: a storage jar, a bowl, or something else. Potsherds bearing graffiti or dipinti must also be attentively examined to avoid confusing them with ostraca, which are potsherds specifically used as a durable material for writing. In ostraca the script, often set in several lines, is arranged to fit within the contour, however irregular, of the sherd.

Inscriptions made on clay artefacts before firing could be incised or stamped, or the whole object could be manufactured in a mould, if its shape and size

---

²⁹⁰ For some examples, see *CIIP* I, 2, nos. 1052-1057; *CIIP* II, nos. 1791-1793, 1795; Ecker 2010: 172, no. 3; *SEG* LVIII, nos. 1795-1807 (from Antinooupolis in Egypt).

²⁹¹ Examples in *CIIP* I, 2, nos. 1059-1062; *CIIP* II, no. 1788; *CIIP* III, no. 2279 (to be read Ἀθανασί[ου] rather than Ἀθανάσι[ς], 'a variation on Athanasius': Ecker).

²⁹² *CIIP* II, nos. 1163-1164. For the chapel, see Patrich 2000, and for the *eulogia* bread stamp, see below.

²⁹³ *CIIP* II, no. 1785; ἁγίου is spelled ἁγήου by iotacism. According to the editor, W. Ameling, 'Though tempting, the reading Hagios (Saint) is unlikely in this inscription. The name Agias is well attested', as indeed it is, though not in Palestine; however, the martyr Theodore was one of the favourite saints in Palestine, with shrines in all major centres and villages.

²⁹⁴ *CIIP* II, no. 1789. According to the editor (Ecker), 'The number is either referring to a quantity, or more likely, an amphora number within a series'; I prefer a different interpretation.

permitted. In the case of incised script, their meaning is not always clear. For instance, the letters ZOY on the neck of an amphora from Tell es-Samaq (Shiqmona), dated to the fourth-seventh centuries, is interpreted by the editor as a potter's mark.[295] This is certainly possible, though potter's marks in this period were usually monogrammed and stamped (see below). If these letters represent the potter's name, the name must be abbreviated, since the amphora neck is completely preserved and shows no other writing: e.g. Ζ(ονεν)ου, or the beginning of a name, e.g. Ζου(ρασιου) or Ζου(βδα), '(Work) of Zonenos/Zourasios/Zoubdas'; but in both cases we would expect an abbreviation mark.[296] Another possibility should be considered, that the letters represent a number, 477: as a date, 477 could correspond to 428/9 CE according to the era of Acco-Ptolemais, in whose territory Tell es-Samaq was included. In other cases the incised words are definitely personal names, but even then their interpretation may be uncertain. A zoomorphic juglet found at Tel Mefalsim near Gaza has ABBA|CWB[- -] incised on its neck, to be read Ἀββᾶ or Ἀββᾷ Cωβ[βιν- or Cωβ[έ-, genitive or dative, rather than Ἀββα|ς Wβ -, as suggested in *CIIP*; also Ἀββασωβ[βου], '(Work) of Abbasobbos', should be considered. The dative would indicate that the juglet was made specially 'for Abba Sobbinos' or Sobeos, or for Abbasobbos, all common names in the region.[297] From the same site a pull-toy (a horse?) also came, on which two names are incised in nominative, Leontakis and Stephanos, perhaps two brothers for whom the toy was made.[298]

Two other types of object with incised inscriptions are worth of mention. One is a sandstone amphora stopper (Fig. 41) inscribed all around the edge Φλά(βιος) Χριστᾶς υ(ἱ)ὸς μ(ακαρίας) μ(νήμης) Αλαφα Ηλαλε φοράριους, 'Flavius Christas, son of Halaf of blessed memory, of Eleale, merchant'.[299] The second

---

[295] *CIIP* II, no. 2160. The Z is retrograde.
[296] Ζονενος is common in the region; for Ζουρασιος and Ζουβδας see *SEG* VIII, no. 45 (Beth Shean); *IGLJ* V, no. 288 (Umm el-Jimal). Semitic names in Greek transcription are best left without accent.
[297] *SEG* XXXIII, no. 1269; *CIIP* III, no. 2527. The *editio princeps* read Ἀββᾶς ['Ι]ώβ, nominative, but the editor in *CIIP* III translated 'Of Father Ob- -', apparently mistaking Ἀββᾶς for a genitive. For Ἀββοσοβος, Ἀββοσουββος, Ἀβεσομβος, Ἀβοσοβεος, and similar variants, see for instance *SEG* VIII, no. 238; XXXVII, nos. 1556, 1562; XL, nos. 1478-1479; the shift A/O is common in southern Palestine. For Σοββινος, *SEG* XXXVII, nos. 1511-1512; for Σοβεος, also spelled Τζοβεος, *SEG* VII, no. 238; XXXIV, no. 1517; XLV, no. 1916; XLVI, no. 2079. If the name was Abbasob- -, it may well have been in genitive, the potter's name.
[298] *SEG* XXXI, no. 1402; *CIIP* III, no. 2528.
[299] Di Segni 2007; *SEG* LVII, no 1869. The item was purchased in the antiquities market and its findspot is therefore unknown, but its origin is certainly from Transjordan, for the home of the merchant, Eleale, is known as a village near Hesban (Schmitt 1995: 140). The alternative reading reported by *SEG* in the commentary (φλαχριστᾳε as an error for φιλοχριστός) is

Fig. 41 – Amphora stopper from Transjordan (*SEG* LVII, no 1869. Courtesy of Mr. Arnold Spaer)

is the bread stamp engraved with a blessing of St. Paul, mentioned above (Fig. 42). The stamp is a disk of well fired reddish clay, 10.4 cm of diameter, broken on the left side. The back has an attached knob serving as a handle. The front is decorated with a cross under an arch flanked by smaller crosses (one of which is lost in the break). Concentric rings run along the edge; the inner contains a row of dots, the outer a zigzag decoration; the middle one bears the inscription Εὐλογία Κ(υρίο)υ ἐ{π}φ' ἡμᾶ[ς καὶ τοῦ ἁγίου Π]αύλο(υ), 'Blessing of the Lord upon us, and of Saint Paul'.[300] The inscription indicates that the object was used to stamp *eulogia* bread, small loaves that were given out to pilgrims at shrines or to the faithful at festivals of a particular saint. The custom of stamping bread goes back to the Roman period: among the material finds of that pe-

---

unacceptable. The word for 'merchant', φοράριος, clearly derives from the Latin *forum*. It appears in Greek inscriptions, but *forarius* is not attested in Latin, as far as I could ascertain. However, the spelling on the stopper reflect the Latin form.

[300] *SEG* L, no. 1475; *CIIP* II, no. 1163. For the archaeological background of the find, see above, n. 292.

Chapter V: Greek inscriptions in the Holy Land in Late Antiquity

Fig. 42a – Bread stamp from Caesarea, restored (Photo A. Hai, Israel Mudeum. Courtesy of J. Patrich)

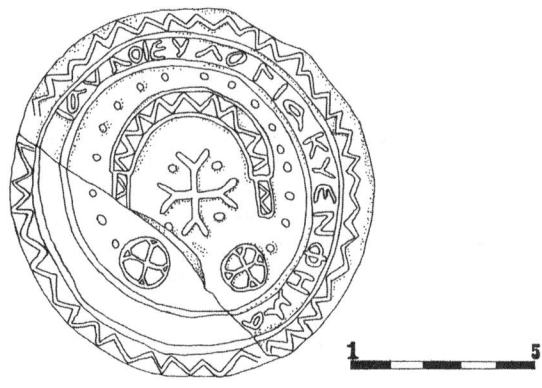

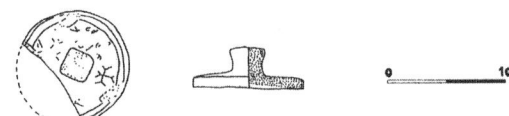

Fig. 42b – Bread stamp from Caesarea (*SEG* L, no. 1475. Courtesy of J. Patrich)

riod are military stamps bearing the name of the soldier who baked the bread for a *centuria* and of the commanding officer of the unit,[301] as well as stamps with Jewish symbols and Hebrew inscriptions, or Greek/Latin inscriptions of Jewish names accompanied by Jewish symbols. Jewish bread stamps continued in use in Late Antiquity.[302] However, the commonest type of bread stamp found in this period is represented by Christian stamps for ecclesiastic use. These stamps first appeared about the fifth-sixth centuries (and continue into the present in the Eastern Churches, especially in Jerusalem). Two types of bread were stamped: the liturgical bread for the Eucharist and small loaves to be given out to pilgrims in certain churches or on special festive occasions. Stamps made of stone, pottery, wood or bronze, found in excavations or in the antiquities market, most often round or square, with a handle on the back, bear inscriptions and decorations on the opposite side, usually engraved in mirror image. This side, once impressed on soft dough, would leave the required design. Stamps for Eucharistic bread typically bear a simple design of crosses with letters between the arms, forming the initials of sentences like IX|AW, Ἰ(ησοῦς) Χ(ριστὸς) ἄλφα ὦ μέγα ('Jesus Christ the beginning and the end', Apoc. 1:8), or Ἰ(ησοῦ)ς Χ(ριστὸ)ς νικᾷ ('Jesus Christ conquers'). Stamps for bread to be given out at churches often bear the inscription *Eulogia...*, 'Blessing', followed by the name of the church or the patron saint, and/or a figure depicting the church, the saint, or the occasion of the festival.[303]

Byzantine pottery was sometimes stamped, either on the handles as in the Hellenistic and Roman periods, or on the body, but unlike Hellenistic and Roman stamped pottery, which has been and is the subject of many studies, no effort has been made until now to collect and classify the impressions on late antique pottery found in our region. Apparently these impressions, usually personal names in genitive, represented the name of the potter, or of the workshop owner. This was rendered in monogrammed form, namely, as a cruciform or square block of ligated letters in which each letter of the name appeared once, even if it occurred twice or more times in the name. Consequently the monograms are often difficult to decipher. Some impressions, not in monogrammed form, represent religious formulas, e.g. Θεοῦ χάρις, 'God's grace'.[304]

---

[301] For some examples, see *CIIP* I, 2, nos. 755-759, 761.

[302] Amit 2006; *CIIP* II, no. 2113A.

[303] For a general treatment of this topic, see Galavaris 1970; Harari 2006; and for examples, see Israeli and Mevorah 2000: 96-97; Coen-Uzzielli 2006; *CIIP* I, 2, nos. 1076-1077; *CIIP* II, no. 1163; *CIIP* III, no. 2526.

[304] For some examples, see Clédat 1916: 20, fig. 11; Bagatti 2002a: 135, pl. 19; Taxel 2009; *CIIP* I, 2, nos. 44*-51*. Some amphora stoppers bear stamped inscriptions of both types: *SEG* XVIII, no. 672; XLVI, no. 2021.

Two types of stamped artefacts industrially produced in this period merit a special mention: mortars and building material – bricks and roof tiles. The former were produced in northern Syria in the third-fourth centuries and imported in large quantities to Palestine, Egypt, Cyprus, Asia Minor, Greece, and even to the west of Europe. These 'Syrian *mortaria*' were stamped on the edge with the name of the potter in the genitive, or – less often – with augural expressions, e.g. εὐτυχῶς, εὐκαρπία ('Good luck', 'Prosperity'). About fifteen names are known, two of them in Latin, the rest in Greek; all were set in two lines within a rectangular frame. Most but not all types are attested in excavations in Israel. These mortars were made of hard, durable material, and may have remained in use for generations: fragments of their inscribed rims are often discovered in layers much later than their date of production.[305] Bricks and roof tiles were manufactured in the legionary kilns in Jerusalem until ca. 200 CE and were stamped with the name of the legion stationed in the city, LEG. XFR, *Legio Decima Fretensis*. At about the end of this period, or perhaps even earlier, ceramic building material stamped *Colonia Aelia Capitolina*, in various abbreviated forms, began to appear, possibly manufactured in municipal potteries. Some of the various types were stamped, others were made in moulds. Another type, as yet attested in very few examples but clearly belonging to a third-century context, bore Latin names written in Latin or in Greek, presumably the names of the makers, most likely veteran soldiers who had learnt the trade in the army and set up their own business.[306] A new type of building material produced by private potteries appeared in Jerusalem in the first half of the fourth century when the city began a rapid growth under the impact of Constantine's policy to transform the half ruined and empty Late Roman Aelia into the focal point of the Christian world.[307] This type bears the stamped name of the workshop owner in Greek, set in two lines within a rectangular frame, just like the stamps on the contemporary Syrian *mortaria*. Eight names are known. The bricks and tiles bearing these stamps are found in many excavations in Jerusalem, including in later assemblages, where they were apparently reused.[308] Some tiles were stamped not with names but with one or two letters or with symbols: those too are mainly found in Jerusalem, but also in its vicinity.[309]

---

[305] Hayes 1967; Groh 1978; Vuk 2021.
[306] For the legionary production, see Barag 1967; for a summary of the early types, with relevant bibliography, see Weksler-Bdolah et al. 2022. Some of these types were not stamped but made in moulds.
[307] On the sorry state of pre-Constantinian Jerusalem, see Di Segni and Tsafrir 2012: 412, n. 26.
[308] For a list and related bibliography see *CIIP* I, 2, App. 52*.
[309] See *CIIP* I, 2, App. 53*.

Another type of clay objects bearing inscriptions, the *eulogiae*, were manufactured in moulds. There were different kinds of *eulogiae*, 'souvenirs' that were given out or sold to pilgrims in churches or holy places, but all shared certain characteristics: they were mass-produced, had negligible material value, and were impressed with a scene or symbol of the holy place and – in certain cases – with an inscription related to it. Since they were acquired by pilgrims, *eulogiae* can be found anywhere, near the site of production as well as far away, along the roads travelled by the pilgrims and in their home countries.[310] They are small disks, 2–4 cm in diameter, some of them poorly fired, others well fired. Among the best known and most widely scattered are the small tokens from Abu Mina, the shrine of St. Menas in Egypt, and from Qal'at Sim'an in northern Syria, the monastic centre where in the fifth century Simeon Stylites lived for thirty-seven years on top of a pillar. The former bear the image of the saint between two kneeling camels, sometimes with the inscription Ἁγίου Μηνᾶ, the latter show St. Symeon Stylite on his column, in many iconographic variants but always featuring a long ladder leaning to the column and two angels around the saint's head. Only rarely the name Συμεώνης appears on the token. Several types of these small *eulogia* tokens are known, picturing different saints or scenes from the gospels. Of the former, some can be traced to shrines of famous saints in Syria or Asia Minor, while the latter surely originated in the holy places of Palestine (Nazareth for the Annunciation, Bethlehem for the Adoration of the Magi, the Jordan for the Baptism of Jesus by St. John the Baptist, and so on), but by the sixth century they were copied and produced in many places. This is indicated by some tokens uncovered in a shop at Beth Shean that was destroyed by fire in the mid-sixth century; the petrographic analysis showed that the clay of these objects came from the Jezreel Valley, not far from Beth Shean.[311] These types of small tokens usually bear no inscription, except for one type, which pictures an unclear tubular object flanked by the inscription Σολο|μών. It was convincingly suggested that the object represented the root of the mandragora plant, by which King Solomon gained his powers over demons: if so, the token may originally have been produced at Bethlehem, where Christian pilgrims visited the tombs of David and Solomon

---

[310] There is a large bibliography on the subject of *eulogiae*, and most studies treat the different types together. Here is a choice of the most relevant to our region and period: Christern 1983; Vikan 1982 (2010); 1998; 2003; Sodini 1989; 2011; Blanc et al. 2011; Foskolou 2012. For illustrated examples, see Israeli and Mevorah 2000: 148-149, 153, 157, 211-212.

[311] Tsafrir 2006. For more similar tokens found in Beth Shean, see Rahmani 1993; 1999.

in St. David's Church, and the *eulogia* might have be acquired not so much as a religious memento as for protection against the Evil One and for healing diseases believed to be caused by demonic possession, like epilepsy or mental illness.[312] In fact, both the tokens and the larger clay cakes – another type of *eulogia* we shall presently describe – were ideally identified with the salvific power of the holy places they represented and were sometimes used as a cure for sickness by administering a small quantity of the ground clay of the *eulogia* to the sick person in a drink.

The larger *eulogiae* are clay disks 8-10 cm in diameter, not fired but only dried, and therefore very brittle, so that very few survived. One, picturing the Annunciation, is part of the collection of the Monza cathedral and probably originated from Nazareth; another, kept in the museum of St. Columbanus Abbey in Bobbio, shows a soldier pursuing a woman with a baby in her arms, while an angel above points to a rock in front of her. An inscription running around the edge of the disk reads Εὐλογία Κ(υρίο)υ ἀπὸ τῆς καταφυγῆς τῆς ἁγ(ίας) Ἐλισαβέθ, 'Blessing of the Lord from the Refuge of St. Elizabeth'.[313] This points to the origin of the *eulogia* at 'En Karem near Jerusalem, where a church, supposedly the house of Zechariah and Elizabeth, John the Baptist's parents, commemorated the Visitation of the Virgin and the miraculous escape of the baby John and his mother from Herod's soldiers (Fig. 43).[314]

A third type of *eulogia* is the ampulla, a tiny flask that could be filled with holy water or oil from a lamp burning in a shrine, or with oil that had been in contact with a relic. Ampullae made of lead or tin, sometimes silvered, representing the holy places of Jerusalem and Bethlehem, are very well known, but clay ampullas (the latter rarely inscribed) are also found. Like other types of *eulogiae*, ampullae reflect the veneration of holy places from Egypt

---

[312] On the Solomon tokens, see especially Rahmani 1999. One of these tokens was discovered in the burnt shop in Beth Shean (Tsafrir 2006: 733, no. 3) but their provenance is mostly unknown, as they come from the antiquities market: see for instance *SEG* XLIX, no. 2091; LXII, no. 1924. These tokens are also discussed by Vikan 1982 (2010), Foskolou 2012 and others within the general discussion of *eulogiae*.

[313] Grabar 1958: 31, pl. XXXI (Annunciation); 44, pl. LVI (flight of St. Elizabeth).

[314] Luke 1: 39-56; Matthew 2: 16. The legend of Elizabeth's flight into a mountain that miraculously opened to receive her and her baby has a popular origin and is not attested in the Scripture. The church of the House of Zechariah can probably be identified with the ruins of a Byzantine chapel under the medieval church of St. John the Baptist in 'En Karem: see *CIIP* I, 2, nos. 849-853. A fragment of an identical *eulogia*, though not made in the same mould, was discovered in excavations in Jerusalem, in a sixth-seventh centuries context: see *SEG* XLIX, no. 2065; *CIIP* I, 2, App. 39*.

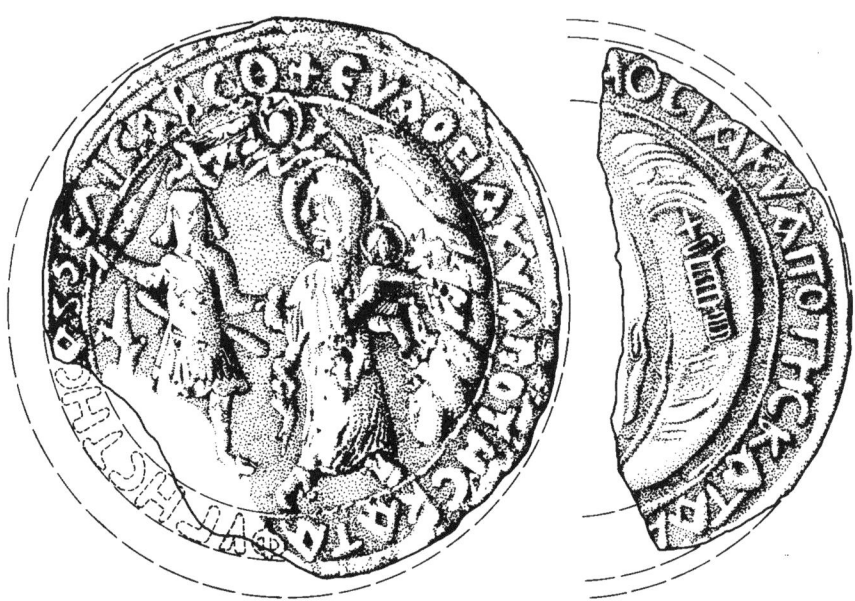

Fig. 43 – Eulogia of the Refuge of Saint Elizabeth (*SEG* XLIX, no. 2065. Drawing Sh. Gibson. Reproduced with the permission of the Institute of Archaeology, The Hebrew University of Jerusalem)

through the Holy Land, Syria and Asia Minor, and after an initial period when each type was manufactured at a particular shrine, they were probably produced and sold in other places.[315] Ampullae depicting the edicule enclosing the tomb in the Anastasis or Christ on the cross flanked by the two robbers, often accompanied by an inscription mentioning the oil of the Cross, were supposed to contain some drops of oil that had been in contact with the wood of the Cross, and therefore they were a memento of the Church of the Holy Sepulchre, but since fragments of this wood were distributed rather liberally, the ampullae with this holy oil might have been produced anywhere, even without casting doubt on the honesty of the producers. Other ampullae with different scenes or inscriptions can be connected to specific churches: e.g., an ampulla featuring the incredulity of St. Thomas and bearing a quotation from John 20: 28 probably refers to the Holy Zion (Hagia Sion), where

---

[315] For the various types of ampullae in clay or metal, with or without inscriptions, see Leclercq 1907; Grabar 1958; Lambert and Pedemonte Demeglio 1994; Israeli and Mevorah 2000: 148-149, 200-203; Anderson 2004. Examples of ampullae of St. Menas with the inscription ✢ Εὐλ(ογία) τοῦ ἁγίου Μηνᾶ: *SEG* XXVI, nos. 1787-1798, 1811; XLIII, no. 1202; XLIV, no. 1444bis; LVI, no. 2018; LX, no. 1818; LXI, nos. 1509, 1653.

the Upper Room was located, where Jesus visited the apostles after the resurrection; scenes of the Ascension of Mary, of the Nativity or the Annunciation respectively to the church of the Tomb of Mary in Jerusalem, of the Nativity at Bethlehem and of the Annunciation in Nazareth.[316]

All the above-described types of *eulogiae* were manufactured in moulds. A few such moulds are known, some from the antiquities market, so that their provenance can only be guessed from their inscription or the scene they depict, but one at least was discovered in a dig in the Mamilla quarter, pointing to Jerusalem as its origin. It is a fragment of a two-faced limestone mould: Face A bears a decoration that cannot be interpreted and the inscription δέχομε (phonetic spelling for δέχομαι), both shallowly incised with a fine pointed instrument; Face B bear the remains of an animal figure (donkey?) and of the same word, in the same shallow script. The understanding of this artefact is assisted by another two-faced stone mould reportedly found near Jerusalem and now preserved at the University of Toronto Art Centre. This shows on one face the visit of the angels to Abraham, on the other an enthroned woman and the inscription Δέχομε χαίρων τὴν Οὐρανίαν, 'I hail rejoicing the Heavenly One', a reference to the Virgin's assumption to heaven rather than to Aphrodite Urania, as some scholars interpreted the figure.[317] The scene of Abraham clearly points to the Oak of Mamre or to nearby Hebron, where the tomb of the patriarch was venerated, while the enthroned figure may be associated with a feast of Mary at her tomb in the Kedron Valley, or at some other Marian sanctuary. In other words, the mould served for the production of different *eulogiae* to be sold in different places and/or occasions. Most likely this type was produced by itinerant artisans who practiced their craft with a number of different and two-faced moulds, moving from one holy place to another according to a calendar of local festivals. This object was erroneously described as a bread stamp, but like the Mamilla fragment, the shallow incision cannot possibly have left an impression on dough – or on clay. The moulds probably were used to cast *eulogiae* in cheap, soft metal like lead or tin, which melt at low temperatures, so that

---

[316] For a terracotta ampulla depicting the crucifixion, inscribed ☩ Ἔλαιον ξύλο[υ ζωῆς τῶν ἁ]γίων Χ(ριστο)ῦ τόπων, see *SEG* XLIX, no. 2384; for a list of inscriptions on ampullae from churches in Jerusalem, *CIIP* I, 2, App. 40*-42*.

[317] See *SEG* LX, no. 1875 for the Toronto mould, and *CIIP* I, 2, no. 1080 and the bibliography there for a discussion of both the Mamilla fragment and the Toronto mould. The interpretation of Urania as Aphrodite led scholars to view this artefact as evidence of the persistence of pagan and Christian (or Jewish) religious practices at the Oak of Mamra, attested by Eusebius, *Life of Constantine* III, 51-53. But the pagan practices had certainly disappeared - or at least gone underground - by the time the *eulogia* mould was made.

itinerant craftsmen could easily carry the minimal equipment required for the job. A mould of unknown provenance kept in a private collection in Munich was used to make two kinds of *eulogiae*: tokens and lead or tin ampullae. It is a small square steatite mould with an image of St. Sergius encircled by an inscription in mirror script on the front and four hollows to cast tokens on the back: two with the same motif as the front, one with Mary enthroned holding the infant Jesus, and the fourth with the adoration of the Magi.[318]

Another stone mould reportedly found in Jerusalem also had a double usage, this time for making ampullae. It has hollows on two opposite faces, each with a different biblical scene framed by two concentric circles. One side depicts the binding of Isaac, with the inscription Εὐλογία τοῦ Ἀβραάμ, "Blessing of Abraham', running within the frame formed by the two circles. The other shows Daniel in the lions' den, with the inscriptions Εὐλογία τοῦ Δανιήλου, 'Blessing of Daniel' running within the frame and Ὁ ἅγιος Δανιήλ, 'Saint Daniel' under it (Figs. 44-45).[319] In the lower part of the mould is a funnel-shaped indentation, through which melted metal could be poured into the mould. Each of the hollows, coupled with an aniconic mould, of which examples are known, served to cast a metal ampulla that would be filled with holy water or oil and sold to pilgrims where and when the memory of Abraham or of Daniel was celebrated.

Besides ampullas and tokens, small and large, inscribed lamps – also made in moulds – can represent a fourth type of *eulogia*. Lamps bearing Christian inscriptions, usually in Greek, but since the seventh century also in Arabic, were produced in several places, but the main area of production was in Jerusalem and in central Transjordan. They were certainly intended to serve their purpose as means of lighting, and as such they bore augural inscriptions, e.g. Φῶς Χ(ριστο)ῦ φένι (φαίνει) πᾶσιν (The light of Christ shines for all), often with the addition Καλὴ (ἑσπέρα) (Good evening), Κύριος φωτισμός μου (The Lord is my light; Ps 26: 1) or Λυχνάρια καλά (Beautiful little lamps); but not a few bear inscriptions of the *eulogia* type, e.g. Εὐλογία τῆς Θεοτόκου μεθ' ἡμῶν (Blessing of the Mother of God upon us' or Τοῦ ἁγίου Ἠλία (‹Blessing› of Saint Elijah), indicating

---

[318] SEG LXI, no. 1414: ✢ Εὐλογία Κ(υρίου) τοῦ ἁγίου Σεργίου. The main centre of the cult of St. Sergius was Resafa-Sergiupolis in northern Syria, but this mould did not necessarily originate there. The martyr was much venerated also in Palaestina and Arabia and at least sixteen churches were dedicated to him, not counting monasteries and churches dedicated to him together with his companion St. Bacchus or other martyrs: see Di Segni and Tsafrir 2015: 406-407, 420.

[319] Piccirillo 1994a; *CIIP* I, 2, no. 1079.

Chapter V: Greek inscriptions in the Holy Land in Late Antiquity   153

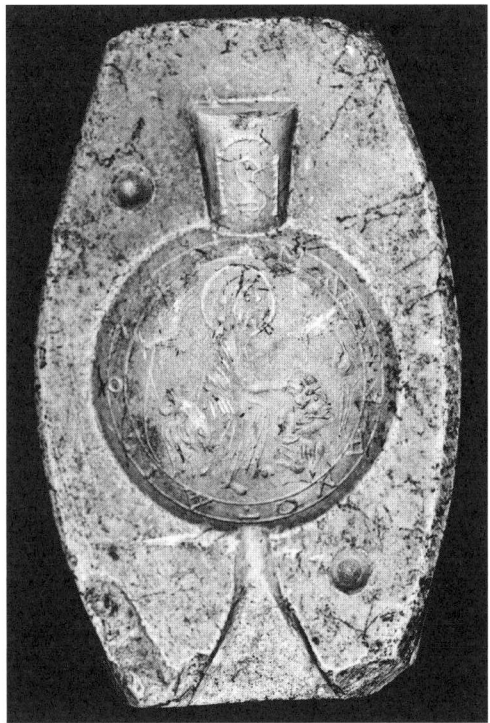

Fig. 44 – Mould for ampullae: Face A (Piccirillo 1994a. Photo M. Piccirillo, SBF Photographic Archive)

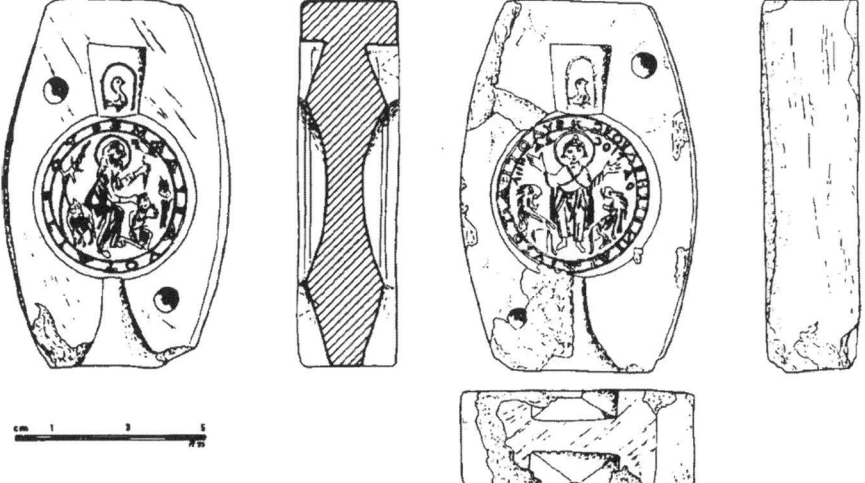

Fig. 45 – Mould for ampullae (drawing E. Alliata, SBF Photographic Archive)

their connection to a church dedicated to Mary Theotokos or to the prophet Elijah.³²⁰ Jewish and Samaritan lamps with Greek or Samaritan inscriptions are also known, albeit rare.³²¹ Churches were lightened with hanging lamps of glass or bronze, as well as with *polykandela*, large plates of metal or terracotta suspended by chains and supporting a number of oil lamps. Some *polykandela* were inscribed with religious formulas and the name of the donor.³²²

Another type of artefact found in churches is the reliquary, a small limestone or marble casket covered with a lid with a hole on top to pour in oil that would be hallowed by contact with the relic within; the oil could then be poured out (in some reliquaries through a second opening on the side of the casket) and used to anoint the sick or to fill ampullae for the pilgrims. The deposition of relics under the altar was an essential part of the consecration of churches, and reliquaries are sometimes discovered *in situ*, or among the ruins of an ancient church where they had been kept in the open, in side rooms or chapels, for the day-by-day use of the hallowed oil. Most reliquaries are not inscribed but several are known which bear inscriptions, usually a reference to the saint or holy place whose relic was preserved in the casket, or a prayer for the donor or the maker of the artefact; some only bear crosses with letters between the arms.³²³ A fragment of limestone box inscribed

---

³²⁰ For examples, see *SEG* VIII, nos. 215-218; XXXIX, no. 1617; XL, nos. 1434-1440; XLII, nos. 1385-1406; XLIV, nos. 1341-1348, 1403; XLVI, no. 1809; XLVIII, no. 1908; LVII, no. 1861; LX, no. 1706; *CIIP* I, 2, App. 54*. For a detailed study, see Loffreda 1989, 1990, 1992, 1994, 1998. *Eulogia* lamps of origin other than Palestine are also known: e.g. *SEG* XLVII, no. 2127. The type with the Theotokos inscription often bears also the signature of the potter: ἐπίγραμ(μ)α Ἰωάννου. They may be linked to the Nea or to the Tomb of the Virgin in the Kedron Valley. The *eulogia* lamps of St. Elias surely refer to a sanctuary dedicated to the prophet Elijah, one of many in Palaestina and Arabia. It has been suggested that this was located at the site of the monastery of Mar Elias between Bethlehem and Jerusalem (Magness 1996: 42*; *SEG* XLVI: no. 1809), but the tradition of the prophet there seems to be later. Unlike the Theotokos lamps, these are rather rare and it is conceivable that they originated in Transjordan, in the church dedicated to the prophet in Madaba (Michel 2001: 319-323, no. 121).

³²¹ For Samaritan examples, see Naveh 1996: 47-50; Barag 2009: 304-311 (Samaritan script); *CIIP* II, no. 2113 (Greek); for Jewish lamps, see Frankel et al. 2001: 11, no. 18 (bronze lamp holder with Hebrew inscription). A pottery lamp with eight holes, decorated with Jewish symbols and the Greek inscription 'Lord, help', was seen in the Deutsch collection.

³²² Examples: *CIIP* I, 2, nos. 1081-1082; *SEG* XLVI, no. 2299 (7); LI, no. 1965; LV, no. 1849.

³²³ For illustrated examples, see Israeli and Mevorah 2000: 76-77. For inscriptions on reliquaries, most from museums or from the antiquities market and thus of unknown origin, see for instance *SEG* XXXVII, no. 1330; XLIII, no. 1024; LIX, no. 1598; LXI, no. 1413; LXII, nos. 1595, 1628-1631, 1633. Silver reliquaries are also known, but none, to my knowledge, was found in our region.

ΗΛΗΟΝΑ was recovered in the excavation of a Byzantine church at Kh. el-Messani (Ḥorvat Miẓna, now in the Ramot neighbourhood of Jerusalem). Eleona is the name of the church built by Constantine over the cave where Jesus taught his disciples, and where the Ascension was also commemorated, before the erection of the Ascension Church. The reliquary may have contained earth or a stone from the cave.[324] The inscription ✝ Ὑπὲρ σωτ(ηρίας) Ἠλία διακ(όνου) υἱοῦ Ἰάννου Σάβα κώμ(ης) Τιρίας ✝ (For the salvation of Elias the deacon, son of Iannes ‹Ioannes› Sabas, from the village of Tiria) was incised on the lid of a marble reliquary found at el-Bassa (Bezeth) in northwestern Galilee.[325] A different type of reliquary, exhibited at the Bible Lands Museum in Jerusalem, is a large block (66 × 71 cm, 55 cm high) with a basin-like hollow on top, with exit for overflow – a type common in Syria, though the material is the *mizzi ahmar*, the red limestone quarried in the Jerusalem region. The block bears two long inscriptions, one on the front (A), the other on the right side (B):

A ✝ Θήκη τοῦ ἁγίου Σεργί[ου]· | ὑπὲρ σωτηρίας Ἀνύσωνος | τοῦ φιλοχρίστου τοῦ ποι⟨ή⟩σαντος

'Repository (of the relics) of St. Sergius; for the salvation of the Christloving Anyson who commissioned this'.

B [?Μνήσθητι Κ(ύρι)ε Μαρί]ας κ(αὶ) Δανιὴλ | [κ(αὶ) -- κ(αὶ) Ἀθα]νασίας κ(αὶ) Σεργίου | κ(αὶ) Πέτρου τοῦ μαρμαραρίου κ(αὶ) Ἀναί[- - -]

'[Remember, o Lord, Mari]a and Daniel [and - - - and Atha]nasia and Sergius and Petrus the marble-worker and Ana[- - -]'.[326]

Metal objects

Until now we have spoken of *instrumenta* made of clay or stone, and only mentioned the existence of similar objects made of metal. Metal objects are not often preserved, for they could be melted and reused.[327] Nevertheless, a great variety of metal artefacts reached us from Late Antiquity, many of them bearing inscriptions made with diverse techniques: some were engraved or punched, some cast, others stamped. The majority of these inscriptions indicate that the object they marked was private property: for instance, rings and other trinkets, including amulets, a type of

---

[324] *CIIP* I, 2, no. 857. For other fragments probably of reliquaries found in the Jerusalem area, see *CIIP* I, 2, nos. 852, 958, 972.
[325] *SEG* XLVI, no. 1803; LV, no. 1696. The village of Tiria is not known from any other source.
[326] Goodnick-Westenholz 2007: 132-133, no. 75 (ph.); *SEG* LVII, no. 1860.
[327] See above, n. 284.

object made or acquired for the personal use of a customer, who in this period might have been of any religion. Rings sometimes bear only the name of the owner but more often were inscribed with an augural or protective formula that made them into proper amulets.[328] Bracelets and pendants featured magic figures, like the Rider spearing a fallen enemy, or animals with a magic significance, accompanied by sacred names, acclamations or invocation to the One God, or scriptural quotations. Copper, bronze and lead were mostly used, but the same objects are also found in silver or gold.[329] Cross-shaped pendants in cheap metal or in silver or gold, inscribed ΦΩΣ ΖΩΗ across the arms, are common. Gold is used for funerary wreaths bearing the formula Θάρσι - - οὐδὶς ἀθάνατος accompanied by a personal name, not that of the deceased but a symbolic one, the most common being Εὐγηνή ('highborn'): 'Courage, Eugene, nobody is immortal'.[330] Lead is the favourite metal for curse tablets, but bronze, silver and gold charm lamellae are also found.[331] Amulets of semiprecious stones with various magic inscriptions are well known.

A special mention should be made of *bullae*, a type of artefact that, though already used in earlier periods, is a much more common find in Late Antiquity, if for no other reason, because of the durable medium of Byzantine *bullae*. These are lead impressions made with a seal engraved with the name and title of its owner, in full or in monogrammed form. In this period a great many persons, from the highest magistrates to notaries and clerks, as well as

---

[328] See for instance *CIIP* I, 2, no. 1086 (copper ring with name of owner); *CIIP* II, no. 1125 (bronze ring, inscribed 'Health for Babosa'); nos. 1686-1687 (copper and bronze rings inscribed 'Lord, help' followed by name of owner). Rings inscribed σφραγίς (θεοῦ), 'Seal (of God)', e.g. *CIIP* II, no. 1693, refer to Solomon's seal that averted evil and are protective devices, as are rings with Samaritan script, sometimes quotations from the Samaritan Pentateuch, sometimes gibberish. These 'Samaritan rings', not necessarily worn by Samaritans but valued for their magic power by followers of other religions, functioned also as amulets.

[329] See for instance *CIIP* I, 2, no. 1085 (bronze pendant inscribed on front 'Holy Mary mother of Jesus, help', on the back a monogrammed name, perhaps Akrisios); *CIIP* II, no. 1682 (lead pendant, inscribed 'One God, help Chairomene'); *CIIP* I, 2, no. 764 (bronze bracelet with two Greek inscriptions: [a] 'One God, save (and) protect your servant Severina'; [b] 'One God who conquers evil'); *CIIP* II, no. 1685 (bronze bracelet with Greek [a] and Samaritan [b] inscriptions: [a] 'One God who conquers evil'; [b] 'There is none like the God of Jeshurun'). The rider identified as Solomon, and later as St. Sisinnius, the formula Εἷς θεὸς ὁ νικῶν τὰ κακά (One God who conquers evil) and a quote or paraphrasis of Ps. 90 (91): 1 (He who dwells in the shelter of the Most High) are common both in pendants and in bracelets.

[330] Nicomachus and Petrus are also found. See *CIIP* II, no. 2094; *CIIP* IV, 1, no. 3104; *CIIP* IV, 2, nos. 3488, 3489 -3494.

[331] See for instance *CIIP* I, 2, no. 1015; *CIIP* II, no. 1679-1680; *CIIP* IV, 1, no. 3103.

religious foundations, had their own seals and attached the *bullae* as tags to documents, letters or packages they sent out. In many cases the monograms are so complex as to be indecipherable.[332]

Some types of metal objects were intended for public usage, though they mostly originated from private offerings to cult buildings, e.g. processional and applique crosses, chandeliers to lighten churches and synagogues, censers, door knockers and similar appliances.[333]

Weights typically belong to the public domain. In the Hellenistic and Roman periods weights were made of lead and sometimes of stone, while in Late Antiquity lead weights were less common. Most weights were made of bronze, sometimes inlaid in silver, decorated with crosses or christograms and bearing inscriptions indicating their mass in νομίσματα (*solidi*, 4.53 g or 1/6 of ounce; abbreviated N with a dot-like omicron on top) or οὐγκίαι (*unciae*, 27.2 g or 1/12 of the Roman pound of ca. 327 g, abbreviated Γ flanked by a dot-like omicron); some weights bore short Christian formulas

---

[332] For some examples of *bullae* found in Jerusalem, Caesarea and Ascalon, see *CIIP* I, 2, nos. 1066-1075; *CIIP* II, nos. 1753-1783; *CIIP* III, nos. 2367-2377. Seals for impressing *bullae* are also known: e.g. *CIIP* I, 2, no. 768 (jasper intaglio gemstone featuring a man driving a quadriga and retrograde inscription Tele(machos), perhaps the seal of a charioteer); *CIIP* II, no. 1724 (carnelian seal of a woman, with Middle Persian inscription). On this special subject, see Laurent 1963-1981; Zacos and Veglery 1972 (re-edited 1984). A collection of 415 monogrammed names on seals is found in Martindale 1992: 1556-1573.

[333] See for instance *CIIP* I, 2, nos. 1084, App. 43* (processional crosses inscribed 'Light. Life' on the cross arms, and 'Saint Mary and Martha, accept the offering of those whose names the Lord knows', and 'Of St. Thomas in Phordision', respectively, on the circular frame); *CIIP* IV, 1, nos. 2838 (bronze candelabra with Aramaic inscription commemorating the offering of a Jewish scribe), 3148 (bronze lamp hanger inscribed 'Of St. Pamphilus'), 3213 (bronze *polykandelon* from Kh. Mird, the site of the Sabaite monastery of Castellion). The *polykandelon* is decorated with a cross and three inscriptions: in the cross arms 'Light. Life', in the circular frame of the cross 'Lord, preserve those ministering together with the beasts of burden of the Cave of Abba Sabas' and on the cross-shaped lower part of the lamp 'For the salvation and the succour of Zacharias the hegumen of the S(pelaion) and Sisinius the deacon'. Despite having been found at Castellion, a monastery active for centuries after the Islamic conquest, the *polykandelon* certainly originated from the Monastery of the Cave (*Spelaion*), founded by Saint Sabas ca. 508 and abandoned much earlier than its confrère. For other bronze objects bearing Greek inscriptions, see *CIIP* IV, 2, no. 3977 (censer inscribed 'For the remembrance and repose of Ephymia and Prosdocia and of those whose names the Lord knows'); *CIIP* II, no. 2115 (plaque with a dedication of the synagogue of Sycamina); *CIIP* I, 2, no. 1087 (door knocker inscribed 'Offering of Antonius'); *SEG* XLIV, no. 1364 (door knocker inscribed 'Offering of - - Marcellina (daughter) of Felefelas for the welfare of her son Barachios; it was written in November 636, indiction 6', corresponding to November 572 by a Pompeian era of 64 BCE – not 63 BCE as reported in *SEG* – probably the era of Scythopolis). The knocker may come from a Jewish or Samaritan synagogue.

(Fig. 23). A few small samples from the territory of Caesarea bear the name of the governor in office at the time the weight was cast, and the mass in γράμματα (scruples, 1.13 g, 1/24 of ounce). Rarely a city official called *ephoros* or *episkopos* (inspector of the markets) is mentioned, while the earlier *agoranomos* completely disappears.[334] Glass weights are also found: they belong to an imperial type, which was cast in a mould and bore the name of the *praefectus Urbis* of the new Rome, Constantinople, or imperial portraits, or the mark of their value. One, discovered at Beth Shean, is inscribed Ἐπὶ Συμεώνου ἐπάρχου Ῥώμης; a twin comes from Salona in Dalmatia.[335] This type of glass weight became very popular under Muslim rule, when they often bore Arab inscriptions with the name of the reigning caliph.[336]

---

[334] For the officials superseding the *agoranomos* in Late Antiquity, see Foster 1970. Examples of late antique weights: *CIIP* II, nos. 1730-1731, 1742-1748, 2153; *CIIP* III, nos. 2261, 2271-2272, 2363-2366, 2619, 2645-2648; *CIIP* IV, 1, no. 2691. For Hellenistic and Roman weights, including stone moulds for casting lead weights, see *CIIP* I, 1, nos. 658-692; *CIIP* II, nos. 1725-1729, 1732; 1733-1740, 1749-1750; *CIIP* III, nos. 2257-2259, 2298-2300, 2358-2362, 2438, 2580-2617, 2620-2643; *CIIP* IV, 1, nos. 2783-2785, 3184, 3279; *CIIP* IV, 2, nos. 3426, 3496, 3671-3686, 3833.

[335] *SEG* VIII, no. 51; XLV, no. 708. A similar imperial weight, but made of bronze, of unknown origin in Syria, is inscribed N° IH (18 *solidi*) and ✝ Ἐπὶ Ζιμάρχου τοῦ ἐνδοξοτά(του) ἐπάρχου Ῥώμης. Zimarchos was prefect of Constantinople in 562 and 565. *SEG* quotes two more bronze weights of the same man, of different values. A glass weight for weighing gold coins was discovered in a fortress on the Danube (*SEG* XXXI, no. 686); four glass weights with imperial portraits, a personal name (that of the official in charge?) and their value are in a Munich museum (*SEG* LV, no. 1915).

[336] Guri-Rimon and Shchori 2005: 25*, 29*, 38-42, figs. 47-54.

CHAPTER VI: TOOLS FOR THE STUDY OF LATE ANTIQUE EPIGRAPHY IN THE PROVINCES OF PALAESTINA AND ARABIA

Many of the available tools for the study of late antique inscriptions in the region have been cited in the pages above. Here we shall sum up in brief the most useful categories.

Corpora (collections of inscriptions from a specific area)

For our region, the old *Corpus Inscriptionum Latinarum* (*CIL*) and *Corpus Inscriptionum Graecarum* (*CIG*) are quite out of date and are being superseded by new collections. For Israel, the *Corpus Inscriptionum Iudaeae/Palaestinae* counts at the moment four volumes: vol. I, divided into two parts, *CIIP* I, 1 (2010) for Jerusalem in the Hellenistic and Early Roman periods and *CIIP* I, 2 (2012) with Jerusalem/Aelia Capitolina in the Roman Imperial and Byzantine-Early Arab periods;[1] *CIIP* II (2011) for Caesarea and the middle coast; *CIIP* III (2014) for the southern coast and *CIIP* IV, 1-2 for Judaea and Idumaea. For Caesarea, see also Lehmann and Holum 2000, still useful for its discussions and a wealth of photographs. More volumes of *CIIP* are expected in the near future. Other corpora deal with the epigraphic yield of a single centre or a limited area. Some of them are small collections or do not aim to completeness and are describes as *corpuscula* (small corpora). Such exist for the Golan (Schumacher 1886, cf. Gildemeister 1888; Gregg and Urman 1996) and for the Negev (Alt 1921; Negev 1981; Figueras 1985, 1996); among those dedicated to single sites are the corpora or *corpuscula* covering Hammath Gader (Di Segni 1997b), Tiberias (Di Segni 1988, updated 1998b), Beth She'arim (Schwabe and Lifshitz 1974; Avigad 1976), Ascalon (Di Segni 1990d, now superseded by *CIIP* III), Gaza (Glucker 1987: 115-161, also superseded by *CIIP* III), Elusa (Kirk and Gignoux 1996), Nessana (Kirk and Welles 1962), Rehovot-in-the-Negev (the Northern Church: Tsafrir 1988: 154-186). A corpus of the inscriptions of Beth Shean-Scythopolis is in preparation (Di Segni et al. forthcoming). Gatier 1999 collected the

---

[1] *CIIP* I supersedes the old corpus compiled by Thomsen 1921, 1941.

Latin and Greek inscriptions from Samra and Rihab in northern Jordan, and Desreumaux 1999 the CPA inscription from Samra. Welles 1938 published the inscription of Gerasa, now to be updated with new finds, for which see *SEG*. Wineland (2001: 69-78) published a *corpusculum* of the inscription of Abila, and Smith (1973: 64, 88-191; 1989: 131-141) one of those of Pella. The epigraphic yield from Mount Nebo, included in *IGLJ* II: 83-113, nos. 71-111, was updated by Di Segni 1998a. Canova 1954 collected the Greek inscriptions from Moab; Piccirillo 1994b those of the ecclesiastical complex of St. Stephen at Umm er-Rasas; Meimaris and Kritikakou-Nikolaropoulou (2005, 2008, 2016) those from the cemeteries in Ghor eṣ-Ṣafi and its vicinity (this rich corpus is still being enriched with new finds, for which see *SEG*); a list of the Aramaic inscriptions from Ghor eṣ-Ṣafi, with chronological notes and earlier bibliography, is offered by Misgav (2006).

Corpora for southern Syria and Jordan appear in the series *Inscriptions grecques et latines de la Syrie* (*IGLS*) and the sub-series *Inscriptions de la Jordanie* (*IGLJ*). For the Hauran, several volumes prepared by Maurice Sartre and Anne Sartre-Fauriat have been published, all in Beirut except for *IGLS* XIII, 1:

XIII, 1 (*Bostra. Nos. 9001 à 9472*, Paris 1982)

XIII, 2 (*Bostra (supplément) et la plaine de la Nuqrah*, 2011)

XIV, 1-2 (*La Batanée et le Jawlā Oriental*, 2016)

XV, 1-2 (*Le plateau du Trachon et ses bordures*, 2014)

XVI, 1 (*L'Auranitide. Qanawāt et la bordure nord-ouest du Jebel al-'Arab*, 2020)

XVI, 2 (*L'Auranitide. Suweidā' et la bordure ouest du Jebel al-'Arab*, 2020)

Volume XVI, 3 (*L'Auranitide. Maximianopolis, la Saccée et le nord du Jebel al-'Arab*) has just appeared (2022). Volumes XVI, 4-5, with the southeastern Auranitis (Hauran) are forthcoming, but for the moment we have to depend on the old collections (Waddington 1870; Ewing 1895; Dussaud and Macler 1901, 1903; Dunand 1932, 1933, 1939, 1950).

For the region properly forming the Holy Land, the relevant volumes published until now are *IGLS* XI (Aliquot 2008) for Mount Hermon and Banyas (Caesarea Philippi); *IGLJ* II, IV and V, 1 (Gatier 1986, Sartre 1993b, Bader 2009) for central, southern and north-eastern Jordan.

Some corpora are dedicated to a particular category of inscriptions. The Jewish inscriptions from Asia and Africa, including a vast majority of inscriptions from Palestine, were collected by Frey in the second volume of his *Corpus Inscriptionum Judaicarum* (*CIJ* II, 1952); the first volume (*CIJ* I, 1936) was dedicated to Europe. This work is now largely superseded by *In-*

scriptiones Judaicae Orientis (*IJO*) I-III, covering Eastern Europe, Asia Minor, Syria and Cyprus, *Jewish inscriptions of Graeco-Roman Egypt* (*JIGRE*) for Egypt and Cyrenaica, and *Jewish inscriptions of Western Europe* (*JIWE*), 1-2, for Italy, Spain, Gaul and the city of Rome. Inscriptions from ancient synagogues in the Land of Israel were collected by Naveh 1978 (Aramaic and Hebrew) and Roth-Gerson 1987 (Greek inscriptions). Dated inscriptions from Palestine and Arabia were collected by Meimaris 1992; for a revised edition of the dated inscriptions from Israel, see Di Segni 1997a. Michel (2001) presents many inscriptions from churches in Jordan (Greek texts and translations, CPA translations only), less than correct as to critical reading but very well documented as to the archaeological context. On the contrary, the collection of epigrams in inscriptions by Merkelbach and Stauber, of which vol. 4 (2002) deals with Palestine and Arabia, is accurate in reading but pays insufficient attention to the archaeological context. Some of the above-mentioned works cover the long period in which Greek, Latin and Aramaic were the vehicular languages in the region, from the Hellenistic to the Early Islamic period; others – particularly those dedicated to Christian inscriptions – focus on Late Antiquity. Works dedicated by definition to subjects exclusively pertaining to earlier periods, e.g. stamped jar handles, ossuaries, milestones, or Hellenistic cities like Marisa, are outside the sphere of our present interest and are therefore omitted from this list.[2]

There are of course a large number of corpora, some in many volumes, like *Inscriptiones Graecae* (*IG*), dedicated to different regions of the Greek-speaking world, but they are not directly relevant to our subject: a full list will be found in the bibliography of the website of The Packard Humanities Institute of Cornell University (see below). We shall only mention Lefebvre 1907, a collection of Christian inscriptions in Egypt, old but still useful.

Updates and research

To keep abreast of new epigraphic discoveries and publications, and for search of inscriptions in past publications by regions, place of discovery, personal names, religious terms, military units and other topics, the main tools are the periodicals *Année épigraphique* (*AE*, Paris, since 1888), also accessible on line (free access in JSTOR), for Latin inscriptions and in late years also for Greek inscriptions reflecting on the Roman world; *Supplementum Epigraphicum Graecum* (*SEG*, Leiden, since 1923), now available

---

[2] Information on these subjects can be obtained from the *Guide de l'épigraphiste* (Paris 1986; 2nd edition 1989) and its Supplements, which can be found on line.

also in the Brill website, by subscription, for Greek inscriptions. Both journals give full texts and editorial comments if needed; in late years, *AE* also provides French translations. Both have detailed indices: *AE* has a compact index for the years 1888-1960, then yearly indices; *SEG* has compact indices for volumes XXVI-XXXV (1976-1985) and XXXVI-XLV (1986-1995), then yearly indices. An annual survey of newly published inscriptions, both Latin and Greek, by region, appears in the section 'Bulletin épigraphique' (BE) of the *Revue des études grecques* (free access in Persée and JSTOR). This bulletin suggests critical comments if needed but provides no texts. For many years – from the Thirties to the mid-Eighties of the last century – it was edited by Jeanne and Louis Robert; at present, the sections dedicated to Syria, Phoenice, Palestine and Arabia are treated by D. Feissel and P.-L. Gatier. Feissel's contributions between 1987 and 2004 were collected in a volume, Feissel 2006a. The chapters dealing with Syria, Phoenice, Palestine and Arabia in BE 2005-2016 were collected in a single publication within *Byzantinische Bibliographie Online*, accessible by subscription (Feissel and Gatier 2005-2016). Most academic institutions have subscriptions to this and other non-free websites.

Websites

Search of inscriptions by region and site, and search of words, combination of words or parts of words can be carried out by using epigraphic databases. Most easily accessible are the Epigraphik-Datenbank Clauss / Slaby (EDCS: https://db.edcs.eu/epigr/epi_ergebnis.php) for Latin inscriptions, the Epigraphic Database Heidelberg (EDH: https://edh-www.adw.uni-heidelberg.de/inschrift/suche) for Latin and Greek; the above-mentioned SEG database, now in the new Brill Scholarly Editions platform (https://scholarlyeditions.brill.com/sego/) and the Searchable Greek Inscription of the Packard Humanities Institute (PHI Greek Inscriptions: https://epigraphy.packhum.org), for Greek.

Special tools

For the decipherment of abbreviations in Greek inscriptions, see Avi-Yonah 1940 (republished by Oikonomides 1974 with useful additions, especially sigla and ligated abbreviations from papyri.[3] The abbreviations used in

---

[3] This work contains also graphic tables of examples from papyri and of ligated abbreviations from early printed Greek books.

Latin inscriptions can be found listed in any manual of Latin epigraphy, but are not relevant here, for hardly any appear in the few Latin inscriptions from Late Antiquity discovered in our region.

The indices of *SEG* and *AE* and the above-mentioned databases are invaluable for a search of all personal names and fragments of names that appear in inscriptions. For finding parallels to personal names, several collections are available for both Greek/Latin and Semitic names. *The Lexicon of Greek Personal Names* (*LGPN*), edited by P.M. Fraser and A. Matthews at Oxford since 1987 and based on all written sources from the eighth century BCE to the Late Roman Empire, counts now six volumes divided into several tomes, covering Greece and the islands, Asia Minor, Magna Graecia and Cyrenaica. *LGPN* is accessible on line.[4] Volume VI, dedicated to the Near and Middle East, is forthcoming, and volumes on Egypt are in preparation. Meanwhile, *Trismegistos Names* (*TM Nam*, https://www.trismegistos.org) is available for Egypt; the names it collects come from papyri, literary sources, Latin inscription and in less measure, from Greek epigraphy. Old dictionaries of personal names may still be useful, like Pape and Benseler (1911) for Greek names, mainly from literary sources, Preisigke 1922 and Foraboschi 1971 for Greek, Egyptian and Semitic names from papyri and ostraca. For Semitic names in Greek inscriptions, see Wuthnow 1930; for names in inscriptions and papyri in the Nabataean sphere, see also Negev 1991 (with references to other collections of Semitic names). Ilan 2002-2012 offers a rich repertoire of Jewish names, but must be used with caution, for a name identified as Jewish by its literary or epigraphic-archaeological context does not guarantee the Jewishness of any person bearing that name.

For prosopography between 260 and 641 CE, see Jones et al. 1971; Martindale 1980, 1992; and between 641 and 867, Martindale 2001. For a collection and identification of scriptural quotations in Greek and Latin inscriptions, see Felle 2006; update for Palaestina and Arabia, Di Segni 2017b.

---

[4] For explanations and search tools go to homepage: http://www.lgpn.ox.ac.uk.

CHAPTER VII: PALAEOGRAPHY

Palaeography is the study of ancient writing, in our case, the changing shape of letters in Greek inscriptions through the centuries. When we observe the changes occurring in letter forms in a great number of dated inscriptions, comparison to particular forms can be a most helpful tool to locate in time other inscriptions, not intrinsically dated by chronological or historical information. This tool, however, has grave limitations: it cannot be used haphazardly, without careful consideration of the entire inscription in all its aspects, including the historical and archaeological. For instance, no dating by palaeography (nor any dating by chronological system!) can be supported if the inscription includes terms (e.g. titles of office or rank) incompatible with the date assigned to it. Furthermore, the way of fashioning letters can vary much from region to region, and no comparison should ever be made between a style popular in the Holy Land in a certain period and an inscription from the same period but a different part of the Roman Empire. In short, though we offer some palaeographic tables (letter forms attested in dated inscriptions from 70 CE to the seventh century, from Israel only) and suggest perusing the tables presented by Welles 1938 for Gerasa and by Russell 1999 for Byzantine Jordan, we add the warning that only experience can teach a wise and reliable utilization of this tool.

Two types of alphabets were used in this period, a square one and a round or oval one, but they coexist to such an extent that lunate and square epsilon and sigma, round, oval and square omicron are often represented in the same inscription. The square script, when used without the intrusion of round characters, is very difficult to date for it hardly shows any changes during the whole period.

Graffiti make much use of cursive letters, sometimes so different from their regular form that their identification is possible only through the context. Useful tables of the varying forms of Greek cursive letters from the third century BCE to the eighth century CE can be found in Thompson 1912.

As will be noticed in the tables below, some letters, e.g. gamma, epsilon, iota, sigma, do not sensibly change throughout the entire period, except for the presence or absence of serifs (small lines attached to the end of one or more strokes in a character), which are popular in some period and absent, or hardly noticeable, in others. Serifs appear in the first, second and early third centuries in the shape of small lines attached to the main strokes of a character at a right angle. In the sixth-seventh centuries we find decorative serifs again: the simplest type consists of a calligraphic widening of the tips, which are finished off with a triangle or a bifurcation. The more elaborate are drooping lines or triangles attached to the ends of the main strokes, triangles inside omega, under the middle bar of alpha or mu, and decorative epaulets across the stem of upsilon, sometimes also of tau.

Here follow some observations on changes that do occur, especially in Late Antiquity, the fourth to eight centuries on which this work focuses, and which is also the time that offers the largest sample of dated inscriptions in our region.

Alpha has two main shapes, with slanting middle bar and with broken middle bar, which coexist throughout the entire period and are often used together in the same inscription. The alpha with horizontal bar appears in inscriptions of the second and third centuries, when it seems to be the prevailing form; then it is found less and less until it disappears in the course of the fourth century. In Gerasa, the alpha with horizontal bar is common also in the first century and we may safely surmise that this shape is absent in our tables only because of the scarcity of dated first-century inscriptions in Western Palestine. First-century alpha, whatever its shape, often has notable serifs at the foot of the diagonal strokes and on top. In the second century the practice of carrying the right diagonal of alpha, delta and lambda across and above the left diagonal appears: this shape and the shape with diagonals meeting in a clean angle coexist up to the seventh century. In the sixth century, the broken bar often acquires a serif reaching down to the base of the letter and even lower. Since the fifth century the alpha with slanting bar appears also in a cursive form consisting of a slanting acute angle or loop, closed off to the right by a diagonal stroke. An open cursive alpha, similar to an English cursive u, is also attested.

Beta does not appreciably change, except for the occasional appearance of a type in which the two semicircles or 'bellies' do not touch (ϐ: earliest examples: mid-fifth century). Two types of cursive beta occur: an 8-shaped one (earliest appearance in the second half of the fifth century), and one open at the top, resembling a cursive u standing on a long leg on the right.

Gamma: no special changes.

Delta is a simple triangle until the prolonged diagonal bar appears in the second century; then the two shapes coexist. In the seventh-eighth centuries some decorative elements appear: e.g. both diagonal bars cross on top, or a small horizontal stroke or a circlet are attached to the vertex of the triangle; or the base is prolonged on both sides. A cursive delta appears in the sixth century, consisting of a loop shut off on the right side by a diagonal, or more rarely a vertical, stroke. This form is mostly used when the delta carries an abbreviation mark, and is therefore most frequent in the word ΙΝΔ(ικτιῶνος).

Epsilon, both lunate and square: no special changes.

Zeta is not a frequently used letter and thus we have less chance to observe changes in its basic form: two horizontal strokes joined by a diagonal one at acute angles. However, a cursive form penetrates in the late fifth century and even more in the sixth and seventh: its base, or both its horizontal strokes, slant down to the right, and sometimes the lower stroke becomes a long curvilinear tail.

Eta shows no special changes, after the disappearance of the early form, with a small detached central bar ending in serifs. Since the sixth century a cursive eta, shaped like an English cursive h, sometimes appears.

Theta is generally oval even in inscriptions with a prevalence of square letters. However, a rectangular theta sometimes appears in the fifth and early sixth century. In the same period another form also appears, narrow and almond-shaped, with two pointed ends. About 540 the drop-shaped or ogival theta comes into use and becomes the dominant form up to the eighth century. In the seventh and eighth centuries this form tends to have a flat base. Theta behaves exactly like omicron in the same periods, except for the presence of the middle bar. The short middle bar ending with serifs of the Hellenistic period and the punctiform one of the Early Roman period are no longer seen after the second century; but even earlier we see a full-length stroke at mid-height of the letter that touches but usually does not cross its contour, until the sixth century: then this and the form with protruding middle bar coexist. In the decorative forms of the late sixth and early seventh centuries the horizontal bar, often of the protruding type, is located in the upper half of the letter.

Iota and *kappa* show no special changes. Kappa carries an abbreviation mark more often than any other letter, both in the abbreviation Κ(αί) and in often truncates words, like ΔΙΑΚ(ονος). The mark is usually a diagonal stroke across the lower leg of the letter, or a small stigma hanging from the same.

Lambda has two shapes: with its two diagonal strokes meeting on top, or with a prolonged right stroke. Like delta, the late, seventh-eighth centuries lambda tends to show a decorative 'roof' on top. Cursive, curvilinear lambdas sometimes intrude in the script throughout Late Antiquity.

Mu appears in a great variety of shapes. In the first-third centuries the types with splaying legs are more common than the upright letter. The legs of the splaying mu may by diagonal or curvilinear strokes, or a combination of both. This type can sometimes be mistaken for a double lambda, while the upright type of mu with a low middle bar often resembles an eta. A middle bar attached to a lower part of the legs is frequently seen in both the splaying and the upright letter. In the fourth-fifth centuries the upright mu becomes the prevailing form, while in the splaying type the slant becomes less noticeable. In the late fifth-early sixth century the broken bar often acquires a serif reaching down to the base of the letter, just like in the alpha; this decorative form can still be seen in the seventh century.

Nu is always upright, with the middle bar attached to the tips of the vertical strokes or at a lower position along one or both legs. These forms coexist and sometimes appear in a single inscription. In the decorative trend of the late sixth century the middle bar may acquire a curl or knot in the middle.

Xi is less frequently used that other letters; therefore it is difficult to trace its development. The Hellenistic xi, made of three parallel horizontal stroked, the middle one smaller than the others, is still seen in the first century CE, but since the second century we find only the four-stroke xi, resembling two joined zetas. This form becomes more and more sinuous until, in the sixth century, it reaches the calligraphic form of two interlacing or 'knotted' curls. This shape coexists with the angular, four-stroke xi.

Omicron is round, square or oval and narrow from the first to the mid-sixth century. The round type is sometimes small and floating above the line. The use of alternate types, the small and the full-size omicron, in the same inscription, is documented as early as the second half of the second century (at Gerasa) and until the second half of the fifth century in the entire region; in the sixth, the tiny omicron is only used in abbreviations, lifted above another letter. The ligature of omicron and upsilon first appears in the early sixth century. About 540 CE the ogival type comes into use, first as an oval omicron slightly pointed on top, then as a fat drop. In the seventh and eighth centuries the drop-shaped omicron often rests on a flat base.

Pi and *rho* do not show significant changes. A rho with an open loop ending in a curl does not seem to be a development of a specific period but rather a calligraphic whim of the designer.

Sigma lunate and square coexist in the first-eighth centuries, showing no changes. The Hellenistic four-stroke sigma is still used in monumental inscriptions of the first century and disappears during the second. A cursive, two-stroke sigma sometimes appears in inscriptions engraved on stone.

Tau shows no changes, apart from the occasional addition of decorative serifs.

Upsilon has two shapes: the commonest with a stem and a rarer, V-shaped one, which is only attested since the fifth century west of the Jordan, but much earlier in Gerasa. In the late sixth and in the seventh century the upsilon with stem acquires decorative serifs: 'epaulets' across the stem or small strokes drooping from the tips of its arms.

Phi is usually round, with a high stem protruding at the top, which may end with a horizontal serif. Square or rhomboid phi occur rather rarely, in inscriptions using the square script.

The basic forms of *chi* and *psi* continue throughout the Roman and Byzantine periods. However, two variants of psi appear in the late sixth century: a candelabrum shape with rounded or squared branches, and a cruciform psi. Both are not frequent.

Omega in the classical and Hellenistic form is still in use, side by side with the uncial form, in monumental inscriptions of the first two centuries CE, then it is superseded by the round uncial omega. Square and angular omegas begin to be seen with the square script in the fifth century. In the second half of the sixth, the round form develops curls, serifs and other decorative elements on the inside.

The characters of the eighth century are not represented in our tables. The decorative trend of the late sixth and seventh centuries continues in several inscriptions of this century. Generally the letters are well spaced and squat, the round ones resting on flattened bases, the upright ones on little triangular 'hooves'. Omicron is plump, with a small pointed top and a flat base.

For the various abbreviation marks and their use throughout Late Antiquity, see Avi-Yonah 1940: 29-39, 119-125.

Ca. 70	70-90	102-117	120-130	141/2	170-172	161-180	187	189/90
Α	Α	Α	Α	Α	Α	Α	Α	Α
Β	Β	Β	Β			Β	Β	Β
Γ	Γ		Γ	Γ		Γ	Γ	Γ
Δ	Δ		Δ	Δ	Δ	Δ	Δ	Δ
Ε	Ε		Ε	Ε	Ε	Ε	Ε	Ε
	Ζ				Ζ		Ζ	
Η	Η		Η	Η		Η	Η	Η
				Θ	Θ	Θ		Θ
Ι	Ι	Ι	Ι	Ι	Ι	Ι	Ι	Ι
Κ	Κ	Κ	Κ	Κ	Κ	Κ	Κ	Κ
Λ	Λ		Λ	Λ	Λ	Λ	Λ	
Μ	Μ		Μ			ΜΗ	ΜΗ	Μ
Ν	Ν	Ν	Ν	Ν	Ν	Ν	Ν	Ν
	Ξ						Ξ	
Ο	Ο	Ο	Ο	Ο	Ο	Ο	ΟΟ	Ο
	Π		Π		Π	Π	Π	
Ρ	Ρ	Ρ	Ρ	Ρ		Ρ	Ρ	Ρ
Σ	C	C	C	C	C	Σ	C	C
Τ	Τ	Τ	Τ	Τ	Τ	Τ	Τ	Τ
Υ	Υ	Υ	Υ	Υ	Υ	Υ	Υ	Υ
Φ					Φ			
Χ	ΧΧ			Χ		Χ		
Ω	ω			ω	ω	ωΩ	ω	

1. North 70-190 CE

	197	210/11	214/15	260-282	297	297	305-311	309-311	333-337
	Α	Α	Α Α	Α	Α Α Α	Α	Α Α	Α Α	Α
	Β	Β		Β	Β Β Β				
				Γ	Γ	Γ	Γ Γ		
	Δ	Δ	Δ	Δ	Δ Δ	Δ	Δ		
	Ε Ε	Ε	Ε	Ε	Ε Ε	Ε Ε	Ε Ε	Ε	Ε
					Ζ				
	Η	Η	Η	Η	Η Η	Η	Η	Η	
		Θ	Θ		Θ Θ	Θ			
	Ι	Ι		Ι	Ι Ι	Ι	Ι	Ι	
	Κ	Κ	Κ		Κ Κ	Κ	Κ	Κ	
	Λ	λ	λ		Λ Λ	λ	λ Λ	λ	λ
	μ	μ	μ	Μ	Μ Μ Μ Μ	Μ		Μ	
	Ν	Ν	Ν	Ν	Ν Ν	Ν Ν	Ν	Ν	Ν
		Ξ		Ξ	Ξ	Σ		Σ	
	Ο	Ο	Ο	Ο	Ο Ο	Ο Ο	Ο Ο	Ο	Ο
	Π			Π		Π	Π	Π	
	Ρ	Ρ	Ρ Ρ	Ρ	Ρ Ρ	Ρ	Ρ	Ρ	
	Ϲ	Ϲ	Ϲ	Ϲ	Ϲ Ϲ	Ϲ Ϲ	Ϲ Ϲ	Ϲ	Ϲ
	Τ	Τ	Τ	Τ	Τ Τ	Τ	Τ	Τ	Τ
	Υ	Υ	Υ	Υ	Υ Υ Υ	Υ	V	Υ	
		Φ			Φ	Φ	Φ		
	Χ				Χ	Χ	Χ		
	ω	ω		ω	ω	ω	ω	ω	

2. North 197-337 CE

Tables   173

358/9	361/2	364-382	385	414/15	432/3	443	455	455
A		A	A	A A	A	A A	A A A	A A
B						B	B B	B
			Γ	Γ		Γ	Γ	Γ
		Δ	Δ	Δ	Δ	Δ Δ	Δ	Δ Δ
Є	Є Є	Є	Є	E	E	E	Є Є	
Z							Z	
H		H	H	H		H	H	H
Θ	Θ	Θ	Θ	⊟	⊟	⊟	Θ	Θ
I	I	I	I	I	I	I	I	I
K		K	K	K	K	K	K	K
Λ	Λ	Λ	λ λ	Λ	λ	Λ	λ	λ
M		μ M	M	μ M	M	M	M	M M
N	N	N	N	N N	N	N	N	N
Ƶ	Ƶ					Ƶ	Ƶ	Ʒ
O °	O	O	O	O · ⊡	⊡	⊡	O	O
Π		Π	Π			Π	Π	Π
P		P	P	P	P	P	P ρ	P
C	C	C	C	⊏ C	⊏	⊏	C	C
T		T	T	T	T	T	T	T
Y	Y	Y	Y	V Y	Y	Y	Y Y	Y
		Φ	Φ	Φ		Φ		Φ
					X	X	X	
						Ψ		
Ш		Ш	ω	W		⊔ Ш	ω ω	ω
				ϛ V		ϗ		ϛ

3. North 358-455 CE

455	ca.460	461/2	478	485/6	489/90	493/4	499	ca.501
A	A	A A	A	A	A	A	A A	A
B		B	B				B	B
Γ	Γ		Γ	Γ		Γ	Γ	Γ
Δ	Δ Δ	Δ	Δ	Δ Δ	Δ		Δ Δ	
Є	Є	E Є	Є	Є	E E	Є	E	Є
		Z				Z		
H	H	H	H			H	H	H
θ	θ	θ θ	θ θ			θ	θ	θ
I	I	I	I	I		I	I	I
K	K	K	K	K		K	K	K
Λ	Λ		Λ	Λ	Λ		Λ	Λ
H	M M	M M	M			M	M	M
N	N	N	N		N	N	N	N
		Ξ						Ξ
O	O	° O	O	O	O ☐	O	O ☐	O
Π		Π	Π	Π	Π	Π	Π	Π
P	P	P	P	P	P	P	P	P
C	C	C	C	C	C C	C	C	C
T	T	T	T	T	T	T	T	T
Y	Y V	Y	Y	V	Y	Y	Y	Y
Φ		Φ	Φ	Φ	Φ	Φ	Φ	Φ
X			X	X	X		X	
Y			Y			Y	Y	
Ш	ω ψ	Ш	W	ω	ψ	ω	ω Ш	ω
		ς	ς ς	ς			Kς ς	ς ς Bι

4. North 455-501 CE

ca.505	512	518-527	519	521/2	522	524-526	526/7	527
Λ Λ	Λ Λ	ΛΛΛ u	Λ Λ	Λ Λ	Λ	Λ	Λ	Λ Λ
B	B		B	B	B		B	B B
Γ	Γ	Γ	Γ	Γ		Γ		
Δ Δ	Δ Δ		Δ Δ	Δ		Δ	Δ	
Є	E	Є E	E	Є	E	Є	Є	Є
								Z
H	H		H	H		H	H	H H
θ	θ	θ	θ		θ	θ θ	θ	
I	I	I	I	I	I	I	I	
K	K	K	K	K	K	K	K	K
λ Λ	λ		λ	Λ λ		λ Λ	Λ λ	λ
MMM	MM	M	MM	M	M	M		
N N	N	N N	N	N	N	N	N N	
Ξ Ξ			Ξ			Ξ		
O	☐	O	o O	O O	☐ ☐	O O	O	O
Π	Π		Π	Π	Π	Π		Π
P	P	P	P	P	P	P		P
C	C	C	C	C	C	C	C	C
T	T	T	T	T	T	T	T	T
Y	Y	Y V	Y	Y	Y	Y	Y	Y
Φ	Φ		Φ	Φ	Φ	Φ	Φ	
X	X	X		X	X	X		X
	Y							
ω ω ω	ω ω	ω	ω	ω		ω	ω	ω
	ς		☌ ϛ ⳤ ο ς ͵ ⳤ		⋔ ς ͵ ⳤ ⳤ		ϒ	ε ρ Ṁ

5. North 505-527 CE

528	536	539/40	522-552	549/50	555	558/9	565	570
A	A	A	A	A	A	A	A	A
B	B			B B	B	B	B	B B 8
Γ	Γ	Γ	Γ	Γ	Γ	Γ	Γ	Γ
Δ	Δ	Δ		Δ	Δ Δ	δ	Δ	Δ Δ δ
Є	Є	Є	Є	E Є	E	Є	Є	Є E
Z						Z		
H	H	H		H		H	H	H
θ	θ θ	θ	θ		θ	θ	θ	θ
I	I	I	I	I	I	I	I	I
K	K	K	K	K	K	K	K	
λ	λ	λ		Λ	λ	λ	λ	Λ
M	M	M		M	M	M	M	M M
N	N	N		N	N	N	N	N
		Z					Z Z	
O	O O O	O	O	O O	O O	O	O O	O O
Π	Π		Π	Π	Π	Π	Π	Π
P	P		P	P	P	P	P	P
C	C	C	C	C	C C	C	C	C C
T	T	T	T	T	T	T	T	T
Y	Y Y	Y	Y	Y	Y	Y	Y	V
Φ	Φ			Φ	Φ Φ		Φ	Φ Φ
		X	X		X	X		
					Ψ			
Ϡ	Ϡ							Ϡ
ω	ω			ω	ω	ω	ω	ω ω

6. North 538-570 CE

584/5	585	591	591	592	604	605/6	637	662
Α	Α Α	Α Α	Α	Α	Α	Α	Α	Α Α
	Β			Β	Β	Β	Β Β	Β Β
	Δ Δ		Γ	Γ	Γ	Γ	Γ	Γ
		Δ	Δ	Δ	Δ	Δ	Δ	Δ
Ε	Ε	Ε	Ε Ε	Ε	Ε	Ε	Ε Ε Ε	Ε
					Ζ	Ζ		
Η	Η	Η	Η	Η	Η	Η	Η	Η
Θ	Θ			Θ	Θ	Θ	Θ	Θ
Ι	Ι	Ι	Ι	Ι	Ι	Ι	Ι	Ι
Κ	Κ	Κ	Κ	Κ	Κ	Κ	Κ	Κ
Λ	Λ	Λ	Λ	Λ	Λ	Λ	Λ	Λ Λ
Μ	Μ Μ	Μ	Μ	Μ	Μ Μ	Μ	Μ Μ	Μ
Ν	Ν	Ν	Ν	Ν	Ν	Ν	Ν Ν	Ν
Ξ			Ξ		Ξ			
Ο	Ο	Ο	Ο	Ο	Ο	Ο	Ο	Ο
Π	Π	Π	Π	Π	Π	Π	Π	Π
Ρ	Ρ	Ρ	Ρ	Ρ	Ρ	Ρ	Ρ	Ρ
	С	С	С	С	С	С	С	С
	Τ	Τ	Τ	Τ	Τ	Τ	Τ	Τ
	Υ	Υ	Υ	Υ	Υ	Υ	Υ Υ	V V
Φ	Φ		Φ		Φ	Φ	Φ Φ	
Χ	Χ	Χ		Χ	Χ	Χ	Χ	
	Ψ	Ψ		Ψ		Ψ	Ψ	Ψ
Ω	ω	ω ω	Ш	ω	ω	Ω	Ω Ω	ω
ϛ ς	ϛ ς	ς		ς	ϞΚϷΣϚ	ϛ	ϛ ΚϚ ς	ϛ ς ς

7. North 584-662 CE

97	179/80	233	241	293/4	411	426	450	452/3
Λ	Λ	Λ	A A	ἀ λ	Λ Δ	Δ Δ	Λ	λ
B B		B	B	β	B B			B
Γ		Γ		Γ	Γ		Γ	Γ
Δ	Δ	Δ	∆	Δ	Δ		Δ	Δ
ϵ	ϵ	ϵ	E ϵ	ϵ	E	ϵ E	ϵ	E
Z			Z	Z			Z	
H		H	H	H	H		H	H
		θ		θ	θ	θ	θ	θ
I	I	I	I	I	I	I	I	I
	K			K	K		K	K
		Λ	Λ		λ	λ	λ	λ
Μ	μ μ	M	M	μ	M		Μ	Μ
N	N	N	N	N	N	N	N	N
X		Ƶ			Ƶ			
O	O	O	o	O O	O □	o ◊	O	O
	Π	Π	Π	Π		Π	Π	Π
P		P	P	P	P	Ρ	P	P
C	C	C	C	C	C	Ϲ C	C	C
T	T	T	T	T	T	T	T	T
Y Y	Y	Y	Y	Y	Y Y	Y	V Y	Y V
			⚘				Ϙ	
X		X	X	X	X			X
							Ψ	
ω		ω		ω	ω		⊎ ω	⊎ ω

1. South 97-452 CE

454/5	464	471	474	475	505	509	510-519	522
Α Α	Α Α Α	Α	Α	Α Α	Α Α	Α Α	Α	Α
Β	8 Β			Β Β	Β	Ϥ Ϥ		Β
Γ	Γ		Γ	Γ	Γ	Γ	Γ	
Δ	Δ	Δ	Δ Δ	Δ Δ	Δ			Δ
Ε	Ε Ϲ	Ϲ	Ε	Ϲ Ε	Ϲ	Ϲ	Ϲ	Ϲ
Ζ		Ζ			Ƹ		Ζ	
Η	Η	Η	Η	Η	Η	Η	Η Η	Η
Β	Β Θ	Θ		Θ	Θ	Θ		Θ
Ι	Ι	Ι	Ι	Ι	Ι	Ι	Ι	Ι
Κ	Κ		Κ	Κ	Κ	Κ	Κ	Κ
Λ	Λ	Λ	Λ	Λ	Λ	Λ		Λ
ΜΜΜ	Μ Μ	Μ Η	ΜΜ Μ	ΜΜ	μ	Μ	Η	Η
Ν	Ν	Ν	Ν	Ν	Ν	Ν		Ν
	Ζ			Ƹ	Ƶ	Ƶ		Ƶ
□	Ο	Ο	□	Ο	Ο	Ο Ο	ο	Ο
Π	Π		Π	Π		Π	Π	Π
Ρ	Ρ	Ρ	Ρ	Ρ	Ρ	Ρ	Ρ	Ρ
Ϲ	Ϲ	Ϲ	Ϲ	Ϲ Ϲ	Ϲ	Ϲ	Ϲ	Ϲ
Τ	Τ	Τ	Τ	Τ	Τ	Τ	Τ	Τ
Υ	Υ Υ	Υ	Υ	Υ Υ	Υ	Υ	Υ Υ	Υ
Φ			Φ Φ		Φ	Φ	Φ	Φ
Χ	Χ		Χ			Χ		Χ
			Ψ			Ψ		
Ш	Ш	Ш	Ш Ш	Ш		Ш		Ш
Ϛ	Ϛ	Ϛ		Ϛ Ϛ		Ϛ		

2. South 454-522 CE

529	531	527-548	541	541	541	543	544	545
Λ	Α Α	Α	Α	Α Α	Α	Α Α	Α	Α
	Β			Β	Β		Β	Β
Γ			Γ		Γ		Γ	Γ
Δ	Δ	ᑯ	Δ	Δ Δ	Δ	Δ	Δ	Δ
Ε	Ε	Ε	Ε	Ε	Ε	Ε	Ε	Ε
Ζ	Ζ			Ζ	Ζ		Ζ	Ζ
Η	Η	Η	Η	Η	Η	Η	Η	Η
Θ	Θ	Θ	Θ	Θ	Θ	Θ	Θ	Θ
Ι	Ι	Ι	Ι	Ι	Ι	Ι	Ι	Ι
Κ	Κ	Κ	Κ	Κ	Κ	Κ	Κ	Κ
Λ		Λ Λ	Λ	Λ Λ	Λ	Λ Λ	Λ	Λ
Μ	ΜΜΜ	Μ	Μ	ΜΜΜ	Μ	Μ Μ	Μ	Μ
Ν	Ν	Ν	Ν	Ν	Ν	Ν	Ν	Ν
Ξ							Ξ	Ξ
Ο	Ο	Ο	Ο Ο	Ο ☐	Ο	Ο	Ο	Ο
Π	Π	Π	Π			Π	Π	Π
Ρ	Ρ	Ρ	Ρ	Ρ	Ρ	Ρ	Ρ	Ρ
C	C	C	C	C Ϲ	C	C	C	C
Τ	Τ Τ	Τ	Τ	Τ	Τ	Τ	Τ	Τ
Υ	Υ	Υ	Υ	Υ V	Υ y	Υ V	Υ	Υ
Φ	Φ	Φ		Φ	Φ			
			Χ		Χ			
ω		ω	ω	Ш	ω	ω		
ϛ	ϛ	ϛ	ϛ	† 岡 ϛ	γ ϛ	ϛ	ϛ ϛ ẟ	ϛ k

3. South 529-545 CE

546	547	548	550	555	555	555-564	561/2	564
Ⲁ	Ⲁ	Ⲁ	Ⲁ	Ⲁ	Ⲁ	Ⲁ	Ⲁ Ⲁ	Ⲁ
	B			B		B B	B	
Γ			Γ		Γ	Γ	Γ	Γ
Δ	Δ		Δ	Δ	Δ	Δ	Δ Δ	Δ
Ε	Ε	E	E	Ε	E	Ε Ε E	Ε	Ε
Z		Z	Z					Z
H	H	H	H	H	H	H	H	H
Θ	Θ	Θ	Θ	Θ	Θ	Θ		Θ Θ
I	I	I	I	Γ	I	I	I	I
K	K	K	K		K	K	K	K
	λ		Λ	Λ	Λ		λ	λ
M	M	M	M M	M	M M	M M	M	M
N	N	N	N	N	N	N N	N	N
			Ξ		Ξ	Ξ		
O	O	O	O	O	O	O	o	O
Π	Π	Π		Π		Π		
P	P	P	P	P		P	P	P
C	C	C	C	C	C	C C	C	C
T	T	T	T	T	T	T	T	T
Y	Y	Y V	Y	Y	V	Y Y		Y
	Φ						Φ	
		X		X			X	X
							Ψ	
	ⲱ			ⲱ			ⲱ	
ς	ⳗ		ς	ϛ ς ϟ ϗ	ς ς	ς ς	ϗ ϡ ϛ ς	ⳉ

4. South 546-564 CE

569	569	576	576-578	581	581	582	584	588
A A	A	A	A	A A	A	A ∂	A A ∂ α	A
B		B	B	B	B		B	B
Γ		Γ	Γ		Γ		Γ	Γ
Δ	Δ	Δ Δ	Δ Δ	Δ	Λ ∂	Δ	Δ ∂	Δ
Є	E	E	Є Є	E	E	E Є	E Є	є
	Z	Z			Z	Z		Z
H	H	H	H	H	H	H	H h	H
θ		θ	θ θ	θ	θ	θ	θ θ	θ
I	I	I	I I	I	I	I	I	I
K	k	K	K	K	K	K	K	K
λ		λ	Λ	λ	λ		λ	λ
M	M	M	M	M	H M M	M	M	M
N	N	N N	N	N	N	N	N	N
Ξ			Ξ	Ξ				
O	O	O	O	O	O	O	O	O
Π		Π	Π		Π	Π	Π	Π
P	P	P	P		P	P	P	P
C	C	C	C	C	C C	C	C	C
T	T	T	T T	T	T	T	T	T
Y		Y	Y Y	Y	Y V	Y	V Y	Y
Φ			Φ Φ			Φ	Φ	
X			X		X	X	X	
			Ψ Ψ					
ω	Ж	ω	W		ω	W ω		ω
ϒ ϚϒϚ	ϷϚ	MϚϚ		☩ ϟ	Ϛ Ϛ	ϒϚϠϒ	ϸΔ Ϛ

5. South 569-588 CE

588	589	595	597	599	601	602	605	607
Α	Ɒ	Α	Α	Α Α	Α Α	Α	Ɒ Α	Α
	Β			Β Β			Β Β	Β
Γ		Γ			Γ	Γ	Γ	Γ
Δ	ϙ	Δ Δ	Δ	Χ ◊	Δ	Δ	ⴷ Δ Δ	Δ
Ε Ε	Ε Ε	Ε	Ε Ε	Ε Ε	Ε	Ε	Ε Ε	Ε
	Ζ			Ζ			Ζ	
Η	Η	Η	Η	Η	Η	Η	Η	
Θ	Θ	Θ	Θ				Θ	Θ
Ι	Ι	Ι	Ι	Ι	Ι	Ι	Ι	Ι
Κ	Κ	Κ	Κ	Κ	Κ	Κ	Κ	Κ
Λ	Λ	Λ			Λ	Λ	Λ	Λ
Μ	Μ	Μ	Μ	Μ	Μ		Μ Μ Μ	Μ Μ
Ν	Ν	Ν	Ν	Ν	Ν	Ν	Ν Ν	Ν
		Ξ						
Ο		Ο Ο	Ο Ο	Ο Ο	Ο Ο	Ο	Ο	Ο
Π	Π			Π	Π		Π	Π
Ρ	Ρ		Ρ	Ρ	Ρ	Ρ	Ρ	Ρ
C		C	C	C	C	C	C C	C
Τ	Τ	Τ	Τ	Τ	Τ	Τ	Τ	Τ
Υ	Ϋ Υ	Υ	Υ	Υ	Ϋ	Υ	Υ	
					Φ		Φ Φ	
					Χ	Χ		
	Ω		Ω	Ω	Ω	Ω Ω	Ω	Ω
ϛ	ϛ ϛ ϥ	ϛ ϛ	ϛ	ϛ ϧ	ϛ ϧ ϛ ϻ	ϫ ϛ	ϛ ϛ ϛ ϥ	ϛ ϛ

6. South 588-6-7 CE

608	609	612	613	614	617	628	630	633
A A A	X A A	A	A A	A	A A	A	A	A A
B	B	B	B		B B 8	B	B	
Γ	Γ			Γ		Γ	Γ	Γ
Δ Δ	Δ Δ	Δ Δ	Δ Δ	Δ	Δ	Δ	Δ	Δ Δ
E ϵ	E	ϵ	E	ϵ	ϵ	E	E	ϵ
								Ƨ
H	H	H	H	H	H	H	H	H
θ	θ	θ θ		θ		θ	θ	θ
I	I	I	I	I	I	I	I	I
K	K	K K	K	K	K	K	K	K
	λ			λ		Λ		Λ
M M	M	M	M M	M M	M	M M	M	M
N	N	N	N	N	H	N	N	N N
	Ξ						Z	
O	O	O O	O	O	O	O	O	O
Π	Π	Π	Π	Π	Π	Π	Π	Π
P	P	P	P	P	P	P	P	P
C c	C	C	C	C	C	C	C c	C c
T	T	T	T	T	T	T	T	T
	Y	Ƴ	Y		Y	Y	Y	V y
Φ		φ		Φ	Φ	φ	φ	Φ
	X			X			X	X
	Ψ							Ψ
ω	ω	ω	ω	ω	ω	ω	W	ω ω
ϛ ϟ	ϛ	ϛ ϟ 𐅵	ϟ 𐅵	ϛ 𐅵		ϡ Ϟ ϟ	ϟ	ϛ ϛ ϟ 𐅵

7. South 608–633 CE

639	639/40	641	641/2	643	643	643	646	679
A	A A	A	A	A A	A	A	A A A A	A
B				B	B	B	B	B
Γ Γ	Γ	Γ	Γ	Δ Δ ɗ	Γ	Γ	Γ	Γ
Δ ∂ A	Δ Δ	Δ	∂		Δ ∂	Δ Δ	Δ Δ ∂	∂
E	E	E	E E	E	E	Ɛ E	E	E
		Z						ʒ
H	H	H	H	H	H	H	H	
θ		θ		θ	ϴ		θ	θ
I	I	I		I	I	I	I	I
	K	K	K	K	K	K	K	K
	λ λ	λ	λ λ	λ	λ	λ	λ	λ
M	H H	M	M	M	M	M	M H H	M M
N	N	N	N	N H	N	N	H	N
				ʒ			ʒ	
O	O	O		O	O	O	◊	O
Π	Π	Π			Π	Π	Π	Π
P	P	P	P	P	P	P	P	P
C	C	C C	C	C	C	C C	C	C
T	T	T	T	T	T	T	T	T
Y	Y	Y		Υ	Υ		Y	Y
φ	φ	φ	φ	φ	φ	φ	φ φ	φ
	X	X						
ω	Ш		ω		Ш	Ш Ш	Ш	ω
ϛ	ϛ Ϗ	ϫ	ϫ ϛ ϫ ϛ	ϫ ϛ	ϫ	ϫ ϛ Ϗ	ϛ	

8. South 639-679 CE

APPENDIX A: CIVIL AND MILITARY ADMINISTRATION

§ 1. The re-organization of the Empire under Diocletian

Under the rule of the emperor Diocletion (284-305 CE) the Roman Empire underwent important political, administrative and fiscal reforms. The huge Empire was divided into two parts, the East and the West, each ruled by an Augustus. To ensure the continuity of power, each Augustus appointed his successor, styled Caesar, who governed half of his part of Empire. The four tetrarchs had each his own capital – Milan and Trier in the West, Nicomedia and Sirmium in the East – and his own chief minister, the *praefectus praetorio*. Constantine moved the capital of the Eastern Empire to Byzantium, which he refounded in 330 CE with a new name: Νέα Ῥώμη, The New Rome, Constantinopolis.

The succession system failed almost immediately but the division of the Roman Empire into East and West continued on and off until the end of Roman rule in the West, and *praefecti praetorio* continued to be in charge of the various portions of the Empire. Both halves of the Empire were subdivided in dioceses, six in the East and six in the West, each under a *vicarius*, 'lieutenant' of the *praefectus praetorio*, with military and judiciary powers. Only the diocese of *Oriens* (Ἕως in Greek), which included the Near East, Egypt and Cyrenaica, was headed by a *comes Orientis* as lieutenant of the *praefectus praetorio* of the East.

§ 2. Diocletian's reform of the provincial administration

Diocletian also carried out a radical change in the administration of the provinces by separating the civil authority from the military command. This reform naturally affected also the Land of Israel, soon to become the Holy Land of Christianity. In 284, most of the country was included in *Provincia Palaestina*, except for Upper Galilee and northern Golan, which belonged to *Provincia Phoenice*, and for the Negev and southern Transjordan, which belonged to *Provincia Arabia* together with most of the Sinai peninsula. To the east, Provincia Arabia extended over modern Jordan and southern Syria, except for a strip along the Jordan River from the Yarmuk to the north to the north-eastern coast of the Dead Sea, the *Peraea*, which was part of Palaestina. All three provinces, Phoenice, Palaestina and Arabia, were included in the diocese of Oriens and formed part of the *limes*, the border regions of the Empire where, following Diocletian's reform, the defence of the Roman lands were entrusted to the holder of a new office, the *dux*.

From the end of the First Jewish revolt to Diocletian's time, Palaestina had been governed by a *legatus Augusti pro praetore* of the senatorial class, who was in charge of military affairs and justice, and by a *procurator* of the equestrian class, in charge of financial and fiscal business. Both were personal representatives of the emperor and appointed by him. Following Diocletian's reform, the command of the army stationed in the province was taken away from the civil governor and entrusted to the *dux Palaestinae*. The civil governor was now responsible for administering justice, levying taxes and controlling the treasury of the province, as well as for maintaining order by means of a limited number of soldiers, a policing rather than a defence force.[1] The importance of the judicial powers of the civil governor is stressed by the title he is given in the literary sources, especially in the first half of the fourth century: *iudex* (in Greek δικαστής), i.e., judge. In that period a provincial governor was usually styled *praeses* (ἡγεμών), an indication that the post was intended for a man of equestrian rank, but soon the sources show that the governor of Palaestina was a *consularis* (ὑπατικός), namely, a man of the upper, senatorial class. In fact, the equestrian rank quickly disappeared and all over the East we find governors (ἄρχοντες) of senatorial rank, differently graded according to the importance of the province, the size of their bureau (*officium*) and the budget they received to pay their officials and their own salary. The governor of Palaestina ranked as *consularis* until the early 380s, when he was promoted to *proconsul*, while the governor of Arabia, a province of lower grade, ranked as *praeses*. In the second half of the fourth century, and for long periods after that, the governor of Arabia also performed the function of *dux Arabiae* and had under him two separate bureaux.[2]

§ 3. The duties of the civil governor

The governor of Palaestina resided in the provincial capital, Caesarea, where he had his tribunal, but he also travelled to the cities of the province with his court to hold assizes there, according to the Roman custom. From Justinian's Novels, however, it appears that governors tried to avoid

---

[1] Jones 1990: 42-52; Isaac 1990.
[2] Sartre 1982; Di Segni and Tsafrir 2017: 779-837.

the troublesome and costly journeys and preferred to despatch deputies (τοποτηρηταί) to the cities with authority to fulfil all the functions of their own office, including the administration of justice and the supervision of tax collection. Edicts forbidding both civil and military governors to appoint such deputies were repeatedly issued during Justinian's rule, a clear sign that they were not obeyed.[3]

Like the governors of the Roman period, he judged both civil and penal cases and could sentence to death. His verdicts could be appealed to the *comes Orientis*, and in some cases even to the imperial tribunal in Constantinople. The governor's court, however, was not the only one in the province. In Late Antiquity a rule called *praescriptio fori* was in force, according to which every person had the right to stand trial or litigate in court according to his status. High-ranking people could only be tried in front of the emperor; soldiers and paramilitary personnel were judged by the *dux*, and people in the religious orders by the bishop of the city in whose territory their churches or monasteries were located. The courts of the *dux* and the bishop dealt with private litigations as well as with criminal offences. And these were not the only available tribunals: since the cost of addressing the governor's court was very high, litigations involving sums of money below a certain limit fixed by law were judged by the *defensor cititatis*, the legal representative of each city,[4] or the litigants could turn to the bishop's court at no cost. Moreover, since Roman law recognized arbitration as a legal means to solve litigations, conditional to both parties' agreement to submit to it, rabbinical courts were also available to all litigants, including gentiles; and they could also judge and punish Jews for infringement of Jewish laws.[5]

Besides administering justice, the civil governor was in charge of the provincial coffer. The taxes collected by the cities (see below), and since Emperor Anastasius' time (491-518) by imperial officials, would in part be forwarded to the office of the *praefectus praetorio* of the East, in part be disbursed in the province itself. The governor was responsible for paying his subordinates, for transmitting to the *dux* the money needed to pay the soldiers and the paramilitary personnel, and in special cases, for financing building activity in the province, conditional to imperial permission. In principle, erection and maintenance of public buildings in the cities were paid for by the city itself, probably under a degree of supervision by the governor (see below), but sometimes imperial benefaction (φιλοτιμία), expressed in

---

[3] Di Segni 1996: 582-584. For the *topoteretai* in the cities, see below, § 6.
[4] Di Segni et al. 2003; Di Segni 2006b.
[5] Rabello 1980: 731-735; Albeck 1987.

the financing of a particular building, is mentioned by literary or epigraphic sources. This usually meant not that gold was sent from Constantinople to the province but rather that the emperor authorized the governor to use tax money levied in the province to pay for the building. The allotted sum would be strictly budgeted and its expenditure supervised by the governor or by another specially appointed personage. An example is provided by the testimony of Cyril of Scythopolis about the benefits granted by Emperor Justinian to Palestine at the request of the saintly monk Sabas after the Samaritan revolt of 529-530. Large sums of money were allotted to the restoration of churches damaged or destroyed by the Samaritans throughout the country, for the building and garrisoning of a fort to protect the monasteries of the Judaean Desert from the incursions of the Saracens, for founding and maintaining a two-hundred bed hospital in Jerusalem, and last but not least, for the erection of the new church of Mary Mother of God, known as the 'Nea'. Although the inscription discovered in the vaults under the Nea speaks of Justinian's *philotimia*, Cyril explicitly attests that all the money was to come from the provincial coffers. Only the architect and some specialized labour were sent from Constantinople, as well as – probably – some of the rich furnishings of the church.[6]

The civil governor was appointed by the emperor for a term of office usually of one year, although we know of governors who stayed in office for longer terms. According to the law he was supposed to be a stranger from a different province;[7] however, inscriptions reveal the names of some governors who were native of the country, like Silvanus of Scythopolis, governor of Palaestina at the end of the fourth century[8] and Flavius Anysius Sergius, another Scythopolitan, who was governor of Second Palestine in 534/5.[9]

---

[6] Cyril of Scythopolis, *Life of Sabas* 73, ed. Schwartz 1939: 177; trans. Price 1991: 186/Di Segni 2005b: 205-207; Di Segni 2012c; Gutfeld 2012: 246-248. This does not mean, however, that there was no real imperial euergetism: see Chapter V. 1. 2 on the renovation of the bathhouse at Hammath Gader, of the city wall of Beth Shean-Scythopolis under Anastasius, and on the building activity at Bostra under Justinian. Money, surely from the emperor's private purse, was bestowed (willed?) by Tiberius Constantine (578-582 CE) to a church in Judaea (Storchan 2021; Di Segni 2021). These largesses did not necessarily come from the capital. The Augusta Eudocia, wife of Theodosius II, who lived in Jerusalem from ca. 443 to her death in 460, funded the renovation of the city wall and the building and endowing of churches and monasteries, most likely from the revenues of the huge imperial estates in Palestine assigned as her apanage when she left Constantinople for the Holy Land.

[7] Jones 1990: 389, 1155, n. 438.

[8] Di Segni and Arubas 2009; *SEG* LIX, no. 1718.

[9] *SEG* XLII, no. 1471.

The governor of Arabia resided in his capital, Bostra, and had similar duties as the governor of Palaestina, but since for long periods he doubled as *dux Arabiae*, he had the additional duties attached to that office, which he fulfilled through a separate bureau.

§ 4. The dux Palaestinae and the dux Arabiae

The *dux Palaestinae* and the *dux Arabiae* were the commanders of the soldiers stationed in Palestine and in Arabia. Their term of office was longer than the term of the civil governor and some of them stayed in office for several years. Besides their responsibility in the defence of the province from exterior attacks, in policing the roads and in crushing revolts, the dux also acted as judge in cases involving military and paramilitary personnel, managed the payment of their salaries, and was also in charge of erecting and maintaining defensive buildings and other buildings that served the army, e.g., hostels for travelling officers.[10]

From Diocletian's reform to the accession to power of Valentinian (emperor of the West, 364-375) and Valens (emperor of the East, 364-378) the dux was a man of the highest equestrian rank, carrying the title *vir perfectissimus* ('most perfect'), lower in rank than the civil governor, a senatorial *vir clarissimus* ('most distinguished'). Only in 364 the dux became *vir clarissimus*, and some time later, possibly already in 372, he was raised to the upper grade of *vir spectabilis* ('most esteemed'). In the sixth century he even attained the uppermost grade of the provincial hierarchy by becoming *vir gloriosissimus* ('most glorious').[11] From ca. 364 to ca. 440, and again from ca. 529 to ca. 535, the *dux Arabiae* served a double function, as both civil governor and military commander, but in Palaestina the two offices remained strictly separated.

An official list from the early fifth century, the *Notitia Dignitatum Orientis*,[12] contains a complete list of the troops under the command of each dux, each regiment with the location of its station, as well as a list of the staff in the *officium* of the dux (*duciani*). From this list we learn that the *dux Palaestinae* had under his command a legion, the *Decima Fretensis*, sta-

---

[10] Di Segni 1995: 320-322.
[11] Jones 1990: 135, 142-143, 526; for Arabia, see Sartre 1982: 105, 112, 117-120.
[12] 'Register of functionaries of the East'. The list was compiled shortly after 395 and revised in the form we possess ca. 411-413. There is also a *Notitia Dignitatum* of the West, also published by Seeck 1876, compiled at the same time but revised at a slightly later date (Jones 1990: 1417-1423).

tioned at Aila (Eilat-Aqaba), and 29 regiments, many of them mounted and most of them stationed in southern Palestine and southern Transjordan.[13] The *dux Arabiae* had under his command two legions, the *Tertia Cyrenaica* based in the provincial capital, Bostra, and the *Quarta Martia* in the legionary camp of Bethhoro (el-Lejjun, northeast of Kerak), as well as 19 regiments, most of them mounted, stationed throughout the province from the Hauran in the north to Wadi el-Hasa, the southernmost ravine descending from Moab to the Dead Sea and the southern border of the province at that time.[14] The regiments under both dux consisted of *limitanei*, namely, soldiers stationed in the *limes* region who – unlike the *comitatenses* who followed the emperor in his military campaigns – permanently resided in the place where they served. They also received land there and spent part of their time in civil pursuits like agriculture, raising cattle and horses, and handicrafts.[15] Each regiment was led by a *tribunus* or, in the absence of this officer, by a lieutenant (*vicarius*).[16]

Since the dux of Arabia also served as civil governor for long periods, and his troops were stations all over the province, no doubt his headquarters was in the capital, Bostra. But where was the headquarters of the *dux Palaestinae*? Most likely not in the provincial capital Caesarea nor in the cities that became capitals when Palaestina was divided into three provinces (see below), or in Jerusalem, which held the status of *metropolis* under Byzantine rule. The presence of a large military camp in Beersheba, together with the epigraphic finds from that city, indicates that in all likelihood the headquarters of the *dux Palaestinae* was there, although Beersheba never attained urban status.[17]

§ 5. Changes of provincial borders and administrative changes

Another important change effected by Diocletian was the division of large provinces into smaller units, a trend he inaugurated and that continued during the entire fourth century. In the case of Palaestina, however, Diocletian did the opposite: he enlarged the province at the expenses of Provincia Arabia by transferring the Negev and the peninsula of Sinai, as well as southern

---

[13] Seeck 1876: 72-74; Jones 1990: 1417-1450.
[14] Seeck 1876: 80-82.
[15] Jones 1990: 649-654; 661-663.
[16] Jones 1990: 643, 675, 1279, n. 158.
[17] Fabian 1995; Di Segni 1996: 580-582; 2000: 787, n. 40; 2004a: 132-133; Gilead and Fabian 2008: 343-349.

Transjordan south of Wadi el-Hasa, from the latter to the former (ca. 295).[18] In all likelihood, the change was made for military reasons. More soldiers were required in the south and the east to protect the region, and the commercial routes through it, from Saracen attacks, and in order to answer this need the Tenth Legion was moved from Jerusalem to Aila[19] and the Sixth, in the second and third centuries based at Legio near Megiddo, to a fort rebuilt ca. 303 at Udruḥ near Petra.[20] Since by 293 Provincia Arabia had already two legions,[21] the move would have put the commander of the Arabian army, the *dux Arabiae*, at the head of a dangerously large force, while leaving Palaestina stripped of defence. By transferring the Negev and southern Transjordan to Palaestina, the usual balance of two legions per province was re-established.

An often-voiced opinion maintains that the regions east and west of the 'Aravah were treated as two separate units and changed hands separately. In one of the most detailed discussions of the issue, Mayerson contested the evidence of the transfer and argued that, even if it did happen, a reversion of the change must have occurred shortly after the Tetrarchic period, for Petra and southern Transjordan belonged to Arabia for most of the fourth century, either never having been detached from it or having rejoined Arabia before 343. Elusa and the Negev would have been separated from Palaestina and reattached to Arabia in 357/8. Both regions, east and west of the 'Aravah, would finally have been detached from Arabia in ca. 390 to become Palaestina Salutaris.[22] A Finnish scholar, Joonas Sipilä, recently developed Mayersons's arguments and maintained that the Negev and southern Transjordan passed from Arabia to Palaestina and back, together or separately, no less than six times in 90 years, between ca. 300 and ca. 390.[23] Both scholars based their conclusions on literary sources, several of which from an ecclesiastical

---

[18] Tsafrir 1983, 1986; Roll 1983; Rubin 1983; Sipilä 2004; 2007; Di Segni 2018a.
[19] Eusebius, *Onomasticon*, transl. Freeman-Grenville 2003: 14.
[20] Kennedy and Falahat 2008.
[21] Speidel (1977: 699) maintains that the *Legio IV Martia* was created by Aurelian shortly after 272 CE, rather than by Galerius in or after 293, as suggested by other scholars, especially for the reinforcement of the Arabian army. A Latin inscription discovered at Meẓad Neqarot in the eastern Negev lists soldiers of this legion, clearly stationed there (Di Segni, forthcoming (b). This indicates that the Martia was already posted in the south – at Udruḥ, where an earlier fort is dated to the time of Trajan? (Killick 1987; Kennedy 2004: 178-180), or even at Aila, before the Tenth Legion was moved there? – when the Negev still belonged to the province of Arabia.
[22] Mayerson 1984, 1987.
[23] Sipilä 2004, 2007.

or biblical background. This complicated question involves also another issue, that of the division of Palaestina into three lesser provinces, which will be discussed below. Enough be to say here, first, that epigraphical evidence from Petra and Udruḥ proves that southern Transjordan was indeed annexed to Palaestina together with the Negev by Diocletian, and second, that ecclesiastical sources pertaining to the fourth century cannot be taken as evidence of administrative realities.[24]

A new change in the provincial borders seems to have occurred about 314, when a province called New Arabia and including the city of Eleutheropolis (Beth Govrin) is mentioned in an Egyptian papyrus and in an early fourth-century list of provinces. The extension and the very existence of this province are a subject of debate among scholars.[25] If it included part of Provincia Arabia (the area between Wadi el-Mujib and Wadi el-Hasa, fronting the territory of Eleutheropolis across the Dead Sea), this might have justified the name 'New Arabia'; but nothing is known of its territory and administration.[26] In any case, New Arabia is not heard of again after the early fourth century.

A new change occurred in the year 357/8. Three epistles sent by the famous rhetor Libanius of Antioch to Clematius, governor of Palaestina, attest that in 357 Elusa and Petra were included in his province (Epistles 315 and 321), while in 358 Elusa was no longer under him (Epistle 334). In 360/1 Libanius refers to Cyrillus as governor of the region that included Elusa (Epistle 166); in 361/2 he congratulates him for his promotion 'from Palaestina to Palaestina, from a governorship to another' (Epistle 686). In that period, therefore, there were two provinces called Palaestina, one of lower grade that included Elusa, the other more important, which must be the original Palaestina whose capital was Caesarea and whose governor was by now a *consularis*.[27]

---

[24] Kennedy and Falahat 2008; Di Segni and Tsafrir 2017: 150-152, 817-818, no. 848. For a further discussion of the views summarized above, see Di Segni 2018a.

[25] Bowersock (1983: 144-146; 1984) locates Nea Arabia in eastern Egypt and Mayerson (1983; 1986a) in Idumaea. For a summary of the scholarly discussion, see Di Segni and Tsafrir 2017: 873-874; Di Segni 2018: 252-254.

[26] The area between the two rivers formed the territory of Areopolis (modern Rabba in the Kerak District, Jordan) and included the legionary fort at Udruḥ. It must be noted that the Dead Sea, regularly crossed by ships and barges, as shown in the Madaba map (Friedman 2012), would not have been considered a barrier, but rather a commodious route for moving goods between the opposite coasts. See Cyril of Scythopolis, *Life of Sabas* 81, ed. Schwartz 1939: 186; trans. Price 1991: 195/Di Segni 2005: 213.

[27] The governor of Palaestina Salutaris or Tertia was always a *praeses*. On Clematius and Cyrillus, see Jones et al. 1971: 213-214; 237-238. For a detailed discussion of Libanius' evidence and its interpretation, see Mayerson 1987; Di Segni 2018a: 254-258.

The commonly accepted assumption is that these epistles attest to the creation of Palaestina Salutaris, consisting of the part of the province – from the Valley of Beersheba southward – that had belonged to Arabia until the late third century. Mayerson, however, rejected this conclusion. Though admitting that a split had occurred in Palaestina in 357/8, he maintained that it represented the separation of the Negev from Palaestina and its re-attachment to Arabia.[28] In his view, Palaestina Salutaris was created only ca. 390, based on a passage in St. Jerome's *Hebraicae quaestiones in libro Geneseos* (21, 30-31, ed. de Lagarde 1959: 26). In this work, written between 389 and 391, Jerome states that 'from Genesis 20-21 we must infer that Isaac was not born at the Oak of Mamre… but in Gerar,[29] where the town of Beersheba is to this very day. Not long ago (*ante non grande tempus*), following a division of the governors, this province has been named Palaestina Salutaris'. Mayerson also notes that in the *Novella* 103, an edict issued by Justinian in 536, by which the governor of Palaestina Prima was raised from the rank of *consularis* to that of *proconsul*, the emperor explained that the governor residing in Caesarea had already enjoyed the proconsular rank in the past, before the division of Palaestina into three provinces, and had been demoted to *consularis* after the division. Hence, Mayerson claims, Palaestina Tertia can only have been created after the 380s, in which years the governor in Caesarea is called *proconsul* and awarded the title of *spectabilis* in written sources and inscriptions. Indeed, the change in the governor's rank probably marked a change in the importance of his province, as reflected in its size. But, since the division attested by Libanius in 357/8 can hardly be explained away, a reasonable solution may be that the southern province, possibly called *Palaestina Salutaris*,[30] was joined again to the northern part, called simply *Palaestina*, and in this occasion the governor of the re-established

---

[28] Mayerson 1987; 1988. Mayerson is followed by Sipilä (2004; 2007). Besides making incorrect use of ecclesiastical sources, both neglect Epistle 166, which proves that, after the split of 357/8, a governor of Palaestina, Cyrillus (see above), was still in charge of Elusa.

[29] That is, in the district called Geraritica in the northern Negev, corresponding to the basin of Naḥal Gerar.

[30] The name Palaestina Salutaris is first documented in the *Notitia Dignitatum*, ca. 395-413, and may not have been the name of the province created in 357/8. However, several provinces were split in the fourth and early fifth century and in each case the main part preserved the original name, while the lesser province was given Secunda or Salutaris as a modifier; for instance, Macedonia was split into Macedonia (Prima) and Macedonia Secunda or Salutaris, Lesser Armenia into Armenia (Prima) and Armenia Secunda, Cappadocia into Cappadocia (Prima) and Cappadocia Secunda, Cilicia into Cilicia (Prima) and Cilicia Secunda, Coele Syria into Syria (Prima) and Syria Salutaris.

greater Palaestina was promoted to proconsul. The first known proconsul was Eucharius, addressee of an imperial rescript dated 22 November 383;[31] the last governor of the united Palaestina was probably Hilarius who, according to the historian Zosimus, was appointed by Theodosius I to govern 'all Palestine'. His term of office can probably be dated to 387/8.[32] The upgrade of the governor's office and the temporary reconstitution of a 'greater Palestine' may be connected with the beginning of the new religious policy of Valens' successor, Theodosius, who supported Nicaene orthodoxy (with the Edict of Thessalonica, 27 February 380) and began to expel Arian clergy. Putting the whole province under a single, more powerful authority could facilitate the success of this campaign, and once it was achieved, *Palaestina Salutaris* was separated again, ca. 389/90, shortly before St. Jerome wrote the passage cited above.

Was this the occasion of the creation also of Palaestina Seconda? The division of the province into First, Second and Third or Salutaris is attested for the first time in an edict of Theodosius II issued on March 23, 409,[33] as well as in the *Notitia Dignitatum* of the East, compiled ca. 395 and updated before 413.[34] But the titulature of a group of governors attested in inscriptions discovered at Beth Shean indicates that in the last years of the fours century and the first years of the fifth the governor bore titles higher than those due to a *consularis* and suited to the rank of a proconsul. It is likely, therefore, that they were not governors of Second Palestine residing in their capital, Beth Shean, but governors residing in Caesarea who still ruled over the whole northern part of the country. One of them was Artemidorus, who erected a statue of Eudoxia Augusta, a title Arcadius' wife held from 400 to her death

---

[31] *Codex Theodosianus* XI, 36, 28; transl. Pharr 1952: 338; Jones et al. 1971: 288. In the list of governors of Palestine reconstructed by Jones et al. (1971: 1108-1109) there is a gap between the consular governors of the 360s and the proconsular governors of the 380s, and the rank of the governors in between is not known. However, the governor in charge of the northern and central part of the country ca. 375-378 was a *consularis*. Palladius (*Historia Lausiaca* 46, 3, ed. Butler 1904: 135) describes the arrest of Melania the Elder by the *consularis* in Sepphoris, where this Roman lady had followed the Egyptian monks and bishops exiled by the Arian emperor Valens. The exile – and Melania's stay in Sepphoris – ended after Valens' death in August 378.

[32] Zosimus, *Historia nova* IV, 41, 2-3. Jones et al. (1971:435, Hilarius 8) date his governorship to 392/3, but this must be wrong, for by that time Palaestina Salutaris was certainly separated from the main body of Palaestina. For the date of Hilarius' governorship, see Di Segni 2018a: 256-257.

[33] *Codex Theodosianus* VII, 4, 30; transl. Pharr 1952: 162.

[34] *Not. Dign. Or.* II, 9, 16-17, ed. Seeck 1876: 5-6. For the date of the text, see Jones 1990: 1420-1421.

in 404 (see Chapter V. 1. 4). This province would therefore have been divided into First and Second Palaestina only after 400 and shortly before 409.[35] From this moment and up to Justinian's reign three governors – a *consularis* and two *praesides* (ἡγεμόνες) of lower rank – resided in three capitals, Caesarea in Palaestina (Prima), Scythopolis (Beth Shean) in Palaestina Secunda and Petra in Palaestina Salutaris, now also called Tertia. They bore the honorary title of *clarissimus* ('most distinguished'), though inscriptions often give them a courtesy title, *magnificentissimus* (μεγαλοπρεπέστατος, 'most magnificent'), which, though higher than *clarissimus*, had no official value. This is the situation attested by the *Notitia Dignitatum* and still reflected in the *Synecdemos* of Hierocles, a list of provinces with their cities and towns compiled ca. 527/8 CE.[36]

A change occurred after the Samaritan revolt that broke out in Samaria and in Scythopolis in spring 529. Possibly because of the failure of the governor of Palaestina Secunda to put down the disorders with the forces at his disposal, after the revolt was crushed it was decided to raise the rank of this officer from *praeses* to *consularis*. This would give his bureau a larger budget and most likely more forces to keep order. There is no edict putting this decision into words, but it is first attested in a notice attached to *Novella* 8, issued in 535, which lists Palaestina Secunda among the provinces ruled by *consulares*. Now the governors of First and Second Palestine held the same rank, in contrast to the traditional primacy of Caesarea. To restore this, and to ensure a proper policing of Second Palestine, where Samaritan unrest was not yet stilled, a new provision was soon applied. In 536 Justinian issued *Novella* 103, which not only enhanced the status of the governor of First Palestine (promoted from *consularis* to *proconsul*, as already mentioned above,

---

[35] Di Segni and Arubas 2009: 116*-117*; Di Segni 2018a: 259-260. This progressive dismemberment of large provinces, with creation of new, smaller ones, and sometimes disappearance of the latter, is not unique of Palaestina. For a similar phenomenon in Syria, see Balty 1980. Coele-Syria, created by Septimius Severus through the separation of Syria Phoenice from Syria, was divided into Augusta Euphratensis and Augusta Libanensis in the fourth century. The names soon went out of usage, but while the northern Euphratensis remained intact, Libanensis, again called Syria, was further divided into Syria (Prima) and Syria Salutaris or Secunda at the end of the fourth century or at the beginning of the fifth. Syria Phonice was also split into Phoenice Paralia ('Along the sea') and Phoenice Libanenis. In the sixth century another small province, Theodorias, was carved out of territories taken from Syria Prima and Secunda; it was in the coastal area of Laodicea (today Latakyia) and was named in honour of Justinian's wife Theodora.

[36] *Not. Dign. Or.* I, 59, 87-88, ed. Seeck 1876: 2-4; Hierocles, *Synec.* 717, 53; 719, 12; 721, 1, ed. Honigmann 1939: 41-43.

with an enlarged bureau and raised pay), but also extended his powers, entrusting him with intervening in Second Palestine when the governor of the latter was unable to put down local disorders. In case of need, the proconsul was to co-opt soldiers from those under the control of the dux.[37] The rank and tasks of the governor of Third Palestine remained unchanged. The main change in this province after its creation – or its second creation, in the late fourth century – was the extension of its border in Transjordan at the expenses of Provincia Arabia. The area between Wadi el-Hasa and Wadi el-Mujib was transferred to Third Palestine, so that a number of settlements in this zone, where the *Notitia Dignitatum* locates regiments under the command of the *dux Arabiae*, are mentioned again in the Beersheba Tax Edict as pertaining to the *dux Palaestinae*. The transfer gave rise to no change in the status of the governor, and its precise date is unknown: seemingly it took place in the mid fifth century.[38] The *terminus ante quem* is the synod of Jerusalem in 518, which was attended by the bishop of Areopolis together with the other bishops of Palestine, in a time when ecclesiastical borders coincided with administrative borders.

§ 6. City administration

By the mid-fourth century the province of Palaestina was completely urbanized. The last headquarters of toparchies, large villages functioning as administrative centres of rural districts, which together with the territories of the cities had formed the substructure of the province in the Roman period, had either been made into cities or their equivalent (see below) or had been absorbed in existing urban territories. Many rural areas in various parts of the country, however, were not included in the territory of any city: they were imperial estates, whose origins went back to the Roman, and in some cases, even to the Hellenistic period. In Late Antiquity these estates were called *saltus* (*salton* in the Greek form) or *tractus* (*klima* in Greek) and occupied large, sometimes huge expanses of land, mainly in peripheral areas.

---

[37] Mayerson (1986b) suggested that the unknown tax whose assessments are listed in the Beersheba edict was meant to cover the cost of the enlarged bureau of the proconsul of First Palestine. This is very unlikely, as the discovery of a new fragment in 1996 proved that the edict was addressed to the *dux Palaestinae*. For a reappraisal of the edict and a critical review of the many hypotheses about its meaning and date, see Di Segni 2004a.

[38] A clue that the transfer may have occurred before 449 can perhaps be found in the list of the bishops who attended the Second Council of Ephesus. Judging by his place in the list, Anastasius bishop of Areopolis sat amidst the Palestinian bishops: Honigmann 1942: 35, no. 72.

For instance, two very extensive imperial estates, the *Saltus Constantinianus* and the *Saltus Gerariticus*, occupied most of the northwestern Negev, and another, the *Klima Gaulanes*, occupied the central part of the Golan Heights. These estates were managed by imperial procurators (ἐπίτροποι) subject to the emperor's patrimony (*res private*), an arrangement of the Roman period still attested in Late Antiquity.[39] With the Christianization of the countryside, the main centres of the saltus acquired bishops of their own, thus achieving quasi-urban status.[40] Also in the Hauran, which formed the northernmost part of the province of Arabia, the largest villages of the imperial estates acquired their own bishops in the course of the fifth and especially of the sixth century. Such a village, known as *metrokomia*, then attained the status of town, but not the administration system of a *polis*.[41] Again, in Palaestina (Prima) four towns – Jericho, former headquarters of a toparchy, Gadora, former metropolis of Peraea, Amathus and Livias (Betharamatha), royal cities of the Hasmonaeans in Peraea – are recorded as centres of *regiones* in the early seventh-century geographical list of Georgius of Cyprus.[42] The term indicates that those districts too belonged to the imperial patrimony.[43] Due to their past history and their strategic location along main roads, these four centres soon became seats of bishops (Jericho and Gadora in the early fourth

---

[39] Jones 1990: 413, 713; Sartre 2001: 206, 406-407, 736-743. A still unpublished inscription from the so-called 'Third-Mile Estate' near Ascalon mentions two personages in charge of the place, an *epitropos*, styled *gloriosissimus*, and another man of lower rank but still rating as *clarissimus*. An *epitropos* of such an exalted rank can hardly have been the stewards of a private estate; it is more likely, therefore, that he was responsible for the *saltus* in the entire province, while the *clarissimus* was the steward of this particular estate.

[40] The bishop of the Saltus Constantinianus most likely resided at Menois, today Ma'on-Nirim, where inscriptions using a Constantinian era were discovered (Meimaris 1992: 324-329). Bishops of Menois attended the second Council of Ephesus (449 CE) and two synods of the Palestinian Church in Jerusalem, 518 and 536 CE (Fedalto 1988: 1027). Another bishop of the Saltus Constantinianus is probably Petrus, mentioned in a mosaic inscription of the Byzantine church unearthed at Kibbutz Magen (*SEG* XXXV, no. 1552). The bishop of Saltus Gerariticus resided at Orda (Kh. 'Irq), or possibly at Birsama (H. Beer Shema', where two bishops of Gerar are mentioned in the splendid mosaic pavements of a church (*SEG* XLVI, nos. 2005, 2009). The bishops of Gerar or Orda attended the council of Chalcedon (451 CE) and the two synods of Jerusalem, 518 and 536 CE (Fedalto 1988: 1023). See also Tsafrir et al. 1994: 91 (Birsama), 183 (Menois), 198 (Orda), 220 (Saltus Constantinianus, Saltus Gerariticus).

[41] Sartre 1999; 2001: 776; 2005: 231.

[42] Georgius Cyprius, *Descriptio*, nos. 1016-1019, ed. Honigmann 1939: 67.

[43] The Arab name of Gadora, es-Salt, preserves the memory of the ancient status of the area as a *saltus*: Avi-Yonah 1976: 60. Another *saltus* mentioned in the geographic list of Georgius of Cyprus, *Salton Batanaias*, an imperial estate in Bashan, is identified with the site called in Arabic Deir es-Salt (*Descriptio*, no. 1076, ed. Honigmann 1939: 68).

century, Amathus and Livias in the early fifth). As bishops became more and more involved in the practical aspects of community leadership, the transformation of a district headquarters into an episcopal seat upgraded it to the equivalent of a city, though without the governing organ of a *polis*, the *boulé*. As we shall see, the administration system of the *polis*, which was introduced in the region in the Hellenistic period, in Late Antiquity was rapidly becoming obsolete.

The autonomous city of the Roman period, the *polis*, was governed by the city council (βουλή, Latin, *curia*), composed of the wealthier citizens, the βουλευταί (*bouleutai*), whose number varied in different cities, from a few dozens to hundreds, and from whose ranks the executive officers, three or more ἄρχοντες (*archontes*), were elected yearly.[44] The council nominated the candidates for the various annual offices (e.g., *agoranomos* in charge of the markets; *gymnasiarchos* in charge of the public gymnasium, the focal place for educating the young; *agonothetes* in charge of the city games; *sitones* in charge of the corn supply). None of the urban offices commanded a salary; on the contrary, the holders were required to finance at least part of the expenses incurred in the course of their term.[45] The city council was responsible for the villages included in its territory, in particular for collecting their taxes and for channelling their applications to the provincial authorities or the emperor. The *bouleutai* were collectively responsible for the yearly amount of taxes imposed by the imperial authorities on the fiscal unit represented by their city and its *chora* (χώρα, territory). In case they could not levy the entire sum, they had to make it up from their own pockets. The

---

[44] In the Roman period, several Palestinian cities received the status of *colonia*. In our region this status granted no special privileges, and the only visible difference in the administration of a *colonia* from that of a *polis* is that the official language of a *colonia* was Latin: thus the council was called *curia* instead of *boulé*, the councilmen *curiales* or *decuriones* instead of *bouleutai*, and *flamines coloniae* (priests of the imperial cult) were added to the city priesthood. Moreover, two *duumviri* (in Greek στρατηγοί) replaced the three or more *archontes*. Except for the *flamines*, who of course disappeared under the Christian emperors, traces of the colonial administrative system survived in Late Antiquity.

[45] An inscription from Gerasa dated between 105 and 114 CE (Welles 1938: 442-444, no. 192) announces the erection of a statue of the *agonothetes* in charge of the first annual festival in honour of Trajan, Titus Flavius Gerrenus, by the guild of the artists, in thanks for his generosity towards its members in prizes, feasting and all necessities. No doubt Gerrenus also showered his largesse on other categories – athletes and spectators of the games – in the same occasion. But service in the council could also be profitable: as responsible for tax collection councilmen could manage to shift the heaviest burden from themselves to others; as responsible for public building, contractors among them could secure the most lucrative projects, and so on.

economic crisis of the third century reduced the wealth of the bouleutic class to such a degree that many councilmen chose flight to avoid being ruined by the obligations of the service. An additional blow was dealt to this class in the fourth century by a series of imperial edicts that forced the cities to give up a large proportion of their revenues to the imperial treasury, depleted by wars and economic crisis. In the Roman period the city revenues, deriving from rents of agricultural lands and real estate belonging to the city, as well as from tolls, customs and various urban imposts, served to build and maintain public buildings and to keep up services and amenities such as heating and providing with oil the public baths, lightening streets, meeting the basic expenses of ceremonies and festivals. By the end of the fourth century the cities were deprived of all but one third of their revenues.[46] From a privilege for which the most prominent citizens were willing to pay, the *boulé* became a hereditary duty from which the councilmen (since the fourth century no longer called *bouleutai* but *politeuomenoi*) tried to escape by any means, such as entering the clergy or a monastery, or striving to secure an imperial office that would carry exemption from the curia. The emperor vainly issued edicts forbidding wealthy councilmen to abandon the curial duty, unless they provided another to take their place. The depletion of the councils became more and more severe during the fifth and sixth century, to the point that in many cities the council ceased to function altogether or continued to exist only formally, while the management of the city passed into other hands. Also the civic offices, once sought after as status symbols, became liturgies imposed by law, or simply disappeared.[47]

In the late antique city of the Holy Land we rarely hear of *bouleuta/politeuomenoii*. From the time of Emperor Anastasius they lost the last important function they had formerly fulfilled, the collection of taxes, which was assigned to imperial officers called *vindices*. The management of the city affairs was now in the hands of a small group of prominent citizens, the πρῶτοι or πρωτεύοντες (*protoi*, *proteuontes*; Latin *primates*, i.e., 'first citizens'), who acted in close collaboration with the bishop. Together, the *protoi* and the bishop appointed the main officers of the city – the *pater civitatis*, the *defensor civitatis*, the *sitones* and the other city functionaries, and together they audited the city accounts at the end of each year.[48] Building inscriptions

---

[46] Jones 1990: 131, 146-147, 732-737.
[47] On changes in the transition from the Roman period to Late Antiquity, see for instance Foster 1970; Whittow 1990; Laniado 1997; 2014. For a detailed study of the city notables in Late Antiquity and an evaluation of their role in urban life, see Laniado 2002; 2021.
[48] *Codex Justinianus* I, 4, 26 (535 CE); *Nov.* 128, 16 (545 CE).

of the fifth century still sometimes mention a councilman as the person in charge of a public project, together with the governor, but in the sixth century the task devolved on the *pater civitatis* or on one of the *protoi*. In building inscriptions the name of the governor always appears first, not only as a dating device but also to stress his supervising role, for public building in a city was to be financed only with the city money, and no money was allowed to come out of the provincial coffers to pay for city expenses.[49]

The office of πατὴρ πόλεως, *pater civitatis*, 'father of the city', the late antique name of the earlier *curator rei publicae* (in Greek λογιστὴς τῆς πόλεως, *logistes tēs poleos*, 'overseer of the city accounts'), originated from the problem of overspending by cities especially in Asia Minor in the Roman period. Already in the early second century cities in need of costly infrastructures, such as aqueducts or public baths, or just eager to compete with neighbouring cities by erecting larger and more splendid public buildings, started spending more than their budget permitted, then turning to the emperor for help. To put an end to crippling expenditure by the cities, since Trajan's time a provincial auditor was appointed by the emperor in every province to inspect city accounts. By the late second century such imperial auditors were appointed to single cities. In Late Antiquity they were nominated by the city from its most prominent citizens, and the nomination was submitted to the emperor for approval. Their duties consisted in managing the city property (such as lands, shops, testamentary bequests and the like) and overseeing the outlay of the city resources.[50] As the father of the city had to authorize all expenditure, under the governor's supervision, no wonder the names of these officials appear in building inscriptions in the late antique cities of the Holy Land, as well as in all the East.

The second important officer of the city was the *defensor civitatis* ('city advocate', ἔκδικος in Greek). Like the *pater civitatis*, he was nominated by the city conditionally to imperial approval. He was the legal representative of the city, but in Late Antiquity he was also invested with the role of judge with jurisdiction on minor civil cases.[51] The city had several other offices, some held as liturgies for a limited period, such as *sitones* and *elaiones* (public buyers of corn and oil) and the *ephoros* or *episkopos* (inspector of the market),[52] others professional and entitled to a salary, such as the *eirenarches*

---

[49] Di Segni 1995: 320-321; 323-326.
[50] Guerber and Sartre 1998.
[51] Di Segni et al. 2003: 286-287; Di Segni 2006b: 113-114.
[52] Laniado and Dashti 1993. This is the functionary called *agoranomos* in the Roman period who, besides generally supervising the market and inspecting the quality of the goods on sale,

('keeper of the peace': a kind of chief of police in charge of public order), the *archiatros* ('chief physician', in charge of public health) and the *zygostates* ('weigher', whose function was to check the quality of the gold coins in the city market).

In some cases inscriptions attest to the involvement of a τοποτηρητής ('deputy) in building activity in a city. In Gerasa, the *magistrianos* and *topoteretes* Flavius Sergius is attested in a building inscription dated August 533 CE; his name follows that of the dux and governor Flavius Anastasius and carries two epithets: καθωσιωμένος, *devotus*, 'devoted', due to his paramilitary status, and λαμπρότατος, *clarissimus*, indicating his personal high status. In Beth Shean-Scythopolis Constantine, περίβλεπτος (*spectabilis*) *topoteretes* was responsible for an unknown building project; the inscription is undated and was found in secondary use.[53] The mere term *topoteretes* provides no clue to the function of this official, for the literary and legal sources offer abundant evidence of 'deputies' (*topoteretai*) of all kinds, including deputies of bishops, and deputies despatched to the provinces by a *praefectus praetorio*, the *comes sacrarum largitionum* and the *comes rerum privatarum*, on missions related to their offices.[54] But both men in the above-mentioned inscriptions fulfilled functions in a city; therefore the scenario behind their appointment must be searched in Justinian's laws pertaining to provincial and urban administration. Several Novels forbid governors, either civil or military, to despatch *topoteretai* to the cities of the provinces they governed. The prohibition has to be repeated several times, between 535 and 556, and reinforced with penalties of heavy fine and exile for both the appointer and the appointee.[55]

As representative of the governor in a city, we would expect a *topoteretes* to be active also in the countryside within the territory of the city in his charge. Indeed, we find an example at Ma'in, in the territory of Madaba, where a πριβάτον (private bath) was built 'under the *clarissimus* and *spect-*

---

also verified and guaranteed the accuracy of weights used by vendors. In some early Byzantine documents the officer is also called *logistes*, which prompted some scholars to suggest that this task too was invested on the *curator civitatis* or *pater civitatis*, but it is more likely that he was a subordinate officer (Foster 1970: 131-139).

[53] Welles 1938: 469-470, nos. 277-278; the inscription from Beth Shean is mentioned by Foerster and Tsafrir 1993: 32.

[54] See for instance *Nov.* 134, 1 (ed. Schoell and Kroll 1954: 677).

[55] *Nov.* 8, 4; 17, 10; 28, 4; 29, 2; 30, 7, 1; 128, 20-22; 134, 1-2 (ed. Schoell and Kroll 1954: 68, 124, 214-215, 220, 230, 644-645, 677).

abilis tribune and *topoteretes* Flavius Martyrius' in the sixth century.[56] The inscription is most clearly a public one, and therefore the 'private bath' cannot have been the appurtenance of a private house, and it not much likely that if was built by the tribune as a business venture. Possibly it was *privatum* as opposed to a δημόσιον, 'public bath', that is, it was not open to all but reserved for a particular category. Military officers under the aegis of the dux built guesthouses and bathhouses for the use of travelling officers and soldiers, who were formerly forbidden to claim access to private bathing facilities as part of their billeting privileges.[57] A process by which a forbidden practice was first tolerated, then regulated by law, is rather typical of legal evolution in Late Antiquity.

The *topoteretes* represented the governor in all his functions, including the administration of justice and the supervision of tax collection, and the involvement of such deputies in building activity in Gerasa, Scythopolis and in the territory of Madaba indicates that their residence in these cities was long-term, not limited for a short period before the arrival of a new governor or during his absence by imperial command, which was permitted by the law. The high status of the men mentioned in the inscriptions implies that their influence in the city was great, as they were equal to, or even outranked, the local leaders. They may have been appointed to help administering cities where leadership was lacking or ineffectual, or, as the language of some Novels hints, the governors' aim was to extort money from the provincials and to divert to their own pockets gold that should have reached the Treasury. In any case, the result of this practice, which imperial enactments could not curb, was to curtail the already limited autonomy of the city.[58]

Another indication of the decline of the city leading class is represented by the growing authority of the city bishop. Not only was his tribunal recognized as early as the first half of the fourth century, but he took over more and more functions, from partecipating in the nomination of the *defensor civitatis* and the father of the city to checking the accounts of the city, from

---

[56] *IGLJ* II, no. 162. Ma'in, ancient Beelmaus (biblical Ba'al Ma'on) was a village in the territory of Madaba, though it is possible that at some late date it was counted as an episcopal see under the name of Dalmounda: Schmitt 1995: 86-87.

[57] The right was reserved only to officers of *illustris* rank by two decrees of *Codex Theodosianus* (VII, 11, 1-2, 406 and 417 CE), revived in *Codex Justinianus* I, 47, 1. On officers, including some styles *topoteretai*, building baths, see Di Segni 1995: 326-327.

[58] Jones 1990: 295, 759; Di Segni 1995: 326-328; Laniado 2002: 83, 85 (civil suits addressed to *topoteretai* in cities of Egypt), 236, 251. The presence of a *topoteretes* even at Scythopolis, the capital of Second Palestine and the seat of its governor, seems to indicate that the appointment aimed to encroach on the authority of the city magistrates.

erecting public buildings to providing for the water supply,[59] from controlling the behaviour of the governors[60] to treating with the invading Muslims on behalf of their city.[61]

§ 7. Village administration

We have very little information about the administration of villages in late antique Palestine,[62] unlike villages in the Hauran, which were managed by a collective leadership and whose communal institutions and numerous magistrates are known from inscriptions.[63] In the provinces of Palaestina we encounter two types of villages: privately owned and communities of free landowners. Privately owned villages were managed by a steward (*epitropos*) on behalf of the owner, a wealthy man usually residing in a city. The phenomenon is well illustrated by the literary sources,[64] and also attested in inscriptions, though the admittedly meagre epigraphic evidence is sometimes misunderstood, possibly because the term *epitropos* suggests a *procurator Augusti* of the Roman period, out of place in a late antique inscription. For instance, an inscription engraved on the base of an obelisk at Beyda near Petra, copied by Musil at the beginning of the twentieth century and republished by Sartre, reads: Τὰ πάντα Νίρου ἐπιτρόπου σπουδῇ ἔτους τι', 'All this (was set up) by the care of Niros, *epitraopos*, year 310'. The date, according to the era of Arabia used throughout this region, corresponds to 415/6 CE, but Musil calculated the year as 2/1 BCE, by the Seleucid era, be-

---

[59] Di Segni 1995: 332; Cyril of Scythopolis, *Life of Sabas* 67, ed. Schwartz 1939: 167-169; transl. Price 1991: 177-179/Di Segni 2005: 199-200.

[60] Laniado 2002: 236.

[61] Mayerson 1964: 175-176.

[62] On the social organization of the Jewish village in the Talmudic period, see Safrai 1995, who however uses a mixture of evidence from village and town life.

[63] MacAdam 1986; Sartre 1993a; on the *metrokomiai*, see above, § 6.

[64] For a steward in the village of Capharzacharia, see Sozomen, *Historia Ecclesiastica* IX, 17; note that all the English translations (E. Walford, London 1855; Ch.D. Hartranft in *Nicene and Post-Nicene Fathers*, II, 2. Buffalo, NY 1890, as well as the revised edition of the latter by K. Knight http://www.newadvent.org/fathers/26029.htm) misunderstood the Greek text and rendered *epitropos* with 'serf'. For an *epitropos* in a private estate near Emmaus, see Cyril of Scythopolis, *Life of Sabas* 35, ed. Schwartz 1939:120-121; transl. Price 1991: 130/ Di Segni 2002: 169. For the description of the purchase of the large village of Porphyreon on the Carmel coast by a rhetor of Caesarea, already a wealthy landowner, for the sum of three *centenaria* of gold (ca. 97 kg), see Procopius, *Secret History* XXX, 18-19, transl. Dewing 1935: 353-355. Wealthy Caesarean Christians owned most of the agricultural lands cultivated by Samaritan tenants: *ibidem* XI, 29-30, transl. Dewing 1935: 139.

cause of the 'pagan nature' of the monument and the mention of an *epitropos*, who was taken for a provincial procurator as a matter of course. Sartre chose to maintain the era of Arabia but to correct the figure from TI to Π, '80', so to give 185/6 CE, on the same assumption that no such procurator was likely to exist in 415. But the correction is unnecessary, and it is much more likely that the man, who boasts of no *nomen gentilicium*, was merely the steward of a private estate.[65] Another inscription, set in a sixth-century mosaic pavement in a church at ed-Deir near Ma'in, southwest of Madaba, mentions an *epitropos* who erected the church 'for the salvation and help of the most glorious *illustris* Theodorus', not a governor or *dux* (of Arabia) as assumed by Gatier, but a man of the new senatorial rank, the top echelon of aristocracy in the Byzantine period.[66] The complex (a basilica with three attached rooms, surrounded by ancient agricultural terraces but no living quarters or installations of any kind) was nevertheless identified by Piccirillo as a monastery;[67] however, since no priest or monk is mentioned in the dedicatory inscription or in the other inscriptions in the church, it is more likely that its was a private church, the *illustris* was the landlord and the *epitropos* his steward.[68]

Villages of free landowners were under the leadership of a head man or of a small council of aldermen who acted as a collective leadership under the primacy of one headman. These officers are known from literary and epigraphic sources under different names: ἄρχων ('chief'), πρωτοκωμήτης ('head man of a village'), πιστικός ('trustee'). In the few testimonies that reached us only one *archon* or *protokometes* is mentioned in any given circumstances, but this does not prove that he was the only holder of that office in his village. For instance, a *protokometes* of Aristobulias near Hebron applied to the saintly monk Euthymius to cure his son, who was possessed by

---

[65] *IGLJ* IV, no. 29; for a critical view, see Di Segni 1993d: 506.

[66] *IGLJ* II, no. 175. The senate in Constantinople served as an advisory body for the emperor and its memberships was composed of only the most experienced and selected men of power, who were obliged to reside in the capital. However, the title *illustris* that distinguished them was sometimes granted *honoris causa* to members of the provincial aristocracy who did not actually sit in the senate, and those were exempt from the obligation to live in the capital.

[67] Piccirillo 1989: 242-246; Michel 2001: 367-370, no. 136.

[68] The absence of any member of the clergy is significant, for in some inscriptions from Syria *epitropoi* appear as executors of works under a bishop or a priest: e.g. *IGLS* II, nos. 270, 279, from villages in Chalcidike; *IGLS* XIII, 1, no. 9128, from Bostra. In these cases they must be stewards of the church, equivalent to the *oikonomos* in Palestine; cf. Di Segni 2004b: 57-58. For another *epitropos* in a context similar to that of ed-Deir but more likely the steward of an imperial estate, see above, n. 39.

an evil spirit.⁶⁹ An inscription not earlier than the seventh century attests that a *pistikos* cared for the erection of a sacred (?) building in the village of Battir (ancient Bethar).⁷⁰ In a papyrus of the Umayyad period from Nessana only one man is described as *archon* in a group of signatories of tax receipts.⁷¹ But in sixth-century papyri from Egypt a body (κοινόν) of *protokometai* is represented as collectively responsible for the payment of the village taxes. The situation may have been similar in Palestine, namely, a body of aldermen designated with different names acted under a headman. The same seems to be true also for Arabia. In Umm er-Rasas, ancient Castrum Mefaa, a dedicatory inscription in the sixth-century Church of Bishop Sergius mentions five *pistikoi*,⁷² while inscriptions in the Church of St. Stephen, dated 718 CE, mention an *archon* of Mefaa and a *pistikos*.⁷³ An inscription from Zizia, east of Madaba, dated 580 CE, refers to the renovation of a building under the *dux*, by the care of an ἄρχων τ‹ῶ›ν τόπων ('chief of these places'), carried out by a man of *clarissimus* rank whose position is not stated.⁷⁴ Here, however, the mention of the *dux* and the fact that – at least in the fifth century – Zizia was the basis of a cavalry unit⁷⁵ make it likely that the renovated building was a fort; therefore the *archon* and the *clarissimus* may have been army officers. A similar situation is known at Shivta. Here the head man of the village appears to have been the commanding officer of *limitanei* stationed there, Ioannes the *vicarius* ('lieutenant'), whose name appears in several inscriptions; in one, he acts as founder of an unidentified building together with the *priores*, the senior NCO of the regiment.⁷⁶ In a settlement whose population in the sixth century must have consisted mostly of *limitanei*, though its name does not appear in the early fifth-century *Notitia Dignitatum*, this arrangement functioned just like the *archon* and the body of

---

⁶⁹ Cyril of Scythopolis, *Life of Euthymius* 12, ed. Schwartz 1939: 22; transl. Price 1991: 18/ Di Segni 2002: 88.
⁷⁰ Avi-Yonah 1932: 142, no. 13.
⁷¹ *P. Nessana* 58, ed. Kraemer 1958: 168-171.
⁷² Piccirillo 1994b: 259-260, no. 15; *SEG* XXXVII, no. 1597.
⁷³ Piccirillo 1994: 244-247, nos. 2, 4; *SEG* XXXVII, nos. 1553, 1555.
⁷⁴ *IGLJ* II, no. 155.
⁷⁵ *Not. Dign. Or.* XXXVII, 16, ed. Seeck 1876: 81.
⁷⁶ Negev 1981: 65-66, no. 75. The date assigned by Negev, 505 CE, is erroneous and should be corrected to 599 CE: Di Segni 1997a: 814-819, no. 323. Ioannes the *vicarius* was a patron of the North Church in Shivta, where two of his sons where buried (Negev 1981: 52, 55, 60-61, nos. 51, 57, 66). Another *vicarius* is mentioned in a fragmentary inscription found near the North Gate of Shivta, adjacent to the North Church (Negev 1981: 62, no. 69). On the military leadership in Shivta see also Hirschfeld 2003.

aldermen in a village of civil peasants, with one main difference: the leaders of a civil settlement would no doubt be elected, while in a settlement such as Shivta or Zizia the army officers would have held the leadership based on their appointed military rank.

APPENDIX B: CHURCH ADMINISTRATION

From its earliest formation, the Christian communities had deacons (διάκονοι, 'attendants'), presbyters (πρεσβύτεροι, 'elders') and bishops (ἐπίσκοποι, 'overseers') who attended to the various needs of the congregation. By the time Christianity was recognized as a tolerated, then as the accepted religion of the Roman Empire, these tasks had long become a close-knitted hierarchy in which each office had its clearly defined duties and status. At the bottom of the pyramid were the lower ranks of the Church: lectors who read the Scripture during the services, deacons, who collected the offerings and distributed alms to the poor, kept the sacred vessels and assisted in the liturgy, but were not allowed to celebrate the Eucharist. There were also female deacons, who cared for the poor and sick and attended the baptism of women. The presbyters, or priests, conducted the cult and celebrated the Eucharistic Mass. A church could have several lectors and deacons but usually had only one priest, unless it was an important church or a pilgrimage site, where several sacred services were performed daily at the main altar and in side chapels. Archpriests, archdeacons and subdeacons are also mentioned in inscriptions and papyri as well as in literary and legal sources.[77] Churches also had lay attendants, such as gatekeepers, wardens and/or stewards in charge of the church property. Not only the laymen in the service of the church, but also all the clergy except the bishop were married persons, unless they were monks, and at least the lower ranks, but often presbyters too, did not follow religion as a profession but had other occupations as well, like land to farm or estates to administer.[78] Bishops were not permitted to live in marriage but had to be unmarried, widowers, or separated from their wives. For this reason, they were often chosen from the ranks of monks. In Late Antiquity the monasteries of St. Sabas and St. Theodosius in the desert of Jerusalem provided bishops to many cities in Palestine, Arabia and beyond.

---

[77] Meimaris 1986: 162-203.
[78] From the correspondence of Barsanuphius of Gaza (*Epistulae* 814-817) we learn that bishops ordained clergy in the villages on the request of the local people. Presbyters so chosen were themselves villagers, surely of some prominence: it is hardly likely that they would abandon their lay business on assuming religious leadership.

In most cases the seat of a bishop was in a city, whence he controlled the churches of the city and its territory; this was his diocese, which from an early date corresponded to the territory of a city or to a *saltus*. However, in the fourth and fifth centuries in Palestine, and even more in Arabia, where urbanization was still incomplete, bishops could also be located in villages. With time, these villages acquired city status, or the see was moved to a nearby city. This was the case, for instance, of Chabulon (today's Kabul in western Galilee), which was the see of a bishop at the time of the Council of Nicaea (325 CE), when the main city of western Galilee, Sepphoris-Diocaesarea, was mostly Jewish and partly pagan. As soon as Diocaesarea acquired a strong Christian community, the seat of the bishop was moved there from Chabulon.[79]

The bishop had authority on all the churches and all the clergy of his diocese, as well as on the monasteries and nunneries, and the monks and nuns therein. His responsibilities, in many aspects extending also to the laity of his diocese, included not only assistance and spiritual guidance but also discipline and judicial power; he had his own tribunal and prison and functioned as one of the chief magistrates of the city (see § 6 above), a task he fulfilled not only because of his authority as shepherd of the Christian community – by the mid-fifth century forming the majority in almost every city in the Holy Land – but also owing to his position as one of the city *possessores*. Thanks to donations of various types, the Church was often one of the largest landowners in any city. The bishop usually had a steward (οἰκονόμος) who took care of the temporal business and of the church property in the diocese.[80] At least in extensive dioceses, the bishop was assisted by a χωρεπίσκοπος ('bishop of the countryside') and/or one or more visitors (περιοδευτής, περιοδευταί), who looked after village communities and are often mentioned in the building inscriptions of rural churches (though not in private ones).[81] The name of the reigning bishop opens many building inscriptions in parochial and sometimes also in monastic churches, both as a dating device and in recognition of his status, possibly also of some help – in guidance, expertise or money – given by the shepherd to his flock.

---

[79] Bishops of Diocaesarea attended Palestinian synods in the sixth century: Fedalto 1988: 1034.
[80] Meimaris 1986: 256-259. For the different offices going under this name, see Di Segni 2004b: 57-58.
[81] Meimaris 1986: 214-217 (*chorepiscopus*); 254-256 (*periodeutes*); Di Segni 2019: 45, n. 7; Di Segni and Ashkenazi 2020: 309-310. For a survey of the functions and appellations of bishops and their assistants in inscriptions, see Feissel 1989; Destephen and Métivier 2007; Hamarneh 2013a; Mazzoleni 2013.

The mention of a bishop's name is precious to the epigraphist or the student of history or historical geography, for his title itself – bishop or archbishop/metropolitan, or patriarch – and the chance of identifying him with a known figure, often permit dating the inscription and/or locating the site where it was found within a specific diocese, which helps to define the boundaries of the urban territories in that area.[82]

Deacons and priests were ordained by the bishop. By the Church canons, it was illegal for a member of the clergy to be ordained by anyone but the bishop of the diocese where he operated, and for a bishop to ordain clergy from outside his diocese. Bishops were consecrated by the bishop of the provincial capital, the archbishop (ἀρχιεπίσκοπος), but in particular cases he could be consecrated by a quorum of three other bishops. Palestine had two archbishops: the bishop of the capital, Caesarea, and the bishop of the ancient metropolis, Jerusalem – a situation that caused not a little tension in the fourth and early fifth century.[83] After the division of the province into three Palaestinae, each of the three capitals – Caesarea, Scythopolis-Beth Shean and Petra – had its own archbishop, now called metropolitan (μητροπολίτης). The province of Arabia had its archbishop or metropolitan, residing in the capital, Bostra. At the time of the Council of Chalcedon (451 CE) the archbishop of Jerusalem obtained the primacy over the archbishops of the three Palaestinae, having been recognized as patriarch, a title and rank held by the bishops of the Churches believed to have been founded by the apostles themselves: Rome (whose patriarch was and is called Pope) and Antioch, both founded by Peter; Constantinople, as the 'New Rome'; Alexandria, founded by Mark the Evangelist, and Jerusalem, founded by James, Jesus' brother. The then patriarch of Jerusalem, Juvenal, aspired to obtain the supremacy also over the provinces of Arabia and Phoenice, but this was denied by the Council and those provinces remained under the supremacy of the patriarch of Antioch.[84]

---

[82] For the use of this piece of information to define territorial borders, see for instance Piccirillo 2005; Di Segni 2008; 2012d; 2019: 49-51. It must be noted, however, that in early inscriptions, and in literary sources even as late as the sixth century, an archbishop could be designated as simply 'bishop', *episkopos*.
[83] Rubin 1996; 2009.
[84] Honigmann 1950.

BIBLIOGRAPHY

References

Literary sources

Antonini Placentini Itinerarium. P. Geyer ed. 1965. In *Itineraria et alia geographica*. CCSL 175. Turnhout: 127–153

Antonius Chozibita, *Miracula Beatae Virginis in Choziba*. C. Houze ed. 1888. *Analecta Bollandiana* 7: 360–370; Italian transl., see Di Segni 1991

Antonius Chozibita, *Vita sancti Georgii Chozibitae*. C. Houze ed. 1888. *Analecta Bollandiana* 7: 95–144, 336–359; Italian transl., see Di Segni 1991

Barsanuphius, *Questiones et responsiones*. F. Neyt and P. de Angelis-Noach eds.; French transl. by L. Regnault 1997–2002. *Barsanuphe et Jean de Gaza. Correspondance* I–III. Sources Chrétiennes 426–427, 450–451, 468. Paris

Codex Justinianus. Corpus Iuris Civilis II. P. Krueger ed. 1954. Berlin

Codex Theodosianus. The Theodosian Code and Novels, and the Sirmondian Constitutions. Transl. C. Pharr 1952, with commentary, glossary, and bibliography. Princeton

Commemoratorium de casis Dei vel monasteriis — see McCormick 2011

Cyril of Scythopolis, *Vita Cyriaci*. E. Schwartz ed. 1939. *Kyrillos von Scythopolis*. TUGAL 49 ii. Leipzig: 222–235. English transl. see Price 1991; Hebrew transl. see Di Segni 2005b

Cyrillus of Scythoplis, *Vita Euthymii*. E. Schwartz ed. 1939. *Kyrillos von Scythopolis*. TUGAL 49 ii. Leipzig: 3–85. English transl. see Price 1991; Hebrew transl. see Di Segni 2005b

Cyrillus of Scythoplis, *Vita Sabae*. E. Schwartz ed. 1939. *Kyrillos von Scythopolis*. TUGAL 49 ii. Leipzig: 85–200. English transl. see Price 1991; Hebrew transl. see Di Segni 2005b. Also available: French translation in A.J. Festugière 1962. *Les moines d'Orient* III, 1. *Les moines de Palestine: Cyrille de Scythopolis, Vie de Saint Sabas*. Paris; Italian translation in Cirillo di Scitopoli. *Storie monastiche del deserto di Gerusalemme*. Traduzione di R. Baldelli e L. Mortari 1990, Praglia: 193–324

Doctrina Iacobi nuper baptizati. V. Déroche ed. and French transl. 1991. *Travaux et Memoirs* 11: 69–219

Eusebius of Caesarea, *Life of Constantine*. Ttransl. Averil Cameron and S.G. Hall 1999. Oxford

Eusebius of Caesarea, *Onomasticon*. E. Klostermann ed. 1904. *Das Onomastikon der biblischen Ortsnamen*. GCS 11 i. Leipzig. Translated by G.S.P. Freeman-Grenville 2003, edited and introduced by J.E. Taylor. Jerusalem

Georgius Cyprius, *Descriptio orbis Romani* — see Honigmann 1939

Hierocles, *Synecdemos* — see Honigmann 1939

Itinerarium Burdigalense. P. Geyer and O. Cuntz eds. 1965. In *Itineraria et alia geographica*. CCSL 175. Turnhout: 1–26

Itinerarium Egeriae. E. Franceschini and R. Weber eds. 1965. In *Itineraria et alia geographica*. CCSL 175. Turnhout: 35–90

Joannes Malalas, *Chronographia*. L. Dindorf ed. 1831. CSHB 13. Bonn; I. Thurn ed. 2000. CFHB 35. Berlin–New York. Excerpts in C. de Boor ed. 1905. *Excerpta historica iussu imperatoris Constantini Porphyrogeniti confecta* 3. *Excerpta de insidiis*. Berlin; also in ed. Thurn 2000

Josephus, *Antiquitatum Iudaicarum libri XX*. B. Niese ed. 1885–1890. *Flavii Iosephi opera* I–IV. Berlin (reprinted 1955); also *Josephus* IV–IX. *Jewish Antiquities*, with English transl. by H. St.J. Thackeray, R. Marcus, A. Wikgren and L.H. Feldman 1930–1965. LCL. Cambridge, Mass.–London–New York

Josephus, *De bello Iudaico libri VII*. B. Niese ed. 1894. *Flavii Iosephi opera* VI. Berlin (reprinted 1955); also *Josephus* II–III: *The Jewish War*, with English transl. by H. St. J. Thackeray 1927–1928. LCL. London–New York

Josephus, *Vita*. B. Niese ed. 1890. *Flavii Iosephi opera* IV. Berlin (reprinted 1955): 321–389; also *Josephus* I: *Life of Josephus*, with English transl. by H. St. J. Thackeray 1926. LCL. London–New York: 1–159

Not. Dign. Or. O. Seeck ed. 1876. *Notitia dignitatum et administrationum omnium tam civilium quam militarium: Notitia Orientis*. Berlin (reprinted Frankfurt a/M 1962)

Nov. Corpus Iuris Civilis III: *Novellae*. R. Schoell and G. Kroll eds. 1954. Berlin

Palladius, *Historia Lausiaca*. E.C. Butler ed. 1898–1904. Cambridge (reprinted Hildesheim 1967)

P. Nessana C.J. Kraemer ed. 1958. H. Dunscombe Colt ed. *Excavations at Nessana III. Non-literary papyri*. Princeton

P. Yadin The documents from the Bar Kokhba period in the Cave of the Letters: Greek papyri. N. Lewis ed. *Aramaic and Nabatean signatures and subscriptions*. Y. Yadin and J.C. Greenfield eds. 1989. Judean Desert Studies 2. Jerusalem

Procopius of Caesarea, *Buildings (De Aedificiis)*. *Procopius* VII, with English transl. by H.B. Dewing 1940. LCL. Cambridge, Mass.–London (reprinted 1954)

Procopius of Caesarea, *Anecdota or Secret History (Historia arcana)*. *Procopius* VI, with English transl. by H.B. Dewing 1935. LCL. Cambridge, Mass.–London (reprinted 1954)

Sozomen, *Historia ecclesiastica*. J. Bidez and G.C. Hausen eds. 1960. *Kirchengeschichte*. GCS 50. Berlin

Theodosius, *De situ Terrae Sanctae*. P. Geyer ed. 1965. In *Itineraria et alia geographica*. CCSL 175. Turnhout: 115–125

Zosimus, *Histoire nouvelle*. F. Paschoud ed. and transl. 1971–1989. Paris

Modern studies

Abel F.-M. 1907. Chronique. Document épigraphique sur le patriarche Eustochios. *RB* 16: 275–276

Abel F.-M. 1909. Mélanges. Épigraphie grecque palestinienne. *RB* 18: 89–106

Abel F.-M. 1926. Inscription grecque de l'aqueduct de Jérusalem avec la figure du pied byzantine. *RB* 35: 284–288

Abu 'Uqsa H. 2006. The excavation at Khirbat el-Batiya (triangulation spot 819). *'Atiqot* 53: 21*–28* (Hebrew), 197–198 (English summary)

Aharoni Y. 1955. Three new boundary stones from the Western Golan. *'Atiqot* 1: 109–114

Akavya A.A. 1945. Contribution of the Zoar inscriptions to chronology. *Kedem* 2: 92–98

Albeck S. 1987. *Law courts in Talmudic times*. Ramat Gan (Hebrew)

Aliquot J. 2008 — see *IGLS* XI

Aliquot J. 2017. Laodicée-sur-mer et les fondations de l'empereur Constance. *Chiron* 40: 61–76

Allan J.W. 2001. Early Islamic glass stamps. In *Measuring and weighing in ancient times*. Haifa: 38–42 (Hebrew), 26*–29* (English)

Alon G. 1945. The Jewish community of Zoar in the Talmudic period. *Kedem* 2: 129–130

Alt A. 1921. *Die griechischen Inschriften der Palaestina Tertia westlich der 'Araba*. Berlin–Leipzig

Amelotti M. 1985. Le costituzioni giustinianee nelle epigrafi. In M. Amelotti and L. Migliardi Zingale. *Le costituzioni giustinianee nei papiri e nelle epigrafi*, second edition. Milan: 87–137

Amit D. 2006. Ancient Jewish bread stamps. In N. Ben-Yossef ed. *Bread: daily and divine*. Jerusalem: 188–189

Anderson W. 2004. An archaeology of late antique pilgrim flasks. *Anatolian Studies* 54: 79–93

Arav R., L. Di Segni and A. Kloner 1990. An eighth-century monastery near Jerusalem. *LA* 40: 313–320

Ariel D.T. et al. 1990. Imported stamped amphora handles. In D.T. Ariel ed. *Excavations at the City of David 1978–1985 directed by Yigal Shiloh* II. Qedem 30. Jerusalem: 13–98

Ashkenazi J. 2018. Family rural churches in late antique Palestine and the competition in the 'field of religious goods': a socio-historical view. *Journal of Ecclesiastical History* 69, 4: 709–727

Ashkenazi J. 2019. Private churches in late antique rural Palestine. In O. Peleg-Barkat, U. Leibner, J. Ashkenazi, M. Aviam and R. Talgam eds. *Between the sea and the desert: On kings, nomads, cities and monks – Essays in honor of Joseph Patrich*, Tsemach: 189-198 (Hebrew)

Ashkenazi J. 2020. Family and religion in the late antique rural Levant: epigraphical observations. *ZPE* 215: 135–146

Augustinovic A. 1951. *Gerico e dintorni*. Jerusalem

Aufrecht W.E. 2001. A legacy of Syria: the Aramaic language. *Bulletin of the Canadian Society for Mesopotamian Studies* 36: 145–155

Avi-Yonah M. 1932, 1933, 1935. Mosaic pavements in Palestine. *QDAP* 2: 136–181; 3: 26–74; 4: 187–193 (republished in M. Avi-Yonah 1981. *Art in ancient Palestine*. Jerusalem: 283–382)

Avi-Yonah M. 1933a. A Byzantine church at Suḥmātā. *QDAP* 3: 92–105

Avi-Yonah M. 1940. *Abbreviations in Greek inscriptions*. QDAP Supplement to Vol. 9. Jerusalem

Avi-Yonah M. 1942. Greek inscriptions from Ascalon, Jerusalem, Beisan, and Hebron. *QDAP* 10: 160–169

Avi-Yonah M. 1954. *The Madaba mosaic map*. Jerusalem

Avi-Yonah M. 1957. A note on the date of the inscription found at Beit Safafa. *'Alon* 5–6: 43 (Hebrew)

Avi-Yonah M. 1963. The bath of the lepers at Scythopolis. *IEJ* 13: 325–326

Avi-Yonah M. 1966. An addendum to the episcopal list of Tyre. *IEJ* 16: 209–210

Avi-Yonah M. 1967. The mosaic pavements. In M.W. Prausnitz. *Excavations at Shavei Zion. The Early Christian church*. Rome: 47–63

Avi-Yonah M. 1976. *Gazetteer of Roman Palestine*. Qedem 5. Jerusalem

Aviam M. 1990. Ḥorvat Ḥesheq — A unique church in Upper Galilee: preliminary report. In G.C. Bottini, L. Di Segni and E. Alliata eds. *Christian archaeology in the Holy Land: new discoveries*. SBF Collectio maior 36. Jerusalem: 351–374

Aviam M. and A. Aharoni 2012. Batei haqvarot shel Ẓippori (The cemeteries of Sepphoris). *Cathedra* 141: 6-26 (Hebrew)

Avigad N. 1960. A dated lintel inscription from the ancient synagogue of Nabratein. *Bulletin. Louis M. Rabinowitz Fund for the Exploration of Ancient Synagogues* 3: 49–56

Avigad N. 1976. *Beth She'arim III. Catacombs 12–23*. Brunswick, NJ

Avigad N. 1993. Beth Alpha. *NEAEHL* I: 190–192

Avner R. 2021. Ḥorbat Ḥanot. *HA-ESI* 133 https://www.hadashot-esi.org.il/report_detail_eng.aspx?id=25933&mag_id=133

Avni G., U. Dahari and A. Kloner 2008. *The necropolis of Bet Guvrin-Eleutheropolis*. IAA Reports 36. Jerusalem

Bader N. 2009 — see *IGLJ* V

Bagatti B. 1969. *Excavations in Nazareth I: From the beginning to the XII century*. SBF Collectio maior 17. Jerusalem

Bagatti B. 2001. *Ancient Christian villages of Galilee*. SBF Collectio minor 37. Jerusalem

Bagatti B. 2002a. *Ancient Christian villages of Judaea and the Negev*. SBF Collectio minor 42. Jerusalem

Bagatti B. 2002b. *Ancient Christian villages of Samaria*. SBF Collectio minor 39. Jerusalem

Bagnall R.S. and K.A. Worp 2004. *Chronological systems of Byzantine Egypt*. Second edition. Leiden – Boston

Baldi D. 1955. *Enchiridion locorum sanctorum*. Second edition. Jerusalem (reprinted 1982)

Balty J. 1980. Sur la date de creation de la *Syria secunda*. *Syria* 57: 465–481

Bar-Asher M. 1988. Le syro-palestinien — études grammaticales. *Journal Asiatique* 276: 27–59

Barag D. 1967. Stamp-impressions of the Legio X Fretensis. *Bonner Jahrbücher* 167: 244–267

Barag D. 1993. Shaalbim. In *NEAEHL* IV: 1338; V: 2110

Barag D. 1994. The dated Jewish inscription of Binyamina reconsidered. *'Atiqot* 25: 179–181

Barag D. 2009. Samaritan writing and writings. In H.M. Cotton, R.G. Hoyland, J.J. Price and D.J. Wasserstein eds. *From Hellenism to Islam. Cultural and linguistic change in the Roman Near East*. Cambridge: 303–323

Baramki D. and S.H. Stephan 1935. A Nestorian hermitage between Jericho and the Jordan. *QDAP* 4: 81–86

Ben-David Ch. 2007. Golan gem: the ancient synagogue of Deir Aziz. *BAR* 33, 6: 44–51

Ben-David Ch. 2011. Toponyms in Eretz Israel written on milestones. *'Al Atar. Journal of Land of Israel Studies* 16: 27-40 (Hebrew)

Ben-Zevi I. and W.R. Albright 1941. The Beit el-Ma Samaritan inscription. *BASOR* 84: 2–4

Benoit P. and M.E. Boismard 1951. Un ancient sanctuaire chrétien à Béthanie. *RB* 58: 200–251

Benovitz N. 2012. Evidence for the "Justinianic plague" in the dated Greek epitaphs of the Byzantine period from the provinces of Palestine and Arabia. Unpublished M.A. thesis. Institute of Archaeology, The Hebrew University of Jerusalem

Benovitz N. 2014. The Justinianic plague: evidence from the dated Greek epitaphs from Byzantine Palestine and Arabia. *JRA* 27: 487–498

Blanc P.-M., D. Pieri, J.-P. Sodini 2011. Nouvelles eulogies de Qalat Seman (fouilles 2007-2010). *Mélanges Cécile Morrisson. Travaux et Mémoires* 16: 761-780

Bowersock G.W. 1983. *Roman Arabia*. Cambridge, Mass.

Bowersock G.W. 1984. Naming a province: more on New Arabia. *ZPE* 56: 221–222

Bowersock G.W. 2004. The mosaic inscription in the Nile Festival Building at Sepphoris: the house of the daughter of the governor Procopius (A.D. 517–18?) and her husband Asbolius Patricius. *JRA* 17: 764–766

Brock S.P. 1977. A letter attributed to Cyril of Jerusalem on the rebuilding of the Temple. *Bulletin of the School of Oriental and African Studies* 40: 267–286

Brock S.P. 1978. Syriac inscriptions: a preliminary check list of European publications. *Annali dell' Istituto Orientale di Napoli* 38: 255–271

Brock S.P. 1989. Three thousand years of Aramaic literature. *ARAM* 1: 11–23

Brown H. 2020. Byzantine church discovered in Banyas nature reserve. https://www.jpost.com/israel-news/culture/byzantine-church-discovered-in-banias-nature-reserve-647223

Cameron A. 1976. *Circus factions: Blues and Greens at Rome and Byzantium*. Oxford

Canova R. 1954. *Iscrizioni e monumenti paleocristiani del paese di Moab*. Rome

Cascianalli D. 2013. Una nuova immagine di Davide da Khirbat al-Mukhayyat? Riflessioni intorno al mosaic pavimentale superiore della cappella del prete Giovanni. *LA* 63: 461–480

Casson L. and E.L. Hettich 1950. H. Dunscombe Colt ed. *Excavations at Nessana II. Literary papyri.* Princeton

Cassuto U. 1945. The dates in the inscriptions from Zoar. *Kedem* 2: 90–91

Chachy R., Y. Kalman and R. Porat eds. Forthcoming. *Herodium final reports of the 1972–2010 excavations directed by Ehud Netzer II. Lower Herodium.* Jerusalem

Christern J. 1983. Die Pilgerheiligtümer von Abu Mina und Qal'at Sim'an. In H. Beck and P. Bol eds. *Spätantike und frühes Christentum. Ausstellung im Lieblieghaus Museum alter Plastik Frankfurt am Main.* Frankfurt: 211–222

Clédat J. 1916. Fouilles à Khirbet el-Flousiyeh (janvier-mars 1914). *Annales du Service des Antiquités de l'Égypte* 16: 6–32

Clermont-Ganneau Ch. 1899. La Palestine au commencement du VIe siècle et les Plérophories de Jean Rufus évêque de Maioumas. *Recueil d' archéologie orientale* III. Paris: 223–242

Coen-Uzzielli T. 2006. Christian bread stamps in the Holy Land. In N. Ben-Yossef ed. *Bread: daily and divine.* Jerusalem: 165–187

Contini R. 1987. Il Hawran preislamico. Ipotesi di storia linguistica. *Felix Ravenna* 133–134: 25–79

Corbo V. 1955. *Gli scavi di Siyar el-Ghanam (Campo dei Pastori) e i monasteri dei dintorni.* SBF Collectio maior 11. Jerusalem

Cotton H.M. and J. Geiger 1989. *Masada II. The Latin and Greek documents.* Jerusalem

Cotton H.M. and J. Price 2001. A bilingual tombstone from Zo'ar (Arabia). *ZPE* 134: 277–283

Crowfoot J.W. 1938. The Christian churches. In C.H. Kraeling, *Gerasa, city of the Decapolis.* New Haven: 171–294

Dan Y. 1981. Circus factions (Blues and Greens) in Byzantine Palestine. *The Jerusalem Cathedra* 1: 105–119

Dar Sh. 2004. *Raqit. Marinus' estate on the Carmel, Israel.* BAR International Series 1300. Oxford

Dauphin C. 1977. Shelomi. *IEJ* 27: 256-259

Dauphin C. 1993. Dor-Dora: a station for pilgrims in the Byzantine period on their way to Jerusalem. In Y. Tsafrir ed. *Ancient churches revealed.* Jerusalem: 90–97

Davenport C. 2010. The building inscription from the fort at Udruh and Aelius Flavianus, tetrarchic *praeses* of *Palaestina*. *JRA* 23: 349–357

De Sandoli S. 1974. *Corpus Inscriptionum Crucesignatarum Terrae Sanctae (1099–1291).* SBF Collectio maior 21. Jerusalem

Decloedt A. 1914. Mélanges. Notes sur des poids grecs et byzantins du Musée biblique de Sainte-Anne. *RB* 23: 549–555

Desreumaux A. 1987a. La naissance d'une nouvelle écriture araméenne à l'époque Byzantine. *Semitica* 37: 95-107

Desreumaux A. (mistakenly Jacques A.) 1987b. A Palestinian-Syriac inscription in the mosaic pavement at 'Evron. *Eretz-Israel* 19: 54*–56*

Desreumaux A. 1999. Les inscriptions funéraires araméennes de Samra. In T. Bauzou, A. Desreumaux, P.-L. Gatier, J.-B. Humbert and F. Zayadine eds. *Fouilles de Khirbet es-Samra en Jordanie I*. Turnhout: 435-509

Destephen S. and S. Métivier 2007. Évêques et chorévêques en Asie Mineure aux IVe–Ve siècles. *Topoi* 15: 343–378

Di Segni L. 1988. The inscriptions of Tiberias. In Y. Hirschfeld ed. *Tiberias – From its foundation to the Muslim conquest*. 'Idan series, Yad Yizhaq Ben Zvi. Jerusalem: 70–95 (Hebrew)

Di Segni L. 1990a — see Arav R., L. Di Segni and A. Kloner 1990

Di Segni L. 1990b. The church of Mary Theotokos on Mount Gerizim: the inscriptions. In G.C. Bottini, L. Di Segni and E. Alliata eds. *Christian archaeology in the Holy Land: new discoveries*. SBF Collectio maior 36. Jerusalem: 343–350

Di Segni L. 1990c. Ḥorvath Ḥesheq: the inscriptions. In G.C. Bottini, L. Di Segni and E. Alliata eds. *Christian archaeology in the Holy Land: new discoveries*. SBF Collectio maior 36. Jerusalem: 379–390

Di Segni L. 1990d. The inscriptions of Ashkelon. In N. Arbel ed. *Ashkelon — 4,000 and forty more years* I. Ashkelon: 67–90 (Hebrew)

Di Segni L. 1991. *Nel deserto accanto ai fratelli. Vita di Gerasimo, Vita di Giorgio di Choziba, Miracoli della Beata Vergine in Choziba*. Magnano

Di Segni L. 1992. The date of the Church of the Virgin in Madaba. *LA* 42: 251–257

Di Segni L. 1993a. A Jewish Greek inscription from the vicinity of Caesarea Maritima. *'Atiqot* 22: 133–136

Di Segni L. 1993b. The Beit Safafa inscription reconsidered and the question of a local era in Jerusalem. *IEJ* 43: 157–168

Di Segni L. 1993c. The Greek inscriptions from the Samaritan synagogue at el Khirbe, with some considerations on the function of Samaritan synagogues in the Late Roman period. In F. Manns ed. *Early Christianity in context. Monuments and documents*. SBF Collectio maior 38. Jerusalem: 231–239

Di Segni L. 1993d. Review of Maurice Sartre, *Inscriptions de la Jordanie*, Tome IV, *Pétra et la Nabatène méridionale du Wadi al-Hasa au golfe de 'Aqaba* (Inscriptions grecques et latines de la Syrie, Tome XXI, Paris 1993). *LA* 43: 496–515

Di Segni L. 1994a. La data della cappella della Theotokos sul Monte Nebo. Nota epigrafica. *LA* 44: 531–533

Di Segni L. 1994b. The date of the Binyamina inscription and the question of Byzantine Dora. *'Atiqot* 25: 183–186

Di Segni L. 1994c. Εἷς θεός in Palestinian inscriptions. *Scripta Classica Israelica* 13: 94–115

Di Segni L. 1995. The involvement of local, municipal and provincial authorities in urban building in late antique Palestine and Arabia. In J.H. Humphrey ed. *The Roman and Byzantine Near East: some recent archaeological research.* JRA Supplementary series 14. Ann Arbor, MI: 312–332

Di Segni L. 1996. Metropolis and Provincia in Byzantine Palestine. In A. Raban and K.G. Holum eds. *Caesarea Maritima. A retrospective after two millennia.*Leiden – New York – Köln: 575–589

Di Segni L. 1997a. *Dated Greek inscriptions from Palestine from the Roman and Byzantine periods.* Ph.D. Dissertation. The Hebrew University of Jerusalem

Di Segni L. 1997b. The Greek inscriptions of Hammat Gader. In Y. Hirschfeld, with contributions by N. Amitai-Preiss et al. *The Roman baths of Hammat Gader. Final report.* Jerusalem: 185–266

Di Segni L. 1998a. The Greek inscriptions. In M. Piccirillo and E. Alliata eds. *Mount Nebo. New archaeological excavations 1967-1997.* SBF Collectio maior 27. Jerusalem: 425–467

Di Segni L. 1998b. Tiberiade romano-bizantina attraverso le sue iscrizioni. In F. Israel, A.M. Rabello and A.M. Somekh eds. *Hebraica. Miscellanea di studi in onore di Sergio J. Sierra.* Turin: 115–163

Di Segni L. 1999a. New epigraphic discoveries at Scythopolis and in other sites of late-antique Palestine. *XI Congresso internazionale di epigrafia greca e latina. Roma, 18–25 settembre 1997. Atti* II. Rome: 625–642

Di Segni L. 1999b. The inscriptions. In Y. Hirschfeld. *The Early Byzantine monastery at Khirbet ed-Deir in the Judean Desert: the excavations in 1981-1987.* Qedem 38. Jerusalem: 97–106

Di Segni L. 2000. Using Talmudic sources for city life in Palestine: D. Sperber, *The City in Roman Palestine* (Oxford-New York 1998). *JRA* 13: 779–788

Di Segni L. 2002a. The water supply of Roman-Byzantine Palestine in literary and epigraphic sources. In D. Amit, Y. Hirschfeld and J. Patrich eds. *The aqueducts of Israel.* JRA Supplementary series 42. Portsmouth, R.I.: 37–67

Di Segni L. 2002b. Greek inscriptions in the Nile Festival Building at Sepphoris. In J.H. Humphrey ed. *The Roman and Byzantine Near East* 3. JRA Supplementary series 49. Ann Arbor, MI: 91-100

Di Segni L. 2003. Christian epigraphy in the Holy Land: new discoveries. *ARAM* 15: 247–267

Di Segni L. 2004a. The Beersheba tax edict reconsidered in the light of a newly discovered fragment. *Scripta Classica Israelica* 23: 131-158

Di Segni L. 2004b. The territory of Gaza: notes of historical geography. In B. Bitton–Ashkeloni and A. Kofsky eds. *Christian Gaza in Late Antiquity.* Leiden: 41–59

Di Segni L. 2004c. Two Greek inscriptions at Horvat Raqit. In Sh. Dar, with contributions by B. Arensburg et al. *Raqit. Marinus' Estate on the Carmel, Israel.* BAR International Series 1300. Oxford: 196–198

Di Segni L. 2005a. A Roman standard in Herod's kingdom. *Israel Museum Studies in Archaeology* 4: 23–46

Di Segni L. 2005b. *Cyril of Scythopolis, Lives of monks of the Judaean Desert.* Jerusalem (Hebrew)

Di Segni L. 2005c. The Greek inscriptions. In Z. Weiss, with contributions by E. Netzer et al. *The Sepphoris synagogue*. Jerusalem: 209–216

Di Segni L. 2005d. The mosaic inscription in the Nile Festival Building at Sepphoris: Response to G. W. Bowersock. *JRA* 18: 781–784

Di Segni L. 2006a. Varia Arabica. Greek inscriptions from Jordan. *LA* 56: 578–592

Di Segni L. 2006b. A schedule of fees (*sportulae*) from Caesarea for official services. *Cathedra* 122: 99–116 (Hebrew)

Di Segni L. 2006–2007. The use of chronological systems in sixth-eighth centuries Palestine. *ARAM* 18–19: 113–126

Di Segni L. 2007. An amphora stopper from Transjordan. *LA* 57: 692–696

Di Segni L. 2008. The Greek inscription from Tel Ashdod — A revised reading. *'Atiqot* 58: 31*-36*.

Di Segni L. 2009a. Greek inscriptions in transition from the Byzantine to the Early Islamic period. In H.M. Cotton, R.G. Hoyland, J.J. Price and D.J. Wasserstein eds. *From Hellenism to Islam. Cultural and linguistic change in the Roman Near East*. Cambridge: 352–373

Di Segni L. 2009b. An unknown "Monastery of the Holy Trinity" on the Mount of Olives — A revision of the evidence. In J. Geiger, H.M. Cotton and G.D. Stiebel eds. *Israel's land: papers presented to Israel Shatzman on his jubilee*. Jerusalem: 131*-145*.

Di Segni L. 2012a. Greek inscription from Deir Qal'a monastery. In N. Carmin ed. *Christians and Christianity* III: *Churches and monasteries in Samaria and Northern Judea*. Judea and Samaria publications 15. Jerusalem: 157–160

Di Segni L. 2012b. Greek inscriptions from the Early Northern Church at Shiloh and the baptistery. In N. Carmin ed. *Christians and Christianity* III: *Churches and monasteries in Samaria and Northern Judea*. Judea and Samaria publications 15. Jerusalem: 209–218

Di Segni L. 2012c. Greek dedicatory inscription from the vaulted structures of the Nea. In O. Gutfeld, with contributions by M. Avissar et al. *Jewish Quarter excavations in the Old City of Jerusalem conducted by Nahman Avigad, 1969–1982. Volume V: The Cardo (Area X) and the Nea Church (Areas D and T). Final report*. Jerusalem: 259–267

Di Segni L. 2012d. Greek inscription in the church of Bishop John at Khirbet Barqa–Gan Yavneh. In L.D. Chrupcala ed. *Christ is here! Studies in biblical and Christian archaeology in memory of Michele Piccirillo, ofm*. SBF Collectio maior 52. Milan: 147–150

Di Segni L. 2013. Il censimento di Quirinio: un nuovo contributo dell'epigrafia. In G. Paximadi and M. Fidanzio eds. *Terra Sancta. Archeologia ed esegesi. Atti dei convegni 2008–2010*. Lugano: 173–191

Di Segni L. 2016. On the contribution of epigraphy to the identification of monastic foundations. In J. Patrich, O. Peleg-Barkat and E. Ben-Yosef eds. *Arise, walk through the land. Studies in the archaeology and history of the Land of Israel in memory of Yizhar Hirschfeld on the tenth anniversary of his demise*. Jerusalem: 185*–198*

Di Segni L. 2017a. Late antique inscriptions in the provinces of Palaestina and Arabia: realities and change. In K. Bolle, C. Machado and C. Witschel eds. *The epigraphic cultures of Late Antiquity*. Stuttgart: 287–320

Di Segni L. 2017b. Expressions of prayer in late antique inscriptions in the provinces of Palaestina and Arabia. In B. Bitton-Ashkelony and D. Krueger eds. *Prayer and worship in Eastern Christianities, 5th to 11th centuries*, London — New York: 63–88

Di Segni L. 2018a. Changing borders in the provinces of Palaestina and Arabia in the fourth and fifth centuries. *LA* 68: 247–267

Di Segni L. 2018b [2020]. A new tetrarchic inscription. *Kölner und Bonner Archaeologica* 8: 145-149

Di Segni L. 2019. The inscriptions in the church of Ḥaẓor Ashdod, and some observations on the boundaries of the territory of Ascalon. In O. Peleg-Barkat, U. Leibner, J. Ashkenazi, M. Aviam and R. Talgam eds. *Between the sea and the desert: on kings, nomads, cities and monks – Essays in honor of Joseph Patrich*, Tsemach. Ostracon: Kinneret Institute for Galilean Archaeology: 41–53

Di Segni L. 2020. Unrecognized and/or misunderstood toponyms in inscriptions. In A. Coniglio and A. Ricco eds. *Holy Land: archaeology on either side. Archaeological essays in honour of Eugenio Alliata, ofm*. SBF Collectio maior 57. Milan: 323–327

Di Segni L. 2021. The inscriptions from the Church of the Glorious Martyr. *Biblical Archaeology Review* 47, 3: 36

Di Segni L. forthcoming (a). The Greek inscriptions in the Northern and Eastern Churches at Lower Herodium. Chapter 14 in R. Chachy, Y. Kalman and R. Porat eds. *Herodium final reports of the 1972–2010 excavations directed by Ehud Netzer II. Lower Herodium*. Jerusalem (forthcoming)

Di Segni L. forthcoming (b). The Inscriptions. In T. Erickson-Gini ed. *Rudolph Cohen's excavations at the Nabatean-Roman sites along the Incense Road in the Negev desert, 1978–1988. Final report* (forthcoming)

Di Segni L. and B.Y. Arubas 2009. An old-new inscription from Beth Shean. In L. Di Segni, Y. Hirschfeld, J. Patrich and R. Talgam eds. *Man near a Roman arch. Studies presented to Prof. Yoram Tsafrir*. Jerusalem: 115*–124*

Di Segni L. and J. Ashkenazi 2020. Newly discovered inscriptions from three churches in Upper Western Galilee. In A. Coniglio and A. Ricco eds. *Holy Land: archaeology on either side. Archaeological essays in honour of Eugenio Alliata, ofm*. SBF Collectio maior 57. Milan: 303–321

Di Segni L. and D. Feissel 2020. From Tyre to Jerusalem: six Greek and Latin asylia inscriptions for churches of Phoenice and Palaestina (6th c.). *Travaux et Mémoires* 24/2: 547–636

Di Segni L. and D. Gellman 2017. A Justinian inscription north of Byzantine Jerusalem, and its importance for the dating of the Nea Chuch inscription. In Y. Gadot, Y. Zelinger, K. Cytryn-Silverman and J. Uziel eds. *New studies on the archaeology of Jerusalem and its region* XI. Jerusalem: 27*–37*

Di Segni L., J. Patrich and K.G. Holum 2003. A schedule of fees (*sportulae*) for official services from Caesarea Maritima, Israel. *ZPE* 145: 273-300

Di Segni L. and Y. Tepper 2004. A Greek inscription dated by the era of Hegira in an Umayyad church at Tamra in Eastern Galilee. *LA* 54: 343–350

Di Segni L. and Y. Tsafrir 2012. The ethnic composition of Jerusalem's population in the Byzantine period (312-638 CE). *LA* 62: 405–454

Di Segni L. and Y. Tsafrir (with the assistance of J. Green) 2015. *The Onomasticon of Iudaea • Palaestina and Arabia in the Greek and Latin sources* I. *Introduction, sources, major texts*. Jerusalem

Di Segni L. and Y. Tsafrir (with J. Green) 2017. *The Onomasticon of Iudaea • Palaestina and Arabia in the Greek and Latin sources* II, part 1: Aalac Mons–Arabia Chapter 4; part 2: Arabia chapter 5–Azzeira. Jerusalem

Dunand M. 1932–1933. Nouvelles inscriptions du Djebel Druze et du Hauran. Nos. 1–63, 64–243. *RB* 41; 397–416, 561–580; 42: 235–254

Dunand M. 1939. Nouvelles inscriptions du Djebel Druze et du Hauran. Nos. 244–310. *Mélanges syriens offerts à M. R. Dussaud* II. Paris: 559–576

Dunand M. 1950. Nouvelles inscriptions du Djebel Druze et du Hauran. Nos. 311–373. *Archiv Orientalni* 18: 144–164

Dunbabin K.M.D. 1989. Baiarum grata voluptas: Pleasures and dangers of the baths. *Papers of the British School at Rome* 57: 6–46

Dussaud R. and F. Macler 1901. *Voyage archéologique au Safa et dans le Djebel ed-Druz*. Paris

Dussaud R. and F. Macler 1903. *Mission dans les régions désertiques de la Syrie moyenne*. Paris

Eck W. 2003. The language of power: Latin in the inscriptions of Iudaea/Syria Palaestina. In L.H. Schiffman ed. *Semitic papyrology in context*. Leiden – Boston: 123-144

Eck W. 2009. The presence, role and significance of Latin in the epigraphy and culture of the Roman Near East. In H.M. Cotton, R.G. Hoyland, J.J. Price and D.J. Wasserstein eds. *From Hellenism to Islam. Cultural and linguistic change in the Roman Near East*. Cambridge: 15-42

Ecker A. 2010. The inscription. In Sh. Kol-Ya'akov, *Salvage excavations at Nesher-Ramla quarry* I. Haifa: 171–173

Ecker A. 2013. The Greek and Latin inscriptions from the Herodian palaces at Jericho and Cypros. Chapter 15 in R. Bar-Nathan and J. Gärtner, with contributions by N. Ahipaz et al. *Hasmonean and Herodian palaces at Jericho. Final report of the 1973–1987 excavations V. The finds from Jericho and Cypros*. Jerusalem: 305–313

Eldar I. and Y. Baumgarten 1993. Malḥata, Tel. Malḥata in the Byzantine period. *NEAEHL* III: 936–937

Eliav Y.Z. 2009. A scary place: Jewish magic in the Roman bathhouse. In L. Di Segni, Y. Hirschfeld, J. Patrich and R. Talgam eds. *Man near a Roman arch. Studies presented to Prof. Yoram Tsafrir*. Jerusalem: 88*–97*

Eriksen E.O. 1989. *Holy Land explorers*. Jerusalem

Ewing W. 1895. Greek and other inscriptions collected in the Hauran. *PEF* 27: 41–60, 131–160, 265–280, 340–354

Fabian P. 1995. The Late Roman military camp at Beer Sheba: a new discovery. In J.H. Humphrey ed. *The Roman and Byzantine Near East: some recent archaeological research*. JRA Supplementary series 14. Ann Arbor: 235–240

Fedalto G. 1988. *Hierarchia Ecclesiastica Orientalis* II. Padua

Feissel D. 1984. Notes d'épigraphie chrétienne (VII), XX. Quelques dédicaces de statues décernées par les empereurs. *BCH* 108: 545–558

Feissel D. 1989. L'évêque, titres et functions d'après les inscriptrions grecques jusqu'au VIIe siècle. In *Actes du XI Congrès d'archéologie chrétienne, Lyon, Vienne, Grenoble, Genéve et Aoste, 21–28 Septembre 1986*. Volume I. Rome: 801–826

Feissel D. 1992. Notes d'épigraphie chrétienne (VIII), XXIV. Trois inscriptions de Justinien Ier a Trébizonde. *BCH* 116: 383– 407

Feissel D. 1993. La reforme chronologique de 537 et son application dans l'épigraphie grecque: années de règne et dates consulaires de Justinien à Héraclius. *Ktema* 18: 171–188

Feissel D. 1995. Épigraphie et constitutions impériales: aspects de la publication du droit à Byzance. In G. Cavallo and C. Mango eds. *Epigrafia medievale greca e latina: ideologia e funzione. Atti del seminario di Erice (12–18 settembre 1991)*. Spoleto: 67–98

Feissel D. 2006a. *Chronique d'épigraphie byzantine 1987–2004*. Paris

Feissel D. 2006b. Les inscriptions latines dans l'Orient protobyzantin. In R. Harreither, Ph. Pergola, R. Pillinger and A. Pülz eds. *Acta congressus internationalis XIV archaeologiae christianae/Akten des XIV. Internationalen Kongresses für christlische Archäologie*. Città del Vaticano – Vienna: 99-129

Feissel D. 2010. Un fragment palestinien de la constitution d'Anastase sur l'administration militaire du diocèse d'Orient. *ZPE* 173: 125–130

Feissel D. 2012. Bulletin épigraphique. Syrie, Phénicie, Palestine, Arabie. *REG* 125: 665–683

Feissel D. and P.-L. Gatier 2005–2016. *Bulletin épigraphique 2005–2016. Syrie, Phénicie, Palestine, Arabie*, accessible by subscription in *Byzantinische Bibliographie Online*

Felle A.E. 2006. *Biblia epigraphica. La Sacra Scrittura nella documentazione epigrafica dell' Orbis Christianus antiquus (III–VIII secolo)*. Bari

Figueras P. 1985. *Greek inscriptions from Beer-Sheva and the Negev*. Beer-Sheva.

Figueras P. 1996. New Greek inscriptions from the Negev. *LA* 46: 265–284

Fischer M., B. Isaac and I. Roll 1996. *Roman roads in Judaea II. The Jaffa–Jerusalem roads*. BAR International Series 628. Oxford

FitzGerald G.M. 1939. *A Sixth-Century monastery at Beth Shan (Scythopolis)*. Philadelphia

Flusser D. 1975. The great goddess of Samaria. *IEJ* 25: 13–20

Foerster G. 1993. Jericho: Khirbet en-Nitla. *NEAEHL* II: 696–697

Foerster G. and Y. Tsafrir 1993.The Bet She'an excavation project (1989–1991). City center (North): excavations of the Hebrew University expedition. *ESI* 11: 3–32

Foraboschi D. 1971. *Onomasticon alterum papyrologicum*. Milano–Varese

Foskolou V. 2012. Blessing for sale? On the production and distribution of pilgrim mementoes in Byzantium. *Byzantinische Zeitschrift* 105: 53–84

Foss C. 1978. Three apparent early examples of the era of creation. *ZPE* 31: 241–246

Foster B.R. 1970. Agoranomos and muḥtasib. *The Journal of the Economic and Social History of the Orient* 13: 128–144

Fraenkel A.H. 1945. Note on a tomb-stone from Zoar. *Kedem* 2: 89

Frankel R., N. Getzov, M. Aviam and A. Degani 2001. *Settlement dynamics and regional diversity in ancient Upper Galilee: archaeological survey of Upper Galilee.* Jerusalem

Friedman Z. 2012. Sailing in the Dead Sea: Madaba map mosaic. In L.D. Chrupcala ed. *Christ is here! Studies in biblical and Christian archaeology in memory of Michele Piccirillo, ofm.* SBF Collectio maior 52. Milan: 341–354

Frösén J., E. Sironen and Z.T. Fiema 2008. Greek inscriptions from the church and the chapel. In Z.T. Fiema and J. Frösén eds. *Petra. The mountain of Aaron 1. The church and the chapel.* Helsinki: 272-281

Galavaris G. 1970. *Bread and the liturgy: the symbolism of early Christian and Byzantine bread stamps.* Madison, Wisc.

Gatier P.-L. 1986 — see *IGLJ* II

Gatier P.-L. 1999. Les inscriptions grecques et latines: Les textes de Samra (N° 1 à 83); Les textes de Rihab (N° 84 à 147). In T. Bauzou, A. Desreumaux, P.-L. Gatier, J.-B. Humbert and F. Zayadine eds. *Fouilles de Khirbet es-Samra, Jordanie I.* Turnhout: 367–431

Geiger J. 1996. How much Latin in Greek Palestine? In H. Rosen ed. *Aspects of Latin: Papers from the Seventh International Colloquium on Latin linguistics, Jerusalem, April 1993.* Innsbruck: 39–57

Geiger J. 2014. *Hellenism in the East: studies on Greek intellectuals in Palestine.* Historia Einzelschriften 229. Stuttgart

Gera D. 2017. Some dated Greek inscriptions from Maresha. *PEQ* 149: 201–222

Gersht R. 2004. The decorated lintel from the synagogue at Raqit. In Sh. Dar. *Raqit. Marinus' estate on the Carmel, Israel.* BAR International Series 1300. Oxford: 178–189

Gibson S. and J.E. Taylor 1994. *Beneath the Church of the Holy Sepulchre, Jerusalem. Archaeology and early history of traditional Golgotha.* London

Gildemeister J. 1888 Bemerkungen zu den griechischen Inschriften Frei's und Schumacher's. *ZDPV* 11: 38–45

Gilead Y. and P. Fabian 2008. 7,000 years of settlement: the archaeological remains in Be'er Sheva from the sixth millennium BCE to the end of the first millennium CE. In Y. Gardos and A. Meir Glittzenstein eds. *Beer-Sheva, metropolis in the making.* Beer-Sheva: 303–331 (Hebrew)

Gitler H. and A. Kushnir-Stein 2004. Date on coins of Marisa in Idumaea and its historical implications. *Swiss Numismatic Revue* 83: 87–94

Glucker C.A.M. 1987. *The city of Gaza in the Roman and Byzantine periods.* BAR International Series 325. Oxford

Goitein S.D. 1975. A court record from Zoar on the Dead Sea. *Eretz-Israel* 12: 200–202 (Hebrew)

Goldfus H., B. Arubas and E. Alliata 1995. The monastery of Theoctistus (Deir Muqallik). *LA* 45: 247–297

Goodnick-Westenholz J. ed. 2007. *Three faces of monotheism.* Jerusalem

Grabar A. 1958. *Ampoules de Terre Sainte (Monza, Bobbio).* Paris

Gregg R.C. and D. Urman 1996. *Jews, pagans and Christians in the Golan Heights.* Atlanta

Griffith S.H. 1997. From Aramaic to Arabic: the languages of the monasteries of Palestine in the Byzantine and Early Islamic periods. *Dumbarton Oaks Papers* 51: 11–31

Groh D.E. 1978. North Syrian mortaria excavated at Caesarea Maritima (Israel). *Levant* 10: 165–169

Grumel V. 1958. *La chronologie*. Paris

Guerber E. and M. Sartre 1998. Un logistès à Canatha (Syria). *ZPE* 120: 93-98

Guri-Rimon O. and R. Shchori 2005. *Measuring and weighing in ancient times*. Haifa

Gutfeld O. 2012. *Jewish Quarter excavations in the Old City of Jerusalem conducted by Nahman Avigad, 1969–1982. Volume V: The Cardo (Area X) and the Nea Church (Areas D and T). Final report*. Jerusalem

Gutman S., Z. Yeivin and E. Netzer 1981. Excavations in the synagogue at Horvat Susiya. In L.I. Levine ed. *Ancient synagogues revealed*. Jerusalem: 123–126

Habas L. 2009. A pair of sandals depicted on mosaic floors in the entrances of private houses and churches in Israel and Transjordan in the Byzantine period. In Ç. Özkan Aygün ed. *SOMA 2007. Proceedings of the XI Symposium on Mediterranean archaeology, Istanbul Technical University, 24-29 April 2007*. BAR International Series 1900. Oxford: 151-159

Habas L. 2015. Crosses in the mosaic floors of churches in Provincia Arabia and nearby territories, against the background of the edict of Theodosius II, *Journal of Mosaic Research* 8: 31–60

Hamarneh B. 2013a. Ruolo del vescovo nella topografia suburbana e nel territorio dell'odierna Giordania, secc. V–VIII. In S. Cresci, J. Lopez Quiroga, O. Brandt and C. Pappalardo eds. *Acta XV congressus internationalis archaeologiae christianae, Toleti 8–12.9.2008. Episcopus, civitas, territorium*. Città del Vaticano: 415–430

Hamarneh B. 2013b. Scene bibliche nella basilica di Ya'amun: una riconsiderazione. In L. Bénou and C. Rognoni eds. Χρόνος συνήγορος. *Mélanges André Guillou* (Νέα Ῥώμη. *Rivista di ricerche bizantinistiche* 9 [2012]). Rome: 5–22

Harari Y. 2006. 'This is my body': bread in the Christian liturgy. In N. Ben-Yossef ed. *Bread: daily and divine*. Jerusalem: 115–141

Hartal M. 2005. *Land of the Ituraeans*. Golan Studies 2. Qazrin (Hebrew)

Hartal M. 2006. The history of Rafid on the background of the history of Northern Transjordan. In D. Urman, edited by S. Dar, M. Hartal and E. Ayalon. *Rafid on the Golan. A profile of a Late Roman and Byzantine village*. BAR International Series 155. Oxford: 269–290

Hayes J.W. 1967. North Syrian mortaria. *Hesperia* 36: 337–347

Hevelone-Harper J.L. 2005. *Disciples of the desert: monks, laity, and spiritual authority in sixth-century Gaza*. Baltimore

Hirschfeld Y. 1990. List of Byzantine monasteries in the Judean Desert. In G.C. Bottini, L. Di Segni and E. Alliata eds. *Christian archaeology in the Holy Land: new discoveries*. SBF Collectio maior 36. Jerusalem: 1–90

Hirschfeld Y. 1992. *The Judean Desert monasteries in the Byzantine period*. New Haven – London

Hirschfeld Y. 1999. *The Early Byzantine monastery at Khirbet ed-Deir in the Judean Desert: the excavations in 1981-1987*. Qedem 38. Jerusalem

Hirschfeld Y. 2003. Social aspects of the late-antique village of Shivta. *JRA* 16: 395–408.

Hirschfeld Y. 2004. The monasteries of Gaza: an archaeological review. In B. Bitton-Ashkeloni and A. Kofsky eds. *Christian Gaza in Late Antiquity*. Leiden: 61–88

Hirschfeld Y. and O. Gutfeld 2008. *Tiberias: excavations in the House of the Bronzes*. Chapter I. Stratigraphy and Architecture. Qedem 48. Jerusalem: 3–33

Holum K.G. 1986. Andreas philoktistes: a proconsul of Byzantine Palestine. *IEJ* 36: 61–64

Honigmann E. ed. 1939. *Le Synekdèmos de Hiéroclès et l'opuscule géographique de Georges de Chypre*, with an introduction by F. Cumont. Brussels

Honigmann E. 1942. The original lists of the members of the Council of Nicaea, the Robber Synod and the Council of Chalcedon. *Byzantion* 16: 20-80

Honigmann E. 1950. Juvenal of Jerusalem. *Dumbarton Oaks Papers* 5: 209–279

Hoyland R. 2010. Mount Nebo, Jabal Ramm, and the status of Christian Palestinian Aramaic and Old Arabic in Late Roman Palestine and Arabia. In M.C.A. Macdonald ed. *The development of Arabic as a written language*. Supplement to the Proceedings of the Seminar for Arabian Studies 40. Oxford: 29–46

Ilan T. 2002–2012. *Lexicon of Jewish names in Late Antiquity* I–IV. Tübingen

Iliffe J.H. 1935. Cemeteries and 'monastery' at the Y.M.C.A., Jerusalem. *QDAP* 4: 70-80

Isaac B. 1990. *The limits of Empire: the Roman army in the East*. Oxford

Isaac B. 1998. Milestones in Judaea: from Vespasian to Constantine. *The Near East under Roman rule – Selected papers*. Leiden: 48-75

Isaac B. and I. Roll 1982. *Roman roads in Judaea* I. *The Legio–Scythopolis road*. BAR International Series 141. Oxford

Israeli Y. and D. Mevorah eds. 2000. *Cradle of Christianity*. Jerusalem

Jones A.H.M. 1990. *The Later Roman Empire, 286–602*. Second paperback edition. Oxford (first published 1964)

Jones A.H.M., J.R. Martindale and J. Morris 1971. *Prosopography of the Later Roman Empire I: A.D. 260–395*. Cambridge

Kelso J.L. and D.C. Baramki 1949–1951. *Excavations at New Testament Jericho and Khirbet en-Nitla*. AASOR 29–30. New Haven

Kennedy D. 2004. *The Roman army in Jordan*. Second revised edition. London

Kennedy D. and H. Falahat 2008. *Castra Legionis VI Ferratae*: a building inscription for the legionary fortress at Udruh near Petra. *JRA* 21: 151–169

Killick A.C. 1987. *Udruh, caravan city and desert oasis: a guide to Udruh and its surroundings*. Romsey

Kirk G.E. 1937. Era problems in the Greek inscriptions of the southern desert. *Journal of the Palestine Oriental Society* 17: 209–217

Kirk G.E. 1938. The era of Diocletian in Palestinian inscriptions. *Journal of the Palestine Oriental Society* 18: 161–166

Kirk G.E. and P. Gignoux 1996. Greek funerary inscriptions and ostraca from Elusa. *'Atiqot* 28: 171–186

Kirk G.E. and C.B. Welles 1962. The inscriptions. In H. Dunscombe Colt ed. *Excavations at Nessana I*. London: 131–197

Kohn-Tavor A., J. Ashkenazi and M. Aviam 2020. Excavations of three Byzantine churches in the Western Galilee: two churches at Ḥorvat Karkara and the Eastern Church at Ḥorvat 'Erav, a preliminary report. In A. Coniglio and A. Ricco eds. *Holy Land: archaeology on either side. Archaeological essays in honour of Eugenio Alliata, ofm.* SBF Collectio maior 57. Milan: 1–10

Kokkinos N. 1998. *The Herodian dynasty: origins, role in society and eclipse.* Sheffield

Kubitschek W. 1893. Aera. *Paulys Realencyclopädia* I, 1. Stuttgart: 606–666

Lambert C. and P. Pedemonte Demeglio 1994. Ampolle devozionali ed itinerari di pellegrinaggio tra IV e VII secolo. *Antiquité tardive* 2: 205–231

Laniado A. 1997. Βουλευταί et πολιτευόμενοι. *Chronique d'Égypte* 72: 130–144

Laniado A. 2002. *Recherches sur les notables municipaux dans l'Empire protobyzantin.* Paris

Laniado A. 2014. From municipal councillors to 'municipal landowners'. Some remarks on the evolution of the provincioal elites in Early Byzantium. In M. Meier and S. Patzold eds. *Chlodwigs Welt. Organisation von Herrschaft um 500*. Stuttgart: 545–565

Laniado A. 2021. Social status and civic participation in Early Byzantine cities. In C. Brélaz and E. Rose eds. *Civic identity and civic participation in Late Antiquity and the early Middle Ages*. Turnhout: 111–144

Laniado A. and B. Dashti 1993. A Byzantine lead weight from the port of Iamnia (Yavneh-Yam) and the title "EFOROS". *Revue des études byzantines* 51: 229–235

Laurence P. 2002. *Gerontius: La vie latine de sainte Mélanie*. SBF Collection minor 41. Jerusalem

Laurent V. 1963–1981. *Le corpus des sceaux de l'empire byzantine*. Paris

Lawlor H.J. 1908. The chronology of Eusebius' "Martyrs of Palestine". *Hermathena* 15, no. 34: 177–201

Leclercq H. 1907. Ampoules. In H. Leclercq, *Dictionnaire d'archéologie chrétienne et de liturgie* I, 2. Paris: 1722–1747

Lefebvre G. 1907. *Recueil des inscriptions grecques-chrétiennes d'Égypte*. Paris

Lehmann C.M. and K.G. Holum 2000. *The Greek and Latin inscriptions of Caesarea Maritima*. The Joint Expedition to Caesarea Maritima. Excavation reports V. Boston, MA

Leibner U. 2018. The synagogue inscriptions. Chapter 5 in U. Leibner, with contributions by D. Adan-Bayewitz et al. *Khirbet Wadi Ḥamam. A Roman-period village and synagogue in the Lower Galilee*. Qedem Reports 13. Jerusalem: 187–194

Lenzen C.J. 2000. Seeking contextual definitions for places: the case of north-western Jordan. *Mediterranean Archaeology* 13: 11–24

Lifshitz B. 1967. *Donateurs et fondateurs dans les synagogues juives*. Paris

Lifshitz B. 1970. Notes d'épigraphie grecque. *RB* 77: 76–83

Limor O. 1998. *Holy Land travels. Christian pilgrims in Late Antiquity*. Jerusalem (Hebrew)

Loffreda S. 1989. *Lucerne bizantine in Terra Santa con iscrizioni in greco*. SBF Collectio maior 35. Jerusalem

Loffreda S. 1990. Nuovi tipi di lucerne con iscrizioni. *LA* 40: 357–363

Loffreda S. 1992. Ancora sulle lucerne bizantine con iscrizioni. *LA* 42: 313–329

Loffreda S. 1994. Dieci lucerne con iscrizioni. *LA* 44: 595–607

Loffreda S. 1998. Lucerna bizantina con iscrizione bidirezionale. *LA* 48: 489–494

MacAdam H.I. 1986. *Studies in the history of the Roman province of Arabia. The northern section*. BAR International Series 295. Oxford

Macalister R.A.S. 1907. Some new inscriptions from Jerusalem and its neighbourhood. *PEF* 39: 234–239

Macuch R. 1985. A new interpretation of the Samaritan inscription from Tell Qasile. *IEJ* 35: 183–185

Magen Y. 1990. The Church of Mary Theotokos on Mount Gerizim. In G.C. Bottini, L. Di Segni and E. Alliata eds. *Christian archaeology in the Holy Land: new discoveries*. SBF Collectio maior 36. Jerusalem: 333–341

Magen Y. 1993a. Samaritan synagogues. In F. Manns ed. *Early Christianity in context. Monuments and documents*. SBF Collectio maior 38. Jerusalem: 193–227

Magen Y. 1993b. Samaritan synagogues. In *NEAEHL* IV: 1424–1427

Magen Y. 2002. Samaritan synagogues. In E. Stern and H. Eshel eds. *The Samaritans*. Jerusalem: 382–443 (Hebrew)

Magen Y. 2010. *The Good Samaritan Museum*. Judea and Samaria publications 12. Jerusalem

Magen Y. 2016. *Monastery of Martyrius. Christians and Christianity* V. Judea and Samaria publications 17. Jerusalem

Magen Y. and E. Aharonovich 2012. The Northern Church at Shiloh. In N. Carmin ed. *Christians and Christianity* III: *Churches and monasteries in Samaria and Northern Judea*. Judea and Samaria publications 15. Jerusalem: 161–208

Magness J. 1996. Blessings from Jerusalem: evidence for early Christian pilgrimage. *Eretz-Israel* 25: 37*–45*

Magness J., S. Kisilevitz, K. Britt, M. J. Grey and C. Spigel 2014. Ḥuqoq (Lower Galilee) and its synagogue mosaics: preliminary report on the excavations of 2011–2013. *JRA* 27: 327–355

Magness J., S. Kisilevitz, M. Grey, D. Mizzi, D. Schindler, M. Wells, K. Britt, R. Boustan, Sh. O'Connell, E. Hubbard, J. George, J. Ramsay, E. Boaretto and M. Chazan 2018. Huqoq Excavation project: 2014–2017. Interim report. *BASOR* 380: 61–131

Maiberger P. 1983. Die syrischen Inschriften als Quelle zur Geschichte der Nestorianer in Palästina. In V. Fritz and A. Kempinski eds. *Ergebnisse der Ausgrabungen auf der Hirbet al-Msas (Tel Masos) 1972-1975*. Volume I. Wiesbaden: 158–185

Maoz Z.U. and Ch. Ben-David 2003. Deir ʿAziz 2000-2001. *HA-ESI* 115: 11-15 (Hebrew); 10*-12* (English)

Maoz Z.U. and Ch. Ben-David 2006. New finds in the Golan: a synagogue at Deir 'Aziz. *Qadmoniot* XXXIX (131): 25–31 (Hebrew)

Marcoff M. and D.J. Chitty 1929. Notes on monastic researches in the Judaean wilderness, 1928–9. *PEF* 61: 167–178

Martin J. 1913. Une inscription romaine de Judée. *Revue des études Juives* 66: 54–59

Martindale J.R. 1980. *Prosopography of the Later Roman Empire II: A.D. 395–527.* Cambridge

Martindale J.R. 1992. *Prosopography of the Later Roman Empire III: A.D. 527–641.* Cambridge

Martindale J.R. 2001. *Prosopography of the Byzantine Empire I: 641–867.* London

Mayerson Ph. 1964. The first Muslim attacks on southern Palestine (A.D. 633–634). *Transactions and Proceedings of the American Philological Association* 95: 155–199 (republished in idem 1994. *Monks, Martyrs, Soldiers and Saracens. Papers on the Near East in Late Antiquity (1962–1993).* Jerusalem: 53–98)

Mayerson Ph. 1983. P.Oxy. 3574: Eleutheropolis of the New Arabia. *ZPE* 53: 251–258 (republished in idem 1994. Ibidem: 204–211)

Mayerson Ph. 1984. "Palaestina" vs. "Arabia" in the Byzantine sources. *ZPE* 56: 223-230 (republished in idem 1994. Ibidem: 224–231)

Mayerson Ph.1986a. Nea Arabia (P.Oxy. 3574): an addendum to *ZPE* 53. *ZPE* 64: 139–140 (republished in idem 1994. Ibidem: 256–257)

Mayerson Ph. 1986b. The Beersheba edict. *ZPE* 64: 141–148 (republished in idem 1994. Ibidem: 258–266)

Mayerson Ph. 1987. Libanius and the administration of Palestine. *ZPE* 69: 251–260 (republished in idem 1994. Ibidem: 284–293)

Mayerson Ph. 1988. Justinian's Novella 103 and the reorganization of Palestine. *BASOR* 269: 65–71 (republished in idem 1994. Ibidem: 294–300)

Mazzoleni D. 2013. Gli appellativi dei vescovi nella documentazione epigrafica fino alla prima metà del VII secolo. In S. Cresci, J. Lopez Quiroga, O. Brandt and C. Pappalardo eds. *Acta XV Congressus internationalis archaeologiae christianae, Toleti 8–12.9.2008. Episcopus, civitas, territorium.* Città del Vaticano: 1580–1600

McCormick M. 2011. *Charlemagne's survey of the Holy Land. Wealth, personnel, and buildings of a Mediterranean Church between antiquity and the Middle Ages, with a critical edition and translation of the original text.* Washington D.C.

McNamee K. 1981. *Abbreviations in Greek literary papyri and ostraca.* Bulletin of the American Society of Papyrologists, Supplements 3. Chico, Cal

Meimaris Y.E. 1986. *Sacred names, saints, martyrs and Church officials in the Greek inscriptions and papyri pertaining to the Christian Church of Palestine.* ΜΕΛΕΤΗΜΑΤΑ 2. Athens

Meimaris Y.E. 1992. *Chronological systems in Roman-Byzantine Palestine and Arabia* (in collaboration with K. Kritikakou and P. Bougia). ΜΕΛΕΤΗΜΑΤΑ 17. Athens

Meimaris Y.E. and K.I. Kritikakou-Nikolaropoulou 2005. *Inscriptions from Palestine Tertia Ia: The inscriptions from Ghor es-Safi (Byzantine Zoora).* ΜΕΛΕΤΗΜΑΤΑ 41. Athens

Meimaris Y.E. and K. Kritikakou-Nikolaropoulou 2008. *Inscriptions from Palaestina Tertia Ib: The inscriptions from Ghor es-Safi (Byzantine Zoora) (Supplement), Khirbet Qazone and Feinan*. ΜΕΛΕΤΗΜΑΤΑ 57. Athens

Meimaris Y. E. and K. I. Kritikakou-Nikolaropoulou 2016, *Inscriptions from Palaestina Tertia Ic: The Jewish Aramaic inscriptions from Ghor es-Safi (Byzantine Zoora)*. ΜΕΛΕΤΗΜΑΤΑ 73. Athens

Merkelbach R. and J. Stauber 2002. *Steinepigramme aus dem griechischen Osten*. Bd. 4. *Die südküste Klein Asien, Syrien und Palästina*, München–Leipzig

Meyers E.M. 1993. Navratein (Kefar Neburaya). *NEAEHL* III: 1077–1079

Michel A. 2001. *Les églises d'époque byzantine et umayyade de la Jordanie*. Bibliothèque de l'antiquité tardive 2. Turnhout

Milik J.T. 1953. Une inscription et une lettre en araméen christo-palestinien. *RB* 60: 526–539

Millar F. 1994. *The Roman Near East 41 BC – AD 337*. Cambridge, Mass. – London

Millar F. 2006. *Rome, the Greek world, and the East*. Chapter 9. Latin in the epigraphy of the Roman Near East. Chapel Hill, NC: 223–242

Miller Sh. and U. Leibner 2018. The synagogue mosaics. Chapter 4 in U. Leibner, with contributions by D. Adan-Bayewitz et al. *Khirbet Wadi Ḥamam. A Roman-period village and synagogue in the Lower Galilee*. Qedem Reports 13. Jerusalem: 144–186

Misgav H. 2006. Two Jewish tombstones from Zoar. *Israel Museum Studies in Archaeology* 5: 35–46

Morgenstern M. 2011. Christian Palestinian Aramaic. In S. Weninger ed. in collaboration with G. Khan, M. P. Streck and J. C. E. Watson. *The Semitic languages: an international handbook*. Berlin: 628–637

Naveh J. 1973. An Aramaic tomb inscription written in Paleo-Hebrew script. *IEJ* 23: 82–91

Naveh J. 1976. Syriac miscellanea. *'Atiqot* 11: 102–104

Naveh J. 1978. *On Stone and mosaic: the Aramaic and Hebrew inscriptions from ancient synagogues*. Tel Aviv (Hebrew)

Naveh J. 1981. A Greek dedication in Samaritan letters. *IEJ* 31: 220-222

Naveh J. 1989a. The Aramaic and Hebrew inscriptions from ancient synagogues. *Eretz-Israel* 20: 302–310 (Hebrew)

Naveh J. 1989b. Did ancient Samaritan inscriptions belong to synagogues? In R. Hachlili ed. *Ancient synagogues in Israel*. BAR International Series 499. Oxford: 61–63

Naveh J. 1996. Gleanings on some pottery inscriptions. *IEJ* 46: 44–51

Naveh J. 1998. Scripts and inscriptions in ancient Samaria. *IEJ* 48:91–100

Naveh J. 2002. Script and inscriptions in ancient Samaria. In E. Stern and H. Eshel eds. *The Samaritans*. Jerusalem: 372–381 (Hebrew)

Naveh J. 2003. Nabatean language, script and inscriptions. In R. Rosenthal-Heginbottom ed. *The Nabateans in the Negev*. Hecht Museum Catalogue 22. Haifa: 15*–16*

Naveh J. 2005. Ktovot be'ivrit ubearamit miZippori (Inscriptions in Hebrew and Aramaic from Sepphoris. *'Atiqot* 49:113*–115* (Hebrew)

Naveh J. and Y. Magen 1997. Aramaic and Hebrew inscriptions from the second century BCE at Mount Gerizim. *'Atiqot* 32: 37–56 (Hebrew); 9*–17* (English summary)

Negev A. 1981. *The Greek inscriptions from the Negev*. SBF Collectio minor 25. Jerusalem

Negev A. 1991. *Personal names in the Nabatean realm*. Qedem 32. Jerusalem

Oikonomides A.N. 1974. *Abbreviations in Greek inscriptions: papyri, manuscripts and early printed books. A manual*. Chicago

Oren E.D. and U. Rappaport 1984. The necropolis of Maresha–Beth Govrin. *IEJ* 34: 114–153

Ovadiah A. 1969. Excavations in the area of the ancient synagogue at Gaza (preliminary report). *IEJ* 19: 193–198

Ovadiah A. 1970. *Corpus of the Byzantine churches in the Holy Land*. Bonn

Ovadiah A. and R. Pierri 2019 [2021]. Inventory of Greek inscriptions from Mount Tabor. *LA* 69: 371–394

Pape W. and G.H. Benseler 1911. *Wörterbuch der griechischen Eigennamen*, I-II. Braunschweig

Patrich J. 1995. *Sabas, leader of Palestinian monasticism*. Dumbarton Oaks Studies 32. Washington D.C.

Patrich J. 2000. A chapel of St. Paul at Caesarea Maritima? *LA* 50: 363–382

Patrich J. 2001. Urban space in Caesarea Maritima, Israel. In Th.S. Burns and J.W. Eadie eds. *Urban centers and rural contexts in Late Antiquity*. East Lansing, MI: 77–110

Patrich J. 2011. *Studies in the archaeology and history of Caesarea Maritima*. Leiden – Boston

Patrich J. and L. Di Segni 1987. New Greek inscriptions from the monastery of Theoctistus in the Judean Desert. *Eretz–Israel* 19: 272–281 (Hebrew)

Patrich J. and L. Di Segni 1990. The Greek inscriptions in the cave chapel at Horvat Qasra. *'Atiqot* 10: 141–154 (Hebrew), 31*–35* (English)

Patrich J. and R. Rubin 1984. Les grottes de el-'Aleiliyât et la laure de Saint Firmin: des refuges juifs et byzantins. *RB* 91: 381–387

Peterson E. 1926. Εἷς θεός: *epigraphische, formgeschichtliche und religionsgeschichtliche Untersuchungen*. Göttingen

Petrantoni G. 2021. *Corpus of Nabataean Aramaic-Greek inscriptions*. Antichistica 28; Studi orientali 11. Ca' Foscari Digital Publishing

Piccirillo M. 1980. Le antichità di Rihab dei Bene Hasan. *LA* 30: 317–350

Piccirillo M. 1982. La Chiesa della Vergine a Madaba. *LA* 32: 373–408

Piccirillo M. 1989. *Chiese e mosaici di Madaba*. SBF Collectio maior 34. Jerusalem

Piccirillo M. 1994a. Uno stampo per eulogia trovato a Gerusalemme. *LA* 44: 585–590

Piccirillo M. 1994b. Le iscrizioni di Kastron Mefaa. In M. Piccirillo and E. Alliata eds. *Umm al-Rasas–Mayfa'ah I: Gli scavi del complesso di Santo Stefano*. SBF Collectio maior 28. Jerusalem: 241–269

Piccirillo M. 2005. Aggiornamento delle liste episcopali delle diocese in territorio transgiordanico. *LA* 55: 377–394

Piccirillo M. 2011. The province of Arabia during the Persian invasion (613–629/30). In K.G. Holum and H. Lapin, *Shaping the Middle East. Jews, Christians, and Muslims in an age of transition 400–800 C.E.* Bethesda, MD: 99–112

Piccirillo M. and E. Alliata 1998. *Mount Nebo: new archaeological excavations 1967–1997*. SBF Collection maior 27. Jerusalem

Piccirillo M. and E. Alliata eds. 1999. *The Madaba map centenary, 1897–1997: travelling through the Byzantine-Umayyad period*. SBF Collectio maior 40. Jerusalem

Ponting M.J. 2008. The scientific analysis and investigation of a selection of the copper-alloy metalwork from Tiberias. Chapter 2 in Y. Hirschfeld and O. Gutfeld. *Tiberias: excavations in the House of the Bronzes*. Qedem 48. Jerusalem: 35–61

Porath Y. 2008. Caesarea. The Israel Antiquities Authority excavations. *NEAEHL* V: 1656–1665

Preisigke F. 1922. *Namenbuch*. Heidelberg

Prentice W.K. 1908. *Publications of an American archaeological expedition to Syria III. Greek and Latin inscriptions*. New York

Price R.M. transl. 1991. *Lives of the monks of Palestine by Cyril of Scythopolis*. Kalamazoo, MI

Rabello A.M. 1980. The legal condition of the Jews in the Roman Empire. In *ANRW* II, 13. Berlin – New York: 662–766 (reprinted Jerusalem 1982)

Radashkovsky I. 2020. Ḥorbat Ḥanot. Final report. *HA-ESI* 132 http://www.hadashot-esi.org.il/report_detail_eng.aspx?id=25769&mag_id=128

Rahmani L.Y. 1993. Eulogia tokens from Byzantine Bet She'an. *'Atiqot* 22: 109–119

Rahmani L.Y. 1999. The Byzantine Solomon 'Eulogia' tokens in the British Museum. *IEJ* 49: 92–104

Robert L. 1946. *Hellenica: Recueil d'épigraphie, de numismatique et d'antiquités grecques*, II–III. Paris

Robert L. 1960. *Hellenica: Recueil d'épigraphie, de numismatique et d'antiquités grecques*, XI–XII. Paris

Roll I. 1983. Comments concerning the southern boundary of Arabia and the camp of the Tenth Legion in Transjordan. *Cathedra* 30: 57–60 (Hebrew)

Roll I. 1989. A Latin imperial inscription from the time of Diocletian found at Yotvata. *IEJ* 39: 239–260

Roll I. and U. Avner 2008. Tetrarchic milestones found near Yahel in the southern Aravah. *ZPE* 165: 267–286

Roll I. and O. Tal 2009, A new Greek inscription from Byzantine Apollonia-Arsuf/Sozousa: a reassessment of the Εἷς θεός μόνος inscriptions of Palestine. *Scripta Classica Israelica* 28: 139–147

Roth-Gerson L. 1987. *The Greek inscriptions from the synagogues in Eretz Israel*. Jerusalem (Hebrew)

Rubin Z. 1983. Was the Tenth Legion deployed in the south to secure the Palestinian frontier or to guard commercial routes to India and Ethiopia? *Cathedra* 30: 61–63 (Hebrew)

Rubin Z. 1996. The see of Caesarea in conflict with Jerusalem from Nicaea (325) to Chalcedon (451). In A. Raban and K.G. Holum eds. *Caesarea Maritima. A retrospective after two millennia*. Leiden – New York – Köln: 559–574

Rubin Z. 2009. The see of Eleutheropolis in the conflict for supremacy between the see of Caesarea and the see of Jerusalem in the fourth and early fifth century CE. In J. Geiger, H.M. Cotton and G.D. Stiebel eds. *Israel's land: papers presented to Israel Shatzman on his jubilee*. Jerusalem: 249–263 (Hebrew)

Russell J. 1999. The palaeography of the Madaba map in the light of recent discoveries. A preliminary analysis. In M. Piccirillo and E. Alliata eds. *The Madaba map centenary, 1897–1997: travelling through the Byzantine-Umayyad period*. SBF Collectio maior 40. Jerusalem: 125–133

Russell K.W. 1980. The earthquake of May 19, AD 363. *BASOR* 238: 47–64

Safrai Z. 1995. *The Jewish community in the Talmudic period*. Jerusalem (Hebrew)

Saliou C. 2000. Gaza dans l'antiquité tardive: nouveaux documents épigraphiques. *RB* 107: 390–411

Saliou C. 2005. L'orateur et la ville: réflexions sur l'apport de Chorikios à la connaissance de l'histoire de l'espace urbain de Gaza. In C. Saliou ed. *Gaza dans l'Antiquité Tardive. Archéologie, rhétorique et histoire. Actes du Colloque international de Poitiers (6-7 mai 2004)*. Cardo/2. Études et Textes pour l'Identité Culturelle de l'Antiquité Tardive. Salerno: 171–195

Saller S.J. and B. Bagatti 1949. *The Town of Nebo (Khirbet el-Mekhayyat) with a brief survey of other ancient Christian monuments in Transjordan*. SBF Collectio maior 7. Jerusalem

Sarris P. 2018. Res privata. In O. Nicholson ed. *The Oxford Dictionary of Late Antiquity* II:1283.

Sartre M. 1982. Les gouverneurs de l'Arabie romaine. In M. Sartre. *Trois études sur l'Arabie romaine et byzantine*. Collection Latomus 178. Brussels: 77–120

Sartre M. 1993a. Communautés villageoises et structures socials d'après l'épigraphie de la Syrie du sud. In A. Calbi, A. Donati and G. Poma eds. *L'epigrafia del villaggio*. Faenza: 117–135

Sartre M. 1993b — see *IGLJ* IV

Sartre M. 1999. Les metrokomiai de Syrie du sud. *Syria* 76: 197–222

Sartre M. 2001. *D'Alexandre à Zénobie: histoire du Levant antique IVe siècle av. J.-C.– IIIe siècle ap. J.-C*. Paris

Sartre M. 2005. *The Middle East under Rome*. Cambridge, Mass. – London

Sartre, *IGLS* — see *IGLS* XIII, XIV, XV, XVI

Schmitt G. 1995. *Siedlungen Palästinas in griechisch-römischer Zeit*. Wiesbaden

Schneider A.M. 1931. Das Kloster der Theotokos zu Choziba im Wadi el-Kelt. *Römische Quartalschrift* 39: 297–333

Schürer E. 1973, 1979, 1987. *A history of the Jewish people in the age of Jesus Christ.* English version revised and edited by Geza Vermes, Fergus Millar, Matthew Black and Martin Goodman, I–III. Edinburgh

Schumacher G. 1886. Der Dscholan. *ZDPV* 9: 165–368

Schwabe M. and B. Lifshitz 1974. *Beth She'arim II. The Greek inscriptions.* Jerusalem

Seeck O. ed. 1876. *Notitia dignitatum et administrationum omnium tam civilium quam militarium: Notitia Orientis*. Berlin (reprinted Frankfurt a/M 1962)

Shalev S. 1998. A Fatimid metal vessel hoard from Caesarea. *Archaeology and the sciences* 6: 31–36

Sharon M. 2018. Witnessed by three disciples of the Prophet: the Jerusalem 32 inscription from 32 AH/652 CE. *IEJ* 68: 100–111

Sipilä J. 2004. Roman Arabia and the provincial reorganisations of the fourth century. *Mediterraneo antico* 7: 317–348

Sipilä J. 2007. Fluctuating provincial borders in mid-4th century Arabia and Palestine. In A.S. Lewin and P. Pellegrini eds. *The Late Roman army in the Near East from Diocletian to the Arab conquest. Proceedings of a colloquium held at Potenza, Acerenza and Matera, Italy (May 2005)*. BAR International Series 1717. Oxford: 201–209

Smith R.H. 1973. *Pella of the Decapolis I. The 1967 season of the College of Wooster Expedition to Pella*. Wooster, Ohio

Smith R.H. 1989. *Pella of the Decapolis II. Final report of the College of Wooster Expedition in Area IX, the civic complex*. Wooster, Ohio

Sodini J.-P. 1989. Remarques sur l'iconographie de Syméon l'Alépin, le premier stylite. *Monuments et mémoires de la Fondation Eugène Piot* 70: 29–53

Sodini J.-P. 2011. La terre des semelles: images pieuses ramenées par les pèlerins des Lieux saints (Terre sainte, Martyria d'Orient). *Journal des savants* (no. 1): 77-140

Speidel M.P. 1977. The Roman army in Arabia. In *ANRW* II, 8: 687–730

Stein A. 1990. *Studies in Greek and Latin inscriptions on the Palestinian coinage under the principate*, Ph.D. Dissertation. Tel Aviv University

Stein E. 1934. Post-consulat et AUTOKRATORIA, *Annuaire de l'Institut de philologie et d'histoire orientales* II (*Mélanges Bidez*). Brussels: 869-912

Stern S. 2014. Ancient and medieval Jewish calendars. Entry 176 in C.L.N. Ruggles ed. *Handbook of archaeoastronomy and ethnoastronomy*. New York: 1883–1888

Stève A.M. 1946. Le désert de Saint Jean près d'Hébron. *RB* 53: 547–575

Stone M. 1990–1991. Armenian inscriptions of the fifth century from Nazareth. *Revue des Études Arméniennes* 22: 315–322

Stone M. 1996–1997. Further Armenian inscriptions from Nazareth. *Revue des Études Arméniennes* 26: 321–327

Storchan B. 2021. A glorious church for a mysterious martyr. *Biblical Archaeology Review* 47, 3: 30–39

Sukenik E.L. 1932. *The ancient synagogue at Beth Alpha*. Jerusalem

Sukenik E.L. 1945. Jewish tomb-stones from Zoar. *Kedem* 2: 83–88

Syon D. 2004. Bet She'an. *HA-ESI* 116: 13–17 (Hebrew); 12*–16* (English)

Syon D. and M. Hartal 2003. A new tetrarchic boundary stone from the northern Hula Valley. *Scripta Classica Israelica* 22: 233-239

Tal O. 2009. A winepress at Apollonia–Arsuf: more evidence on the Samaritan presence in Roman–Byzantine southern Sharon. *LA* 59: 319–330

Tal O. 2015. A bilingual Greek-Samaritan inscription from Apollonia-Arsuf/Sozousa: yet more evidence of the use of ΕΙΣ ΘΕΟΣ ΜΟΝΟΣ formula inscriptions among the Samaritans. *ZPE* 194: 169–175

Talgam R. 2014. *Mosaics of faith: floors of pagans, Jews, Samaritans, Christians, and Muslims in the Holy Land*. Jerusalem – University Park, PA.

Taxel I. 2009. Late Byzantine/Early Islamic stamped jar handles from Jerusalem and Tell Qatra. *IEJ* 59: 185–193

Taylor J. 1990. The Bethany cave: a Jewish-Christian cult site? *RB* 97: 453–465

Tchekhanovets Y. 2017. The 1930s excavations at the YMCA site in Jerusalem and the Byzantine 'Monastery of the Iberians'. *LA* 67: 427–448

Tchekhanovets Y. 2018. *The Caucasian archaeology of the Holy Land: Armenian, Georgian and Albanian communities between the fourth and eleventh centuries CE*. Leiden

Tepper Y. 2018. A church from the Byzantine, Umayyad and Abbasid periods and remains from Iron Age I at Tamra (ez-Zu'abiyya) in Ramat Issakhar, *'Atiqot* 90: 75*–106* (Hebrew), 168–171 (English summary)

Thompson E.M. 1912. *An introduction to Greek and Latin palaeography*. Oxford

Thomsen P. 1917. *Die römische Meilensteine der Provinzen Syria, Arabia und Palästina*. Leipzig

Thomsen P. 1921. Die lateinischen und griechischen Inschriften der Stadt Jerusalem und ihrer nächsten Umgebung. *ZDPV* 44: 1–61, 90–168

Thomsen P. 1941. Die lateinischen und griechischen Inschriften der Stadt Jerusalem und ihrer nächsten Umgebung. 1. Nachtrag. *ZDPV* 64: 203–256

Tsafrir Y. 1981. A new reading of the Samaritan inscription from Tell Qasile. *IEJ* 31: 223–226

Tsafrir Y. 1983. Why were the Negev, southern Transjordan and Sinai transferred from Provincia Arabia to Provincia Palaestina? *Cathedra* 30: 35–56 (Hebrew)

Tsafrir Y. 1986. The transfer of the Negev, Sinai and southern Transjordan from Arabia to Palaestina. *IEJ* 36: 77-86

Tsafrir Y. 1988. *Excavations at Reḥovot-in-the-Negev I. The Northern Church*. Qedem 25. Jerusalem

Tsafrir Y. 1993. The Early Byzantine town of Reḥovot-in-the-Negev and its churches. In Y. Tsafrir ed. *Ancient churches revealed*. Jerusalem: 294–302

Tsafrir Y. 2006. Four eulogia tokens found in Bet Shean-Scythopolis (Israel). In R. Harreither, Ph. Pergola, R. Pillinger and A. Pülz eds. *Acta Congressus internationalis XIV archaeologiae christianae/Akten des XIV. Internationalen Kongresses für christliche Archäologie, Wien 19.–26. 9. 1999*. Città del Vaticano – Vienna: 731-734

Tsafrir Y. 2012. Between David's Tower and Holy Zion: Peter the Iberian and his monastery in Jerusalem. In L.D. Chrupcala ed. *Christ is here! Studies in biblical and Christian archaeology in memory of Michele Piccirillo, ofm*. SBF Collectio maior 52. Milan: 245–264

Tsafrir Y., L. Di Segni and J. Green 1994. *Tabula Imperii Romani – Judaea • Palaestina*. Jerusalem

Tsafrir Y. and Y. Hirschfeld 1993. The Byzantine church at Ḥorvat Berachot. In Y. Tsafrir ed. *Ancient churches revealed*. Jerusalem: 207-218

Tzaferis V. 1987. The Greek inscriptions from the Early Christian church at 'Evron. *Eretz-Israel* 19: 36*–53*

Tzaferis V. and S. Bar Lev 1976. A Byzantine inscription from Khisfin. *'Atiqot* 11: 114-115

Tzori N. 1967. The ancient synagogue at Beth-Shean. *Eretz-Isreal* 8: 149–167 (Hebrew); 73* (English summary)

Urman D. 1972. Jewish inscriptions from Dabbura in the Golan. *IEJ* 22: 16–23

Urman D. (edited by S. Dar, M. Hartal and E. Ayalon) 2006. *Rafid on the Golan: a profile of a Late Roman and Byzantine village*. BAR International Series 1555. Oxford

Ustinova Y. 2005. Ktovet du-leshonit miZippori (Bilingual inscription from Sepphoris. *'Atiqot* 49: 117*–118* (Hebrew)

Ustinova Y. and J. Naveh 1993. A Greek-Palmyrene Aramaic dedicatory inscription from the Negev. *'Atiqot* 22: 91–96

Vikan G. 1982 — see Vikan G. 2010

Vikan G. 1998. Byzantine pilgrims' art. In L. Safran ed. *Heaven on earth. Art and the Church in Byzantium*. University Park, PA: 229-266

Vikan G. 2003. 'Guided by land and sea': pilgrim art and pilgrim travel in Early Byzantium. In G. Vikan. *Sacred images and sacred power in Byzantium*. Aldershot: 74–92

Vikan G. 2010. *Early Byzantine pilgrimage art*. Dumbarton Oaks Byzantine Collection Publications 5. Washington, D.C. (revised ed. of *Byzantine pilgrimage art* 1982)

Vincent L.H. and F.-M. Abel 1932. *Emmaüs*. Paris

Vuk T. 2021. The so-called Syrian clay mortars with stamp inscriptions: general classification and first edition or re-edition of some exemplars. *LA* 71: 289–341; https//www.academia.edu/78167689/The_so_called_Syrian_clay_mortars_with_stamp_inscriptions_general_classification_and_first_edition_or_re_edition_of_some_exemplars_Re_editon_of_the_article_corrected_by_the_author_

Weiss Z. 2005. *The Sepphoris synagogue*. Jerusalem.

Weiss Z. 2008. Sepphoris. *NEAEHL* V: 2029–2035

Weiss Z. 2016. Decorating the sacred realm: biblical depictions in synagogues and churches of ancient Palestine. In U. Leibner and C. Hezser eds. *Jewish art in its late antique context*. Tübingen: 121–137

Weiss Z. and E. Netzer 1994. Zippori— 1992/1993. *ESI* 14: 40–46

Weiss Z. and R. Talgam 2002. The Nile Festival Building and its mosaics: mythological representations in Early Byzantine Sepphoris. In J.H. Humphrey ed. *The Roman and Byzantine Near East* 3. JRA Supplementary series 49. Ann Arbor, MI: 55–90

Weksler-Bdolah Sh., R. Bar-Nathan, A. Cohen-Weinberger and L. Di Segni 2022. '*[Work of] Cilo*' – A private stamp impression of the Roman period from the Western Wall tunnels. '*Atiqot* 106: 239–256

Welles C.B. 1938. The inscriptions. In C.H. Kraeling ed. *Gerasa, city of the Decapolis*. New Haven: 355–615

White R. 1993. Bet al-Ma. In AD. Crown, R. Pummer and A. Tal eds. *A companion to Samaritan studies*. Tübingen: 39

Whittow M. 1990. Ruling the Late Roman and Early Byzantine city: a continuous history. *Past and present* 129: 3–29

Wiesenberg E.J. 2007. Calendar. *Encyclopedia Judaica* (second edition) IV. Detroit – Jerusalem: 354–358

Wineland J.D. 2001. *Ancient Abila: an archaeological history*. BAR International Series 989. Oxford

Wilkinson J. 1977. *Jerusalem pilgrims before the Crusades*. Jerusalem

Wilkinson J. 1981. *Egeria's travels to the Holy Land*. Revised edition. Jerusalem

Wuthnow H. 1930. *Die semitischen Menschennamen in griechischen Inschriften und Papyri des vorderen Orients*. Leipzig

Yeivin Z. 1993. Susiya, Khirbet. The synagogue. *NEAEHL* IV: 1417–1421

Zacos G. and A. Veglery 1972. *Byzantine lead seals*. Basel (re-edited by J.W. Nesbitt, Bern 1984)

Zerbini A. 2017. The Area III inscription. In U. Rothe, A. Zerbini and F. Kenekel. Excavations in Area III of Tall Zar'a. *ADAJ* 58: 268–270

Zissu B. and A. Ecker 2014. A Roman military fort north of Bet Guvrin/Eleutheropolis? *ZPE* 188: 293–312

TABLE OF CONTENTS

Preface	V
Acknowledgements	IX
Abbreviations and Sigla	XI
Chapter I: Introduction	1
The geographical framework	1
The chronological framework	2
A general survey of the epigraphic yield in the Holy Land	4
Chapter II: Chronological systems in use in the Holy Land	7
Calendars	8
The Macedonian calendar(s)	8
Julian calendar	9
Babylonian-Aramaic calendar	10
The sabbatical year (*shevi'it*)	13
Eras in use in the Hellenistic-Roman period and in Late Antiquity	13
The innovations of Late Antiquity	24
The indictional cycle and the use of indiction in dates	32
Chapter III: Aramaic dialects and scripts	35
Chapter IV: Latin inscriptions in the Holy Land in Late Antiquity	41
Chapter V: Greek inscriptions in the Holy Land in Late Antiquity	49
Types of finds in the epigraphic yield of the country in Late Antiquity	51
V. 1 Public inscriptions	51
V. 1.1 Imperial edicts	51
V. 1.2 Building inscriptions in civil and military buildings	59
V. 1.3 Building inscriptions in cult buildings	69
V. 1.4 Honorary inscriptions	69
V. 1.5 Acclamations	71

V. 1.6 Other inscriptions in public buildings	77
V. 1.7 *Instrumenta*	81
V. 2 Private inscriptions	83
V. 2.1 Inscriptions in ecclesiastical buildings	83
A. Monasteries and charity foundations	83
B. Building and dedicatory inscriptions in churches	100
C. Other inscriptions in churches and monasteries	114
V. 2.2 Inscriptions in synagogues	120
V. 2.3 Inscriptions in private buildings	127
V. 2.4 Funerary inscriptions	129
V. 2.5 *Instrumenta*	140
Ceramic and similar objects	140
Metal objects	155

Chapter VI: Tools for the study of Late Antique Epigraphy in the provinces of Palaestina and Arabia — 159

Chapter VII: Palaeography — 165
  Tables 1–7 North — 171
  Tables 1–8 South — 178

Appendix A: Civil and military administration — 187
  § 1. The re-organization of the Empire under Diocletian — 187
  § 2. Diocletian's reform of the provincial administration — 187
  § 3. The duties of the civil governor — 188
  § 4. The *dux Palaestinae* and the *dux Arabiae* — 191
  § 5. Changes of provincial borders and administrative changes — 192
  § 6. City administration — 198
  § 7. Village administration — 205

Appendix B: Church administration — 209

Bibliography — 213